CONFRONTING
FIJI FUTURES

EDITED BY A. HAROON AKRAM-LODHI

Australian
National
University

eVIEW

Published by ANU eView
The Australian National University
Acton ACT 2601, Australia
Email: enquiries.eview@anu.edu.au
This title is also available online at eview.anu.edu.au

National Library of Australia Cataloguing-in-Publication entry

Title:	Confronting Fiji futures / A Haroon Akram-Lodhi (editor).
ISBN:	9781921934292 (paperback) 9781921934308 (ebook)
Subjects:	Fiji--Politics and government. Fiji--Economic conditions. Fiji--Social conditions.

Other Creators/Contributors:
           Akram-Lodhi, A. Haroon (Agha Haroon), 1958- editor.

Dewey Number: 320.099611

Cover design and layout by ANU Press. Cover photograph by M M (padmanaba01): www.flickr.com/photos/43423301@N07/3997565309/

First published 2000 by Asia Pacific Press
This edition © 2016 ANU eView

Stop Press

Confronting the Present: The Coup of May 2000

A Haroon Akram-Lodhi

On 19 May 2000, as *Confronting Fiji Futures* went to press, a group of 7 men armed with machine guns entered the Parliamentary Complex in Suva. They took the Prime Minister, Mahendra Chaudhry, members of the Cabinet, and other members of the Fiji Labour Party-led People's Coalition Government hostage, including Ganesh Chand, a contributor to this book. A previously little-known figure, George Speight, took responsibility for the attempted coup, stating that he had assumed executive power in order to represent the interests of indigenous Fijians. It was later revealed that rogue elements within the Fiji Military Forces' Counter Revolutionary Warfare Unit were directing the attempted coup. Indigenous Fijian youths rampaged through Suva and other communities, smashing windows, looting shops, setting fire to buildings, and terrorising their fellow citizens. Despite the declaration of a state of emergency by the President, *Ratu* Sir Kamisese Mara, the police and the army seemed unable to contain the violence.

With widespread doubt about who was in charge of the country, the Great Council of Chiefs met. On 25 May, following an intensely divided meeting, the council authorised the President to establish, pending the release of the hostages and the resignation of the Prime Minister, a new interim administration drawn from a council of advisers. Although common law was used to justify the authorisation, the suggested arrangements were clearly extra-constitutional. Speight rejected the arrangements.

The coup is an unfortunate reminder of the salience of the issues raised in *Confronting Fiji Futures*. Robbie Robertson argues that Fiji has witnessed only a partial retreat from the exclusionary communalism that shaped the politics of the country in the aftermath of the 1987 coups, despite the achievements of the 1997 Constitution and the 1999 elections. The limited extent of this partial retreat has been vividly illustrated by the coup, which has also illustrated, as both Yash Ghai and Satendra Prasad note in this book, that support for the 1997 Constitution and the cross-community politics that it suggested was not universal. It can be argued that the failure of the senior members of the government to recognise and seek to strengthen the fragility of the political consensus helped create a climate that made the coup possible. Even backbenchers and grassroots members within the indigenous Fijian parties that formed part of the Coalition did not support the 1997 constitutional settlement, or did so grudgingly. It would appear that the rapid movement demonstrated by the government at times on sensitive issues was an unnecessarily dangerous course of action. Rapid movement on sensitive issues overrode the positive achievements of the government, such as the maintenance of macro-economic stability. It overrode a number of major policies to assist the poor, significantly Fijians. It helped create the ground upon which the *Taukei* movement could be revived, and the politics of exclusion resurrected as a viable political strategy.

Land is a particularly sensitive issue. Indigenous Fijians own the land, but it is worked by Indo-Fijians. The government had been seeking to deal with the issue of land during its term of office. Biman Prasad and Sunil Kumar examine the complexity of the issue here. Speight has made it clear that indigenous Fijians wanted 'their' land back. The land issue is seen by many indigenous Fijians as the answer to the economic backwardness and social exclusion faced by some within their community— the 'Fijian question' (William Sutherland). Yet, as Sutherland makes clear, land will not resolve the Fijian question. During the course of the 1990s the Fiji state undertook an extensive program of structural reform, examined in detail in this volume. A central component was economic affirmative action for the benefit of the indigenous Fijian community as a whole but which, as is documented by Steven Ratuva, ended up benefiting a minority within the indigenous Fijian community. Structural reform and economic affirmative action stood in contradiction, and the result, as discussed in different ways in the contributions by John Cameron, Jacqueline Leckie, Sepehri and Akram-Lodhi, Chand, Sutherland, Robertson and Ratuva, was a deepening of social inequality. This created the material circumstances in which a violent reassertion of what Simione Durutalo termed the 'paramountcy' of indigenous Fijian interests in Fiji could take place. Historically, communalism has been a viable political strategy to maintain the façade of unity in the face of difference, as the events of May 2000 demonstrate.

The irony is that the presumed homogeneity of the indigenous Fijian community is now very much a fiction. Social inequality occurs not just between communities; it occurs within them. The contributions by Holger Korth, Steven Ratuva, William Sutherland and Robbie Robertson demonstrate the sharp social, economic and geographical differentiation that has occurred within the indigenous Fijian community since 1987. While some have prospered, many have not, and the result of these economic differences has been a fracturing of the culture of the indigenous Fijian community. Add to this the difficulties described by Robertson in even defining an indigenous Fijian. The leader of the coup embodies the contradictions. Speight, who is of indigenous Fijian and Euro-Fijian parentage, is a foreign-educated failed businessman who both benefited from the economic affirmative action policies of previous governments while at the same time being unable to navigate the treacherous waters of structural reform. He is an atypical indigenous Fijian.

As stressed by Martin Doornbos and Haroon Akram-Lodhi, Fiji in 2000 is a very different country from Fiji in 1987. The most important social cleavage in Fiji now lies within the indigenous Fijian community, demonstrated at length by the contributors to this book. Differences of status, region, and class have fostered conflict within the indigenous Fijian community, and it is this conflict which explains the origins of the coup, an expression of attempts within the indigenous Fijian community to establish political ascendancy. In particular, the coup has witnessed the indigenous Fijian *nouveaux riches* that emerged, as described by Steven Ratuva, out of the economic affirmative action policies since 1987 come into conflict with the economically connected aristocracy that ruled Fiji between 1970 and 1992. Both groups have used indigenous Fijian nationalism in an effort to unite themselves with the indigenous Fijian community from which they have become increasingly cut off. It is the deepening recognition of social cleavage within the indigenous Fijian community that has led more indigenous Fijians to accept the basic multiethnic and multicultural reality of their country than at any time in its history. It is these people who, along with the members of the other communities of Fiji, tried to oppose the coup. Indeed, it is the extent of the opposition to the coup across the communities of Fiji that can give rise to a guardedly cautious optimism as Fiji confronts its futures.

Contents

Contributors   x

Preface

A Haroon Akram-Lodhi   xii

Part I: Politics, economics and social inequality   **1**

1. Introduction: Confronting the future, confronting the past

   Martin Doornbos and A Haroon Akram-Lodhi   3

2. The implementation of the Fiji Islands Constitution

   Yash Ghai   21

3. Fiji's 1999 general elections: outcomes and prospects

   Satendra Prasad   50

4. Fiji's economy: the challenge of the future

   Ardeshir Sepehri and A Haroon Akram-Lodhi   71

5. Institutional rigidities and economic performance in Fiji

   Biman Prasad and Sunil Kumar   111

6. Confronting social policy challenges in Fiji

   John Cameron   133

7. Labour market deregulation in Fiji

   Ganesh Chand   152

8. Women in post-coup Fiji: negotiating work through old and new
   realities

   Jacqueline Leckie   178

Part II: The 'Fijian' question   **203**

9.   The problematics of reform and the 'Fijian' question

     William Sutherland   205

10. Addressing inequality? Economic affirmative action and
     communal capitalism in post-coup Fiji

     Steven Ratuva   226

11. Ecotourism and the politics of representation in Fiji

     Holger Korth   249

12. Retreat from exclusion? Identities in post-coup Fiji

     Robbie Robertson   269

     References   293

     Index   310

Tables

Table 3.1   1999 election results for 'Fijian communal seats'   59

Table 3.2   1999 election results in the open seats   62

Table 3.3   Party representation in Cabinet after the 1999 elections   65

Table 4.1   Selected macroeconomic indicators, 1971–96   73

Table 4.2   Specification of the three-gap model   92

Table 4.3   Econometric results of the structural equations and the
            three-gap equations   96

Table 4.4   Projected growth path scenarios, 1997–2001   102

Table 5.1   Categories of land ownership in Fiji   118

Table 5.2   Land use classification in per cent, 1965 and 1978   119

Table 5.3   Sugarcane production in the Labasa mill area, 1986–95   120

Table 5.4   Percentage of Indo-Fijian and indigenous Fijian farmers
            in the Seaqaqa project, 1981–93   121

Table 5.5   Classification of native land in Fiji   122

Table 5.6   Distribution of rents collected by the NLTB   124

Table 6.1   Active life profiles in years for men in Fiji around 1980   139

Table 7.1   Unionisation rate by sector, per cent   165

Table 7.2   Strike activity, 1970–97   167

Table 7.3   Number, nature and composition of disputes   168

Table 7.4   Dispute resolution   169

Table 7.5   Real wage ratios   170

Table 7.6   Real salary ratios   170

Table 7.7   The sectoral composition of employment by gender   171

Table 7.8   Wage and salary structure by gender   172

Table 9.1   Distribution of Fiji Development Bank commercial loans
             to indigenous Fijians by sector, 1989–96, per cent   212

Figures

Figure 4.1   Foreign exchange, saving and fiscal gaps   98

Symbols used in tables

n.a.   not applicable

..   not available

-           zero

.   insignificant

Abbreviations

ALTA	Agricultural Landlord and Tenant Act
ALTO	Agricultural Landlord and Tenants Ordinance
ANC	All National Congress
AV	Alternative Vote
CEDAW	Convention on the Elimination of All Forms of Discrimination Against Women
CLFS	Commercial Loans to Fijian Scheme
DP9	Ninth National Development Plan
EEC	European Economic Community
EIMCOL	Equity Investment Management Company Limited
EU	European Union
FAB	Fijian Affairs Board
FAGW	Fiji Association of Garment Workers
FAP	Fijian Association Party
FAWG	Fiji Association of Women Graduates
FCRC	Fiji Constitution Review Commission
FDB	Fiji Development Bank
FEMM	Forum Economic Ministers Meeting
FFI	Fiji Forest Industry
FHC	Fijian Holdings Company Limited
FLP	Fiji Labour Party
FNA	Fiji Nursing Association
FTUC	Fiji Trades Union Congress
FWCC	Fiji Women's Crisis Centre
FWRM	Fiji Women's Rights Movement
GDP	Gross Domestic Product
GNP	Gross National Product
ILO	International Labour Organization
ISS	Institute of Social Studies
JPSC	Joint Parliamentary Select Committee
MFA	Ministry of Fijian Affairs
MOT	Ministry of Tourism
NBF	National Bank of Fiji
NEP	New Economic Policy
NFP	National Federation Party
NIE	new industrialising economies

NLCPPSC	Native Lands Conservation and Preservation Projects Steering Committee
NLTB	Native Lands Trust Board
NUFCW	National Union of Factory and Commercial Workers
NVTLP	Nationalist *Vanua Takolavo* Party
NZODA	New Zealand Official Development Assistance programme
OECD	Organisation for Economic Cooperation and Development
PAFCO	Pacific Fishing Company
PANU	Party of National Unity
PIB	Prices and Incomes Board
PSA	Fiji Public Service Association
SEAPAT	South East Asia and the Pacific Multidisciplinary Advisory Team
SPARTECA	South Pacific Regional Trade and Economic Cooperation Agreement
SPOCTU	South Pacific and Oceanic Council of Trade Unions
SVT	*Soqosoqo Ni Vakavulewa Ni Taukei* or Fijian Christian Party
UGP	United General Party
UNDP	United Nations Development Programme
USP	University of the South Pacific
VKB	*Vula ni Kawa Bula*
VLV	*Veitokani Ni Lewenivanua Vakaristo*
WTO	World Trade Organization

Contributors

A Haroon Akram-Lodhi teaches rural development economics at the Institute of Social Studes, The Hague, The Netherlands and has written on and lived in Fiji.

John Cameron teaches at the School of Development Studies, University of East Anglia, Norwich, UK and was a member of the 1984 Fiji Employment and Development Mission.

Ganesh Chand is Minister for National Planning, Local Government, Housing and Environment in the Government of Fiji.

Martin Doornbos is Professor of Political Science at the Institute of Social Studies, The Hague, the Netherlands and a former external assessor of the University of the South Pacific, Suva, Fiji.

Yash Ghai is the Sir Y. K. Pao Professor of Public Law at the University of Hong Kong.

Holger Korth works in the Department of Anthropology at the University of Otago, Dunedin, New Zealand.

Sunil Kumar teaches economics and statistics at the University of the South Pacific, Suva, Fiji.

Jacqueline Leckie teaches anthropology at the University of Otago, Dunedin, New Zealand. She has worked extensively on labour and gender in the South Pacific region in general, and Fiji in particular.

Biman Prasad is an economics lecturer at the Fiji Centre, which is part of the Extension Services section of the University of the South Pacific, Suva, Fiji.

Satendra Prasad teaches in the Department of Sociology at the University of the South Pacific, Suva, Fiji.

Steven Ratuva works at the Institute of Development Studies, University of Sussex, Brighton, UK, and is a former journalist in Fiji.

Robbie Robertson is a development historian at La Trobe University, Melbourne, Australia who lived and worked in Fiji for nearly ten years. He co-authored *Fiji: shattered coups* and more recently wrote *Multiculturalism and Reconciliation in an Indulgent Republic: Fiji after the coups, 1997–1998.*

Ardeshir Sepehri teaches economics at the University of Manitoba, Winnipeg, Canada and has conducted research on behalf of the United Nations' World Institute for Development Economics Research, Helsinki, Finland.

William Sutherland has lectured in political science at the Australian National University in Canberra. He previously taught at the University of the South Pacific, Suva, Fiji, resigning in 1987 to become Secretary to the late Prime Minister, Dr Timoci Bavadra. From 1992 to 1995 he was Deputy Secretary General of the South Pacific Forum. He is now with the Aboriginal and Torres Strait Islander Commission (ATSIC) in Canberra.

Preface

A Haroon Akram-Lodhi

Fiji is one of the largest Pacific Island countries. With a per capita GNP in 1997 of US$2470 Fiji is classified by the World Bank as a lower–middle income developing country. Further, with an average life expectancy of 72 years, infant mortality of approximately 22 per thousand, and an adult literacy rate of 91 per cent, Fiji has a high level of social development, being ranked number 46 in the United Nations Development Programme's 1997 human development index. However, despite what has been in regional and comparative terms a reasonably enviable record of 'development', Fiji has not been at peace with itself. In common with countries as diverse as Scotland, Canada, Belgium, South Africa, Rwanda, Burundi and Bosnia–Herzegovina, Fiji has witnessed, over the post-independence period, the increasing politicisation of identity. More specifically, in Fiji social dissent and conflict commonly use the identity politics of ethnicity. As a direct consequence, in 1987 the seeming tranquility of Fiji was shattered by two military coups—the first in the South Pacific region.

Since the coups there have been dramatic changes in Fiji's society, politics and economy. The period has witnessed four governments: an unelected, military-backed Interim Government between 1987 and 1992; two governments elected under the 1990 Constitution and led by Sitiveni Rabuka, the leader of the 1987 coups; and the government elected in 1999 under the provisions of the 1997 Constitution and led by the Fiji Labour Party (FLP). Fiji's governments between 1987 and 1998 altered the structure of the economy, primarily by encouraging the production of garments in tax-free factories and by seeking to integrate Fiji increasinglyinto the global economy through a reduction in trade barriers. At the same time the labour force has changed: the feminisation of the waged labour force has occurred with the expansion of the garment sector, skilled Indo-Fijian labour has emigrated and urbanisation has increased sharply. There has also been a reassertion of élite politics, a reassertion that stands in sharp relief to social change in a vigorous civil society. The end of the 'Sunday ban' and the introduction of television have most vividly illustrated this change. In 1999 Fiji is a very different country from that which was traumatised by the 1987 coups.

Moreover, change will continue to confront Fiji in the future. The new constitutional settlement agreed to in 1997, alterations in agrarian relations emerging out of the termination of land leases, the further erosion of trade preferences as a consequence of a new round of multilateral world trade negotiations and continued globalisation have major implications for the country in the next fifteen years. For those interested in Fiji, these changes and the challenges they create need to be understood. Recent scholarship on Fiji has however often tended to look back, focusing on the changes which occurred in the twelve years following the coups. Necessary as a sound historical perspective is, it is also necessary to use historical understanding to seek to grasp the implications for present and for the future. This is especially the case in a society that has been as divided as Fiji.

That such an approach has been largely lacking indicates, in academic terms, a gap in the literature on Fiji. This gap was identified by Haroon Akram-Lodhi and Robbie Robertson in 1997 and led to the development of an informal collaborative research project based at the Institute of Social Studies (ISS) in The Hague, the Netherlands. The choice of the ISS as the base for the project might at first glance appear odd, being situated such a long way from the South Pacific region. However, a fortuitous set of circumstances meant that over the course of eighteen months the ISS was host, for varying periods of time, to seven of the contributors to the current volume. Moreover, the ISS has a long if somewhat understated tradition of collaborative teaching, research and advisory services in the South Pacific region. Thus, rather than being an odd choice, the ISS was in fact an ideal choice to serve as the base for the project.

A second fortuitous coincidence has reinforced the need for the forward-looking research contained in this book. The primary editorial work on the book was completed around the time of Fiji's 1999 general elections, the outcome of which came as a surprise to many local and international observers. In the 1999 general elections the peoples of Fiji resoundingly rejected both the government and the two parties which were largely responsible for steering the 1997 constitutional settlement through parliament, the *Soqosoqo Ni Vakavulewa Ni Taukei* (SVT) and the National Federation Party (NFP). In a vivid repudiation of the legacy of the coups, victory went to the FLP, which obtained an outright majority. The victory of the FLP led to the elevation of its leader, Mahendra Chaudhry, to the post of Prime Minister—the first Indo-Fijian to hold that position in the history of the country.

It is unlikely that those who framed the 1997 constitutional settlement could have envisaged a situation in which one party would achieve an overall majority of parliamentary seats at this stage in Fiji's political development, garnering limited but nevertheless significant support from across the multiplicity of Fiji's ethnic communities. However, despite the surprise of the outcome, the Cabinet which has emerged is a multiparty one, in line with the principles of the Constitution and the political processes which it has engendered, and with a greater range of representation than that of any previous government in Fiji—a situation sought by those who framed the Constitution and welcomed by the peoples of Fiji.

The FLP was elected on a platform of social and economic justice. Such a platform stands in sharp relief to the policies of structural adjustment pursued by successive governments since 1986. However, it is unclear whether the FLP will be able, in the context of multiparty government and in the context of the probable end of the country's preferential market access for most of its exports, to formulate independent policies that address the country's remarkably poor economic performance. Yet the need for fresh, forward-looking economic policy is urgent: Fiji's rate of growth of GDP per capita has fallen from 4.2 per cent per annum between 1965 and 1980 to only 0.5 per cent per annum between 1980 and 1993, and the political consequences of deepening economic insecurity could be significant. Nonetheless, it remains to be seen whether Fiji's new government will be able to 'adjust' structural adjustment.

At the same time, it remains to be seen whether the victory of the explicitly multiethnic FLP represents the bold leap into the dark which is needed to move beyond the primacy of the politics of identity in Fiji. Granted, the signs from the new government have appeared promising. As Mahendra Chaudhry said on 19 May 1999, after having been sworn in as Prime Minister, 'I, and my government, are committed to promoting multi-racialism in our country, multi-racialism that brings our different communities together'. In such circumstances, it is to be hoped that a forward-looking assessment of the broad social, economic and political issues facing Fiji in the present and the future of the sort contained in this book will be useful to individuals and to policymakers seeking to bring communities together. Nonetheless, the contributors to this book recognise the limits of their intervention. Obviously, no book can foster the emergence of genuinely united Fiji community. Rather, the emergence of a united Fiji community depends upon all the peoples of Fiji realising that they have changed, that Fiji has changed, and that the only way in which they can move forward into their collective futures is together.

Part I

Politics, economics and social inequality

Introduction: Confronting the future, confronting the past

Martin Doornbos and A Haroon Akram-Lodhi

'Things fall apart'[1]: a personal retrospective of Fiji in 1987

It was October 1987, and one of the authors was at a social gathering in Suva. One of the guests told the gathering: 'there is the body of a dead soldier lying in the morgue, but the relatives are not being informed'. The guests being addressed allowed the announcement to sink in for a moment. The key point was then made: 'the question of course is why not?'.

This was evidently not an unknown soldier. However, this made the question only more compelling. One of the others present provided further details, which sharpened the point: 'apparently, they are having some difficulty with the cause of his death. Will (Colonel Sitiveni) Rabuka be facing greater public embarrassment if the man has been killed by an opponent of the coup, or if he turns out a victim of a liquidation within the army?'. A third speaker reflected: 'Rabuka evidently cannot use either. Yet, an internal reckoning strikes me as the most likely explanation; who else has weapons in this country, or at least at this point in time?'.

It was a month since the second coup of 1987. In the absence of newspapers and uncensored radio, rumour and speculation was passed on and exchanged continuously. That is, until the evening, when everybody rushed home before the nine o'clock curfew. Before reaching home, one had to pass more than one checkpoint, a new experience to all who lived in Fiji. A spokesman for the military government on the radio offered the encouraging news that the number of burglaries had gone down since the curfew was introduced.

The announcement of new decrees by the military government was greeted with an air of sceptical misgiving. If someone had the texts, people found out that the army and the police were allowed to shoot at people that had caused disturbances, and could not afterwards be held liable for murder. People found out that suspected elements could be detained by the security forces without prior notice. People found out that if they were detained, a panel would be constituted with the power to give non-binding advice about possible release after a month's detention. If the advice was ignored, the panel would meet again in six months.

People, such as several members of staff of the University of the South Pacific (USP), were detained, and thrashed, without justification. The regime did indeed use harsh methods to intimidate its opponents, and this no doubt muted broad open protest, which was surprisingly absent. Thus, about 120 names were entered on a list of people who were prohibited to leave the country, out of fear for the damage they might cause to Fiji's image abroad. The perversity of the situation was apparent. As one of those listed asked, 'would not the existence of that list itself be much more damaging to the national image?'. Despite this, though, there were relatively few acts of violence, in large part because a structural basis for violence did not exist. There was, admittedly, some social friction, particularly in informal contexts. At the time though there seemed little doubt that both Indo-Fijians and most indigenous Fijians were not particularly happy with the installation of the military regime.

Despite the lack of opposition, the tranquility of Fiji had been shattered, and the desperation that came in the wake of the new situation was pervasive. 'It is inconceivable and incomprehensible', a Dutch lecturer at USP remarked, 'to see such a wonderful and truly multicultural society collapse within such a short while. I cannot and I will refuse to believe that all this will really be destroyed'. A British physicist recounted how after eleven years of work in Fiji he had decided to apply for citizenship. 'At the moment of the first coup I stood in the queue for the immigration office. It was like hearing God's voice. Now, after the second coup, I have resigned.'

Indo-Fijians felt the most desperation. Their future appeared very gloomy, with every day bringing new, deeply demoralising measures. Calls such as 'throw Indians out' and 'Fiji for Fijians' were heard, reflecting sentiments which from time to time had been articulated amongst a particular sub-stratum of indigenous Fijians. Though Rabuka's military government did not quite echo these calls, it made it clear by various means that it intended to regard Indo-Fijians—who, after all, comprised fifty per cent of the population—as no more than second rate citizens. For example, Rabuka formally 'allowed' Hindu Indo-Fijians to celebrate Diwali, but without firecrackers, out of 'security' considerations. With every passing day Indo-Fijians were dismissed from civil service positions to make room for the followers of the new order. Within the service sector, the granting of work permits was increasingly beset by discriminatory hurdles. Fiji's economy was highly dependent on the cultivation of sugarcane by Indo-Fijian farmers operating small holdings, and it appeared that the new regime was intent to keep them in that position, though as working ants without political rights. Parallels to South Africa and apartheid were continually being suggested.

'It was all inevitable' opined a student at an improvised panel discussion, 'the differences were too big and they were becoming bigger and bigger; it had to come to an explosion at some point'. An older expatriate said that he too had seen it coming for quite some time: 'the rapid growth, especially from the early 70s onwards, of a professional class of Indo-Fijians on the one hand, and of almost exclusive recruitment of indigenous Fijians into the army on the other, sooner or later was bound to lead to confrontations'. He continued: 'it was a big mistake for Fiji to have gone in for those Unifil tasks in Lebanon. That has led to much too rapid an expansion of the army, based on (indigenous) Fijian recruitment as an easy employment project'.

The inevitability of an ethnic confrontation was however widely disputed, by both indigenous Fijians and Indo-Fijians. 'Ethnic conflict is not what is at issue', one person argued, 'but it serves the new power holders—and some of the old ones—to portray it that way'. Who were these power holders? People knew. As one indigenous Fijian student said, 'it is not true that Fijians and Indians are living here in tension with one another. It is those other islanders who are making that up'. He was referring to the people of the Lau archipelago, and his insight pointed in two directions. In the first place there was a fundamental contradiction between the east and the west of Fiji. The 'west' comprises mainly the west of Viti Levu. It was here where the country's wealth was concentrated—sugar, gold, pine plantations, and tourism. In the west, indigenous Fijians and Indo-Fijians had been co-habiting for generations, perhaps out of economic necessity, but nevertheless generally on good terms. Yet the west had no political power. It was the 'east', comprising the Lau archipelago and part of Vanua Levu, which was the origin of many political power holders. For example, most members of the Great Council of Chiefs, a neotraditional political body set up by the colonial power and which had had its powers substantially expanded over time, came from the east. The divide ran roughly parallel to the distinction between the Melanesian and the Polynesian politico-cultural spheres of influence, which met in Fiji: Polynesian, with hierarchical political traditions in the east; Melanesian, with more egalitarian structures, in the west.

'Rabuka's coup is not supported in the western part, but it opens the door for a direct confrontation between east and west', noted an observer with a deep understanding of Fiji. If such a confrontation had occurred, it would not have been the first. It is well established that the west of Fiji was subjugated and brought under colonial control by a coalition of the British and chiefs from the east of Fiji. Moreover, and this was the second insight of the indigenous Fijian student mentioned above, the dominance of the east in Fiji's politics had increasingly allowed it to establish a grip on the sources of wealth in the west. As a consequence, some voices in the west spoke cautiously of secession and the establishment of a separate state in the west of Fiji, but the instruments needed to achieve anything of the sort were totally lacking. While a further expansion of the army was to take place, as always recruitment occurred primarily in the east.

The accumulation of economic and political power amongst a top layer of indigenous Fijians from the east of the country had been rapid and substantial, especially during the last term of office of the Alliance Party, which had witnessed a whole series of excesses and corruption scandals. 'It is the Alliance administration's poor performance and the new dichotomies it created which brought about increasing dissatisfaction among Fijians as well as Indians', a close observer quietly remarked. This in turn was a key factor leading to the emergence of the Fiji Labour Party (FLP) in 1985, and finally to the successful coalition of the FLP with the largely Indo-Fijian National Federation Party (NFP). Together, the FLP-NFP Coalition won the April 1987 elections and toppled the Alliance, putting an end to seventeen years of uninterrupted government control by *Ratu* Sir Kamisese Mara, a powerful figure with evident political talents but who during the last years of Alliance rule had become the centre of an increasingly tainted government.

The Coalition government led by Dr Timoci Bavadra was not radical or revolutionary. While it declared itself in favour of a nuclear-free Pacific, during its short time in office it pursued largely *ad hoc* solutions to immediate problems, particularly in the area of employment. Indeed, many insiders had felt that the Coalition government would not last long, falling apart as a result of internal contradictions between the FLP and the NFP. However, upon the formation of Bavadra's government, events moved rapidly. Soon after the Coalition's electoral victory sounds of protest were heard from the emergent *Taukei*, or 'native Fijian', movement, which accused Indo-Fijians of seeking to take over power in Fiji. The *Taukei* movement appeared at first a rather obscure entity, but when, after the elections, they provoked a series of disturbances and clashes, they reminded some older expatriates of the Nazi German 'brownshirts' prior to World War II. For others, they appeared reminiscent of Haiti's 'tom-toms'. Certainly, there were affinities. 'The *Taukei*', said a political scientist at the time, 'constitutes lumpenproletariat, consisting of fighting gangs arising from amongst unemployed youth with a vague sense of alliance with people from the Lau islands. They themselves also largely originate from there'. The *Taukei* undoubtedly prepared the climate for Rabuka's 14 May 1987 coup, and indeed following the coup Rabuka conducted a kind of public dialogue with the *Taukei*. As he put it, 'we are pursuing the same ends, but with different means'.

In common with the *Taukei*, Rabuka emphasised the indigenous Fijian character of Fiji's identity. However, indigenous Fijian identity was itself, in part, the product of the colonial encounter. This was most clearly witnessed in the introduction of the 'Sunday ban'. Following the coup, an absolute observance of Sunday as a 'day of rest' came into force. At a stroke, nothing was allowed on Sundays: no sports, no games, no picnics, no gardening nor car washing. No taxis or buses ran, and all shops were closed. However, the Sunday ban, despite appearing to be a bow to Christian fundamentalism, had a political objective. Rabuka's relationship with the Great Council of Chiefs was unclear. Rabuka's relationship with the politico-economic power bloc around Mara was also hazy. Indeed, Rabuka's relationship with the indigenous Fijian community as a whole was unclear. As one indigenous Fijian student, struggling to comprehend political changes that he really did not understand, put it: 'what is really being engineered here? What else is waiting us?'. Rabuka needed to solidify his position. The Sunday ban gained the support of many Methodist preachers and their congregations. It also offered Rabuka an opportunity to broaden his ideological base within the *Taukei* movement, many of whom were, paradoxically, actively practicing Christians, even if the macho jogging *Taukei* and the properly necktied Methodists appeared to be emotional antipoles.

The regime may have been trying to expand its base of support, but the competence within Rabuka's government to tackle the problems which it had both inherited and created, or indeed to even to acknowledge them, was extremely poor. 'One half of his team has a criminal record, while the other half has probably managed to escape it', judged a trained observer of Fiji's political scene and its actors. 'The economy is in crisis, and is running into a head-on disaster' was how one person saw it, while a policy researcher at the Reserve Bank of Fiji observed that following successive devaluations of the Fiji dollar 'the reserves have been reversed'. Everywhere, talk was of an economic 'nose-dive'. Whoever could afford to leave at least considered it, and in some sectors, particularly education and the public service, departures assumed massive proportions. Many companies retrenched staff, with instant effects in terms of people's ability to pay for rent, schools and buses; within a short space of time, noticeably fewer children were going to school. Tourism came to a standstill, notwithstanding spectacular budget offers being made to the US market. Several pine plantations went up in flames, in quiet protest. Indo-Fijian and indigenous Fijian sugarcane producers tried to protect themselves against potential food scarcities by reserving larger parts of their plots to grow food crops. Wealthy Indo-Fijian merchants and rich indigenous Fijians made sure their capital was out of the country as quickly as possible. 'If need be, we'll go back to the countryside, and to our traditional way of life', the *Taukei* claimed. 'But we don't want to go back to the land, and we would not even know how to cope there', a third generation urban indigenous Fijian woman stated. It was a heavy price to pay, not for democracy, but for its denial.

Words and meaning

Many living in Fiji made caustic remarks about the reporting of the coup by foreign journalists. 'Most of them took it easy. They settled themselves in the lounge of the Grand Pacific Hotel and wrote a simplistic story about ethnic conflict between Indians and Fijians, exactly how Rabuka—and others behind him—would like to see it. We had hoped that at least the foreign press would correct that perverse image.' The reality was of course more complex, as was demonstrated to one of the authors when visiting USP as an external advisor to the History/Politics Department just a few weeks after the second coup. Towards the end of the visit the time came to share some impressions with members of the Department before drafting the final report. A staff meeting was thus arranged, just prior to departure, and quite central to the issues which were raised for discussion was, as a result of declining student enrolments and the changed political climate, the increasingly vulnerable position in which the History/Politics Department found itself within the university. The situation called for a new strategy, in which, through the offering of regionally specific, non-traditional history courses and policy-oriented politics courses, the Department would seek to build an interdisciplinary, development-focused approach. It thus seemed opportune for the History/Politics Department to dilute its disciplinary identity and, metaphorically, go 'underground'. This viewpoint was verbally communicated to the members of the Department during the course of the meeting.

Several weeks later, back in Europe, a clipping arrived in the mail from the *Fiji Post* of 31 October 1987. Under the bold headline 'Fight rages over Dutch scholar's activities', the paper carried a lengthy article on a controversy between the government and the university, which, at first glance, seemed to originate from another planet:

> A verbal war continued yesterday between the Education Ministry and the University of the South Pacific over allegations that a visiting Dutch scholar had been advising USP staff to teach Marxism and Communism 'undercover'.

> Yesterday, Education Minister *Ratu* Filimone Ralogaivau reiterated what he said early this week that the visitor had advised staff in the Social Science department to go 'underground' and teach the two subjects. *Ratu* Filimone said he had been reliably informed of these

developments by a member of the staff who had been 'part of the discussions'. He said the move was designed to 'undermine the traditions of the Fijian people and thwart their present struggle in their own country'.

'I am surprised that this type of activity is being deliberately permitted in an institution funded by the taxpayers of Fiji. It appears that those who administer USP are setting out to force the hand of the present government...The leadership of the university continues to be insensitive about the inspirations of the Fijian people...The Vice-Chancellor must understand that the Laucala Bay campus stands on the sovereign territory of Fiji and that the university is subject to the laws of Fiji...'

In retrospect, what was interesting about this mini-crisis was not the different connotations of the word 'underground', but rather why its meaning was twisted. This was done to try and ensure that the external advisor's report was not considered, and thus ward off any possible attacks to the offering of an undiluted, 'traditional' history of Fiji and Pacific culture within the History/Politics Department. Moreover, it was clear that the government's information had come from a staff member engaged in the teaching of traditional Fiji history and culture. That teaching had been done with the pre-colonial, colonial and the post-colonial periods all grasped within a single perspective of historical continuity, and with the colonial period being viewed as an interlude.

The interesting point about the controversy however was that it linked a perceived threat to departmental continuity and hegemony in the offering of traditional history courses to the threat to the integrity of the indigenous Fijian community imagined by the supporters of the new regime. Developing course offerings on the wider economic and social transformations to which Fiji had been subject during colonial times and after would have implied recognition of the roles that Fiji's various peoples—migrant as well as indigenous—had come to play in these transformations. It would have had to address the new social and political context that had come into existence in the wake of these historical changes. In contrast, restricting history courses to a focus on the continuity of traditional Fiji institutions to the present day made it possible to negate the vastly changed social and economic situation that had emerged through Fiji's history—as indeed the *Taukei* and Rabuka's government also appeared intent to do. The parallel between the micro politics in the Department and the macro situation in the country could hardly have been closer. Indeed, the politicisation of the issue at the particular time directly linked the question of course offerings to the central issue at stake in the country: identity in Fiji at the time and thereafter.

Crisis and identities

Until the time of the coups, identities in Fiji had appeared quite simple and straightforward. It was generally clear who could be referred to as 'Fijian' and it was similarly clear who could be identified as 'Indian' or 'Indo-Fijian'. Fuller integration had simply not been on the agenda. Distinct identities were largely reflective of the separate niches the two main ethnic groups occupied within Fiji's economy and society. Social contacts across communities were relatively limited: except for some sections within the urban milieu, most indigenous Fijians and most Indo-Fijians interacted primarily amongst themselves rather than with members of a range of ethnic communities. Without any overt enmity or direct confrontations taking place, social relations had largely seemed unproblematic, and Fiji could readily be portrayed as a Pacific paradise by tour operators and others.

At another level, though, it was precisely this non-integration—consciously engineered and preserved as it had been—which could be said to have constituted Fiji's main problematic feature. Superficially a multicultural society, its separate identities also signified unfulfilled social integration, social distance, differential access to political power and, though perhaps remotely, potential friction. Despite its various institutional mechanisms to ensure continued separate social and economic positions, such as in land, it is doubtful whether Fiji society in the longer run would have been able to sustain its seemingly appealing image alongside its lack of social integration.

The coups ruptured the seeming tranquility that people had been enjoying and brought to the fore this simmering issue. As a consequence, over the last decade Fiji has been deeply engaged in a process of re-appraising itself, which is leaving its imprint in terms of changing self-images and changing collective understandings about the future. Numerous questions about the shape of social and political relationships have been raised, and continue to be articulated from different perspectives. At one end of the spectrum, they range from querying continued separate designations which might be employed to keep ethnic groups apart, to asking whether ultimately all of Fiji's people may come to feel encouraged to call themselves 'Fijians'. At the other end of the spectrum, questions concern the preservation of authenticity, closely followed by a concern with the maintenance of the status quo. What both ends of the spectrum share is that they imply questions and concerns about the scope for power sharing and equity in any future constellation of social, cultural, political and economic arrangements in Fiji.

At the same time, probably more aspects of Fiji's society and economy have been subjected to probing analysis during this period than has happened at any time before. Moreover, at the policy and political level, numerous interventions—aggravating, ameliorating, or just sustaining the situation—have been undertaken following identification of the 'problem' in the wake of the coup. All this added substantially to changing relations, and perceptions of relations. Clearly, the period has not been an easy one. Indeed, in socio-psychological terms it is easy to see how the damage could have been irreparable.

Appraising the aftermath

Time has now come to recognise the importance of this aftermath; that is, to re-assess the net effects of all the self-searching and restructuring that has taken place during these twelve years, coupled to the equally significant social and political transitions that have been taking place on the ground. None of these have been minor and by themselves they signal the major differences, and possibly also the major gains, between the Fiji of today and that of twelve years ago—socially, economically, and politically.

Significantly, recognising the transformations that have occurred over the last decade or more also places a different light on Fiji's condition today, thus allowing the coups and their aftermath to be viewed within a broader historical and comparative perspective. From such a perspective some fresh reinterpretations might well suggest themselves. One overriding way of viewing the crisis so far has been—quite naturally—to equate it with a shattering of earlier expectations of progressive and peaceful co-habitation and integration, even though only a few people at the time may actually have been giving any thought as to how that might be brought about.

Viewed from such a perspective, most of the different labels of national identity which have since been proposed either officially, such as 'Fiji Islanders', or unofficially, such as 'aboriginal' or 'ethnic' Fijians, could be seen as either reflecting fragmentation, or, at best, as perhaps rather feeble attempts at repair.

Dominant and natural as this range of interpretations has been, in due course they might possibly make room for different kinds of understanding, including some that might have appeared out of the question or contentious at an earlier stage. Notably, given the complex and virtually unprecedented demographic situation with which the colonial experience had left Fiji, the relative outsider, for one, might wonder whether the confrontations signaled by the coup and after could not be viewed as a kind of inevitable or 'necessary' crisis the country would have to pass through: necessary in the sense of being needed before the country would be able to arrive at a painful recognition of the common destinies which its peoples must share. Reflecting on the present, it is also necessary to remember from where Fiji has come. Colonial rule had left a country singularly handicapped to be handled as a unit, and a unity, thus potentially ranking it among the 'impossible' nation-states, countries such as Sudan, South Africa, Cyprus, and others. With a near even balance between the two main ethnic groups, with the two groups having largely separate economic spheres, with the two groups governed through institutions which emphasised separateness, and with powerful élites keen to preserve institutionally entrenched positions, Fiji evidently had a long way to go. Against that background, 1987 constituted a major, unprecedented shock which, it appears, has served as a prelude to the intensive soul-searching conducted over the past twelve years. If this reading is valid, it would just underscore the imperative, for Fiji's societal development and change, of constructing sound strategies oriented towards the country growing together, rather than growing apart.

Surely, though, such speculative thinking has its limits, and social science as a matter of principle will only sparingly offer space for it. Nor should any such reflections be construed to imply more generally that army coups can provide reliable routes towards possible reconciliation. Nonetheless, what is important is that due attention should be given to the many ways in which, provoked by the coups, segments of Fiji society and government during its aftermath have been attempting to come to terms with the country's basic realities—

whether from narrowly competitive, even retrogressive, or from more genuinely constructive angles—thus beginning to address issues about Fiji's future in a more head-on fashion than they probably had done at any time earlier.

Confronting Fiji futures

The present volume reflects this ongoing search for alternatives and direction, and aims to make a contribution to the debates by illuminating a range of relevant issues from several strategic vantage points. Therefore, the volume is divided into two sections. The first section is entitled 'Politics, economics and social inequality' and begins with Chapter 2, 'The implementation of the Fiji Islands Constitution' by Yash Ghai. Ghai examines both the process by which the new 1997 Constitution of Fiji Islands was constructed, as well as its objectives, before going on to focus on three issues: the electoral system; multi-party government; and accountability. Some questions are raised concerning how the new Constitution will be implemented, using the word 'implementation' to denote the dynamics of the inner logic of the Constitution, the directions in which it compels, promotes or facilitates change, as well the contradictions within it which may obstruct the achievement of its objectives. Ghai stresses that the ultimate success of the new Constitution will depend upon the extent to which civil society becomes committed to its norms and values, and on this critical factor there are as yet no guarantees.

Chapter 3 is by Satendra Prasad and is entitled 'Fiji's 1999 general elections: outcomes and prospects'. The chapter demonstrates that the alternative voting system used in the 1999 general elections has been able to foster cooperation amongst Fiji's political parties, and that this cooperation has been reinforced by the introduction of multiparty government. However, the new voting system has not been able to eliminate the recourse to ethnicity as a tool of political mobilisation. Ironically, the use of ethnicity may not have occurred in those seats 'reserved' for Fiji's main ethic communities; rather, it may have occurred in those seats for which the entire electorate is eligible to cast its vote. Moreover, where it has fostered cross-community cooperation, this has been amongst élites; it has not occurred amongst the people. Nonetheless, as a national referendum on the 1997 Constitution, the 1999 general elections demonstrate that it has received an overwhelming mandate from the peoples of Fiji.

Chapter 4 is entitled 'Fiji's economy: the challenge of the future' and is by Ardeshir Sepehri and Haroon Akram-Lodhi. The chapter begins by providing an overview of the evolution of Fiji's macroeconomic structure during the post-independence period, placing particular emphasis on changes occurring during the period between 1987 and 1992. It then focuses upon assessing the impact of domestic savings, public sector spending and external resources, including Fiji's preferential access to the European Union for its sugar exports, on the growth path of the Fiji economy by specifying a three-gap model of growth in Fiji for the period 1971 to 1996. Once the three-gap model is estimated, the parameters of the model are used to simulate the period between 1997 to 2001 under four alternative growth path 'scenarios'. These scenarios examine the impact of a gradual elimination of Fiji's preferential access to the European Union, and thus a substantial reduction in the availability of foreign resources, which, should it occur, would have a major affect on the growth of the economy. Sepehri and Akram-Lodhi demonstrate that the challenge for Fiji's policy makers is to intensify export diversification efforts. They suggest that in order to develop a set of coherent and consistent policies to promote export diversification there is a pressing need to reduce the 'ethnicisation' of economic policy, arguing that a reduction in the role played by ethnicity in the formulation and implementation of economic policies may improve the efficiency of state intervention in the economy and in so doing contribute to enhanced economic performance.

Chapter 5, 'Institutional rigidities and economic performance in Fiji', is by Biman Prasad and Sunil Kumar. Consistent with Chapter 4, Prasad and Kumar argue that the key constraints to improved economic performance in Fiji are a set of institutional rigidities. Supply-side structural adjustment policies in Fiji have, according to Prasad and Kumar, been based upon a neoclassical model which assume institutional structures as given and thus fail to consider their potential role as a constraint. Yet, argue the authors, institutional rigidities pervade the Fiji economy. Long-term growth will only increase if these institutional rigidities are addressed and resolved. Prasad and Kumar provide a case study of property rights in land to illustrate their main argument, arguing that key land tenure institutions are inefficient, and suggesting that this inefficiency has implications for investment, production and distribution.

Chapter 6 is by John Cameron and is entitled 'Confronting social policy challenges in Fiji'. Cameron examines the extent of the challenge confronting civil society and the state in Fiji in seeking to redistribute social and economic uncertainty, improve the degree of equality within society, and in so doing build 'social wealth'. Adopting a perspective similar to that found in Chapter 5, Cameron offers a critique of the neoliberal approach to social inequality and argues that the new institutional economics offers a countervailing approach rooted in distinctive moral and political perspectives which emphasise the interaction between civil society, state institutions and imperfect markets in facilitating improvements in the degree of equality within a society. In light of this framework, Cameron argues that the challenge confronting the state in Fiji is not in the detail of policy design but rather in the need to build on and invest in existing social wealth so as to institutionalise positive socio-economic processes. Three possible policy interventions which could institutionalise positive socio-economic processes are briefly examined: health and nutrition, education and community relations. Cameron argues that the construction of a less unequal, more socially-inclusive, multicultural polity requires that state social policy actively support those civil society institutions in both major ethnic groups which have facilitated social wealth formation and a good quality of life for many of Fiji's peoples.

Chapter 7, by Ganesh Chand, explores an important source of social inequality in its examination of 'Labour market deregulation in Fiji'. Chand looks at the background to deregulation policies, the objectives of the deregulation drive, the key mechanisms for deregulating the labour market, and some consequences of deregulation. Chand argues that the deregulation process was part of a wider set of structural adjustment policies which Fiji began adopting in the mid 1980s. The military coup and the subsequent collapse of the economy provided the opportunity for Fiji to push ahead with the adjustment program. As the gist of the new policy package was export-oriented industrialisation, deregulation was to align the labour market with this objective. The consequences of deregulation are demonstrated by Chand to have been a continuing decline in the unionisation rate, most notably in the manufacturing sector but more generally in the private sector; a rise in industrial disputes but a fall in the number and intensity of strikes; a fall in real wages; and an increasing prominence of female workers in wage employment. Chand notes that the new Constitution has repealed some of the decrees which were promulgated during 1991 and 1992, stressing that this suggests that the institutional framework structuring labour market outcomes in the early 1990s was regarded by many of the peoples of Fiji as unjust. However, Chand argues, repeal has occurred after a significant transformation in Fiji's labour market has already occurred. Labour market deregulation has therefore already had an impact that will be felt in the years to come.

Chapter 8, entitled 'Women in post-coup Fiji: negotiating work through old and new realities', examines a second source of social inequality, that of gender relations. Written by Jacqueline Leckie, the chapter explores the ways in which the political economy of post-coup Fiji has profoundly shaped women's lives, expectations and identities. Predicated on the proposition that it is futile to separate work from other component's of women's lives, Leckie argues that change has been a reflection of women's cultures, the legacy of colonialism, the education system, the impact of the post-coup regime, and globalisation. According to Leckie, for women gender is the central thread through these changes; but they are also linked to other identities and hierarchies, and especially those of ethnicity and class. In part, she argues, this sheds light on the contradictory responses to change from women. For most women these responses are not polarised choices but rather represent what may seem to be a never-ending balancing act between old and new realities, in which personal and collective identities are negotiated to varying degrees. Contestation over tradition, culture and political rights has thus been on going since the coups, although it was not given legitimate public space until the review of the 1990 Constitution. Leckie concludes by arguing that given the cultural and economic realities of the present, how Fiji's new constitution will improve women's rights remains a vitally important question.

In Chapter 8 Leckie introduces the idea that social identity is rooted in political and economic processes. This idea is explored in more detail in the second section of *Confronting Fiji Futures*, 'The "Fijian" question', which offers detailed analysis on the political economy of indigenous Fijian identity. The section begins with Chapter 9, 'The problematics of reform and the "Fijian" question', by William Sutherland. Sutherland is concerned with the impact of post-coup reforms on the 'Fijian' question which, at its most elementary,

comes down to a simple question: who is a Fijian? Sutherland argues
that up to the early 1990s the state's economic reform agenda was
driven primarily by nationalist indigenous Fijian demands but that
from the mid 1990s, faced with increasing external pressures for
greater liberalisation, the state not only picked up the pace and scope
of reform but also increasingly had to distance itself from its nationalist
agenda. In so doing the state alienated the political constituency on
which it depended most critically. By the late 1990s the level of
indigenous Fijian disaffection had grown, and the Fijian question
remained unresolved. Sutherland concludes by demonstrating that
how the Fijian question is managed in the future will be critical to the
country's prospects for economic growth and political stability.

Chapters 10 and 11 offer two case studies of the 'Fijian' question.
Chapter 10 is entitled 'Addressing inequality? Economic affirmative
action and communal capitalism in post-coup Fiji' and is by Steven
Ratuva. Having defined 'communal capitalism', Ratuva provides an
overview of the economic affirmative action policies intended to
benefit indigenous Fijians in the wake of the 1987 coups. A case study
of communal capitalism, that of the Fijian Holdings Company
Limited, is presented by Ratuva because it is the flagship of
indigenous Fijian communal investment, and is seen as a success story
in as far as communal capitalism is concerned, yet it manifests some
fundamental contradictions, which are explored in the chapter. In
these explorations, Ratuva is able to substantiate the profound doubts
he has about the benefits of economic affirmative action in Fiji, in large
part because they have primarily benefited a small minority of
indigenous Fijians.

In Chapter 11, Holger Korth examines 'Ecotourism and the politics
of representation in Fiji'. Korth demonstrates that the main thrust
behind ecotourism development in Fiji has been the re-invention of Fiji
as a 'destination image' which, in its production and consumption,
centers on nature and indigenous Fijian ethnicity. Seemingly
progressive in its environmentalist sensitivities, Korth shows that the
development of ecotourism in Fiji has been driven by segments of the
state apparatus. However, ecotourism development in Fiji has,
according to Korth, been predicated upon the conservation of the
social, cultural and natural ecology. Korth argues that while sustainable
development requires this, it also requires more: the democratisation
of decision-making processes, the equitable distribution of resources,

and equal opportunities across the age and gender divide. Ecotourism has failed to contribute to these. Closely examining certain aspects of ecotourism development, Korth shows that such development reflects ethnic divisions and prevalent post-coup political sentiments. Korth notes that it is, in this light, not surprising that ecotourism has had minimal economic impact.

Chapter 12, by Robbie Robertson, concludes the volume. Entitled 'Retreat from exclusion? Identities in post-coup Fiji', Robertson argues that Fiji has only partially retreated from the extremist nationalism that underlay the 1987 coups. Robertson notes that despite considerable achievements in the new 1997 Constitution, the nation still has to come to terms with its past. In particular, Robertson highlights issues of identity—including ownership of the national name—which remain largely unresolved. Robertson illustrates the complex paradox of identity in Fiji by examining the changing views of Sitiveni Rabuka on inter-community relations. This paradox, Robertson argues, means that the potential remains for powerful but fractious class interests to exploit ethnocentrism in order to maintain advantage, and thereby once more push the country back towards heightened communal division.

The chapters offered in this collection represent a stocktaking of the rethinking processes that have been underway in Fiji since the coups. They point to the significant ways in which social, economic and political relations have been shifting since 1987, as well as to emerging changing perspectives on these relations and their future. In this regard, the chapters by Robertson, Sutherland, Ratuva, Leckie and Chand, amongst others, represent thoughtful discussions of different levels of post-coup transition and the re-interpretations to which they have given rise. The picture that emerges is one of a society that seems much better equipped now than it was twelve years ago to face and take up the challenges it is confronted with, and to recognise that integration on various fronts is going to be arduous, but nevertheless the only route worth going.

The book's timeliness in this respect has been underscored by the spectacular and largely unexpected outcomes of the 1999 Fiji elections. The election results themselves have been indicative of the significant social re-orientation that has occurred in recent years in response to, or despite, all the governmental and non-governmental doctoring that was done. Satendra Prasad contributes an insightful analysis of the elections in this volume. Evidently, changing social realities have given rise to a new and autonomous social dynamic which, more emphatically than ever before, begins to defy the ethnic categorisations once thought descriptive of basic social divisions. The importance of changing social realities in the Fiji context also lies in demonstrating that even complex institutionalised strings and knots cannot keep voters' feet tied all the time. As Robertson remarks, what official resources have failed to do, the popular vote may possibly achieve.

Naturally, the drastically changed political constellation the elections have inaugurated invites another fresh wave of rethinking on the key issues confronting Fiji. It is hoped that the chapters that follow can serve as an aid in that process: many of the questions explored by the authors will no doubt feature prominently on the policy agenda and in public debate in the years to come.

Endnote

1. From W.B. Yeats *The Second Coming*:
   Turning and turning in the widening gyre
   The falcon cannot bear the falconer;
   Things fall apart; the center cannot hold;
   Mere anarchy is loosed upon the world.
   All quotations contained within this chapter are taken from the field notes of Martin Doornbos, collected and collated during his 1987 visit to Fiji.

CHAPTER 2

The implementation of the Fiji Islands Constitution

Yash Ghai

This chapter[1] examines some questions concerning the implementation of the new Constitution of Fiji Islands, adopted in 1997. It might be thought that in light of the successful completion of the 1999 general elections such an examination is redundant. However, the chapter does not use 'implementation' in the narrow sense of the legislation and the administrative measures which give effect to some or all of the provisions of the Constitution. Rather, it employs it in a teleological sense, to denote the achievement of the objectives of the Constitution. In this sense, 'implementation' also denotes the dynamics of the inner logic of the Constitution, the directions in which it compels, promotes or facilitates change, as well the contradictions within it which may obstruct the achievement of its objectives. In this wider sense, it does not solely refer to measures taken by official bodies alone, important though they are, for various institutions must be funded and resourced, and various policy initiatives taken. Civil society institutions must also play a crucial role in this wider sense. Such a broad view of 'implementation' requires discussion of the objectives of the Constitution and the instruments it has provided for their achievement. Thus, after sketching the framework of analysis, the process by which the Constitution was constructed, and its objectives, the chapter will focus on three issues: (i) the electoral system; (ii) multiparty government; and (iii) accountability.

The Constitution as a paradox

The 1997 Constitution of Fiji Islands is a rich and complex document.
Paradoxically, it represents both an affirmation of liberalism—
especially significant after the repudiation of liberalism in the 1990
Constitution—and a major qualification on it. This paradox is less the
result of confusion on the part of the Fiji Constitution Review
Commission (FCRC) (referred to henceforth as the Reeves Commission,
after its chair) as rather the legacy of Fiji's constitutional and political
history. Nevertheless, the interest of the 1997 Constitution lies precisely
in this paradox, for the paradox reflects not only the tortured ethnic
history of Fiji but also the more global concern of how to accommodate
ethnic and cultural diversity within liberalism (Kymlicka 1989, 1995;
Taylor 1994; Tully 1996). The Constitution also marks a break, in
different ways, with both earlier Fiji constitutions and with dominant
liberal constitutionalism. For those familiar with Fiji's history, the
previous sentence itself may seem paradoxical, for earlier constitutions
themselves were a negation of liberalism. However, the fact is that the
Constitution does not lend itself to simple accounts or explanations. It
is rooted both in Fiji's specificity and in more general debates on
'ethnic constitutionalism'.

The new Constitution can be located within contemporary
approaches to the constitutional settlement of ethnicity. In the classical
liberal paradigm, no distinction is made between members of different
ethnic communities. The key organising concept is that of citizenship,
which carries with it rights and responsibilities on the basis of the
equality of all. Cultural diversity can sometimes be accommodated
through federalism, as in Canada for the Francophone community.
However, such autonomy is generally fortuitous. For example, US
federalism has been rigorously opposed to ethnic federalism, as is
manifested in its attitude, until recently, to Puerto Rican claims to
statehood, as Puerto Rico's Hispanic traditions were widely
considered to be incompatible with the dominant traditions of the
United States. In the classical liberal paradigm culture and religion are
seen as belonging by and large to the private sphere, and should thus
not intrude upon the public domain. More accurately, classical
liberalism assumed cultural homogeneity and these possible dilemmas
were not fully recognised. It is fair to say that in the negotiations for
independent Fiji's first constitution, the leading party of Indo-Fijians,

the National Federation Party (NFP), pressed for a settlement rooted in the classical liberal paradigm, with its advocacy of the election of the entire legislature by a common roll electorate, a procedure which was also deeply rooted in the history of the Indo-Fijian community in Fiji.

The other approach is to recognise diverse ethnic communities in public law. Within this broad approach, there are three different frameworks, which have little in common. The first is to adopt constitutional provisions designed to provide specific and limited recognition for ethnic groups, particularly minorities, typically through special representation in the legislature, property rights, and/or personal laws. Many such provisions tend to be transitional, for they are located within a constitution which is based on equal citizenship, and which thus aspires to liberalism. Thus, although liberal constitutions seek to disregard cultural and ethnic differences, they may nonetheless reflect an underlying concern with the promotion of national integration. To this end, such a constitution may include provisions such as ethnic equity, independent commissions to remove ethnic discrimination or disabilities, and electoral systems that provide incentives for inter-ethnic cooperation. In some respects Fiji's first Constitution of 1970 seems to fall in this category, for its provision of communal seats was seen as temporary, even though other non-liberal aspects of that Constitution, and particularly the system of administration based on the separation of indigenous Fijians from other groups, were permanent and entrenched.

The second framework proceeds on the assumption of the hegemony of one ethnic community over others (Lustick 1980). Ethnic hegemony ensures political order and stability through the subordination by one community of other communities, who are either disenfranchised completely or are grossly under-represented in the apparatus of the state. Control is a dominant concern of such a system, and as such it operates typically through various forms of coercion, political as well as economic. Colonialism and apartheid South Africa have been classical examples in recent history; while the Jewish dominance of Arabs in Israel, the Protestant dominance of Catholics in Northern Ireland, and the Malay dominance of other ethnic groups in Malaysia are contemporary examples. Such an approach is not inconsistent with the recognition of the culture of the subordinated; indeed, in many instances the recognition in public law of cultural diversity is a central device for subordination.

The third framework, consociationalism, may be said to be the exact opposite of this control model (Lijphart 1977). It is a response to the inadequacies of the liberal, majoritarian approach in ethnically divided states, which fails to recognise and protect the specific interests of minorities or even significant ethnic groups or to provide a place for them in the decision making of the state apparatus. Consociationalism recognises different communities as corporate groups, with rights and responsibilities. It is premised on the principle that each community should be allowed to participate in the affairs of the state—legislative, executive and public services—in some acceptable proportion. It thus uses a system of pillars and quotas. The leaders of each community have a veto over decisions that they regard as affecting the community's interests adversely. It advocates maximum autonomy for each community over its internal affairs, whether through federalism or some other form of autonomy. Consociationalism is sometimes a description of constitutional arrangements that confer a corporate status on communities, for example by providing communal electoral rolls and/or internal autonomy. It also provides for the cooperation of community leaders in government, as in Bosnia–Herzegovina or the first constitution of independent Cyprus. At other times the term is used to refer to the way a constitution actually works, even though it may not have formal consociational features. For a period of years, Malaysia would have been an example of the latter.

Few constitutions fall neatly into these categories. However, as will be demonstrated below, while the 1970 Fiji Constitution had clear elements of consociationalism, its consociationalism was neither thorough nor equally just to all communities. By way of contrast, the 1990 Constitution provided directly and explicitly for the 'control' system that was in many ways implicit in the 1970 Constitution. The 1997 Constitution is different. Hovering between these paradigms, one may say that the 1997 Constitution uses consociationalism, but in an effort to achieve multiethnic integration. In that sense both the 1970 and 1997 Constitutions were dynamic, in that they sought to restructure ethnic political relationships, as opposed to both the 1990 Constitution and indeed the pure consociationalist model, which do not. However, before turning to the examination of the 1997 Constitution, the process of its making is discussed.

The role of the Constitution: process

As conceived by the Reeves Commission, an essential role of the 1997 Constitution of Fiji Islands was to establish and consolidate a national consensus on how the country should be governed. If it succeeded in this aim, it would help to put aside the divisions and the bitterness of 1987 coups and subsequent policies of discrimination. For this purpose it was important to adopt a procedure which would enable a critical examination of the 1990 Constitution. As a part of this, it was also important to give a wide opportunity to individuals, political parties and civic groups to express their views of the past, and their aspirations for the future.

The process underpinning the formulation and the adoption of the 1997 Constitution thus provides a vivid contrast to the procedures used in producing the 1970 and the 1990 Constitutions. The former was drawn up in a series of closed meetings between the political parties, principally the Alliance and the NFP. Differences between them that could not be resolved were settled by the British, particularly at London conferences. There was little public discussion of constitutional issues. The assumption underlying this procedure was that the only way to narrow and resolve ethnic differences was to make the necessary compromises among the élite in private. By way of contrast, the 1990 Constitution was made after the public was invited to make representations to a committee. Public hearings were held to provide legitimacy on the process and the outcome. However, the committee itself was packed with supporters of the coups, and was thus widely perceived by Indo-Fijians to lack impartiality. Consequently, it enjoyed little legitimacy among them.

The Reeves Commission rejected a proposal for its hearings to be held in private, although it allowed a few individuals to present their views on a confidential basis (Fiji Constitution Review Commission (henceforth FCRC) 1996:4.4). It instead promoted a wide consultative process, itself travelling extensively in the country. At the same time, the Commission also believed that it was important to learn from the experiences of other multiethnic countries. Finally, it valued the views of both local and foreign scholars. Consequently, it commissioned and eventually had published a number of studies relevant to its terms of reference, analysing local circumstances and policies, and foreign experiences, including Malaysia, Mauritius and South Africa (Lal and Vakatora 1997a, 1997b).

The Reeves Commission received in all 852 submissions (FCRC 1996:4.5). Representations were made not only by political groups, but also by religious organisations, trade unions, academics, women's groups, and the Citizens Constitutional Forum, a non-governmental organisation established specifically to promote public discussion of constitutional options, which had itself held consultations with a wide variety of groups before preparing its submission. It is probably fair to say that the issues were reasonably well understood, that all views were canvassed, and there was a high degree of interest in the issues and the process. There was also a thorough review of the 1990 Constitution. As such, there had never before been such an opportunity for all the peoples of Fiji to participate in the constitution-making process.

Thoroughness was also manifested in the report and recommendations of the Reeves Commission. The report provides an impartial summary of the submissions it received, particularly from the major political parties. It builds on an emerging local consensus where that is appropriate, but it is not afraid to make innovative proposals that depart from the submissions to it. The report is moreover informed by developments in the international regime of rights and the experiences of other countries. Drawing from a careful analysis of its terms of reference, and without ignoring history, reality and constraints on change in Fiji, the Commission sets out in clear and forthright terms a framework of recommendations which are forward looking and which provide clear directions for change. Granted, the Reeves Commission could only achieve the objectives of its terms of reference through a series of compromises. Nonetheless, its vision for the future of Fiji had a remarkable degree of coherence.

The recommendations of the Commission provided the basis on which the Joint Parliamentary Select Committee made its recommendations to Parliament. Although the Select Committee seems to have accepted the primary national goals spelled out by the Commission, it did not adopt all the recommendations of the Commission, especially on systems of elections and government. However, while the Select Committee did not articulate its own vision or the reasons for it deviating from the Reeves Commission recommendations, it does still seem to have been animated by the overall approach of the Reeves Commission. The Select Committee did produce a consensus, which was rapidly transformed into a draft constitution which was given the force of law by a unanimous vote of Parliament, after the recommendations of the Select Committee had received the agreement of the Great Council of Chiefs. The work of the Select Committee and of Parliament, urged on by the leaders of all political parties, was rightly hailed as a breakthrough. It seemed to represent a reconciliation of sorts, but more importantly, a consensus on how Fiji should be governed and how its different communities should relate to each other. It was seen to mark a significant break from past policies and the institutionalisation of ethnic difference, although not as decisively as the Reeves Commission had recommended. In this light, it is not surprising that the 1997 Constitution was widely welcomed in Fiji and abroad.

Although the outcome of the process is to be welcomed, it is not possible to say that the process succeeded in completely reconciling ethnic communities. The terms of reference of the review, concluded after difficult and hard negotiations, had indeed provided a basis for reconciliation and a cooperative search for national consensus. The principal objective of the review was the promotion 'of racial harmony and national unity, and the economic and social advancement of all communities' (FCRC 1996:754–55), goals which seemed to override other virtues like 'democracy'. This objective had been agreed upon after protracted discussions between the government and the opposition, which resulted in support for the review in Parliament. Having been agreed, it might have been expected that it represented an important consensus under which the details of the constitution would have been worked out. However, the 'consensus' was criticised by many Indo-Fijians and indigenous Fijians as a 'sell out'. As a result, and perhaps not surprisingly, a spirit of consensus or amity was not much in evidence as the process unfolded, aggravating the task of the Reeves Commission as it received highly opposed submissions and as the drama of ethnic animosity was rehearsed before it daily. Far from political parties using the process to bring their supporters around the consensus of the terms of reference, some of them incited their supporters to further animosities against other communities. Nor did they try to use the process to establish rapport with leaders of other communities and parties. The lack of that spirit, or what seemed the absence of commitment to the terms of reference by some major groups, threatened at times to sabotage the entire review. When agreement was finally reached on the constitution in the Joint Committee as well as in Parliament, it was grudging and half-hearted, with speeches belying the vote many cast, as if many members were acting under coercion. That lack of a complete commitment to the new constitutional dispensation will most probably act as a brake on its full and proper implementation.

Nevertheless, it would be unrealistic to ignore the value of agreement on the Constitution. Even if not all the parties were wholeheartedly behind it, the agreement was based on the recognition that a generally acceptable constitution had to be a compromise; that no community or party could get all of what it wanted. The fact of unanimity, even if some members had reservations, was perhaps demonstrative of a broad recognition of the justice of the Constitution.

The role of the Constitution: objectives

The purpose of the 1997 Constitution is to provide a basis, on which all of Fiji's communities could agree, for the peoples of Fiji to live together under a system of government. It is intended to bring to an end the social and political stalemate that had resulted from the 1987 coups and the constitutional system that was established as a consequence of the coups. That system was seen to be divisive, apart from its other defects, in failing to provide effective scrutiny of government or a proper system for the protection of rights. As part of its aim to promote a multiethnic ethic and national unity, the Constitution introduced a new electoral system and a new system under which multiparty politics is now conducted. In addition to providing a foundation for inter-ethnic harmony, it is also intended to strengthen the protection of rights and freedoms, bringing the scheme of rights in Fiji into conformity with the international regime of rights. It finally seeks to harmonise group rights with individual rights.

The Constitution goes considerably further than previous Fiji constitutions in establishing a national ethic. It does so by strengthening the protection of human rights, regulating the conduct of leaders to ensure they behave responsibly and honestly, and committing the nation to social justice and the care of the disadvantaged. It also seeks to inculcate values of tolerance and compromise, through respect for the culture and traditions of others. It thus moves away from the stereotypes that have so bedevilled ethnic relations.

The Constitution was moreover intended to bring Fiji fully back into the community of nations, particularly the Commonwealth. In recent years the Commonwealth has developed a set of norms of rights and democracy to which it seeks to hold its members. It was well understood that Fiji would be re-admitted to the Commonwealth only if its constitution conformed to these norms and to the general international regime of human rights. To that end, a Commonwealth consultant prepared a review of the constitution, noting its substantial conformity with these norms, before Fiji was re-admitted.

The orientation of the 1997 Constitution can be highlighted by contrasting it with its predecessors. The 1970 Constitution was based on the separation of races. Its centrepiece was the electoral system, which was dominated by communal seats and communal voting. Although there was provision for national seats, which had been intended to provide a basis for non-ethnic politics, the logic of communal seats prevailed over the logic of national seats. Moreover, while there was parity of seats between the two major communities, the over-representation of seats for the 'General Electors' roll—that is, those who were deemed to be neither indigenous Fijian nor Indo-Fijian—was a device designed to ensure the dominance of the executive by indigenous Fijians. In this way the rather deformed Westminster system of the 1970 Constitution not merely kept communities apart politically, but also tended towards the dominance of one group over others.

The 1970 Constitution had clear elements of consociationalism in the establishment of communal rolls. However, its consociationalism was neither thorough nor equally fair to all communities. It did not directly provide for inter-ethnic cooperation; in so far as that was considered desirable, it was left primarily to the voluntary cooperation of ethnic leaders, although the requirement that the Prime Minister consult with the Leader of the Opposition on various state appointments also provided a basis for limited cooperation. The proportionality principle, which was established for the legislature, was not extended to the executive. It was much more solicitous of the interests, property and institutions of indigenous Fijians and of the political interests of 'others' than of Indo-Fijians.

At the same time, it was also possible to regard liberalism as the dominant framework of the 1970 Constitution, for the system of national seats was to be catalyst by which communal politics and communal parties would be transcended. This was reinforced by the understanding that the electoral system would be reviewed, in order to provide further incentives for inter-ethnic cooperation. Even if the forward looking recommendations of the electoral review by the Street Commission, which proposed an increase in the number and nature of national seats, making them non-communal and elected on a system of proportional representation, had been adopted, integration would however have been problematic because the separate administrative structure governing indigenous Fijians, termed the 'Fijian Administration', entailed a considerable separation of communities. The rejection of the Street Commission's recommendations shows that the 1970 Constitution may have been perceived by some politicians less in liberal terms than in terms of 'control', whereby political stability, and a measure of multiethnic stability, would be achieved under the hegemony of indigenous Fijians. Indeed, it can be argued that the disenchantment of some politicians with the 1970 Constitution in 1987 arose precisely from the realisation that its liberal impulses were at least as strong as its 'control' orientation.

The silent agenda of the 1970 Constitution, that of political order and stability under the dominance of one ethnic group, made it perhaps comparable to apartheid South Africa and contemporary Malaysia and Israel. However, the 1970 Constitution was constantly under threat from the vagaries of elections for national seats. The overt basis of the 1990 Constitution was to maintain the previously silent agenda while eliminating the threat posed by elections for national seats. The 1990 Constitution therefore removed any vestiges of cross-community voting, completing the political separation of ethnic groups, and thus making politics almost exclusively ethnic. In so doing, the 1990 Constitution aimed to ensure the permanent and undisputed rule of indigenous Fijians. It gave a disproportionately large representation to them in both houses of Parliament. Thus, in the House of Representatives 37 out of 70 seats were reserved for indigenous Fijians. In addition it provided that a Prime Minister always had to be an indigenous Fijian. Preferential treatment in, for example, education, public service, and commerce, was to benefit only the indigenous Fijian community (Ratuva, this volume). It also elevated other indigenous Fijian institutions, placing them in important respects over state institutions. As a consequence, it dispensed with the rather awkward, residual agenda of the 1970 Constitution, which had as its explicit ultimate aim the development of a multiethnic society in Fiji. The sidelining in this way of Indo-Fijians had an effect that was predictable: factionalism within the indigenous Fijian community, which had been largely contained under the more balanced allocation of communal seats in the 1970 Constitution, emerged.

By contrast, the 1997 Constitution is based on a recognition of Fiji's multiethnic character. It seeks to promote national unity so that all communities are respected and their interests protected. Its electoral system provides clear incentives for multiethnic politics, either through the collaboration of ethnic parties or indeed their replacement by multiethnic parties. It requires a multiparty government, in the expectation that leaders from all ethnic groups will participate in the government. However, although it is easy to distinguish the 1997 Constitution from its predecessors, its orientation towards multiethnic politics and government is not without ambiguities. It has not, and realistically could not, disregard entirely the burden of the constitutional and political history of the country. In the language of scholars of ethnic relations, it is neither fully consociational nor fully integrative. The entrenchment of extensive provisions for the Fijian Administration and the eminent role given to the Great Council of Chiefs serves to separate ethnic groups and privileges one against all others. Moreover, by providing a framework for indigenous Fijian politics somewhat detached from the national framework, it hinders inter-ethnic integration. Hovering between these paradigms, one may say that the 1997 Constitution uses consociationalism to achieve integration, but for the present consociationalism is more evident. These ambiguities complicate the task of the implementation of the Constitution.

It is clear that the objectives and structure of the 1997 Constitution differ in significant respects from the earlier constitutions. As has been demonstrated, it was adopted after a more participatory process than had previously been the case. As will be seen, it seeks to accommodate shared executive power amongst the major communities, a principle of proportionality in other institutions of the state, and ethnic equity. Its goals are ethnic harmony and national unity, to be achieved by adherence to a national ethic of reconciliation and compromise. Whether political habits generated by previous constitutions can be changed to accord with these new goals and methods is a central question in any examination of implementation.

Implementing the Constitution

Several provisions of the Constitution are 'non-executing' and require legislation to be implemented. At the time of writing, some progress had already been made. In addition to legislation concerning the electoral system, including the mechanism for drawing up boundaries, which was used in the 1999 general elections, there is now legislation on: Emergency Powers; an expanded jurisdiction for the Ombudsman; citizenship; the Human Rights Commission; and the Freedom of Information Act. Legislation and administrative machinery have yet to be made for the scheme of chapter 5, which provides for social justice; and the Code of Conduct for senior state office holders, including Members of Parliament. Consideration of these questions is beyond the scope of this chapter. However, it should be stated that it is important that the necessary legislation and the resources to implement them be provided as soon as possible. The Constitution cannot be separated into compartments. All its parts are integral to its purpose, orientation and method. For example, the strengthening of the protection of rights should be seen as counterbalancing a possible loss, namely parliamentary supervision of government, which may occur with the establishment of multiparty government.

In this section, key provisions of the Constitution relating to the electoral process, multiparty government and accountability will be discussed. Commentary will be offered on some issues relating to their implementation. To recapitulate, the Constitution seeks to establish a multiethnic Fiji, which is understood to be, in the political field, a system in which there is less pre-occupation with ethnicity and a clearer focus on social and economic issues from a broader, national perspective. It is a system in which political parties should coincide decreasingly with ethnicity, and should increasingly be organised along different alignments, such as class or region, however problematic such alignments may be. It is a system in which the concept of citizenship, the Fiji Islander, will replace that of ethnicity.

The electoral system

The Commission considered that these objectives would be achieved through a combination of rules for institutions and a national ethic, which would animate the functioning of these institutions. There are various provisions in the Constitution which seek to achieve this objective. So far as institutions are concerned, it provides for 25 of the 71 seats in the House of Representatives to be open to candidates of any ethnic group and for which all voters resident in the constituency may vote. The voting for these, as for communally reserved seats, is by alternative vote (AV). Under the AV system, a voter has to rank their preference among all the candidates. A winning candidate has to have an absolute majority; if no candidate obtains an absolute majority after the count of first preferences, the second—or subsequent—preferences of those who voted for candidates who came bottom of the poll on the first count are taken into account. The second and subsequent preferences of a voter can thus be crucial in determining the result (Prasad, this volume). In communal seats this method of voting principally serves the purpose of ensuring that the winning candidate enjoys clear majority support. In non-communal 'open' seats, however, its purpose is to provide incentives for political parties to cooperate across ethnic frontiers by opening up possibilities of arrangements between political parties whose core support comes from different ethnic groups. By making recommendations to their supporters concerning second and subsequent votes in open seats, parties can, in effect, try to 'trade' the second and subsequent preferences of their supporters. The trade off can of course take place between parties of the same ethnic group, but since they will be in competition in open constituencies where the members of that ethnic group predominate, trade between political parties of different ethnic groups makes better political sense. Indeed, the logic of the system might well lead to a multiplicity of multiethnic parties; this was the expectation of the Reeves Commission, which recommended it. Additionally, it was expected by the Commission that candidates with moderate views would have an advantage over those espousing extreme views, as they would have a chance of capturing more second preferences (FCRC 1996:9.150–52, 10.31–109; see also Horowitz 1997). The outcome of elections held under the provisions of the Constitution should thus either be coalition government or, better still, government by a party with multiethnic membership.

The Reeves Commission strongly believed that the AV system would operate in this way in open seats; indeed, it was content to propose this system as the only device for a multiethnic government. Since the incentives for cooperation between or the integration of parties would lie in the voting for open seats, it recommended that a predominant number of seats—45 out of a total of 70—should be open seats. Even the 25 communal seats were seen as a transitional arrangement, to be eventually replaced by open seats.

The Joint Parliamentary Select Committee was less willing to take such a bold step. Its indigenous Fijian members wanted to retain a larger number of communal seats. It thus decided, having agreed on a total membership in the House of Representatives of 71, on 46 communal and 25 open seats. Nonetheless, like the Reeves Commission, the Select Committee also favoured a party of government that was multiethnic—a so-called government of national unity. However, in a major dissent from the thinking of the Reeves Commission, it sought to achieve that government by a more direct way—by the Constitution mandating a multiparty cabinet. The Constitution provides that any party with at least 10 per cent of the seats in the House of Representatives is entitled to a proportionate share of cabinet posts. The Reeves Commission recommendation would have retained the essential principle of majority government as in the standard Westminster model, to which it was strongly committed (FCRC 1996:22). By way of contrast, the Constitution creates a major modification of parliamentary government, which will over time undoubtedly raise problems in its operation.

Some implications of the deviation of the Select Committee from the Reeves Commission recommendation can be noted. For a start, although it may sound logical it is not self-evident that the Reeves Commission proposal would have led to cooperation between parties with different ethnic bases, much less to multiethnic parties. Apart from some confusion on the part of the Commission on the technical details of how the proposed system would operate (Arms 1997), the proposed system would have required a very major re-drawing of constituency boundaries to achieve a significant mix of ethnic populations. At best, it would have been difficult to avoid constituencies where one community was not a majority, although it might have been possible to have a number of constituencies with different ethnic majorities, thus facilitating some trade off. Moreover, even if such constituencies were achieved, old habits of ethnic voting would have been likely to continue, and the supporters of a party might well have ignored the advice of the party as to how they should cast their second and subsequent votes, preferring to vote for other candidates of their own ethnicity (Ghai 1997a).

In the different arrangements under the Constitution, the probability of the AV system working over time in the way that was envisaged by the Reeves Commission becomes even less likely. The number of open seats is only about a third of the total membership of the House of Representatives. Winning open seats thus becomes less crucial to the right to form a government. A party, particularly if rooted in one of the two major ethnic groups, might well decide in future elections to adopt a strategy directed towards winning the more numerous communal seats. If old habits were to persist, the chances are that the strategy would be designed to exploit ethnic divisions by attacking politicians of one's own ethnic affiliation for being soft on other communities.

A better understanding of how the new system might work over time can be obtained through an examination of the electoral experience under the 1970 Constitution. Granted, the new electoral arrangements differ from the 1970 Constitution. However, it remains to be seen whether its logic is significantly different. Under the 1970 Constitution the House of Representatives consisted of 52 members, elected on a combination of 27 communal and 25 national seats. National seats were ethnically allocated but all the voters in the relevant constituency voted for them—hence the system came to be known as 'cross voting'. There were three electoral rolls: for indigenous Fijians, which included Rotumans and other Pacific islanders; for Indo-Fijians; and for General Electors. Indigenous Fijians and Indo-Fijians each had 12 communal and 10 national seats, while the General Electors had 3 communal and 5 national seats. Communal seats were contested on the basis of single member constituencies on a 'first past the post' basis, using communal electoral rolls. For national seats each voter had three votes to cast: one for an indigenous Fijian, one for an Indo-Fijian, and one for a General Elector. 'First past the post' operated in constituencies where three such members were to be elected.

The logic of the political system was dictated by the communal rather than the national seats. Political parties were organised essentially on ethnic lines, in order to compete for communal seats. There was one dominant party for each of the communities. While the need to contest national seats compelled each of the major parties to extend its appeal beyond the community they principally represented, for the most part this was not successful: each party was content to field a few candidates from other ethnic groups. National seats were decided principally by communal votes; thus, indigenous Fijian candidates sponsored by the dominantly Indo-Fijian NFP were successful as a result of Indo-Fijian votes, and so on. This was possible because of the concentration of Indo-Fijians and indigenous Fijians in different parts of the country. Consequently, national seats won by candidates who relied on the vote of the other sponsoring community had little support in their own community, while those who relied on votes from their own communities had little support in other communities. In this way cross-voting seats became an extension of communal seats.

The Alliance Party in the years immediately following independence was a partial exception to this trend. It attracted a significant percentage of Indo-Fijian votes, especially for the cross-voting seats, in which it often achieved over 20 per cent of the vote. By way of contrast, the NFP commonly gained less than 5 per cent of indigenous Fijian votes. However, the Alliance Party had to maintain its support amongst indigenous Fijians if it was to remain a serious political contender, especially as militant indigenous Fijian parties were bidding for the support of its principal electorate. The logic of the system compelled the Alliance Party to progressively champion exclusively indigenous Fijian interests. The disregard by it of Indo-Fijian interests gradually led to the attrition of its Indo-Fijian support, so that by 1977 it had lost most of it and the parties settled back to relying on their old ethnic constituencies.

The electoral provisions and general circumstances of the 1997 Constitution are sufficiently different that the analogy of earlier experience may be misleading. Nonetheless, it should be noted that in future elections conducted under the 1997 Constitution the incentive to appeal across ethnic frontiers may be reduced by provisions for multiparty government. Any party, which obtains at least 10 per cent of the seats—that is, 8 seats—is entitled to be represented in the government. Even an extremist party has a chance to get into the cabinet. Just as a proportional representation system for the legislature tends to produce a multiplicity of parties, so too the low threshold proportionality rule for the cabinet could have the same effect. There is thus a possibility that a multiparty government could in the future emerge in which the partners were somewhat incompatible, if not actually hostile, and the result would be the transference of bitter and fundamental differences from the public arena, via the legislature, to the cabinet.

Of course, a party with the higher ambition of directing government by providing the Prime Minister would aim for bigger representation. The President appoints as Prime Minister the member of the House of Representatives who, in the President's opinion, can form a government that has the confidence of that House. This formulation, taken from the traditional Westminster system, may not appear to be entirely appropriate for multiparty government if, following an election, the partners were incompatible. However, it would seem that in circumstances where no party obtains an absolute majority of seats the President would need to judge which party leader would be most likely to be acceptable to the other parties which would be eligible to form a government. In normal circumstances the party with the largest representation in the House of Representatives would probably be invited to assemble a cabinet. There is thus still a clear incentive for a party to broaden its appeal across ethnic divides, unless of course it considers that such broadening would alienate its own ethnic supporters. This suggests that politicians wanting to broaden their base of support for the open seats will do so through cooperation between, rather than the integration of, parties. However, even if only that limited progress were made in future elections held under the provisions of the Constitution, it would be an advance upon previous electoral systems.

Multiparty government

Multiparty government as provided in the Constitution is a new concept for Fiji. It is also rare in other parts of the world. The Fiji provisions are drawn to a large, but not complete, extent from the interim South Africa constitution, on which the joint submission of the NFP-Fiji Labour Party (FLP) to the Reeves Commission was based (NFP-FLP 1995). While the Constitution is relatively specific on the method for the formation of multiparty government, it has few provisions for its operation. In such circumstances, a few cautious speculations on how multiparty government may function can be offered.

In Section 97 the Constitution establishes the principle that the government must have the confidence of the House of Representatives. As already noted, the process of the formation of government starts with the appointment by the President of a member of the House of Representative who, in the President's judgement, can form a government that has the confidence of the House. This rule, contained in Section 98, is no different from previous constitutions, but its operation may not be as straightforward as before, particularly as the configuration of parties will change under the impetus of the new electoral system. The concept of 'the confidence of the House' may also take on a new colouration because of the fact that all the major parties are entitled to be part of government. It would be normal for the President to appoint the leader of the largest party as Prime Minister-designate, as happened following the 1999 general elections. However, if in the future the largest party does not have a majority in the House, and instead two smaller parties, who had formed an electoral pact under which they had agreed to support for appointment to the prime ministership the leader of the larger of the two parties in the House, had a majority between them, the President would in all likelihood call upon that leader to form a government. The bargaining between parties which was witnessed following the 1999 general elections has thus in all probability become embedded within the process under which a government in Fiji is formed. Indeed, in the future the President may have to engage in much more extensive consultations with party leaders before deciding whom to appoint as Prime Minister. It is to be hoped that this will not lead to the horse trading and bribery that has become endemic in Papua New Guinea before the vote for the Prime Minister on the floor of the House (Ghai 1997b).

Sections 99(5) and 99(7) of the Constitution entitle but do not compel any political party to join the cabinet. The Prime Minister has to invite eligible parties to join government, but they may decline, as occurred after the 1999 general elections. It is important to underscore this point; although there is an element of voluntariness in the arrangements, much of the analysis of the possible difficulties facing multiparty government in the future is based upon the assumption that every eligible party will join the cabinet. Constitutionally, it does not appear that the Prime Minister can impose conditions on the invitation to other parties to join the cabinet. If the Prime Minister's party needed the support of other parties to form a government, these parties would then be in a strong position to negotiate policies that would bind the government. However, if the Prime Minister's party had a majority or substantial numbers, it might exercise a hegemonic role, and other parties might be compelled into compliance with its priorities.

It is clear that despite the outcome of the 1999 general elections smaller parties—that is, those with less than 8 members—will in all likelihood be less favourably placed than before, for previously they might have held the balance between two major and opposing groups. Now their support will seldom be crucial, unless a major party opts to stay out of government and to oppose it, as happened following the 1999 general elections, or unless their support was crucial for a major party during elections. Moreover, such smaller parties will not be entitled to enter the cabinet. Granted, Section 99(6) of the Constitution does permit the Prime Minister to appoint as minister a member of such a party, but only by sacrificing a ministerial post from the quota of the Prime Minister's party. This provision was designed, it would seem, for the benefit of those parties which seek to represent General Electors. While a concern for minorities is no doubt commendable, the provision betrays a continuing obsession on the part of those who framed the Constitution with ethnically based parties, and goes against the logic of multiparty government.

According to Section 99(1), the Prime Minister decides on the appointment of ministers. However, when appointing persons from participating parties the Prime Minister has to consult with the leader of that party. Section 103 holds that the Prime Minister alone decides on the allocation of portfolios, while Section 99(1) holds that the Prime Minister also decides on the dismissal of ministers. Obviously, in both cases the Prime Minister will do well to consult with the leaders of other parties in the cabinet. The Prime Minister would effectively have to do so in the case of dismissal, for the post that becomes vacant would have to replaced after consultation with the leader of the relevant party. In most Westminster systems, the Prime Minister is no longer *primus inter pares* (one member of a collective leadership), as in constitutional theory, but effectively the one who makes the key policy and administrative decisions of the government. Such is not the case under the 1997 Constitution, and while this would not create a major constitutional problem if the government consisted of one party, it could become problematic in case of coalitions. Moreover, in the case of the Fiji Constitution the problems and difficulties may be even greater, for two reasons. The first reason is that the purpose of multiparty government is power sharing, which could be negated if the Prime Minister were not to consult other partner parties. The second reason is that multiparty government is mandated by the

Constitution, and is not a voluntary arrangement. A 'forced' marriage of this kind requires utmost sensitivity, consultation and compromise, and therefore effectively changes the nature of the office of the Prime Minister.

The Constitution provides relatively few rules for the functioning of the cabinet. It is not clear, for example, how far the Prime Minister has to consult with or act in accordance with the advice of the cabinet in the exercise of functions directly vested in the Prime Minister's Office. The Prime Minister plays an important role in the appointment of key officers such as the Ombudsman, the Human Rights Commission, heads of departments and secretary to the cabinet, presidents of certain tribunals, and the Chief Justice. The Prime Minister exercises other powers as well, including the important one, introduced through a 1998 amendment, Section 5(2), of advising the President on the dissolution and proroguing of Parliament. Through Section 102 the cabinet is collectively responsible to the House for the governance of the state, which means that all ministers must support the policy decided by the cabinet, even if the minister or the party the minister represents has voted against that policy in the cabinet. The collective responsibility of the cabinet may deprive representatives of these parties from voicing in public their disagreement with official policies. This may put them in a dilemma, for to retain the support of their followers they may need to distance themselves from the government of which they are a part. Alternatively, since the lure of office is so powerful in Fiji, as in other states, politicians may seek to stay in government and yet criticise it in public. However, this would put a strain on cabinet unity and effectiveness. Yet it would seem that the Prime Minister could not expel such a party from the government, for the sanctions for breach of collective responsibility are political and not legal. This is in and of itself interesting, in that in other respects the Constitution transforms many issues and decisions that are political in the traditional Westminster system into legal ones.

It would seem, following from the above discussion, that inadequate attention was paid in the drafting of the Constitution to the operation of multiparty government. For example, the rules for individual and collective responsibility of ministers owe more to the traditional Westminster system than to one that enjoins power sharing. The difficulty may have arisen from slavishly adopting the Reeves Commission's proposal on the parliamentary system, which, as has already been mentioned, was not well disposed towards compulsory power sharing, favoured a traditional Westminster system, and was in any event rather conservative on recommendations for the executive. It will be necessary, for the proper functioning of multiparty government, to establish agreement amongst the parties or develop conventions or even possibly laws as to the method of decision making in the cabinet and the way in which the Prime Minister can exercise directly vested functions. The proper functioning of multiparty government will require that such decisions be made in consultation with the cabinet, or at least with leaders of political parties participating in government. It is also necessary to reconsider the role of collective responsibility. One function served by the rule of collective responsibility is to maintain the unity of the government in the face of an opposition ever keen to replace it through a vote of no confidence. A vote of no confidence against the kind of government established by the Constitution is however unlikely, unless the participating parties fall out, and it may be that they are more likely to fall out due to the presence of the collective responsibility rule than its abolition. On the other hand, some modified rule of collective responsibility or some convention will be needed to ensure that there is basic respect for policies adopted by the cabinet, especially if the rules for decision making become more consensual. Multiparty government provides the possibility of moving away from adversarial to more consensual modes of parliamentary business as well, which would also provide for a more meaningful role for backbenchers, as discussed in the next section.

Even with such conventions, there may be problems. Discipline within the government may come under strain because of the multiplicity of parties within it. There may be tendencies towards 'inner' and 'outer' groups in the cabinet. The budgetary process, and the special role of the minister of finance, may lead to the exclusion of some political groups or change the nature of the process. Consensus may be hard to establish. Parties which, once in the cabinet, are expected to cooperate, may have fought against each other in the elections, perhaps leaving resentment and bitterness in their train. If extremist parties eventually find their way into government, they will make ethnic accommodations difficult, for the probability is that they will be quick to accuse other parties of their own ethnic affiliation of selling the community 'down the river'. Instead of consensus and cooperation, there may be veto and blockage.

It therefore has to be acknowledged that despite the outcome of the 1999 general elections constitutional provisions for elections or for multiparty government by themselves will not necessarily achieve ethnic cooperation or harmony. Indeed, it is seldom that constitutions have such an ineluctable outcome. Their provisions are meditated by and through institutions, the judiciary and the public service, and perhaps most importantly, by politicians and their parties. This is particularly true of the two sets of provisions that have been examined above—the electoral system and multiparty government. It was for this reason that the Reeves Commission emphasised the ethics of the nation under the new dispensation. It said that

> Racial harmony is not merely an absence of conflict. It connotes a positive attitude by the members of each community towards those of other communities, based on mutual respect and trust, a sympathetic appreciation of one another's values and traditions, and tolerance of different beliefs, customs and cultural attitudes (FCRC 1996:3.45).

> National unity connotes a willingness of all communities to work towards common goals. It must be built on the existing foundation of shared interests and values, including the loyalty and commitment to the country of all its citizens. The shared citizenship of the members of the indigenous and the non-indigenous communities alike gives them the right to participate in national life and the conduct of government (FCRC 1996:3.47).

> Racial harmony and national unity should be promoted by reducing or eliminating sources of tension between communities. Their shared interests values and priorities should be recognised. All communities are interdependent. Every community should therefore regard the major concerns of another community as national concerns, whose solution is essential in their own interests, as well as the interests of the whole country (FCRC 1996:3.50).

So important did the Commission consider these attitudes to politics and to inter-ethnic relations that it proposed to make them part of the national ethic—and a constituent part of national political morality—by incorporating them in a Compact to be included in the Constitution. Paragraphs 7 and 8 of the Compact are of special interest. Paragraph 7 says that in 'forming a government, and in that government's conduct of the affairs of the nation through the promotion of legislation or the implementation of administrative policies, full account should be taken of the interests of all communities'. Paragraph 8 says that to 'the extent that the interests of different communities are seen to conflict, all interested parties should enter into negotiations in good faith in an endeavour to reach agreement'.

The Commission also considered that the behaviour of leaders is fundamental to the improvement of inter-ethnic relations, although there is no express provision in the Compact on this point. Nonetheless, its views are worth quoting in full since they are so central to the conduct of electioneering and the exercise of power. It said

> Political, religious and other community leaders, together with individual community leaders, have a responsibility, both in public and in private, to show good sense, moderation and sensitivity in their comments on, and behaviour towards, members of other communities. They should refrain from attributing characteristics to the members of other communities on the basis of a stereotype or the behaviour of a particular person. They should also refrain from displaying racial prejudice themselves or attributing racial prejudice to others (FCRC 1996:3.50).

Short of the non-binding Compact, the Commission found no way to institutionalise these roles and norms. They establish a social agenda, the responsibility for which lies in large part with civil society. This point is discussed in the conclusion, highlighting the role of many private institutions and processes in the implementation of the Constitution.

Accountability

Understandably, most of the negotiations over the Constitution and much of the discussion since its adoption have focused on its ethnic dimensions. Consequently, not much attention has been paid to one of the major objectives of the Constitution, particularly as recommended by the Reeves Commission, which in turn built upon the recommendations of the Citizens Constitutional Forum and the joint submission of the NFP-FLP. This objective is to enhance the accountability of the government; to ensure clean and honest government and officials; and to promote parliamentary as well as public participation in the processes of decision making and supervision of the conduct of government. Various measures have been adopted for this purpose: Section 174 requires freedom of information legislation; Section 156 requires a Code of Conduct to regulate the behaviour and conduct of politicians and senior officials, in order to ensure integrity and honesty; Section 74(3) promotes an increased role of parliamentary back benchers through sector standing committees; and Section 42 strengthens the office of the Ombudsman and establishes the Human Rights Commission.

It could be argued that despite these provisions there might be less scrutiny and supervision of government under the new Constitution, as the leaders of all the key political parties are in most instances likely to be in the cabinet. Various factors suggest why there is likely to be less of the traditional type of accountability than before. For a start, there will be a lesser role for the opposition, or more accurately, the opposition will not be able to play an effective role. No party may accept clear responsibility for government policy, since this would entail blaming its partners. The electorate may not be offered a clear choice; and even if it is, the platform on which a party may have fought the election may need to be modified in cabinet to produce a consensus. Decision making may become less open, being made in the secrecy of the cabinet, while at the same time being protected from scrutiny by the principle of collective responsibility. Finally, because all major political parties may, at some point in the future, be in the cabinet the effectiveness of backbenchers may decrease, especially if party procedures for expulsion of its members are invoked or are threatened to be invoked.

The new mechanisms for participation and accountability introduced by the Constitution, if properly implemented, will to some extent make up for the loss of accountability that may emerge over time as the new arrangements for multiparty government are implemented. However, it is unlikely that they will be sufficient by themselves. It is necessary to reflect on the new arrangements to consider how the political process itself can be modified to enhance accountability. The following measures would help towards, and some are essential for, effective accountability.

Political parties play an enhanced role under the new Constitution. Unless the parties are well organised and are themselves democratic and accountable, the chances of wider parliamentary or executive accountability are slim. The Reeves Commission probably overrated the stability and vibrancy of political parties in Fiji when it said that it believed that 'the party system is deeply embedded in the political culture' (FCRC 1996:2.75; for a critique, see Ghai 1997a:155–6). For either that reason or for its general conservatism in legal policy, the

Commission rejected the proposal of the NFP and FLP that the Constitution should provide for the regulation of political parties. Perhaps Parliament could now be persuaded to enact appropriate legislation.

A particular problem regarding the role of political parties is that under Section 71(1) (h) a political party can disqualify any of its parliamentary members from their seat in the House by the simple expedient of expelling them from the party. The only exception to this wide rule is if the member was expelled for action taken by them in their capacity as a member of a parliamentary committee, in which case they retain their parliamentary seat even though no longer a member of that party. As section 71 is formulated, MPs are not protected against expulsion for their views on the floor of the House. However, freedom of expression and the acceptance of dissent by MPs are particularly necessary under the new arrangements. Another way to deal with party intolerance is firm legislation to regulate the process and procedure of political parties, which was urged on the Commission by both the NFP and FLP.

There are other ways too in which backbenchers can help in the supervision of the executive. The role of parliamentary select committees, to cover the scrutiny of the administration and of Bills and subsidiary legislation, can be a vital factor in creating an active role for backbenchers. No minister can be a member of a select committee, which means not only that the committees should be more independent of the government, but also that its members, particularly the chair, should develop their own expertise in order to be more effective. The select committees can also enhance public participation in supervision as well as policymaking by, for example, holding public hearings and consultations, giving a platform to individuals, trade unions, non-governmental organisations and other groups to make submissions to them on government policies and legislative proposals. These hearings should be open to the public and should be broadcast. Of course, if the committees are to discharge their responsibilities effectively they must be supplied with the necessary resources, including training. This in turn requires that some of the conventions of the traditional Westminster system need to be modified, as in the Standing Orders, or rules of party discipline in Parliament, in recognition of the significantly new system set up by the Constitution.

Public participation in law making can also be enhanced through changes in the process of law making. As is customary in many countries, a consultative paper containing an explanation and justification should precede legislative proposals. The paper can be used by all interested parties as the basis by which consultations are held. Ample time should be allowed for public comments. The government should set up machinery to review these comments and should be open to the revision of the policy accordingly. It may be argued that this process would slow down law making—but this may be precisely its virtue, for laws made with deliberation and after full consultation not only result in more acceptable laws, but also more effective laws.

Then there is the role of the Leader of the Opposition. What role they play will depend greatly on whether there is a party with substantial public and parliamentary support which is willing to forgo its participation in the government and to assume the role of the opposition. The formal role of the Leader of the Opposition is not much different from that under the 1970 Constitution. For example, under Section 64(1) (c) the Leader of the Opposition nominates 8 members of the Senate; under Section 132(1), the Leader of the Opposition has to be consulted on the appointment of the Chief Justice; under Sections 75(3)(4) and 78(8) respectively, the Leader of the Opposition must be consulted on the Constituency Boundaries and Electoral Commissions. In addition, the functions given to the Leader of the Opposition under the Standing Orders would presumably continue, as would the resources provided to the office for the discharge of its responsibilities. While it is important for the objectives of the Constitution that all major ethnic groups should be in the cabinet, it is not necessary that all major parties should also be in the cabinet. Indeed, it could be argued that the objective of honest government, which is effectively accountable to Parliament and the public, needs an effective Leader of the Opposition. Moreover, in keeping with the multiethnic aspirations of the Constitution it is important that the opposition party strives to include all ethnic groups so that criticisms are not seen, nor can they be dismissed, as merely ethnically motivated. The salience of this issue was highlighted in the aftermath of the 1999 general elections, when an ethnically based party emerged as the principal opposition to a multiethnic government.

However, above all else there is a challenge to civil society to ensure fair policies by, as well as accountability of, government. Social and non-governmental organisations should follow the conduct of government and proceedings in Parliament, they should provide audits of departments and parastatal bodies, use reports of the Auditor-General to raise questions about the probity of government, ensure that the Freedom of Information legislation is put to good use, that education about human rights is disseminated to the public, and that they supplement the work of the Ombudsman and the Human Rights Commission in appropriate ways. They have to highlight arbitrariness and corruption within government when it occurs. An informed and concerned citizenry is the ultimately the best safeguard against these practices. No democracy can function or survive without their vigilance.

Conclusion

Constitutional provisions are a mix of rules, norms and institutions. Perhaps the easiest part of implementation is the setting up of institutions. It is much harder to ensure that institutions and their office holders follow the norms that have been established. Much depends on the balance between the institutions of the executive and the institutions of control and accountability. Some assistance can be had from the rules; some rules are more likely to generate the results desired of them, others less so. For example, it is generally said that electoral laws are very efficacious, for politicians make an effort to understand them and are influenced in the pursuit of power by the incentives or disincentives provided by them (Sartori 1968), a view which had much influence with the Reeves Commission. The implementation of a constitution also depends on the commitment of citizens to its values and the ability of civic groups to mobilise in support of its objectives. The dominance of ethnic consciousness can have a major impact on how the constitution operates, particularly its electoral laws; and a rights ideology is particularly hard to inculcate, for the outrage that might otherwise be felt at the violation of rights is channelled into building ethnic hostilities. A constitution does not, as a rule, break down if its norms and values are not honoured; rather, it then works in quite different, and perverse, ways from that originally envisaged and desired (Ghai 1997b). This analysis suggests that there are no guarantees that the 1997 Constitution of Fiji Islands will achieve its goals.

While the 1997 Constitution represents a consensus, it does not have universal approval. The terms of reference of the review represented agreement between the government and the opposition as to the future direction for the governance and development of Fiji. The process by which the Constitution was made ensured the careful consideration of all alternatives. It was based on the unanimous recommendations of the Reeves Commission, on which there were nominees of the two major communities who pursued the interests of both their community as well as that of Fiji as a whole. The Great Council of Chiefs sanctioned it. It was adopted unanimously by Parliament. Most have welcomed it as being best able to tackle Fiji's contemporary problems.

The Constitution provides a framework and institutions. These seek to direct policymaking and the manner of the exercise of state power, but they cannot by themselves determine how politics will be conducted. The Constitution may be hard to operate without goodwill and flexibility, as it is based on compromises, balances, and even contradictions. There will be need for frequent negotiations. It is now the obligation and responsibility of all involved in the process, and particularly politicians, to support the Constitution and to ensure that it is implemented in the spirit that animates it. A particularly heavy responsibility lies on political parties.

Nonetheless, unless public attitudes and practices support a constitution, there is no guarantee that its purposes will materialise. Constitutional provisions are dependent on wider community commitment and practices; they depend on the view the public takes of the values the Constitution seeks to promote. Political and religious leaders must behave responsibly, promoting tolerance of and respect for other communities. Any person, and even more so a leader, who seeks to inflame racial animosity is in gross violation of the Constitution. While there is of course a limited role for the law in establishing these norms and values, it is, in the final instance, Fiji Islanders who must exercise their rights of citizenship to ensure the accountability of government and the observance by leaders of the spirit of the Constitution.

The prospects for the success of the Constitution are promising, especially in the aftermath of the 1999 general elections. In the near future there is bound to emerge be a new set of leaders from within Fiji's communities. These leaders are likely to have studied together and forged some kind of friendship during their student days. Many of them will enjoy the multiethnic and cosmopolitan nature of Fiji society. Moreover, the process of the review of the 1990 Constitution and the adoption of the 1997 Constitution have produced a new understanding of the problems facing the country. The awareness of the social, economic and political costs of the coups is now clear. Public support for inter-ethnic equity and social justice has thus grown. At the same time, the imperatives of globalisation are incompatible with a return to some form of narrow ethnicism. Further, the demography of Fiji is changing, to the clear advantage to indigenous Fijians. This should make indigenous Fijian leaders more relaxed about the political process, regardless of electoral and parliamentary rules. Perhaps most importantly, there is a palpable pride among key leaders, their supporters and people at large at having achieved a fair and popular constitution in difficult circumstances, and perhaps, as a result, a commitment to making Fiji as the world should be.

Endnote

1. This chapter was written before the 1999 general elections, being based on the inaugural Citizens Constitutional Forum 'Constitution Matters' Lecture, held on 27 August 1998 at the University of the South Pacific, Suva, Fiji. The chapter was not revised in light of the outcome of the elections, in large part because the results have reinforced the salience of the analysis contained in the chapter. The author is grateful to the Committee on Research and Conference Grants of the University of Hong Kong for a grant. He also wishes to thank Peter Larmour for valuable comments on a draft of the chapter.

CHAPTER 3

Fiji's 1999 general elections: outcomes and prospects

Satendra Prasad

Introduction

For Fiji, the May 1999 general elections have been exceptionally significant and historic.[1] They were the first elections held under the provisions of the 1997 constitutional settlement, which was a product of unprecedented negotiation and compromise between the main political actors in Fiji (Ghai, this volume). As a consequence, the outcome of the elections provides some basis for interpreting the validity of certain key assumptions underpinning the 1997 Constitution. At the same time, the outcome of the 1999 elections can also provide some indication of the commitment of different political actors to the 1997 constitutional settlement, in part because the 1999 general elections were the first since 1987 in which there was a real possibility of removing the dominant political party—in this case, the *Soqosoqo Ni Vakavulewa Ni Taukei* (SVT)—from power. Finally, the 1999 general elections were held in an environment where successive governments had, since 1986, made strong commitments to pursuing policies of structural adjustment and trade liberalisation (Sepehri and Akram-Lodhi, this volume). The outcome of the 1999 elections can provide some guide as to the extent to which these commitments have been accepted by the peoples of Fiji, which will undoubtedly affect Fiji's political and economic prospects as it negotiates global economic challenges.

These aspects of the 1999 general elections have a bearing on some of the issues raised in other contributions to this collection. As a consequence, Fiji's 1999 general elections may help us assess how some of the issues raised in this collection are likely to play themselves out over the next decade. In part, this is because a reflection on the outcome of the elections and an evaluation of some of the key voting trends that were witnessed may provide clues which facilitate an understanding of how dominant structures of ethnicity and class may effect the developmental prospects of this small, vulnerable and globalising economy. It is in this light that this chapter discusses the outcome of the 1999 general elections in Fiji. Following this introduction, the next section examines how some key features of the 1997 Constitution may have affected the 1999 elections in ways other than those of electoral processes. The chapter then discusses the main political parties that engaged in the 1999 election and examines the strategies of the parties in light of the voting system that was used. The process that led to the formation of the Cabinet is also examined. In the context of these outcomes the chapter critically assesses the success of the alternative vote (AV) system, particularly in terms of its capacity to foster a more multiethnic politics in Fiji. The chapter concludes by examining whether the new Government will be able to respond to the challenge of the future in light of its constitutional obligations.

The 1997 Constitution and the 1999 general elections

During the review of the 1990 Constitution much of the debate on the set of possible constitutional arrangements capable of dealing with ethnic divisions in Fiji came to revolve around three principal issues. The first issue was whether there should be a guarantee of indigenous Fijian advantage in the allocation of parliamentary seats, so as to allay any possible fears about the dilution of indigenous Fijian interests. The second issue followed: what was an acceptable ratio between ethnically reserved, 'communal' parliamentary seats and non-reserved, 'open' parliamentary seats? The third issue tied the other two issues together: what was to be the electoral process under which members of parliament were to be elected to open and reserved seats? As will be seen, these issues had an impact on the particular strategies used by political parties during the course of the 1999 elections, and in so doing helped shape the outcome of the elections.

The Fiji Constitution Review Commission (FCRC) argued that particularly but not exclusively in light of the events of the late 1980s and early 1990s it was necessary to move Fiji gradually but decisively away from the 'politics of race'. To that end, the FCRC recommended that the predominant feature of the electoral system which was to emerge out of the constitutional review should be that parliamentary seats would be 'open': that is, all voters residing in a particular constituency would be free to contest and vote in an election. The FCRC therefore proposed that Fiji's parliament have 12 seats reserved for indigenous Fijians; 10 seats reserved for Indo-Fijians; 2 seats reserved for 'general electors', that is to say those voters who were neither indigenous Fijian nor Indo-Fijian; and 1 seat reserved for the Rotuman community. Thus, the FCRC recommended that 25 parliamentary seats be reserved on the basis of ethnicity. Concurrently, the FCRC recommended that there be 45 open seats. The FCRC argued that the proposed ratio between open and reserved seats would ensure that political parties contesting elections would mainly focus their attention and hence their political strategies on winning the open seats, and indeed the FCRC's recommendations represented a major window of opportunity for Fiji to reduce the ethnic orientation of its politics.

However, the Joint Parliamentary Select Committee (JPSC), which was charged with developing a parliamentary consensus on the constitutional amendments to emerge out of the review process, rejected this ratio. Indeed, the JPSC favoured a reversal of the ratio of open to reserved parliamentary seats. The JPSC thus proposed that 23 parliamentary seats be reserved for indigenous Fijians, 19 parliamentary seats be reserved for Indo-Fijians, 3 parliamentary seats be reserved for general electors, and 1 parliamentary seat be reserved for the Rotuman community. The JPSC further proposed that in addition to 46 reserved parliamentary seats there be 25 open parliamentary seats. The reversal in the ratio of open parliamentary seats to reserved parliamentary seats clearly favoured those political parties which were organised on the basis of ethnicity, and thus apparently compromised an explicit objective of the FCRC: namely, movement away from the 'politics of race'. In this light, it is perhaps not surprising that the main political parties in the JPSC were the SVT and the National Federation Party (NFP). Both are almost exclusively organised on the basis of ethnicity, with the SVT having been a key political actor amongst the indigenous Fijian community during the 1990s and the NFP having been a key political actor amongst the Indo-Fijian community since the 1960s. At the same time, as will be seen the domination of reserved parliamentary seats in the allocation of total parliamentary seats had a critically important yet possibly unexpected impact on the strategies employed by the political parties during the 1999 general elections.

Despite an allocation of open to reserved parliamentary seats which favoured political parties organised on the basis of ethnicity, the 1997 Constitution did introduce an additional mechanism which had as its explicit rationale the objective of reducing the role of ethnicity in Fiji's politics. This mechanism is power sharing. Under the 1997 Constitution, all parties having 10 per cent or more of the membership of parliament are guaranteed representation in the executive arm of government, the cabinet. Membership in cabinet was to be in proportion to the overall number of parliamentary seats held. This provision of the 1997 Constitution, which represented a major departure away from the approach espoused by the FCRC, was designed to ensure that political parties would co-operate after the general elections.

The 1999 general elections were conducted using an AV system. Under Fiji's AV system, voters must rank their preferences amongst the candidates for both open and reserved parliamentary seats. If no candidate secures an absolute majority of the first preferences expressed by the voters, those candidates at bottom of the poll are eliminated and the second preferences of those voters who voted for candidates at the bottom of the poll are counted. If no candidate secures an absolute majority of first and second preferences, the process is repeated until an absolute majority is secured for one candidate.

Despite its apparent complexity, and the concomitant possibility that voters would not really understand the electoral system that they were using, the AV system was nevertheless adopted in order to overcome the excessively ethnic orientation of the elections which had been conducted under both the 1990 and the 1970 Constitutions. Granted, the processes at work in mobilising votes under the AV system for reserved and open seats were likely to be different. In reserved seats, it was to be expected that political mobilisation would follow those processes witnessed in elections under the 1990 and 1970 Constitutions; namely, the main parties would emphasise ethnic interests and make appeals to 'ethnic unity'. However, for open seats it was hoped that the AV system would facilitate the deployment of less ethnically exclusive strategies by giving clear incentives to political parties in the pursuit of power to seek out votes from a multiplicity of ethnic communities (Ghai, this volume). Indeed, the FCRC envisaged that the introduction of the AV system would in the long term promote the emergence and consolidation of multiethnic parties, while in the short term the introduction of the AV system would facilitate the emergence of cooperative arrangements and alliances between ethnically based parties (FCRC 1996). Thus, the promotion of inter-ethnic cooperation was an explicit aim of the AV system. Through the promotion of inter-ethnic cooperation, the electoral system was to have a key role in moving Fiji gradually but decisively away from the 'politics of race' and towards an underlying goal of the 1997 Constitution, namely the promotion of racial harmony and national unity (Prasad 1999). Thus, while the choice of the voting system clearly has had an impact on the outcome of the 1997 elections, assessing the overall consequences of the introduction of the AV system is more complex, in large part because the assumptions that have underpinned its choice as a method of electing parliamentary representatives have had a significant effect on the final results of the election.

Clearly, the provisions of the 1997 Constitution have had a deeper effect on the political processes underpinning the1999 general elections than a first glance at its stipulated electoral procedures might appear to indicate. In particular, the ratio of open to reserved parliamentary seats, the statutes governing the formation of the executive arm of government, and the electoral system have effected the outcome. This effect however has not been linear; rather, it has been refracted through the strategies of the political parties that contested the election. Party strategies and the outcome of the 1999 general election is the subject of the next section.

The results of the 1999 general elections

The parties

The main parties that contested the 1999 general elections were the
1. *Soqosoqo Ni Vakavulewa Ni Taukei* (SVT). The SVT was the dominant political party to emerge after the coups of 1987. Its support was derived almost exclusively from the indigenous Fijian community, and it formed the Government after both the 1992 and 1994 general elections. The SVT was the predominant indigenous Fijian party engaged in the

constitutional review process. It was also the central indigenous Fijian party in the JPSC, and as such took a large measure of responsibility for negotiating the new constitution.

2. National Federation Party (NFP). The NFP was the oldest of the parties that contested the 1999 elections, having been formed in the 1960s during the agitation for independence. Since independence the NFP had remained in opposition, deriving its support largely from the Indo-Fijian community. It became an exclusively Indo-Fijian party after the 1992 general elections, when it emerged as the largest Indo-Fijian political grouping. After the SVT, the NFP was the key player in the JPSC, and as such it also took a large measure of the responsibility for the new constitution.

3. Fijian Association Party (FAP). The FAP emerged as a parliamentary breakaway from the SVT after the 1992 elections, when the SVT's Sitiveni Rabuka, leader of the 1987 coups, and the late Josefata Kamikamica, Finance Minister under the military-backed Interim Government and eventual founder of the FAP, clashed over who should become prime minister. The support base of the FAP is largely concentrated among indigenous Fijians from the central and southeastern provinces on Viti Levu.

4. Fiji Labour Party (FLP). The FLP party was created in 1985, with strong support from the Fiji Trades Union Congress. It won the 1987 general elections in coalition with the NFP, under the leadership of the late Timoci Bavadra. The victory of the FLP-NFP coalition in 1987 led to two military coups. The coalition was ruptured by the 1992 elections. In both the 1992 and 1994 elections the FLP won a minority of the seats reserved for the Indo-Fijian community. Nonetheless, despite drawing a large measure of support from within the Indo-Fijian community, of all the political parties only the FLP has maintained some semblance of cross-community support and multiethnic orientation since the 1987 coups.

5. *Veitokani Ni Lewenivanua Vakaristo* (VLV). This exclusively indigenous Fijian party evolved during the lead up to the 1999 general elections. It draws its support and enthusiasm from a powerful segment within the Methodist Church.

6. Party of National Unity (PANU). The PANU was in some senses a successor to the defunct All National Congress (ANC). It emerged in the run up to the 1999 elections. Like the ANC, the PANU draws its support mainly from indigenous Fijians in western Viti Levu.

7. Nationalist *Vanua Takolavo* Party (NVTLP). The NVTLP is the successor to the Fijian Nationalist Party. Like its predecessor, the NVTLP has developed a strongly nationalistic, if not indeed openly chauvinistic, indigenous Fijian platform, which is explicit in its anti-Indo-Fijian agenda. The NVTLP finds its main support in the central and southern provinces on Viti Levu.

8. United General Party (UGP). The UGP sought to represent the interests of the 'general electors', that is to say that portion of the population who were neither Indo-Fijian nor indigenous Fijian, and who are predominantly the descendents of European and Chinese migrants.

In addition to these parties, a large number of smaller parties emerged in the lead-up to the elections. Moreover, a number of independent candidates stood for elected office.

However, despite the multiplicity of parties, in the 1999 general elections the primary contest was between two groupings of parties: a more formal SVT/NFP/UGP coalition; and a looser, FLP/FAP/PANU combination. Both groupings consisted of individual parties that presented themselves as 'mainstream', capable of providing leadership to their supporters within the indigenous Fijian and Indo-Fijian communities and capable of entering into 'deals' on behalf of their supporters. At the same time, both groupings collectively had a reasonable degree of internal discipline, and as such could be treated as 'unitary actors', able to produce a cohesive pre-election alliance with the capability to form a plausible government.

The SVT/NFP/UGP coalition consisted of what might be considered the 'mainstream' ethnic parties. The coalition was consolidated during the period of the constitutional review, when the SVT and the NFP, the bulk of the coalition, worked closely together, and was considerably strengthened after the passing of the Constitution Amendment Act in 1997. During the elections, both the leaders of the SVT and the NFP, Rabuka and Jai Ram Reddy respectively, were correctly projected as the principal driving force behind the revised constitution, having undertaken the principal negotiations, rallied the support of the elected members of the two ethnic groups for the constitutional settlement (Robertson, this volume), received the endorsement of the Great Council of Chiefs, and ensured the implementation of the necessary provisions of the new Constitution in the run up to the 1999 general elections. As such the two leaders were able to enter into pre-electoral agreements of importance to the two main ethnic groups in Fiji. From such a perspective, it is not surprising that ethnic unity became a principal theme of their campaigns and a key means by which they sought to mobilise political support. Economic issues, on which the parties largely agreed, such as the need to push ahead with policies of structural adjustment, were relegated to a secondary status.

This contrasted with the FLP/FAP/PANU combination. The principal source of strength for this combination was the FLP, which had a pre-existing support base amongst Indo-Fijian sugarcane farmers and a narrower, but nonetheless significant, multiethnic support base amongst the trade unions. By way of contrast, the FAP's appeal was more regionally specific and was also perhaps apparent amongst a comparatively small segment of the liberal indigenous Fijian middle class (Ratuva, this volume). Similarly, the PANU was also a regional party. Thus, within this combination, and with the exception of the FLP, the other parties were less unitary, with weaker leadership and less unified platforms. This combination thus reflected the pattern of a looser, 'post-election' arrangement.

The FLP/FAP/PANU combination concentrated its campaign upon economic and social issues, including low rates of economic growth, declining investment rates, and high unemployment (Sepehri and Akram-Lodhi, this volume). The FLP's emphasis on these issues was understandable, given both its origins and its support base. At the same time, both the PANU and the FAP also identified with these issues because economic stagnation and the impact of unemployment are, in Fiji, experienced more intensely in the urban areas and on Viti Levu, both of which served as the principal geographical base of support of the two parties. Notwithstanding a common overall agenda, there were clear policy differences between the FAP, the PANU and the FLP. The FLP demonstrated a consistently hostile attitude to policies of structural adjustment, while the FAP and the PANU were more sympathetic to the need to continue the structural adjustment process even as they sought to reassure those that had lost out in the process that they would have recourse to social safety nets. However, despite these differences, in their emphasis on economic issues the second combination could be said to have been more class based, although it must be admitted that organisationally it remained a combination of three largely ethnically based parties.

The 1999 general elections thus displayed a strong undercurrent of the tensions caused by alternative forms of political mobilisation. On the one hand there were two primarily ethnic parties, the SVT and the NFP, which had nonetheless been able to negotiate a new constitutional arrangement. On the other hand there was a more class based political momentum, which could be associated with the FLP-led combination, even though the organisational basis for this form of mobilisation was largely based upon ethnic groups. As will be seen, the impact of these factors will have been felt in the outcome of the election.

Serious concerns were raised in advance of the elections about the capacity of the electoral authorities to administer elections under such a complex electoral system. Some doubts were also aired about the fairness of elections given the complexity of the AV system. It is however possible to assess the fairness of elections, using a set of agreed guidelines. These guidelines include: the independence of the electoral authorities; the respect for the law by the election administrators; the transparency and accuracy of the administration of the elections; and the 'voter-friendly' nature of the administration of the election (Institute for Democracy and Electoral Assistance 1998). With the exception of the final point, both the peoples of Fiji and independent observers have generally regarded the 1999 general elections as having fulfilled these guidelines. Thus, the result has been seen as being by and large legitimate, and not capable of being challenged.

Results in reserved seats

As agreed by the JPSC and embedded within the 1997 Constitution, in the 1999 general elections there were 23 parliamentary seats reserved for indigenous Fijians ('Fijian communal seats'), 19 parliamentary seats reserved for Indo-Fijians ('Indian communal seats'), 3 parliamentary seats reserved for general electors, and 1 parliamentary seat reserved for the Rotuman community.

Considering first those seats reserved for the indigenous Fijian community, overall the SVT received 38 per cent of the first preferences, while the FAP and VLV both received 18 per cent of the first preferences. The PANU and the NVTLP received 10 and 9 per cent of first preferences respectively. However, as a consequence of the AV electoral system, the distribution of first preferences and the distribution of parliamentary seats were very different. Table 3.1 demonstrates the distribution of parliamentary seats amongst those parties that contested seats reserved for the indigenous Fijian community. As is demonstrated in Table 3.1, while the SVT received 38 per cent of the first preferences, this was only translated into 5 parliamentary seats, some 22 per cent of the total. The FAP, which received 18 per cent of the first preferences, won 9 parliamentary seats, some 39 per cent of the total, while the VLV, which also received 18 per cent of the first preferences won only 13 per cent of the parliamentary seats.

Turning to the seats reserved for other communities, amongst the Indo-Fijian community the FLP obtained 66 per cent of the first preferences, while the NFP received 32 per cent of the first preferences. Again however the distribution of first preferences was very different from the distribution of parliamentary seats: all 19 seats reserved for the Indo-Fijian community were won by FLP. Finally, the UGP won one of the 3 parliamentary seats reserved for the general electors; the other two seats reserved for the general electors as well as the seat reserved for the Rotuman community were won by independent candidates.

Examining the results for the reserved parliamentary seats three points in particular stand out. The first point was the overwhelming support for the FLP amongst the Indo-Fijian electorate, which, by winning a clear majority in all seats reserved for the Indo-Fijian

Table 3.1 1999 election results for 'Fijian communal seats'

SVT	5
VLV	3
FAP	9
Independent	1
PANU	4
NVTLP	1
Total number of seats	23

community, effectively wiped out the NFP. The success of the FLP can be attributed to its broad appeal amongst the Indo-Fijian community throughout the country: unlike 1987 and 1992, the FLP was successful in both rural and urban constituencies. Clearly, the effort to focus its policies upon the interests of smallholder Indo-Fijian farmers and urban working classes by articulating an anti-structural adjustment agenda worked. In a sense then although the use of reserved seats was expected to foster appeals to ethnic identity, in the case of the FLP voter choices may have been governed by factors other than ethnic identity alone.

The second point to stand out from the results for the reserved parliamentary seats was the extent to which provincial loyalties appeared to strongly affect voting outcomes within the indigenous Fijian community. The SVT's support was quite strong in Cakaudrove and Kadavu. Similarly, the PANU won all its reserved parliamentary seats in Ba. The FAP also won all of its reserved parliamentary seats on Viti Levu. Thus, no indigenous Fijian political party in the 1999 general election was able to attract a wide base of support across the rural and urban regions of Fiji; provincialism appeared to overwrite the ideological appeals of the different political parties. Again, although the use of reserved seats was expected to facilitate the use of ethnic identity as a tool of political mobilisation, in the case of the indigenous Fijian electorate voter choices appeared to be governed by factors other than ethnic identity alone. This in turn helps explain, to a degree, the collapse of the ruling SVT, which won only 5 of the 23 parliamentary seats reserved for the indigenous Fijian community.

The third point to stand out from the results for the reserved parliamentary seats is more speculative. It may be the case that the policies pursued by the SVT while in power, both in the field of economic development and in its support for the consociational settlement between Fiji's ethnic communities (Ghai, this volume), contributed to a strengthening of provincial loyalties and a weakening of the role played by ethnicity in political mobilisation. The policies of structural adjustment pursued by the SVT while in power have had geographically uneven effects both within and between Fiji's ethnic communities. Thus, different provinces are differentially positioned within the national political economy, which may have fostered a provincialism which has been simmering for a very long time and which to an extent may have been able to override appeals to ethnic unity.

At the same time, both Cakaudrove and Kadavu, where the SVT won decisive victories, are largely populated by indigenous Fijians. In these provinces there is little interaction between the two main ethnic communities and while there was clear support for the SVT this may not have represented support for one of its key policy initiatives, the consociational settlement, because in these provinces the SVT was, perhaps simplistically, seen as *the* party of indigenous Fijians. By way of contrast, in the western provinces of Viti Levu the PANU and the FAP did well. These provinces are far more ethnically mixed and there is considerable economic, social and political interaction between the ethnic communities. In these regions, therefore, the electoral arrangement reached between the PANU and the FAP on the one hand and the FLP on the other hand was perhaps more acceptable to the indigenous Fijian electorate, in part because of an acceptance of the need for a consociational settlement. If such an argument were accurate, the acceptance of the need for a consociational settlement would in all likelihood have weakened the electoral usefulness of an appeal to ethnic identity. In order to assess the veracity of these speculations there is a need for further scrutiny. In order to do this it is necessary to assess the results of the 1999 election in the 25 open seats.

Results in open seats

The results for the 25 open parliamentary seats are summarised in Table 3.2. Table 3.2 demonstrates the dominance of the FLP in the electoral contest for the open parliamentary seats, winning 72 per cent of the seats. The SVT, the FLP's nearest rival in the contest for the open parliamentary seats, could only win 12 per cent of the seats.

The results presented in Table 3.2 have some bearing on understanding whether the AV electoral system was capable of promoting the broader objectives envisaged by the FCRC: namely, increased inter-ethnic cooperation between and within political parties. In only four of the open seats did the parties win on the first preference. Three of these seats were won by the FLP, while one was won by the SVT. In order to demonstrate then that the AV system encouraged inter-ethnic cooperation in the short term it would be necessary to show that parties engaged in electoral contests for the 21 open seats which were not won on the basis of first preferences were able to come to arrangements concerning the 'sharing' of preferences.

Table 3.2 1999 election results in the open seats

FLP	18
SVT	3
FAP	1
Independent	1
NVTLP[1]	1
UGP	1
Total number of seats	25

Note: [1] This seat has been subject to a recount following an appeal to the High Court by the FAP candidate.

This in turn makes it necessary to think about the extent and type of cooperation between parties. In short, it becomes necessary to evaluate the strategies of Fiji's political parties during the 1999 elections.

A first step in evaluating the strategies of Fiji's political parties in the open seats is to evaluate the ethnic composition of the open seats. As has already been demonstrated in the reserved seats, the FLP's support amongst Indo-Fijians was overwhelming. This can be contrasted with the regional concentration of support for indigenous Fijian parties, and particularly the SVT, the PANU, the FAP and the VLV. Nonetheless, it is possible that while voter choice for the reserved seats may have been determined by factors other than ethnicity, for the open seats ethnicity may have remained the dominant logic governing voter choice. In order to gauge whether this was in fact the case it is necessary, as a first step, to assess the ethnic composition of the open seats that were contested.

The Constituency Boundaries Commission defined the boundaries of all seats, including the open seats. In defining the open seats the Commission had to take into regard geographical factors as well as the ethnic composition of the constituency. This was because in order for the open seats to work effectively under the AV system there was a need to ensure a reasonable ethnic mix in each of the open seats. Despite this however in 14 open seats the proportion of the voting population attributable to one ethnic group exceeded 60 per cent. Of these 14 seats, in 8 the indigenous Fijian share of the voting population exceeded 60 per cent of the total voters. In these the SVT did well, winning three seats. At the other end of the spectrum, in 6 of the open seats the Indo-Fijian share of the voting population was in excess of 60 per cent of the total voters. The FLP won all 6 of these seats, and indeed won 3 on the basis of first preferences. The AV system may thus have had a curious effect on these 14 open seats. Despite the fact that in the reserved seats voter choice may have been guided by factors other than ethnicity, in 14 of the open seats parties which focused on winning a large majority of the votes of the dominant ethnic community had an apparently reasonable chance of winning outright. These open seats may thus have witnessed voter choice being guided by ethnicity.

In the remaining 11 seats the share of the population between the two dominant ethnic communities was relatively more even: no community had more than 60 per cent of the electorate in any of these seats. It can be argued that the real contest in the 1999 general elections was in these 11 seats, because it was only in these seats that the allocation of preferences required that parties rooted in one ethnic community appeal to voters in other ethnic communities. The need to appeal to voters across the ethnic divide necessitated cooperation between parties, as envisaged by the FCRC, and led to pre-electoral arrangements between the political parties. Thus, as has already been noted, the SVT, the UGP and the NFP entered into a firm pre-election coalition. The FLP however operated somewhat differently. The FLP, the FAP and the PANU fielded candidates against each other in the open seats. Indeed, in several seats the competition between the FAP and the FLP candidates was particularly intense. The preference-swapping deal arranged between the FLP, the FAP and the PANU was thus reserved for second preferences, in order to capitalise on the regional concentration of indigenous Fijian support for both the FAP and the PANU and more general Indo-Fijian support for the FLP. Working in this way not only denied the SVT/UGP/NFP candidates chances of gaining a majority on the first count, it also increased the FLP/FAP/PANU chances of winning on second and later counts. Overall then the FAP, the PANU and the FLP parties worked more realistically as a 'vote-pooling block' than did the SVT/NFP/UGP coalition.

In addition to the advantages derived from the preference sharing arrangement and a majority of Indo-Fijian support, the FLP is estimated to have won in excess of 10 per cent of the indigenous Fijian vote outright in at least 6 of the remaining open seats. Thus, the FLP was well positioned to win a majority of the open seats where the distribution of the population was relatively even between the two main ethnic communities. Given this, it is then not surprising that the FLP did very well in these seats. Overall, the FLP won 36 parliamentary seats out of a total of 71.

Two further comments on the election results can be offered. The first recalls the point that the AV system was designed to promote increased cooperation between parties. Clearly, an examination of the results in the open seats shows that the type and level of cooperation between parties is crucial to understanding the outcome of the election. On this account then the AV system fulfilled its objective, albeit in ways which those who had designed the system probably did not envisage. The second comment concerns the overall outcome. Despite having misgivings about particular aspects of the Constitution, the SVT, the NFP, the FLP, the PANU and the FAP all support the broad parameters of the Constitution. Votes for these parties therefore may be taken to at least translate partially into support for the Constitution, and the 1999 elections can be considered to have been a national referendum on the Constitution. In this light, the mandate received in support of the 1997 Constitution is overwhelming by any account.

Representation in cabinet

The number of seats won by the FLP gave it the ability to form a government on its own. However, the Constitution required that the FLP invite other parties to participate in the executive. Table 3.3 therefore presents the overall distribution of parliamentary seats by party, together with the resulting entitlement to cabinet seats as set out in the 1997 Constitution, as well as the proportion of cabinet seats actually held by individual parties.

Particularly through its provisions for multiparty government the 1997 Constitution seeks to institutionalise power sharing amongst Fiji's ethnic communities. Broadly, the concept of power sharing has been operationalised in the aftermath of the elections, albeit through some difficult negotiations and in a manner that is probably somewhat different from that envisaged by those who framed the Constitution. Initially, power-sharing negotiations focused on the FLP's proposed candidate for Prime Minister, its leader Mahendra Chaudhry. At first the FAP and the PANU refused to accept an Indo-Fijian as the Prime Ministerial candidate. Following the negotiation process, the FAP and the PANU conceded the designation of an Indo-Fijian as Prime Minister in exchange for being over-represented in the Cabinet. This outcome was designed to allay fears about an Indo-Fijian dominated government. It was also a reward for the preference sharing arrangements that gave the FLP victory in several open seats.

In line with constitutional obligations, the Prime Minister-designate invited the SVT to become a part of the cabinet. Initially, the SVT responded to this invitation favourably. However, the SVT also indicated that its participation was to be tied to a number of conditions, over which the Prime Minister was not prepared to negotiate (*Fiji Times*, 20–29 May 1999). As a consequence, the SVT is not participating in the cabinet even though it has cleared the threshold for cabinet representation.

A power-sharing executive is likely to act as a safety valve against the outright domination of government by a single ethnic group. Indeed, this outcome is an implicit objective of the 1997 Constitution. However, power sharing at this level may also act in another, possibly more important, manner. Power sharing may prevent a single party from dominating the policy agenda. As a consequence, while the FLP went into the elections on a platform of social and economic justice, it is possible that it will not be able to implement the full range of its social and economic agenda, given the need to maintain the support of other political parties in the executive arm of government. Granted, Chapter Five of the 1997 Constitution directs the state to make provisions for programs designed 'to achieve for all groups or categories of persons who are disadvantaged effective equality of

Table 3.3 Party representation in Cabinet after the 1999 elections

Party	Total seats in Parliament	Per cent entitlement to Cabinet seats	Actual per cent of Cabinet seats as share of 22 ministers
FLP	36	50	59
FAP	10	14	18
SVT	8	11	0
VLV	3	B/t	9
PANU	4	B/t	9
UGP	2	B/t	0
NVTLP	2	B/t	0
Independent and Rotuma	5	B/t	5

Note: B/t - Below threshold

access to education, land, housing, and participation in commerce'
(Ghai, this volume). Although this commitment is 'non-justiciable',
were it to be enforced, the neoliberal direction of economic policy that
came to be associated with the SVT over the past decade would
certainly come into question. Despite this however the reality of
power sharing may well result in the FLP's aversion to orthodox
policies of structural adjustment being diluted to accommodate the
more pro-liberalisation orientation of its partners in Cabinet, such as
the VLV and the FAP.

Reflections on the AV system

Many commentaries in the local dailies and responses by political
leaders following the swearing-in of the Cabinet have continued to
raise concerns about an Indo-Fijian dominated government. After all,
it was the emergence of Indo-Fijian power in the cabinet that led to the
coups in 1987. Although public opposition is considerably more muted
than that which was observed following the FLP-led victory in 1987, it
remains a cause for concern. Many appear to blame the AV system as
the primary cause of the downfall of the SVT government and the
cause of 'disunity' amongst indigenous Fijians. Some further remarks
about the operation of this system of voting are therefore in order.

The AV system used in the 1999 general elections was introduced
in order to generate effective government and effective political
parties capable of serving national constituencies. At the same time,
it was argued that the AV system provided the best incentives for
cooperation between ethnically based political parties (FCRC 1996).
Moreover, to reinforce the pursuit of inter-ethnic cooperation the JPSC
tried to back up the strengths of the AV system by introducing
constitutional provisions for multiparty government. However, the
AV system did not work as it was thought it would.

As has already been demonstrated, the political parties that
contested the 1999 general elections attempted to maximise their
strength by trying to win reserved seats. However, in trying to win
such seats, while all the main parties relied upon obtaining support
from within particular ethnic communities, those that were successful
may not have used an appeal to ethnic identity as the means of
obtaining that support. Rather, they may have used other forms of
identity as the basis of electoral mobilisation. Thus, indigenous Fijian

parties relied heavily upon provincial loyalties, while the FLP relied heavily upon its support base amongst Indo-Fijian farmers and workers. The possible weakness of ethnic politics in the reserved seats was not expected of the AV system.

Paradoxically, in open seats where one ethnic community dominated the voter population there was probably a wider implicit reliance upon ethnic identity as a central part of political mobilisation. This is probably true even as regards the most multiethnic of the major parties, the FLP. Granted, the FLP's capacity to skilfully deploy its policy platform meant that its appeal to the Indo-Fijian vote in such seats did not have to be couched in ethnic terms. Nonetheless, even the FLP did not have to try and increase its support amongst the indigenous Fijian community in these seats; it could rely upon its support amongst Indo-Fijian farmers and workers to win seats. Such an outcome was not what the FCRC had expected of the AV system. Moreover, such an outcome is obviously not in the long term interest of a class-based party such as the FLP.

Finally, in those open seats where no one community dominated the voter population, cooperation between parties was fostered in the form of efforts to share preferences. Thus, the AV system did indeed promote increased cooperation between parties. However, the type of cooperation between parties is also important to consider. The SVT and the NFP, the two principal actors in the constitutional review process, entered, along with the UGP, into a formal coalition. The voters rejected this. The FLP, on the other hand, entered into an agreement with the PANU and the FAP regarding second preferences, and were rewarded handsomely. It can thus be cautiously argued that when given appropriate alliance structures and incentives, communities in Fiji may be willing to vote for parties other than those rooted in their own ethnic group.

However, the depth of the commitment to cross-community politics engendered amongst ordinary voters by party strategies designed to maximise first and second preferences can be questioned when the parties are themselves largely ethnically based. The 1999 general elections illustrate the point. Both the groupings were groupings of largely ethnically based political parties. To that end, the individual parties of these groupings organised their own campaigns. As a consequence, interaction between workers and supporters of different ethnically based political parties and indeed between voters of different ethnic groups was limited. In this light, it is not surprising that during the elections there was little change in the mindset of voters: obviously, while the AV system did promote greater cooperation between parties, this occurred at the level of the élites who controlled the parties. That there was little change in the mindset of voters can be illustrated by the pattern of voting. Under the electoral procedures, voters could either indicate the political party of their choice or they could register their own individual preferences amongst the candidates of those parties. In most constituencies, less than 5 per cent of voters exercised their individual preferences, which would have demonstrated a greater willingness to engage in the messy realities of cross-community politics. Thus, the AV system may not have helped consolidate openness to multiethnic politics amongst ordinary party workers, supporters and voters. As a consequence, the AV system was not really able to break down the ethnicisation of politics in Fiji. Indeed, by fostering cooperation only amongst élites it may well be the case that the AV system harms the prospects for cross-community, ideology-based parties.

In addition to not working as those who introduced it thought it would, the AV has had a clearly unfavourable impact upon the principle of proportionality in parliamentary representation. This is obviously demonstrated by the parliamentary representation of the SVT and the NFP. The SVT received 38 per cent of first preferences from within the indigenous Fijian community. This translated into only 11 per cent of overall seats in the House of Representatives. The NFP received 32 per cent of Indo-Fijian first preferences. This translated into no parliamentary seats. It is ironic that both the SVT and the NFP, which actively opposed proportional systems of parliamentary representation during the review of the constitution, would have been better represented in parliament under proportional representation. At the same time, the pooling of preferences which initially went to smaller, more independent parties and candidates in favour of one of the constituent parts of one of the larger party groupings may contribute to a loss of confidence in parliamentary democracy. Certainly, the AV system has severely weakened the parliamentary representation of the more extreme ethnic nationalist parties such as the NVTLP, and while a first reaction to such an outcome might be to welcome it, it is also necessary to be aware of potentially adverse consequences in the longer term should more extreme parties become disenfranchised from parliamentary representation as a consequence of the AV system.

Conclusion: confronting the present and the future

Fiji's 1999 general elections were a national referendum on the 1997 Constitution. Given that the SVT, the NFP, the FLP, the FAP and the PANU all supported—albeit with some reservations—the 1997 Constitution, the mandate that it has received from the peoples of Fiji is overwhelming. However, despite this mandate, and despite the clear objectives of the Constitution in seeking to promote multiethnic politics in Fiji, it is clear that significant tensions remain between those who would use ethnicity as a primary means of political mobilisation and those who would use class as a primary means of political mobilisation. While the AV system has been able to foster cooperation amongst the political parties, and while multiparty government may reinforce this cooperation, the AV system has not been able to expunge the recourse to ethnicity as a tool of political mobilisation. It has possibly permitted a 'de-ethnicisation' of politics in reserved seats. However, it is indeed ironic that under the AV system the use of ethnicity may have been reinforced in those seats specifically designed to foster the emergence of a multiethnic politics: the open seats. Moreover, where it has fostered cross-community cooperation, this has been amongst élites; it has not occurred amongst people. In this light, two suggestions emerge. The first is that Fiji would do well to critically reassess the suitability of AV system. Electoral systems which respect the proportionality of parliamentary representation are also capable of breaking down inter-ethnic boundaries, and perhaps these should be considered anew in light of the outcome of the 1999 general elections. The second is that the ratio of open to reserved seats must be re-examined and possibly reversed if Fiji is to move decisively towards a less ethnically based system of politics.

Clearly, as is evident in the other contributions to this volume, the tension between the use of ethnicity and the use of class as primary means of political mobilisation will continue to define the parameters of Fiji's politics. In this light, it is significant that the main challenges that any Fiji government will confront over the next decade are likely to emerge from factors associated with economic globalisation. It is unclear whether a consociational arrangement that may work to consolidate and indeed reify contested categories of ethnicity favours or undermines the capability of national governments to negotiate in an increasingly open, unforgiving and undiscriminating international environment.

What is of a more immediate concern to the peoples of Fiji, however, is the level of commitment of the new government to the implementation and operation of the new Constitution. To a large extent it was the leaders of the NFP and the SVT who were able to negotiate a constitutional settlement, rally the support of the elected members of the two ethnic groupings for the constitutional 'deal', receive the endorsement of the Great Council of Chiefs, and ensure the implementation of the electoral provisions of the Constitution. The situation has now changed. Following the elections, the mantle of political leadership has passed on to leaders whose parties were less central to the negotiation of the Constitution. It remains to be seen whether the new government will accord a similar degree of importance to the implementation of all the provisions of the Constitution. It also remains to be seen whether the new government is committed to promoting the consensus amongst Fiji's main political parties regarding social and economic policy, which is implicit in the constitutional provisions regarding the formation of the executive. The extent of the commitment to policy consensus will be seen most prominently in the attention which is paid by the new government to indigenous Fijian rights and interests. Indeed, it is possible that the FLP's electoral commitment to delivering an ambitious social package may collide with the commitment to enhancing indigenous Fijian rights and interests that is a core pillar upon which the Constitution rests. Were such a collision to occur, it would undermine the potential that the FLP-led government has to radically transform Fiji's economy and its politics. Fiji's politics have entered a new era, and what the future may hold has yet to unfold.

Endnote

1. This chapter is a substantially revised version of Prasad (1999).

CHAPTER 4

Fiji's economy: the challenge of the future

Ardeshir Sepehri and A Haroon Akram-Lodhi

Introduction

Following a decade of relatively high rates of economic growth during the 1970s, Fiji's economic performance declined considerably in the 1980s. Economic growth both slowed down and became increasingly erratic, and for many policymakers it appeared that the country's decade-old experience with an inward-looking import-substituting industrialisation strategy had reached its limits. In an effort to restore economic growth Fiji embarked upon an orthodox structural adjustment program which sought, among other things, to redirect industrial policy towards export-led growth while pursuing macroeconomic stabilisation, external trade liberalisation and internal deregulation, including changes in agricultural markets, public sector restructuring and financial sector reform (Akram-Lodhi 1996; Elek, Hill and Tabor 1993). While the adjustment program was apparently successful, to the extent that it reversed the decline in the trend rate of growth of output, diversified exports and restored macroeconomic balances, it fell short of policymakers' expectations in other aspects. The adjustment program did little to reverse the declining trend in the rate of growth of investment, failed to achieve a reasonably high rate of growth of output, and did little to spur a generalised increase in job creation.

While Fiji's economic difficulties and their causes have been studied, these studies have been mainly descriptive; no recent attempt has been made to quantify the main constraints upon economic growth in Fiji. This chapter addresses this shortcoming. It assesses the role and significance of domestic private and public sector savings, as well as foreign savings, on the growth path of output by formulating and estimating a simple structural three-gap model of growth similar to that suggested by Bacha (1990) and Taylor (1991). According to the three-gap model, the utilisation and growth of productive capacity is constrained not only by domestic and foreign savings, as was initially discussed by Chenery and Strout (1966) in the context of the two-gap model, but also by the availability of public sector resources. There can be little doubt that public sector resources have played a crucial role in the economy of independent Fiji. Public sector savings and investment have been vital in determining the productive capacity of the economy and its growth rate, both directly through public enterprises and indirectly through investment in physical, social and human infrastructure. Therefore, this chapter estimates a three-gap model for the period 1971–96. The estimation results are then used to conduct simulations of the period 1997–2001. Four distinctive policy simulations are conducted. These simulations assess the impact of a gradual elimination of Fiji's preferential access to the European Union (EU) for its sugar exports as well as the amount of foreign resources that would be needed if Fiji were to achieve a socially desirable growth rate.

The economy of Fiji, 1970–98

Table 4.1 provides a summary of the major macroeconomic indicators during four main periods: the first post-independence decade, 1971 to 1981; the crisis period of 1982 to 1986; the adjustment period under the Interim Government (1989–92)[1]; and the most recent period of 1993 to 1996. In what follows, developments in the main macroeconomic indicators, and the underlying policy changes surrounding such developments, are examined.

Economic policy and performance, 1970–81[2]

Fiji inherited a colonial economic structure which changed little in the decade after independence in 1970, as the government pursued a development strategy based upon seeking to secure full employment through the continued use of the country's natural resources. Thus, as in the pre-independence period, agriculture continued to be the major

Table 4.1 Selected macroeconomic indicators, 1971–96

	1971–81	1982–86	1989–92	1993–96	1993	1994	1995	1996
Growth rates (% per annum)								
Real GDP (constant 1977 factor cost)	5.2	1.3	5.5	2.8	1.2	4.5	2.6	3.1
Per capita GDP	3.2	-0.7	4.2	1.4	-0.5	2.8	1.3	1.9
Consumer price index	11.6	5.0	6.4	2.8	5.2	0.6	2.2	3.1
Annual share of GDP (current factor cost)								
Agriculture	25.7	19.4	19.5	20.0	19.8	20.9	19.9	19.4
Manufacturing	11.5	9.8	11.4	14.8	14.6	15.0	14.8	14.8
Gross fixed investment	23.2	20.8	14.9	13.5	15.8	12.9	13.0	12.1
Private fixed investment	12.6	11.3	5.6	5.0	5.5	4.9	4.9	5.0
Government deficits	5.3	6.1	4.4	4.9	6.2	4.0	3.3	5.9
Net exports[a]	-7.4	-2.5	2.5	4.3	-2.8	1.6	9.2	9.2
Annual share of merchandise exports								
Sugar and molasses	74.5	63.9	40.1	39.3	39.9	38.9	38.9	39.5
Garments	n.a[b]	n.a	19.8	22.6	21.9	21.2	24.2	23.1
External debt (as % of GNP)[c]	28.6	32.4	21.4	14.0[d]	20.5	17.0	14.0	n.a.
Mean daily real wage rates (1985 prices)								
'all industries'	13.2	12.4	9.7	9.8[e]	9.7	9.9	n.a.	n.a.
'manufacturing'	13.3	12.5	8.4	8.4[e]	8.3	8.5	n.a.	n.a.

Sources: Real variables such as GDP, investment, exports and imports, and government expenditures and revenues were obtained from the Fiji Bureau of Statistics *Current Economic Statistics* (various issues). All real variables are measured at 1977 prices. Balance of payments and foreign debt data were obtained from the Reserve Bank of Fiji *Quarterly Review* (various issues) and the World Bank's (1997) *Global Development Finance: Country Tables*. Capital and intermediate imports data were calculated by the authors using the import data by SITC as reported in the United Nations *International Trade Statistics Yearbook* (various issues). Our thanks to Kishor Chetty for his help in obtaining certain data from the Fiji Bureau of Statistics.
[a] exports of goods and non-factor services less imports of goods and non-factor services; [b] negligible; [c] at the end of each period; [d] at the end of 1995; [e] for the period 1993–94 only

economic activity, accounting, as Table 4.1 illustrates, for over 25 per cent of gross domestic product (GDP) over the period 1971–81. Indeed, since 1970 agriculture has accounted for between 20 and 25 per cent of GDP. In 1996, agriculture provided almost a fifth of Fiji's GDP and employed, on a full-time or a part-time basis, more than 75 per cent of all households. Within agriculture, sugarcane continues to be the dominant crop. As late as 1996 sugar production accounted for over 12 per cent of GDP, more than 40 per cent of the agricultural sector, 30 per cent of the manufacturing sector, and provided direct employment for more than 25 per cent of the country's economically active population (Fiji Bureau of Statistics (various issues): Table 3.3). In 1996 the sugar industry provided about 40 per cent of exports by value (Table 4.1). Granted, the importance of the sugar sector has declined as independent Fiji has diversified its economic activities; for example, other significant natural resource-based activities currently include tourism, gold, fisheries and timber. Nonetheless, sugar production still plays a critical role in the performance of the overall economy.

In theory, Fiji's sugar industry has been subject to the dictates of the international economy. However, in practice the impact of international economic conditions on Fiji's sugar industry has been muted because of quota arrangements with the EU. The Sugar Protocol agreed between the then European Economic Community (EEC) and the Africa, Caribbean and Pacific countries came into force in 1975 under the auspices of Protocol 3 of the Lomé Convention (Prasad and Akram-Lodhi 1998). The Sugar Protocol committed Fiji to delivering specific quantities of sugar to the EEC at prices which were guaranteed and which were based upon the price of sugar set annually under the EEC's Common Agricultural Policy. In 1975 Fiji was allocated a quota of 163,600 metric tons of sugar, equivalent to 13.4 per cent of the total preferential quota. For the period 1990–92 Fiji's quota allocation amounted to an average of 42 per cent of the country's total sugar production and 46.6 per cent of the country's total sugar exports (MacDonald 1996). Fiji received a price which not only averaged between 2.5 and 3 times the world market price but which was also significantly more stable than the world market price (Hermann and Weiss 1995).

In contrast to natural resource-based economic activities, the manufacturing sector has been small in size and subordinate in terms of its economic importance. The limited industrial development that occurred during the first post-independence decade was largely based upon import-substitution, which protected domestic industries through a complex regulatory regime deploying quota, license and tariff protection. Thus, the contribution of manufacturing to GDP rose slightly from less than 11 per cent at the time of independence to about 13 per cent by the end of first post-independence decade. The lower priority attached to industrialisation partly reflected the widely shared view that very small economies have only a limited potential for industrialisation. It also reflected an emphasis on employment-generating labour-intensive activities as a means of maintaining communal relations between a population almost equally divided between indigenous Fijians and Indo-Fijians.

However, despite trade barriers the economy always had a comparatively high degree of openness to the international economy. Fiji relied upon a vast range of imported consumption, intermediate and capital goods to meet the demands of consumers and firms. Thus, in the period between 1971 and 1981, imports accounted for about 57 per cent of GDP, exports for almost half of GDP, and net exports for - 7.4 per cent of GDP (Table 4.1). Post-colonial Fiji was therefore a hybrid: an economy with elements of *dirigisme* which was nonetheless deeply insinuated into the world economy (Narayan 1984).

State regulation was not confined to external trade. Indeed, it can be argued that the most important intervention by the government was the regulation of factor and product markets within the economy. A Prices and Incomes Board (PIB) was established to monitor and control the wholesale and retail prices of many goods and some services. In addition to the PIB, several ministries, including the present Ministries of Tourism and Transport, Works and Energy, Commerce, Business Development and Investment, Public Enterprises, and Labour and Industrial Relations, and several quasi-autonomous government institutions like the Native Land Trust Board and the Fijian Affairs Board, were empowered to regulate product and factor markets, including land and labour. The post-colonial government also exercised considerable power over productive activity, both directly, by establishing public enterprises in agriculture, manufacturing and services, as well as indirectly, by planning and setting production targets. Finally, the state intervened heavily in financial markets: interest rates were controlled, and the exchange rate was fixed.

Economic crisis, 1982–86

Overall economic performance, as measured by the rate of growth of GDP, has varied considerably since 1970 (Table 4.1). In the first decade following independence, economic performance was generally good, as Fiji witnessed real GDP growth of 5.2 per cent per year and removed 'some of the worst elements of the colonial inheritance' (Cameron 1994:420). However, this performance was not sustained through the first half of the 1980s. In the early 1980s 'Fiji was undergoing a multi-dimensional crisis' (Cameron 1994:420) consisting of drought, cyclones, the 1979 oil price rise, and unexpected turbulence in international sugar prices. As a consequence, real GDP growth dropped to 1.2 per cent per annum during the period between 1982 and 1986; over the same period, real per capita GDP contracted by 0.7 per cent per year. As might be expected, the stagnation of output was accompanied by increasing fiscal imbalance: the fiscal deficit rose from 5.3 per cent of GDP during the period between 1971 and 1981 to 6.1 per cent during the period between 1982 to 1986. Foreign debt also continued to grow. Foreign debt as a percentage of gross national product (GNP) rose from 28.6 per cent at the end of 1982 to 32.4 per cent by the end of 1986 (Table 4.1).

In light of what was clearly an economic crisis, in late 1986 the Finance Minister outlined the beginning of a change in Fiji's industrial policy by announcing the creation of tax-free factories, a form of export-processing zone (Akram-Lodhi 1992). This initiative was meant to be a first decisive step in a shift in industrial policy away from import-substitution and towards export promotion, a shift which had an extremely long gestation period, having been first mooted in Development Plan 6 published in 1970 (Chandra 1985). However, the 1986 shift in industrial policy became a much deeper transformation in economic strategy in the wake of two coups led by Lieutenant-Colonel Sitiveni Rabuka in May and September 1987.

The 1987 coups were a severe economic shock. Tourism dropped by some 36 per cent, while farmers disrupted the sugar cane harvest in protest. The cessation of concessional credit, a sharp fall in inflows of foreign direct investment, and the flight of an estimated F$120 million (US$83 million) out of the country in 1987 and 1988 all reduced considerably the availability of foreign financial resources and hence imports. Given that some 40 per cent of budget revenues came from customs and excise, the impact of the coups was quickly experienced by government: between 1986 and 1987 the budget deficit increased by over 12.5 per cent, to stand at almost 8 per cent of GDP. It was partly in response to the deepening crisis that the newly-appointed, military-backed Interim Government 'pinpointed industrialisation as being of prime importance to Fiji's future development' (Chandra 1989:170) in that it could both stabilise and indeed expand the economy, and thus act to offset possible political unrest.

Embedding structural adjustment, 1987–92

In transforming economic strategy the Interim Government was not only claiming to respond to the higher costs, excess capacity and resource misallocation associated with Fiji's attempt at import-substitution, problems initially identified in the government's review of Development Plan 7 (Fiji Ministry of Finance, Central Planning Office 1979). It was also 'responding both to the international trend towards economic liberalisation and export-oriented industrialisation and to specific advice from its consultants and international agencies' (Chandra 1989:170). This advice had argued that Fiji needed to radically improve its export potential by reducing unit labour costs if it was to continue to grow (World Bank 1986; Fiji Employment and Development Mission 1984). Given that much of this advice had been received prior to the coups, and given that the initial creation of tax-free factories predated the coups, the transformation in Fiji's economic strategy that occurred after 1987 should not so much be seen as a dramatic break with the past as rather a confirmation of policy processes which had already been initiated prior to the coups.

The central themes in Fiji's transformation of economic strategy were embedded in the formulation and implementation of an orthodox structural adjustment program that by and large shared many features of World Bank and International Monetary Fund-sponsored programs. The important exception to this rule was that Fiji received no financial transfers from either multilateral institution in exchange for initiating the program. The adjustment program aimed at a far reaching economic change through macroeconomic stabilisation, external trade liberalisation and internal deregulation, including changes in agricultural markets, public sector restructuring and financial sector reforms. These policy reforms were to facilitate economic restructuring and transform Fiji from an 'inward looking, high tax, and slow growth economy to a dynamic outward looking, low tax and high growth economy' (Fiji Ministry of Finance 1991).

Macroeconomic stabilisation

The increase in the budget deficit brought about by the collapse in tourism and the disruption of the sugar cane harvest necessitated the stabilisation of the economy. The government did this by implementing deflationary fiscal and monetary policies. On the fiscal side, the government imposed a 15 per cent wage cut on all civil servants. It also slashed public investment in real terms by a third. On the monetary side, the central bank, the Reserve Bank of Fiji, severely restricted the availability of private sector credit and imposed additional restrictions on outflows of foreign exchange.

However, undoubtedly the most important component of the Interim Government's stabilisation package was a devaluation of the Fiji dollar (Akram-Lodhi 1996). The value of the Fiji dollar is fixed by the Reserve Bank relative to a weighted basket of the currencies of Fiji's principal trading partners. A two-stage devaluation in June and October 1987 reduced the value of the dollar in nominal terms by some 33 per cent. When combined with the decline in real wages the impact was to bring about a fall in the real effective exchange rate of almost 28 per cent in the period between 1986 and 1988. The effect was to reduce further the attractiveness of capital flight and improve the competitive position of the economy by reversing the decline in output and investment caused by the coups.

However, the government did not stop at stabilisation. It used economic crisis to cement macroeconomic reform by restructuring Fiji's fiscal stance. In the 1990 budget the Finance Minister felt confident enough to cut income tax rates by 20 per cent, leaving the highest rate at 40 per cent. At the same time exemptions and allowances were increased. To compensate for the loss of revenue and to ease the transition to a new value-added, tax existing indirect taxes were raised and the tax base was broadened by bringing some 40,000 peasants into income tax for the first time. Plans to 'corporatise' several state-owned enterprises also moved forward. While this effort to force state-owned enterprises to follow commercial practices was envisaged to be a prelude to privatisation, the more immediate positive impact from the government's point of view was on its own accounts.

In the Interim Government's final 1992 budget further cuts in income tax and corporation tax were announced, the number of income tax bands was reduced, corporation tax was simplified, income tax thresholds were increased and the requirement that those below the threshold pay tax was ended. Finally, despite the resignation of the Interim Government prior to the May 1992 election, a key policy initiative, the much-debated value-added tax, was introduced on schedule in July by the newly elected government.

Trade liberalisation

The most visible aspect of the Interim Government's adjustment program was that of external trade liberalisation. Tax-free factories quickly became an important feature of Fiji's industrial and export policy (Akram-Lodhi 1992). Tax-free factories received substantial tax concessions in exchange for a commitment to export 95 per cent of output. Such concessions were available to both Fiji and international firms, thus placing both within a similar regulatory regime. Of the 119 firms engaged in tax-free manufacturing by the end of 1992, 70 per cent were in garment production. Despite the fact that garment exports had started to increase prior to the introduction of tax-free factories, the performance of the garment factories was impressive: by 1990 garment production for export comprised over 55 per cent of manufacturing production, over 22 per cent of total domestic exports, and over 37 per cent of all manufacturing employment (Akram-Lodhi 1992; Elek, Hill and Tabor 1993). Almost half of those firms operating tax-free factories in 1992 were transnational corporations, albeit from a narrow group of countries. Economic changes in Australia and New Zealand in particular forced garment producers from those countries to seek to source production offshore in countries such as Fiji. In order to attract such businesses, the Interim Government eased and simplified approval procedures for foreign direct investment while at the same time expanding the resources available to the Fiji Trade and Investment Board so that it could enhance its capacity to attract foreign direct investment. Thus, the share of foreign direct investment in GDP was 27 per cent higher under the adjustment period of 1989 to 1992 as compared to that of the immediate pre-adjustment period of 1982 to 1986. The increase in international investment flows directed into Fiji might be taken to be a sign of confidence in the irreversible nature of the change in Fiji towards a liberal, export-oriented economic regime. It also indicates the extent to which trade and investment are complementary phenomena.

As regards imports, external trade liberalisation has meant an effective end to import licensing. The licensing regime used to sustain import substitution was largely eradicated as Fiji switched to an open general license scheme covering most consumption, intermediate and capital goods. Thus, prior to 1989 over 47 commodities required licenses; in 1991, only 9 commodities required licenses (Elek, Hill and Tabor 1993). The government replaced import licensing with a simplified structure of tariffs. Maximum tariff levels were progressively cut, so that by 1992 most imports had attached to them a fiscal duty of 30 per cent. Indeed, the last budget of the Interim Government held out the prospect of a maximum tariff of only 20 per cent in 1993, in part due to the introduction of a value-added tax designed to assist in reducing the dependence of revenue upon customs levies.

Internal deregulation

External trade liberalisation was accompanied by extensive internal deregulation. The overall thrust of the changes involved a reduction in barriers to entry in domestic markets, thereby potentially enhancing competitive discipline. Obviously, the shift to an open general license scheme was an important component of a reduction in barriers to entry. So too was the reduction and simplification of customs duties and corporation tax. However, internal deregulation went further than these obvious changes. Detailed sectoral economic targeting was eliminated after the coups. This reduced the non-market, linkage-enhancing planning requirements that had been placed upon some firms. An enhancement of the role of markets was furthered by the elimination of price controls on a range of items. Indeed, the need for price controls was to some extent eliminated by the introduction of enforceable trading standards by the Ministry of Trade and Commerce in the last year of the Interim Government.

Barriers to market entry were further diminished by attempts at reforming state-owned enterprises. Under the auspices of the Public Enterprise Unit in the Ministry of Finance and Economic Planning, the government corporatised several large public enterprises. This placed some state-owned enterprises on the same legal and commercial basis as private sector firms, with the government theoretically committed to simply acting as the majority shareholder. Corporatisation led some firms to conduct efficiency-enhancing internal reforms. At the same time, the process did in theory open up protected markets to competition. However, only one seriously unprofitable firm was closed, while industrial action in several corporatised companies resulted in the kind of government intervention that corporatisation was supposed to prevent.

The final major internal deregulation initiative of the Interim Government was to enhance the flexibility of the labour market (Chand, this volume). In 1991 statutory wage guidelines were abolished in order to strengthen the position of employers in establishing the relationship between pay and productivity. This was followed by changes to labour legislation, which substantially increased government intervention in the internal affairs of unions. The effect of these changes to labour legislation was to make it less likely that the 80 per cent of the formally employed labour force which belonged to trades unions, professional associations or other, similar, organisations would assert their right to withdraw their labour.

There can be no doubt concerning the impressive stabilisation of the economy in the period following the coups. Although real per capita GDP shrank by over 7 per cent in 1987 and inflation peaked at 12 per cent in November 1988, by mid 1988 the economy was recovering. As demonstrated in Table 4.1, the economy grew at an average annual rate of 5.5 per cent over the period between 1989 and 1992, fiscal deficits were reduced to 4.4 per cent of GDP, and net exports turned positive for the first time. Recovery was fuelled by higher sugar export earnings and by a gradual expansion of private sector credit. The recovery of the sugar sector was accompanied by a return of tourists; thus, government revenues increased. Buoyant government revenues permitted 1987 public sector wage cuts to be restored in real terms in 1988 and 1989. At the same time, higher earnings from sugar exports and tourism, combined with higher export earnings from garment and increasing foreign direct investment, helped to raise foreign reserves and reduce foreign debt. Net foreign direct investment increased from US$6.3 million in 1987 to an average annual net inflow of US$43 million during the period between 1989 and 1992.

While the structural adjustment program of 1987–92 was quite instrumental in restoring economic growth, it did little to reverse the decline in the trend rate of growth of investment, and particularly private investment. The share of fixed investment in GDP declined from 23 per cent during the period 1971–82 to just under 15 per cent during the period 1989–92 (Table 4.1). Indeed, it dropped to as low as 12.1 per cent in 1996. Private investment as a percentage of GDP almost halved, dropping from its peak value of 14 per cent during the period 1977–81 to 7.4 per cent during the period 1987–92. The economic crisis of the early 1980s, combined with fiscal restraints during the adjustment period, growing uncertainty over property rights in land and the future direction of government policy reforms, put severe constraints upon the growth of investment.

Economic policy under Rabuka, 1993–98

In 1992 elections were held under the provisions of the discriminatory 1990 Constitution. Rabuka, the leader of the coups and now a Major General, became Prime Minister at the head of a *Soqosoqo Ni Vakavulewa Ni Taukei*-General Voters' Party coalition government. Under Rabuka's leadership the explicit commitment to structural adjustment did not change: economic policy remained committed to macroeconomic stabilisation, external trade liberalisation and internal trade deregulation. Nonetheless, the exigencies of electoral politics—however flawed—meant that the context had certainly shifted. While policy reform continued, the pace of reform slowed. Moreover, the impact of fluctuating fortunes in the sugar and tourism sectors sustained continued efforts by the government to diversify the pattern of economic activity, especially through the encouragement of manufacturing.

Between 1993 and 1996 the economy grew at an annual average rate of 2.8 per cent—much less than that achieved in the decade following independence (Table 4.1). As they had since the mid 1980s, sugar, garment manufacturing and tourism dominated economic performance between 1993 and 1996. Sugar was responsible for 42 per cent of agricultural production in 1996. Moreover, between 1993 and 1996 sugar comprised over 39 per cent of total exports (Table 4.1). At the same time, the redirection of industrial strategy towards export-led growth in the mid 1980s led to a steady increase in manufacturing's contribution to GDP. By 1996 manufacturing accounted for almost 15 per cent of GDP (Table 4.1). While sugar remained responsible for 22.4 per cent of manufacturing production in 1996, the sector was in fact dominated by garment production for export in 120 tax-free factories, which in 1997 were responsible for two-thirds of all manufacturing employment. Garment exports increased from 4.1 per cent of total exports in 1986 to 23.1 per cent of total exports in 1996. Indeed, the efforts of successive governments to transform Fiji into an export-oriented economy were, by the late 1990s, clearly successful. Exports went from 16.2 per cent of GDP in 1985 to 28.2 per cent of GDP in 1994. Sugar and garments between them were responsible for over 60 per cent of all merchandise exports in 1996, and well over 60,000 jobs (Table 4.1). Tourism, which provided around 20 per cent of GDP in 1996, also made an important contribution to net exports. The steady improvement in trade balances during the early 1990s led net exports, which had been in deficit for most of the post-colonial period, to move into surplus. The improvement in the trade balances helped to restore foreign reserves—which in 1997 stood at US$347 million—and reduce foreign debt. Total foreign debt dropped from an average of 21.4 per cent of GNP in 1992 period to 14 per cent in 1995 (Table 4.1). Inflation, which in Fiji is mainly determined by import prices and the exchange rate, was also significantly cut, averaging 2.8 per cent between 1993 and 1996.

However, the public finances of low growth, export-driven Fiji were not particularly strong between 1993 and 1996 (Table 4.1). The government ran consistent budget deficits, which over the period between 1993 and 1996 averaged 4.9 per cent of GDP. Moreover, while the public finances did begin to improve in 1994 and 1995 (Table 4.1), it was subsequently discovered that the state-owned National Bank of Fiji (NBF), the largest domestic commercial bank, had, as a consequence of financial mismanagement and possible corruption, accumulated bad debts of more than F$200 million (US$143 million) and was near to collapse. In order to restructure the NBF the government was forced to give it a F$213.3 million (US$152 million) injection of capital. The impact of the rescue of the NBF on the budget deficit was enormous: the budget deficit reached an unsustainable 9.2 per cent of GDP in 1997, of which over 12.3 per cent was a direct result of the rescue.

At the same time, consistent budget deficits had other, less contingent, causes. A first factor was that the government had to meet accumulated debt repayment obligations. In 1996 accumulated debt repayments accounted for 16 per cent of government spending and over the period between 1993 and 1996 debt repayments often exceeded the size of the budget deficit. Nonetheless, the strength of exports implied that the debt burden, while heavy, was manageable: the debt-service ratio fell from 11.2 per cent in 1991 to 5.9 per cent in 1995.

A second factor was that the government was continuing to restructure its tools of revenue acquisition. In order to boost domestic competitiveness, the government sought to reform pricing in water, power and telecommunications utilities. In order to boost international competitiveness, increase simplicity and transparency, and in order to comply with World Trade Organization (WTO) non-discretionary policies, the 1998 budget reviewed the tariff structure. Tariffs were cut on many imported non-locally produced goods. Some 97 non-locally produced goods were subjected to a new tariff of 10 per cent, while some goods were moved onto a zero-tariff band. For those imported goods that competed with locally produced goods, tariffs were increased to 35 per cent. However, such a tariff fell within the WTO bound rate of 40 per cent. Moreover, it was promised that tariffs for imported goods that competed with locally produced goods would fall by 3 per cent a year every year to 2002.

Fiscal weakness also contributed to budgetary deficits. Privatisation proceeds had been expected during the 1990s to improve the public finances. However, the first privatisation attempted by the government, that of the Government Shipyard, was a mess. One of the partners in the buyout went into receivership and government had to spend time and money searching for a new partner. At the same time, attempts to speed up privatisation required large budgetary outlays in order to meet the initial expenses of reorganising corporatised state-owned enterprises and in order to locate possible purchasers of the assets.

Fiscal weakness was exacerbated by tax non-compliance. The Finance Minister in the 1998 budget estimated that some 13 per cent of government revenues were lost due to non-compliance. In part, non-compliance may have been a result of corruption as, in addition to the NBF scandal, in 1997 the police had launched corruption probes into the Customs Department, the Companies Office, the Registrar-General's Department and the Fiji Housing Authority. There can be little doubt that the perception that corruption in Fiji was becoming both wider and deeper was at least in part responsible for the Finance Minister's 1998 decision to set up an autonomous and independent Fiji Revenue and Customs Authority.

Within the context of a low growth, export-driven, fiscally weak economy, the government relied heavily upon monetary policy. Between 1993 and 1996 the Reserve Bank allowed the M1 measure of the money supply to grow at an annual average rate of 11 per cent, well above both the nominal rate of growth of the economy and the real interest rate, in order to encourage growth. In order to offset the pressure on the exchange rate caused by monetary expansion, in 1997 the government relaxed foreign exchange controls in an effort to increase inflows of foreign direct investment. However, in order to relax foreign exchange controls, the process of liberalising the current account was begun. While this had the affect of delegating current account transactions to commercial banks and increasing the share of retained export proceeds, it also had the affect of increasing the size of permissible company profit remittances and easing the capacity to invest offshore, both of which served to put further pressure on the exchange rate.

However, unlike 1988, when an easing of monetary policy contributed to expansion, monetary policy failed to sustain an increase in the rate of growth of output. The government could not sustain the unsustainable, and in January 1998 the most important shift in monetary policy of the decade occurred when the Reserve Bank devalued the Fiji dollar by 20 per cent. Ostensibly, the basis of the decision to devalue was the need to mount a defensive reaction to the East Asian crisis, which had led to substantial depreciations in Thailand, Malaysia, Indonesia, South Korea and the Philippines. In the wake of these depreciations, Fiji's two largest trading partners, Australia and New Zealand, had seen their currencies depreciate. In Fiji's low growth, import-dependent, export-driven economy, the relative appreciation of the Fiji dollar against the currencies of the country's two largest trading partners meant a loss of competitiveness and a reduced capacity to export. This had the potential to dramatically destabilise the economy. At the same time, movements in the gold price had worked against the economy.

Nonetheless, it is clear that devaluation in and of itself will not resolve the weaknesses of the Fiji economy in the short and medium term. It is true that devaluation will boost domestic production, as locally produced products become cheaper than imports with which they compete. However, the scope for import-substitution in Fiji's small, open economy is clearly limited. Both exports and imports are very insensitive to changes in relative prices: price elasticities of the demand for exports and imports are estimated to be as low as -0.44 and -0.27 respectively (Reddy 1997: Tables 1 and 2). Fiji's import dependence must severely restrict the benefits of devaluation. Consider, for example, the three principal export industries. Sugar earnings from exports in Fiji dollar terms will rise as a result of the devaluation. However, so too will the cost of essential production and processing inputs that have to be imported, as well as the cost of transport. Similarly, devaluation might make the Fiji tourist industry more competitive. However, the sector as a whole is highly import dependent (Korth, this volume), and devaluation has raised the price of imports. The net benefits are thus likely to be much smaller than anticipated by policy makers. Finally, while the garment industry will have been given a competitive boost by the devaluation, the fact that labour is the only domestically provided input in the industry would serve to offset the competitive boost. Moreover, in those sectors where Fiji competes directly with East Asian countries and companies, the devaluation is, in many instances, less than the depreciation of their currencies, meaning that Fiji after the devaluation has lost a competitive advantage. This applies particularly to garments and tourism.

At the same time, with increases in the prices of imports, inflation will rise in the short term and consumers will have to bear the brunt of the increase. The decline in real wages arising out of increased inflation should mean that the devaluation would impact upon domestic demand. Thus, it is clear that devaluation is an unimaginative means of dealing with a stagnant economy. The need to devalue also makes clear that after more than a decade of structural adjustment, the economy of Fiji is still plagued by structural weaknesses. That this is recognised by policymakers is clear from comments on the imperatives facing the Fiji economy in the wake of devaluation: government stressed the need for producers to reduce unit labour costs by improving efficiency and cutting costs. There are two routes by which lower labour costs could be secured in Fiji. The first is by cutting real wages; however, as already noted, cuts in real wages would serve to restrict domestic demand and economic growth. The second is by increasing investment and hence labour productivity; however, the prospect for an improvement in productivity remains poor as long as the share of investment in GDP continues to fall, in the manner illustrated in Table 4.1.

Although per capita income grew at an average annual rate of 4.2 and 1.4 per cent during the periods 1989–92 and 1993–96 respectively, the benefits of growth were not equitably distributed. It is estimated that 25 per cent of Fiji's households in general and 32.8 per cent of urban households in particular lived in poverty in 1990. Moreover, the proportion of the population in poverty between 1977 and 1990 increased by about 10 percentage points amongst households overall, and by 21 percentage points amongst urban households (Prasad and Asafu-Adjaye 1998). According to the United Nations Development Programme, this situation had deteriorated by 1996, especially as a result of rapid food price rises, rises which will accelerate in the wake of the 1998 devaluation (United Nations Development Programme/ Government of Fiji 1997). Other indicators of income inequality, such as the Gini coefficient, also show a worsening of income distribution. The estimated Gini coefficient for Fiji suggests that, nationally, income inequality deteriorated by about 10 percentage points between 1990 and 1997 for households overall, and by as much as 19 percentage points for urban households (Prasad and Asafu-Adjaye 1998). Moreover, as illustrated in Table 4.1, mean daily real wages in 'all industries' declined from an average of F$12.40 during the period 1982–86 to F$9.70 during the period 1989–92. The decline in real wages was consistent over the entire period between 1982 and 1992. It was more pronounced in the manufacturing sector, where mean daily real wages declined from an average of F$12.52 in the period 1982–86 to an average of F$8.40 in the period 1993–94, a decline of 33 per cent. Stagnant real wages sit alongside poor employment prospects for many. By the year 2000, 11,000 annual entrants onto the labour market will be chasing 5,000 annually created new jobs. Clearly, the current situation is a recipe for social conflict that can only be averted by job-creating, demand-enhancing investment.

Yet, as Table 4.1 indicates, investment continued its trend decline between 1993 and 1996, dropping to as low as 12.1 per cent of GDP in 1996. The government, in the wake of low levels of investment, has explicitly sought to increase foreign direct investment, usually through the deployment of tax concessions. This is especially so in the tax-free factories, where 120 factories are responsible for two-thirds of all manufacturing employment and 23 per cent of exports. However, the impact of the tax-free factories on the Fiji economy is reduced by leakages: half of all garment exports go to Australia, but non-labour inputs into garment production come from Australia. The result is that for some garment exports Australian content may reach 67 per cent of the product's value. Net exports from garments are therefore low. Fiji has been seeking revisions to the South Pacific Regional Trade and Economic Cooperation Agreement's (SPARTECA) rules of origin, which dictate 50 per cent local content. It has long been realised that the rules of origin discourage efficiency improvements by discouraging investment (Akram-Lodhi 1992).

Tax concessions have also been used to little effect in the tourist industry. The government's most recent policy package was designed to increase the stock of five-star hotels in the country. To that end, investors were offered a 20-year corporate income tax holiday, the duty free entry of all capital goods, other concessions, and the option to sell privately-generated electricity to the national grid. The impact on investment has however been limited. Tax concessions have also been used in the timber industry, but although it has became an important export earner, in producing exports one-seventh the value of those generated by sugar, it has been, to policymakers, a disappointment. The only sector where investment has been increasing has been in gold production, in which Emperor Gold Mines has expanded even as Pacific Island Gold has begun operating the new Mount Kasi mine. Gold generated 9.9 per cent of exports in 1996; however, the recent slump in the world gold price will affect further investment. Moreover, the scope for expansion is clearly limited.

The current policy of granting concessions to investors has thus proven to be ineffective in boosting investment. Moreover, it may be fiscally unsustainable. As Elek, Hill and Tabor (1993:763) observe in the context of tax concessions to the garment industry, '[i]f, as is likely, the relative share of export firms in the economy continues to expand, then it will become increasingly difficult to finance the physical infrastructure they need, or to assure an adequate supply of skill unless they make a contribution—through taxes—to the cost of providing them'.

The next decade

The need to boost investment is also a priority because of the major challenges facing Fiji's economy in the next decade. Under the Uruguay Round's Agreement on Agriculture, the market access provisions of the Sugar Protocol were locked into the tariff schedules inspected and agreed upon by all signatories to the Agreement and subsequently all members of the WTO. The Agreement did not however make specific provisions in favour of Fiji. This means that the main continued benefit of the Protocol lies in its quota allocations and the price it offers for Fiji's sugar. However, it is likely that after 1999 there will be major downward pressure on the EU's internal sugar price, and thus the price received by Fiji for its sugar, as a result of two factors. The first is the reform of the EU's Common Agricultural Policy, which is becoming increasingly likely. The second is the next round of WTO-initiated multilateral trade negotiations in agricultural products, which under the terms of the Agreement on Agriculture are due to begin in 1999. These negotiations 'will set in train a more powerful impetus to change than may at first sight seem obvious' (Roberts 1996:6). Negotiations

> can be expected to broadly follow the lines of the Uruguay Round: further reductions of support, increases in market access (e.g. through further reduction of tariffs and tariff equivalents) and further reduction in export subsidies and subsidised export quantities (Roberts 1996:5).

Downward pressures on the sugar price received by Fiji will only be reinforced if, in the negotiations to construct a successor arrangement to the Lomé Convention, negotiations that commenced in 1998, Article 24 of the General Agreement on Tariffs and Trade is more strictly interpreted. A stricter interpretation is probable, in an effort to achieve WTO consistency. The implication of Article 24 is that the successor arrangement would have to move towards free trade over a specified time period and include all significant economic sectors, including sugar (Prasad and Akram-Lodhi 1998). If such were to be the case, the Sugar Protocol would become redundant, and would, in all probability, be scrapped, an outcome which would represent a severe economic shock to Fiji.

In addition, it is likely that SPARTECA will be revised over the course of the next decade, in part because Fiji has been seeking a bilateral agreement with Australia which strengthens its access to the dominant economy in the region, and in part because Australia has been considering enhancing its trade-based assistance. However, new agreements might not be as beneficial as might be thought. Australia and Fiji are both members of the WTO and thus agreements covering their trading relationships must be consistent with the rules of the WTO, and in particular Article 24. This implies that any revised agreements would have, as a final outcome, free trade over a specified time period, which would exclude no significant economic sector. It is difficult to envisage the circumstances under which an economy as small as Fiji's could avoid the trade-reducing impact of Australia's absolute advantage.

A three-gap model[3]

Domestic investment, foreign resources and government resources have all played a major part in Fiji's economic performance since independence. Clearly, economic performance has, in the aggregate, not been good, especially in the 1990s. Thus, the low growth, export-driven, fiscally weak, import-dependent economy of Fiji faces major challenges over the medium term. There is in particular an urgent need to improve the share of investment in the economy if the poor economic performance of the 1990s is not to be replicated. In order to assess the significance of the level of government resources and foreign resources, as well as domestic savings, on the growth path of output and investment in Fiji, in this section a structural three-gap model of growth along the lines suggested by Fanelli, Frenkel and Winograd (1987), Bacha (1990) and Taylor (1991) is specified and estimated.

The three-gap model provides a general framework by which to assess the role and significance of domestic private and public sector saving, as well as foreign saving, on the growth path of output and investment. At the same time, the three-gap model explicitly considers the interaction between capacity expansion and capacity utilisation. Finally, the three-gap model has minimal data requirements for both estimation and simulation. These three features make the three-gap model a more suitable means of understanding macroeconomic growth processes than that provided by other open economy macroeconomic models. Granted, the three-gap model is a highly aggregated one-sector growth model in which price variations, including exchange rate variations, are not explicitly incorporated. Although it is possible to incorporate absolute prices into the three-gap model (Solimano 1993), it is not yet possible to incorporate relative prices. This obvious limitation of the three-gap model should however be weighed against the already-mentioned benefits of the model. At the same time, the use of the three-gap model for understanding economies under adjustment is limited by the assumption that the structure of the economy is not changing. It should be noted though that this shortcoming is not particular to the three-gap model; most open economy macroeconomic models suffer from the same shortcoming.

According to the three-gap model, the utilisation and expansion of existing productive capacity is constrained not only by domestic and foreign savings, as was initially discussed by Chenery and Strout (1966) in the context of the two-gap model, but also by the impact of fiscal limitations on government spending and thus on its public investment choices. In the absence of well-developed financial markets, the available methods of financing public investment are mostly confined to foreign borrowing, budget surpluses and inflation. Foreign resources can play a particularly significant role, especially if cutting current expenditures and inflation-based financing are not possible, either due to political circumstances or to external pressures on the fiscal authorities to curtail inflation.

The model's formulation is presented in Table 4.2. All variables in the model are defined as a percentage of potential output (Q), which was estimated by passing a linear line through output peaks for the period between 1971 and 1996.

Equation 1 defines real output (X) as the sum of gross domestic product (GDP) and real intermediate imports $(M_k)^4$ Capacity utilisation (u) is defined by Equation 2 as a ratio of output (X) over potential output (Q). The rationale for working with X and Q as separate variables is that many developing economies often operate at less than full capacity, mainly as a result of the unavailability of foreign exchange and other structural bottlenecks. The capacity utilisation rate, then, allows an exploration of the way the three gaps interact in the process of economic growth.

Table 4.2 Specification of the three-gap model

Real output	$X = GDP + M_k$	(1)
Capacity utilisation	$u = X/Q$	(2)
Growth rate	$g = g_0 + k\,i$ $\quad\forall\, g_0;\ k>0$	(3)
Equilibrium	$i = s$	(4)
Total investment	$i = i_p + i_g$	(5)
Total saving	$s = s_p + s_g + s_f$	(6)
Private investment	$i_p = i_0 + \alpha\, i_g + \beta\, u$ $\quad\forall\, a;\ b>0$	(7)
Private saving	$s_p = \sigma_0 + \sigma_1 u$ $\quad\forall\, \sigma_0;\ 0<\sigma_1<1$	(8)
Public sector saving	$s_g = z - \zeta\, j^*$ $\quad 0<\zeta<1$	(9)
Fiscal effort	$z = z_0 + z_1 u$ $\quad\forall\, z_0;\ z_1>0$	(10)
Public sector borrowing		
requirements	$\pi u = i_g - s_g$	(11)
Intermediate imports	$m_k = a_0 + a_1 u$ $\quad\forall\, a_0;\ 0<a_1<1$	(12)
Capital goods imports	$m_z = m_0 + m_1 i$ $\quad\forall\, m_0;\ 0<m_1<1$	(13)
Foreign saving	$s_f = m + m_k + m_z + j^* - e = \phi = \Delta\delta + \delta g + r$	(14)

Three-gap equations

Growth-investment equation	$i_g = [1/(1+\alpha)][(\bar{g} - g_0)/k - (i_0 + \beta\, u)]$	(15)
Savings gap	$(1+\alpha)\, i_g - (\sigma_1 + z_1 - \beta)\, u = z_0 - \zeta\, j^* + \sigma_0 + \phi - i_0$	(16)
Foreign exchange gap	$m_1(1+\alpha)\, i_g + [a_1 + m_1\beta]\, u =$	
	$= \phi - m - j^* - m_0 - m_1 i_0 - a_0 + e$	(17)
Fiscal gap	$i_g - (\pi + z_1)\, u = z_0 - \zeta\, j^*$	(18)

Output growth is determined along Harrod-Domar lines, according to which the rate of growth of potential output (g) is specified in Equation 3 as a linear function of the investment rate (i), which is in turn defined as investment as a percentage of potential output. The parameter (k) denotes the incremental output-capital ratio, while (g_0) denotes other factors affecting the rate of growth of output, such as labour productivity growth. Equation 4 states the equilibrium condition, or savings constraint, according to which investment (i) is equal to savings (s). Total investment in Equation 5 is specified as the sum of private investment (i_p) and government investment (i_g), with government investment defined as excluding investment by state-owned enterprises. Equation 6 specifies total savings as consisting of private saving (s_p)[5], public sector saving (s_g) and foreign saving (s_f). Private investment is defined in Equation 7. It is assumed that private investment varies with changes in demand conditions, as measured by (u), and with government investment. Private sector investment can vary positively with government investment, a 'crowding-in' effect, or negatively with government investment, a so-called 'crowding out' effect, depending on whether these two types of investment are complements or substitutes. Private savings are defined in Equation 8 and are specified in a standard way, according to which savings are assumed to vary positively with the capacity utilisation variable (u).

Public sector savings, investment and borrowing requirements are explained by Equations 9 to 11. Public sector savings are defined in Equation 9 as the difference between the fiscal effort variable (z) and interest payments on the government's foreign debt ($\zeta j^\cdot$), where ($j^\cdot$) denotes interest payments on foreign debt and (ζ) the government's share. In Equation 10 the variable (z) defines the fiscal effort rate, also known as the public sector operating surplus, as the difference between current revenue net of transfers and subsidies plus the operating surpluses of public enterprises less government consumption expenditures and interest payments on the public sector's domestic debt. According to Equation 10, the public sector operating surplus is assumed to be primarily determined by the capacity utilisation rate (u), in that taxes, surpluses from public enterprises, and other receipts rise more rapidly than current spending when economic activity goes up. The strength of this response is measured by the parameter (z_1), the marginal fiscal effort rate. In addition to the rate of capacity utilisation, the fiscal effort rate is influenced by other factors such as size of the tax base and the effectiveness of tax collection system. The strength of these other factors is captured by the parameter (z_o). Equation 11 defines the public sector borrowing requirement (πu), or the public sector saving constraint, as the difference between government investment (i_g) and public sector saving (s_g). Note that in Equation 11 the public sector borrowing requirement (π) is measured as a proportion of output (X), while (πu) denotes the public sector borrowing requirement as a percentage of potential output (Q).

The external sector is summarised by Equations 12 to 14. The import demand for intermediate goods (m_k) is specified as a function of the capacity utilisation rate (u) in Equation 12, while import demand for capital goods (m_z) is specified as a function of domestic investment (i) in Equation 13. Equation 14 defines foreign savings, or the balance of payments constraint. The first part of Equation 14 defines the current account deficit as competitive imports (m) plus intermediate imports (m_k) plus capital goods imports (m_z) plus interest payments on foreign debt (j') less exports (e). The capital account is presented in the second part of Equation 14, where ($\Delta\delta$) denotes changes in the ratio of foreign debt over potential output, (δg) changes in official reserves, (r) the ratio of other capital inflows—such as foreign direct investment—over potential output, and (ϕ) total capital inflows as a percentage of potential output. Exports and capital inflows are treated as exogenous variables.

The growth-investment equation, the savings gap equation, the foreign exchange gap equation, and the public sector savings gap equation are obtained from Equations 1 to 14 and are presented as Equations 15 through 18.[6] In Equation 15, government investment (i_g) and the capacity utilisation rate (u) are treated as variables which can be traded off to give macroeconomic equilibrium, meaning that the growth rate of capacity output (g) can be treated as a target policy variable. While the focus of Equation 15 is on government investment and capacity utilisation and not on growth, which, as documented earlier, has been weak, treating the growth rate of capacity output as a target policy variable is clearly attractive given poor economic performance. Equation 15 thus relates government investment (i_g) to the capacity utilisation rate (u) and targeted potential output growth ($\bar{g}$). The savings gap Equation 16 gives the maximum government investment attainable from a given rate of capacity utilisation (u) that satisfies the equilibrium condition defined in Equation 4. Higher government investment increases private investment and capacity utilisation and thereby generates sufficient savings to finance the higher investment. According to the foreign savings gap Equation 17, there is a trade off between government investment (i_g) and the capacity utilisation rate (u). Higher capacity utilisation generates a higher demand for intermediate imports that can only be met, given available foreign exchange, by cutting into capital goods imports and hence by lowering the growth rate of capacity. Lastly, the fiscal gap

Equation 18 shows government investment (i_g) and the capacity utilisation rate (u) to move together as higher capacity utilisation generates more net fiscal revenue that can be channeled into capital formation.

Econometric results

The model specified in Table 4.2 was estimated using annual data for the period between 1971 and 1996 and using an ordinary least-squares technique.[7] Since capacity utilisation (u) is estimated separately, simultaneity does not pose any problem. The results of the estimated behavioural equations are presented in Table 4.3. However, the parameter estimates presented in Table 4.3, as well as the simulation results presented in Table 4.4, should be treated as highly tentative. The model specified in Table 4.2 is, as already noted, a highly aggregated one-sector growth model in which price variations are not explicitly incorporated. Projected growth rates are in particular very sensitive to changes in world sugar prices and the performance of Fiji's non-sugar exports. Finally, and obviously, the quality of the data can always be better.

Structural equations, three-gap results and policy implications

Considering first the private investment equation presented in Table 4.3, the estimates generated by Equation 7 suggest that both the capacity utilisation rate and government investment are statistically significant determinants of private investment, explaining altogether about 95 per cent of the variation in the private investment rate. However, the estimated coefficient of government investment suggests that higher government investment tends to crowd out private investment. It should be noted that such crowding out need not be detrimental to the economy. The impact of crowding out on the economy would depend upon the extent of crowding out, and the relative productivity of government and private investment. The results indicate that the crowding-out effect is incomplete, while the results do not convey any information about relative productivity.

The capacity utilisation variable also appears to be a statistically significant determinant of private saving, fiscal effort and intermediate imports. Thus, the greater the degree of productive activity in the economy, the greater the rate of private savings which

can be used to finance investment, the greater the rate of government
revenue collection, and the greater the rate of imports which are used
as inputs in productive activity. It can be noted that the marginal fiscal
effort rate is considerably smaller than that reported for other middle-
income countries (Taylor 1993: Table 2.3). It can also be noted that the
estimates for intermediate imports indicate a high degree of
dependence on imports. Finally, the estimates for imports of capital

Table 4.3 Econometric results of the structural equations and the three-gap equations[a,b]

Private investment[c]	$i_p = 0.031 + 0.062\,u - 0.547\,i_g$	
	(1.31) (4.46) (-2.32)	$R^2 = 0.95$
Private saving	$s_p = 0.011 + 0.17\,u$	
	(0.71) (11.08)	$R^2 = 0.92$
Fiscal effort	$z = -0.084 + 0.117\,u$	
	(-2.33) (2.88)	$R^2 = 0.42$
Import demand		
intermediate goods	$m_k = -0.116 + 0.316\,u$	
	(-2.43) (5.87)	$R^2 = 0.72$
capital goods[d]	$m_z = 0.101 + 0.39\,i$	
	(0.44) (2.29)	$R^2 = 0.80$
Three-gap equations		
Savings gap	$i_g = -0.381 + 0.495\,u$	
Fiscal gap	$i_g = -0.127 + 0.183\,u$	
Foreign exchange gap	$i_g = 1.59 - 1.924\,u$	

Notes:
[a] t-statistics are given in parentheses under the coefficients, and the coefficients of determination (R^2) are adjusted R^2. All equations were tested and corrected for autocorrelation.
[b] All equations were estimated using a dummy variable representing the coup of 1987 and the period under the Interim Government, 1987 to 1992. The dummy variable was not statistically significant in any estimated equations, and hence is not reported here.
[c] The private investment equation was estimated using annual data for the period 1977 to 1996. Due to the high degree of correlation between private investment and potential output, the private investment equation was estimated using the level of private investment and actual output rather than their normalised ratios. Both current and lagged values of public sector investment were included in estimating the private investment equations. The lagged values were however not statistically significant, and are therefore not reported here.
[d] Due to the high degree of correlation between capital goods and imports and potential output, the equation for capital goods imports was estimated using the level of imports and investment rather than their normalised ratios.

goods demonstrate that the marginal propensity to import with respect to fixed capital formation is statistically significant. It is also relatively large, indicating Fiji's high degree of dependence on imported capital goods. Thus, the greater the rate of investment, the greater the extent of capital goods imports.

Using the estimated values of the parameters and the values of the exogenous variables, the model was calibrated for 1996. The resulting three-gap equations are shown in Table 4.3 and visually displayed in Figure 4.1. Figure 4.1 demonstrates a sharp trade-off between government investment—which is to say, publicly funded capacity creation—and capacity utilisation under the foreign exchange constraint. The savings constraint line is steeper than the fiscal constraint line. This indicates that the government budgetary constraints are more binding than the savings constraint as more foreign capital becomes available. In such circumstances, an attempt to raise government investment in order to stimulate economic growth will put the government in fiscal difficulties, even though savings are in principle available to finance additional investment.

The fiscal limitations on the government, as well as the crowding-out effect of government investment, should be interpreted with great care. This is because of the highly aggregated nature of the model. Nonetheless, two possible explanations for these results can be suggested. The first is more 'economistic', in that it seeks to explain why government investment crowds out private investment. The crowding-out effect of government investment might be explained, amongst other factors, by the government's low savings rate, its massive budgetary appropriations to public enterprises,[7] and the preferential access to commercial credit that has been granted to public enterprises. At the same time, the government's increasing use of tax holidays to attract both domestic and foreign investment into the export sector, and most notably the garment, tourism and minerals sectors, when considered in light of a relatively small marginal fiscal effort rate, may have in fact exacerbated fiscal weakness. As a consequence, government deficits have had to be primarily financed by domestic borrowing. However, the financing of chronic government deficits by domestic borrowing has reduced private non-financial investment, through a process of crowding out. There is therefore a need to recognise the impact of government spending on capacity utilisation, both in its impact on investment, through the

Figure 4.1   Foreign exchange, saving and fiscal gaps

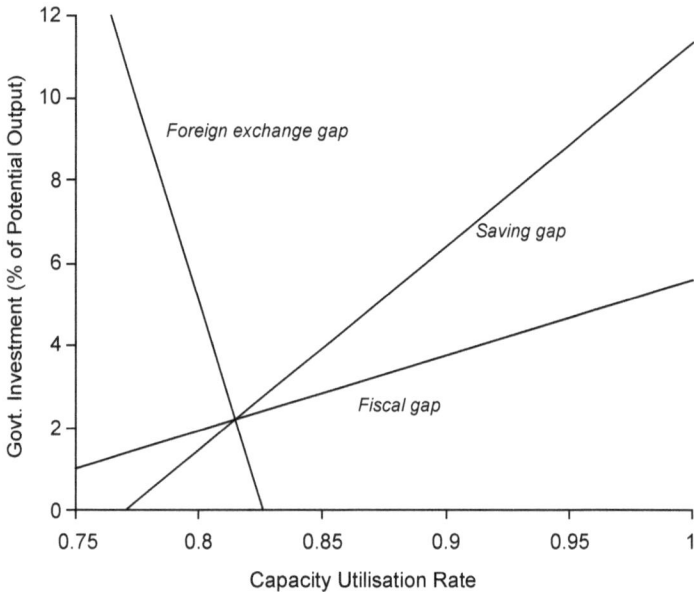

crowding-out effect, and in its generation of savings, through the inefficiency of public enterprises. In light of these possible mechanisms, it could be suggested that it is necessary to increase private domestic and foreign investment in order to enhance capacity creation and its utilisation. This in turn suggests two policies. The first deals with the monopolisation of domestic savings by the public sector, and the answer is both clear and orthodox: much deeper deregulation of the financial sector, primarily through privatisation. The second is consistent with existing government policy: the need to further mobilise external resources through the promotion of greater inflows of foreign direct investment.

However, this economistic response is not satisfactory. This is because it diagnoses symptoms without giving an understanding of underlying causes. In order to understand underlying causes, it is necessary to try and explain why there may be fiscal limitations on the government and why government intervention in capacity creation and utilisation may be detrimental to Fiji's economy. In order to address this broader issue, it is important to recognise that the state in Fiji through the late 1980s and 1990s has sought to establish a delicate balance between promoting private sector growth and safeguarding the interests of its principal constituency, the indigenous Fijian community (Elek, Hill and Tabor 1993). As Sutherland points out in his contribution to this volume, the pursuit of this balance has been highly contradictory. Contradictions in the pursuit of this balance may in turn have had economic consequences. Recent work on Africa has established 'strong and specific mechanisms whereby ethnically fractionalised societies were liable to have worse economic performance than more homogenous societies' (Collier 1998:12).[8] This is because ethnic fragmentation may be 'bad for...macroeconomic policy, (local) government performance, public sector wage determination, and the determinants of trust' (Collier 1998:3). Granted, the negative economic implications of ethnic diversity can be overcome. Collier (1998:12) stresses that 'political institutions matter more where a society has a potential problem of ethnic fractionalisation than in homogenous societies. Democracy has the capacity almost completely to offset the economic damage which can be done by a high level of fractionalisation'. Nonetheless, ethnic diversity—and particularly, according to Collier, moderate ethnic diversity of the type experienced in Fiji—may reduce the efficiency of government in circumstances where there is a lack of political rights.

There is good reason to suspect that these kinds of mechanisms may have contributed to Fiji's economic performance during the late 1980s and 1990s. On the one hand, the state sought to maintain its political base amongst the indigenous Fijian population by reducing the political rights of the Indo-Fijian community (Sutherland, this volume; Robertson, this volume). On the other hand, the state pursued explicit and implicit policies designed to promote economic affirmative action on behalf of the indigenous Fijian community (Ratuva, this volume). These policies have expanded the scope of ethnically based patronage within the state and society, and may have given rise to rent seeking on the part of individuals. The collapse of the National Bank of Fiji illustrates the capacity for rent seeking in post-coup Fiji. Ethnic preferences in post-coup Fiji may also have contributed to other inefficiencies in the public sector. Certainly, ongoing losses in many public enterprises have been acceptable to the state, in part because of the 'ethnicisation' of economic policy. It is thus a reasonable hypothesis that the 'ethnicisation' of economic policy in Fiji has played a pivotal role in reducing the effectiveness of the state and has contributed to the creation of circumstances in which state intervention may be detrimental to the economy.

Simulation results

The estimated model can be used to simulate the effects of alternative policies by altering the values of individual variables such as the targeted growth rate of output, investment, exports and imports and then assessing the effect of such a change on the other variables contained in the model. In what follows, the model was simulated for the period between 1997 and 2001. These simulations were undertaken under four growth path 'scenarios'. While the first two simulations assume that Fiji's preferential access to the EU for its sugar exports will terminate by 2001, scenarios I and II differ in terms of their underlying export growth rates. Scenario I follows a rather optimistic growth path, according to which the gradual elimination of Fiji's preferential access to the EU for its sugar is matched by a corresponding and offsetting export diversification effort, as a result of which the country's export earnings remain unchanged. This rather optimistic export growth rate is adjusted under simulation II to reflect the most recent data on Fiji's non-sugar export performance and the recent slow down in the economic growth of Fiji's main trading partners.

Scenarios III and IV explore two quite different and distinctive growth paths: a growth rate that is most likely to occur; and a growth rate that meets 'socially desirable' ends. The most likely growth path scenario assumes that Fiji's preferential access to the EU remains in place until the end of 2001 and that Fiji's non-sugar export growth rate falls considerably short of those rates achieved during the early 1990s. Thus, Fiji's successful achievement in diversifying its exports during the early 1990s is assumed to come to an end. This occurs because of the low projected growth rates of Fiji's East Asian trading partners, as well as because of the domestic difficulties facing the country in its transition from the first, comparatively easy, phase of export-led growth to the next, more difficult, phase, under which the basis of such growth must be deepened in order for it to be sustained. Particular domestic issues include that of land leases (Prasad and

Kumar, this volume), as well as the future evolution of inter-
community relations in light of the new Constitution and the 1999
general elections. By way of contrast, according to the 'socially
desirable' growth path scenario, potential output and per capita
output are assumed to grow at an average annual rate of 5.2 per cent
and 4 per cent respectively. These rates of growth are almost identical
to those rates achieved by Fiji during the 1970s. Unlike the first three
scenarios, external resources are assumed to be both available and
adequate under growth scenario IV, so that foreign exchange gaps, if
any, can be filled. The results of these simulations are summarised in
Table 4.4.

Scenario I: Successful export diversification

Considering first growth path scenario I, it is necessary to begin by
noting that over the 10 year period between 1985 and 1994 Fiji
received a price for its sugar exports to the EU which was, on average,
65 per cent greater than the world market price. This preferential
market access provided Fiji with an implicit subsidy amounting to
about 3.5 per cent of Fiji's GDP per year over the period between 1985
and 1994. The effect of a gradual elimination of this preferential
market access between 1997 and 2001 on economic growth,
investment, government revenues and borrowing requirements, and
imports and external debt depends on the performance of non-sugar
exports. For Fiji to continue to grow at the same rate as the rate of
growth of output experienced in the 1996 base year—3.1 per cent—
and with no change in savings and investment ratios and government
borrowing requirements, it is projected under scenario I that non-
sugar exports will have to grow at an annual average rate of 3.9 per
cent between 1997 and 2001. This is noted in Table 4.4. Higher non-
sugar export earnings and moderate import growth are then projected
to produce a small current account surplus, equivalent to 2.5 per cent
of total export earnings, and a reduction in external debt from 5.3 per
cent of exports in 1996 to an average annual rate of 2.9 per cent
between 1997 and 2001. However, this rate of growth of non-sugar
exports appears to be unattainable, especially in light of the recent
slowdown in economic growth in the East Asia and Pacific region, as
well as the exhaustion of the first and easy stage of Fiji's export
diversification drive.

Table 4.4 Projected growth path scenarios, 1997–2001

	Base year 1996	Growth path scenarios		Most likely	Socially desirable
		End of Sugar Protocol			
		successful export diversification	limited export diversification		
		I	II	III	IV
Real growth rate					
(% per annum)					
Actual GDP	3.1	3.1	-0.3	1.3	5.2
Per capita GDP	1.9	1.9	-1.5	.1	4.0
Potential GDP	1.3	3.1	0.9	0.9	2.0
Imports	7.7	1.9	-0.5	1.3	4.2
Exports	15.5	3.9[a]	1.3[a]	1.1	1.1
As % of potential GDP					
(period average)					
Actual output					
(capacity utilisation rate)	81.5	81.5	78.6	82.6	89.5
Fixed investment	8.0	8.0	7.8	8.5	10.8
Govt. borrowing requirements	5.4	5.4	5.4	5.0	4.7
As % of exports					
(period average)					
Imports	97.7	97.7	98.1	100.6	107.3
External debt	17.0	10.3	17.0	17.0	24.5
Debt services	5.3	2.9	5.3	5.3	11.3

Note: [a] Non-sugar exports only.

Scenario II: Limited export diversification

In growth path scenario II, export growth rates are adjusted downward to reflect the most recent export performance of Fiji as well as the developments in East Asia. Using the latest Organisation for Economic Cooperation and Development (OECD) forecasts for Fiji's main export markets and Fiji's most recent export performance, non-sugar exports are assumed to grow at an average annual rate of only 1.3 per cent between 1997 and 2001. It is also assumed that only moderate inflows of foreign direct investment are available, there is limited access to foreign financing and there is no change in Fiji's external debt to potential output ratio between 1997 and 2001. Under these assumptions, imports and output growth will have to be compressed in order to make do with reduced export earnings and limited capital inflows. This compression, as reflected in the decline in output growth and the capacity utilisation rate is, as shown in Table 4.4, considerable. Reduced imports, including imports of capital and intermediate goods, make the foreign exchange constraint more binding as the gradual elimination of implicit subsidies under the Sugar Protocol pushes the foreign exchange constraint line in Figure 4.1 towards the origin. Lower export earnings also reduce the maximum achievable rate of investment. As a consequence, actual output and per capita income are projected to shrink at an average annual rate of 0.3 and 1.5 per cent respectively between 1997 and 2001. The decline in actual output combined with a slow rate of growth of potential output lowers the average rate of capacity utilisation to 78.6 per cent, and fixed investment to 7.8 per cent of potential output, over the period between 1997 and 2001. Although lower capacity utilisation reduces government tax revenues, an increase in the fiscal effort, such as the broadening of the tax base, leaves government borrowing requirements almost unchanged—the fiscal effort parameter rises from 0.117 in the base year of 1996 to 0.125 by 2001.

Scenario III: The most likely growth path

Unlike the previous two growth path scenarios, scenario III, the most likely growth path, assumes Fiji's preferential market access will remain in place at least until the end of 2001. Making similar assumptions about the growth rates of non-sugar exports and capital inflows as those made under scenario II, the maximum achievable output and investment growth rates are reported in Table 4.4. Low rates of growth of export earnings, combined with limited capital inflows, are projected to reduce the growth rate of actual output from 3.1 per cent in 1996 to an average of 1.3 per cent per annum over the period between 1997 and 2001. With a population growth rate of about 1.2 per cent per annum, per capita income remains stagnant over the period. Fixed capital formation rises slightly, from 8 per cent of potential output in 1996 to 8.5 per cent of potential output over the period between 1997 and 2001. The small increase in fixed capital formation reflects an increase in the capacity utilisation rate from 81.5 per cent in 1996 to 82.6 per cent over the period between 1997 and 2001. This slight increase in investment is primarily brought about by an increase in government investment, which rises from 2.2 per cent of potential output in 1996 to 2.6 per cent of potential output over the period between 1997 and 2001. However, despite this slight increase in government investment, government borrowing requirements decline from 5.4 per cent of potential output in 1996 to 5 per cent of potential output over the period between 1997 and 2001 as additional public revenue efforts, such as a broadening of the tax base and improvements in tax collection, are achieved. Imports of capital and intermediate goods rise as a result of the increase in both capacity utilisation and fixed capital formation. These higher imports are financed partly by growing export earnings and partly by moderate capital inflows. As it has been assumed that there is limited access to foreign financing and moderate inflows of direct foreign investment, external debt and debt service as a percentage of exports remain unchanged over the period between 1997 and 2001.

Scenario IV: The socially desirable growth path

Given Fiji's low rates of economic growth during the past decade, projected economic growth under scenario III, the most likely growth path, will fall short of meeting the population's expectations and aspirations, as well the growth rates achieved by Fiji during the 1970s. Scenario IV examines the implications of a socially desirable growth path, in which actual output is assumed to grow at an average annual rate of 5.2 per cent, a rate that was achieved by Fiji in the 1970s. Potential output is also assumed to grow at annual average rate of 2 per cent. These assumptions imply a steady increase in the capacity utilisation rate over the period between 1997 and 2001, so that by 2001 capacity utilisation reaches almost 98 per cent. Higher capacity utilisation, combined with improvements in the socio-political environment, including a satisfactory resolution of land lease issues, reverse the steady decline in the investment rate experienced by Fiji during the past decade. Fixed capital formation rises from 8 per cent of potential output in 1996 to an average rate of 10.8 per cent of potential output per annum in the period between 1997 and 2001, while private investment similarly rises from 3.5 per cent of potential output in 1996 to 4.3 per cent of potential output over the period between 1997 and 2001. It should be noted that these investment rates fall considerably short of the investment rates achieved by Fiji in the 1970s, and are hence achievable. So too is the projected increase in government investment. Following years of low government investment and the gradual deterioration of physical infrastructure, government investment rises slightly from 2.2 per cent of potential output in 1996 to an average annual rate of 2.8 per cent over the period between 1997 and 2001. Higher government investment is partly financed by higher capacity utilisation and partly by additional public revenues—the fiscal effort parameter rises from 0.118 in 1996 to 0.125 in the period between 1997 and 2001 as the tax base is broadened and the collection of taxes is improved. As noted in Table 4.4, these higher tax revenues slightly reduce government borrowing requirements. Higher rates of capacity utilisation and investment also increase imports of capital and intermediate goods. To fill the foreign exchange gap, export earnings are supplemented by a moderate increase in foreign direct investment as well as by an increase in foreign debt. External debt is projected to grow from US$217 million in 1996 to US$431 million by the end of 2001; debt servicing also grows. However, relative to potential output, this foreign borrowing is not large, amounting to an average of 17.5 per cent of potential output over the period between 1997 and 2001. It is thus sustainable.

The policy implications of the simulation results

The size of the foreign financing gap under all four scenarios illustrates quite vividly the centrality of the foreign exchange constraint in general, and preferential access to the EU sugar market in particular, on the medium-term growth rate. It thus helps to explain why the Fiji government has been trying to promote and diversify exports. In the absence of compensatory financing a gradual elimination of Fiji's preferential market access will considerably reduce output growth and the capacity utilisation rate. This would have potentially destabilising consequences. For a country which has had a decade of slow growth and deepening economic insecurity, resulting, amongst other things, from the implementation of an orthodox structural adjustment program, low growth in output, investment and capacity utilisation are not without their own significant socioeconomic costs, both in the short and the long term. Moreover, given the short-term pain associated with the implementation of an orthodox structural adjustment program, these low rates of output and investment growth make it even harder to sustain the adjustment program. Finally, despite the implementation of a new constitution (Ghai, this volume), the 'ethnicisation' of economic policy may continue to have an effect on the growth rate. This rather bleak outcome applies not only to an extreme scenario, such as scenario II, under which Fiji's preferential market access for its sugar exports is assumed to end. It also applies, to some extent, to scenario III, under which Fiji's preferential market access is assumed to be maintained until 2001.

Clearly, if a socially desirable growth rate is to be achieved in the short and medium term, there is a need to overcome the two most binding constraints facing the Fiji economy, namely the foreign exchange constraint and the fiscal constraint. The former requires an increase in foreign capital inflows and the latter an improvement in government savings. Since increases in concessional aid for a middle-income economy such as Fiji are unlikely, the government is left with borrowing on international markets and attracting foreign direct investment in order to meet the foreign exchange requirements of a socially desirable growth path. Borrowing on the international market has its own costs, as the recent experience of East Asia clearly indicates. By way of contrast, Fiji has undoubtedly been relatively successful in attracting foreign direct investment during the adjustment period. However, the record of the adjustment period is that the government sought to attract foreign direct investment in order to 'remake' Fiji into a low-income economy. Thus, its export drive has been predicated upon attracting capital into low value-added activities such as the low-wage, semi-skilled garment industry. This is clearly the wrong kind of export diversification, in that it is not based upon Fiji's comparative advantage. Fiji's comparative advantage surely does not lie in low value-added activities. Rather, Fiji's advantage is its workforce: well educated and comparatively well skilled. At the same time though the country is spatially isolated. The impact of spatial isolation can however be offset if Fiji uses the comparative advantage of its workforce to attract foreign direct investment into skill-intensive, higher value-added activities which are not affected by transport costs. International knowledge-based and information technology-utilising services offer one possibility which could utilise Fiji's comparatively skilled labour force and which would not necessarily be affected by Fiji's spatial isolation. Data processing is but one example of such services. Even in these circumstances though, greater care should be paid when seeking to attract international capital into Fiji. The state should seek to encourage joint ventures with local capital, along the lines encouraged in China, Vietnam and India, so that that technology and know-how which is transferred into the economy is predicated upon deepening the human capital available to the Fiji economy and as such building competitive advantage.

However, achieving the socially desirable path requires not only an increase in foreign capital inflows but also an improvement in government savings. This can be achieved in part by: redirecting investment, including foreign direct investment, into higher value-added industries; by raising the fiscal effort rate and the public sector operating surplus; and by improving the efficiency of government revenue generation. Improved efficiency amongst public enterprises requires, amongst other things, greater market-based autonomy, greater managerial accountability, and a stronger link between performance and remuneration. Improvements in the productivity and operating surpluses of public enterprises would contribute to improved efficiency in government revenue generation. So too would the granting of tax concessions more wisely, the broadening of the tax base and improvements the tax collection system. Improvements in the efficiency of tax concessions requires, among other things, a shift away from the current policy of granting tax concessions across the board and towards granting them on a case-by-case basis, with the evaluation of each case based upon the extent to which the concession helps fulfil strategic priorities specified by the state.

One final point can be made. It has been hypothesised in this chapter that the 'ethnicisation' of economic policy in Fiji may have played a role in reducing the effectiveness of state intervention. Clearly, more research needs to be done on this issue. Nonetheless, if the use of ethnicity in the allocation of resources has reduced the efficiency of resource allocation by the state, there is a clear need to end the 'ethnicisation' of economic policy in Fiji.

Conclusions

The purpose of this chapter has been to review Fiji's macroeconomic performance and assess the relative significance of foreign exchange, domestic savings, and public sector resources on Fiji's economic growth. Using annual data for the period between 1971 and 1996 a three-gap model has been formulated and estimated. The estimated foreign exchange gap equation indicates a sharp trade-off between investment, or capacity creation, and capacity utilisation. The government savings constraint also appears to be more binding than the savings constraint as more external resources become available. In such circumstances, attempts to raise government investment in order to stimulate economic growth will put the state into fiscal difficulties even though savings are in principle available to finance additional investment.

To assess the significance for Fiji of the foreign exchange constraint in general, and Fiji's preferential access to the EU sugar market in particular, the model has been simulated for the period between 1997 and 2001 under four growth path scenarios. The first two growth path scenarios assume that Fiji's preferential market access to the EU is eliminated over the period between 1997 and 2001 but differ in their assumptions concerning the success of export diversification. The third and fourth growth path scenarios assume that Fiji's preferential market access remains in place until 2001 but differ in their assumptions concerning growth in actual output, exports and capital inflows.

The results from the first two scenarios suggest that in the absence of high growth rates of non-sugar exports, and with an absence of compensatory financing, the decline in output growth and capacity utilisation rates may be so considerable as to be potentially destabilising: the maximum achievable growth rate of per capita income was found to be -1.5 per cent per year for the period between 1997 and 2001. Even if Fiji's preferential market access were to remain in place until the end of 2001 the results of the most likely growth path scenario suggest stagnant per capita income over the period between 1997 and 2001. Given the short-term pains associated with the implementation of an orthodox structural adjustment program and the slow growth in per capita income over the past decade, these low rates of output and investment growth would make it even harder to sustain policy credibility.

However, the results suggest that the external financing required to achieve a socially desirable growth path is modest, amounting to an average of 17.5 per cent of potential output over the period between 1997 and 2001. In addition to a moderate increase in direct foreign investment, foreign debt is projected to grow from US$217 million in 1996 to US$431 by the end of 2001. The size of the foreign financing gap under the socially desirable growth path illustrates quite vividly the centrality of the foreign exchange constraint in general, and preferential market access in particular, on Fiji's ability to achieve a modest rate of growth in the medium term. Clearly, the challenge for Fiji's policymakers is to intensify export diversification efforts and to improve the government savings rate. The former requires, among other things, a set of coherent and consistent export promotion efforts directed at utilising Fiji's comparatively well-educated and skilled workforce and attracting foreign direct investment into joint ventures in international services. Such a strategy, focused as it is on higher value-added activities, might serve to increase the rate of capacity utilisation in the economy and increase the rate of growth of the economy. Export diversification efforts should, however, be accompanied by an improvement in government savings if a modest rate of growth is to be achieved in the short and medium term. Finally, it has been suggested in this chapter that in order to improve the efficiency of state intervention in the economy, and thus government savings, there may be a need to reduce the 'ethnicisation' of economic policy. Clearly, achieving a socially desirable growth path in Fiji in the medium term is a major challenge for the new government.

Endnotes

1. Neither the year of the coups, 1987, nor the immediate catch-up year of 1988 have been used in calculating the period averages in this chapter, in an effort to garner a better understanding of the relative economic performance of the Fiji economy under adjustment. It can be noted that making some alterations to the years included in the period averages does not shift the direction of change but rather only affects the magnitude of change, and only then to a small degree.
2. The following three subsections draw heavily on Akram-Lodhi (1996).
3. Less mathematically inclined readers may want to skip this section.
4. Output is here defined in somewhat non-standard fashion, reflecting the importance of intermediate imports in production for a developing country such as Fiji.

5. Private savings (s_p) were estimated as a residual from the Keynesian national income identity, which can be written in normalised form as:

$$s_p = i_p + i_g - s_g + e - m - m_k - m_z - j^*$$

where other terms are as they are defined in the text.

6. The growth-investment Equation 15 is obtained by substituting the total investment Equation 5 into the growth Equation 3 using the private investment Equation 7. The savings gap Equation 16 is obtained by substituting Equations 7 to 10 and 14 into Equation 3. Substituting Equations 12 and 13 into the foreign savings Equation 14 yields the foreign savings gap Equation 17. Finally, the fiscal gap Equation 18 is obtained by substituting Equations 9 and 10 into Equation 11, the public sector borrowing requirement.

7. Budgetary appropriations to public enterprises amounted to about 55 per cent of total public sector capital expenditure over the period 1985–90 (Elek, Hill and Tabor 1993: Table 2).

8. Our thanks to David Styan for directing us to Collier's work on ethnicity and economic performance.

CHAPTER 5

Institutional rigidities and economic performance in Fiji

Biman Prasad and Sunil Kumar

Introduction

It has been argued that the increased commitment towards structural adjustment policies in Fiji following the two military coups of 1987 were an important step in placing Fiji in a position to cope with the deepening globalisation of the world economy. However, the performance of the Fiji economy over the last decade has been poor (Sepehri and Akram-Lodhi, this volume). Some would argue that this poor economic performance is because Fiji has not gone far enough in pursuing its structural adjustment policies, in large part because of political uncertainty. Now, a new constitution is in place (Ghai, this volume). Many political and business leaders believe that the new constitution will resolve uncertainty and in so doing provide a climate conducive to investment and growth, especially if the pace of structural adjustment in Fiji picks up.

However, it has been pointed out by Dunning (1997) that there are no universal prescriptions available to a country responding to the forces of globalisation. Each country has different institutional and economic structures, which will affect how it responds to global economic forces. As one of those institutions, the role of the state is vital in determining the economic performance of countries, both in its own direct interventions and in facilitating the development of the complementary economic, political, social and cultural institutions which can supplement performance. Fiji is no exception in this respect, and this helps explain why the performance of the state in Fiji has been in the spotlight.

In this chapter it is argued that the state in Fiji has paid insufficient attention to the institutions which provide the framework within which economic growth takes place. As such, the state has not addressed institutional rigidities that constrain growth. The chapter makes this argument by focusing on one particular institutional constraint to growth: property rights in land in Fiji. In the next section, the relationship between institutions and economic performance is discussed. The character of property rights in land in Fiji is critically examined and ways of transcending institutional rigidities in the assignation of property rights in land are evaluated. The final section provides some tentative conclusions.

Institutions and economic performance

The 'new institutional economics'

Institutions in a society determine the way in which social, cultural, political and economic relations are conducted. They thus constitute the framework by which relations are structured. In structuring relations, institutions shape the various rules and procedures applied in a given set of circumstances. For example, when conducting economic activities, institutions can affect incentives and thus outcomes. Therefore, institutions and what they do are, as Adams (1993) notes, important when seeking to understand and affect the changes taking place in an economy or in a society. As a consequence, institutions and what they do need to be a central part of the policy process. This is increasingly being acknowledged by policy makers, who are coming to accept that within the economy growth is affected by the institutional framework and social practices which structure the process of development (Maki 1993; Hodgson 1989).

Development economics pioneers such as Hirschman (1958), Leibenstein (1957), Myint (1965), Fei and Ranis (1964), Myrdal (1957) and Nurkse (1953) all gave attention to institutions when explaining economic development. However, as Adams (1993) points out, what is now called the 'new institutional economics' is different from both mainstream and development economics. It clearly differs from the former, with its challenge to the neoclassical theory of individualistic optimisation in competitive markets, a theory that does not accept the pervasive nature of institutional constraints. As for the latter, Adams writes that

> despite much agreement and interaction, an important division remained between institutional economists and development economists: the former stressed the importance of institutions and the dysfunctions of the market capitalist system in all settings, while the latter generally held to the tenet that institutions mattered and markets are meaningfully flaw-ridden only in relatively underdeveloped areas (1993:250).

A focal figure in the emergence of the new institutional economics is that of Nobel Laureate Douglass North. As Libecap notes,

> Douglass North has been one of the foremost economists in asserting that much more attention must be directed to the institutional structure of a society in general, and to its property rights arrangements in particular, for explaining variations in economic performance across societies and across time (1992:227).

North's contribution can be traced from as early as 1955, when he first sought to explain economic growth by reference to the specific institutional structures present in a developed capitalist state (North 1955:243). Subsequently, North sought to explain the role of institutions in the overall performance of economies by differentiating between efficient and inefficient institutions and then attempting to demonstrate how these affected variables such as rate of growth of gross domestic product or the investment rate (North and Thomas 1973:127).

Within the new institutional economics that North has helped to foster, issues such as property rights, the role of the state, the character of the bureaucratic structure and the control of technology have all occupied analytical prominence. At the same time however the new institutional economics has not been unaware of the role of social power in affecting the performance of an economy. Institutions reflect social power. Thus, the basis by which power is created, accessed and used has been seen by new institutional economists as being an important factor in determining the kind of institutional structures that emerge in a society and which thus have an impact upon the economy.

Property rights as an economic institution

As North (1990:11) has written, neoclassical theory is based on the fundamental assumption of scarcity and hence competition. Its harmonious implications come from its assumptions about a frictionless exchange process in which property rights are perfectly and costlessly specified and information is likewise costless to acquire. Standard neoclassical theory thus assumes that a set of private property rights already exists and that such a set of rights governs the control and use of all resources. Moreover, neoclassical theory assumes that individuals engage in economic activities when the cost of information concerning the exchange, enforcement and policing costs of contractual activities are zero. It is under this set of assumptions that individuals become free to pursue the utility-maximising activities that ensure an efficient allocation of resources.

However, this set of assumptions is exceedingly stringent. For example, in the process of exchange there is usually an unequal distribution and accumulation of information, which may lead to asymmetrical information (Riker and Weimer 1994). Under conditions of asymmetrical information, exchange generates an inefficient outcome. Similarly, Tietenberg (1992) and Randall (1987) both argue that the application of neoclassical theory demands that property rights are universal, exclusive, transferable and enforceable. This too is quite stringent: costs may be involved in the maintenance of the private property rights structure, and such costs may generate an inefficient outcome. Clearly, the neoclassical framework, and particularly its assumptions concerning the structure and maintenance of property rights, may not be witnessed in the real world.

Cost considerations underlie the inclusion of property rights into economic analysis. Coase (1960) was instrumental in facilitating such an inclusion, arguing that market distortions and hence costs arising from externalities could be eliminated by a clear definition of property rights. A clear definition of property rights would result in resources being allocated to those agents that placed the highest value upon such resources, and this would facilitate economic efficiency. However, interventions in the economics of property rights such as those of Cheung (1970), Demsetz (1967), Alchian (1974), Wallis and North (1986), Barzel (1989) and Pejovich (1990) have all noted that any system of property rights entails an ancillary set of costs pertaining to enforcement. These costs need to be integrated into any economic analysis. Clearly, private property is only secure and its owner can only reap the benefits of ownership if others are prevented from the unauthorised use, appropriation or expropriation of the private property. In the words of Adam Smith (1937:862), 'commerce and manufacture can seldom flourish long in any state which does not enjoy a regular administrative justice in which people do not feel themselves secure in possession of their property, and in which faith of contracts is not supported by the law'.

Governance and property rights

Thus, for property rights to be secure, contracts must be enforced. As a consequence, there emerges a pivotal role for the state: maintaining and enforcing the property rights of individuals. Moreover, as Binswanger and Rosenzweig (1984:139) point out, 'as contracts and property rights enforceability becomes institutionalised, free trade and capitalist development is promoted'. This is because where property rights are undefined, insecure or are not enforced by the state, people have less incentive to invest or undertake innovative, entrepreneurial initiatives (Scully 1988; Scully and Slottje 1991; Torstensson 1994). However, in many developing countries there is a lack of security of property rights. There thus emerges a link between property rights and economic performance: the inability of governments to ensure the enforceability of property rights weakens investment, weakens entrepreneurial activity, and acts as an impediment to economic efficiency and growth.

Riker and Weimer (1994) indicate the four characteristics of property rights that the state must enforce: allocation, trespass, alienation and credibility. The capacity of the state to enforce these four characteristics is a question of governance. The World Bank has defined governance as 'the state's management of economic and social resources' (World Bank 1994). The governance capacities of the state may be higher in a country which is politically stable (Riker and Weimer 1994), where democratic principles are highly valued in civil society, and where the security of property has become socially and morally institutionalised. Conversely, the governance capacities of the state may be lower where the rule of law is weaker. In part, this is because the potential for corrupt rent seeking by individuals within the state structure is greater where the rule of law is weaker (Tullock 1980). Such 'directly unproductive profit-seeking' (Bhagwati and

Srinivasan 1980) activity generates income which is not based upon making a contribution to productivity improvements, and thus leads to a loss in the welfare of a society.

Thus, governance affects economic performance, in part because the effectiveness of governance determines the extent to which property rights are enforced and this in turn affects investment. Property rights are thus an extremely important economic institution. Given this importance, in those developing countries that have significant agricultural sectors—countries such as Fiji—it is to be expected that property rights in land are an economic institution that has implications for economic performance. If property rights in land are, to paraphrase North (1990), institutionally efficient, growth will be enhanced. If property rights in land are institutionally inefficient, growth will be reduced. In order to assess the efficiency of property rights in land, it is necessary to examine land tenure institutions, as these are the basis by which property rights are assigned, and as such will have an impact on productivity.

In the following section, the theoretical insights of the new institutional economics are applied to a case study of property rights in land in Fiji. This is done in order to assess the implications of economic institutions on economic performance in general, and in particular to assess whether institutional rigidities in property rights in land have had an impact on economic performance in Fiji.

Property rights in land in Fiji

Agriculture in Fiji[1]

For most of the post-independence period, agriculture has provided around a fifth of Fiji's gross domestic product. Agriculture is also a major employer, with more than 75 per cent of all households working on a full or part-time basis in crop production, livestock, forestry and fisheries (World Bank 1995a). Sugarcane farming and processing dominates commercial agricultural activity, and has done since its introduction in the 1880s. Sugarcane farming accounted for more than 40 per cent of the total agricultural sector in 1995. At the same time, sugarcane processing accounted for almost 30 per cent of the total manufacturing sector in 1995 (Fiji Bureau of Statistics (various issues): Table 3.3). As a consequence, the sugar industry was worth more than

12 per cent of GDP in 1995. Moreover, the sugar industry remains the largest single source of employment in Fiji, providing direct employment for more than 25 per cent of the economically active population. Finally, sugar provided some 40 per cent of exports by value in 1992.

In 1993 sugarcane farming in Fiji was done on 23,454 registered farms. According to the World Bank (1995a), the average size of a sugarcane farm was 4.2 hectares. The average area harvested was 3.11 hectares, the average cane yield was 48 tonnes per hectare, and the average gross revenue received was F$8,314. Most sugarcane farms are thus small production units. Operating for most of the year with household labour, 61 per cent of sugarcane farms produce on average less than 150 tonnes of cane per year. Moreover, 24 per cent of sugarcane farms have operational holdings of one hectare or less and produce on average 50 tonnes or less of cane a year.

Sugarcane farming is subject to long production cycles, inflexible resource allocation and the uncertainty of the weather. In Fiji, production uses self-provided seed cane, animal draught power and limited quantities of agro-chemical fertilisers. In addition to family labour, hired labour is used during the harvesting season. Cane harvesting is performed manually under a complex gang system that involves farmers working alongside some 13,500 seasonal harvesters, many of whom are landless migrants. Cane harvesters receive an average rate of F$7.50 for every tonne of cane cut. This translates into an average daily wage paid of approximately F$8.50, almost 40 per cent below the mean average for all industries in Fiji. However, in addition to wage costs the farmer hiring the cane harvesters often bears the cost of providing housing and meals for the temporary labour.

Access to land

Given the importance of agriculture in the Fiji economy in general, and the importance of sugarcane production in particular, the institutional structures that govern the access of farmers to land are of critical importance. This is because arable land, in Fiji as elsewhere, is scarce. According to a survey by Twyford and Wright (1965) the total land area of Fiji is about 7,000 square miles. Table 5.1 indicates the composition of land ownership in Fiji, as indicated by Nayacakalou (1971). Land can be owned by indigenous Fijian land-owning groups,

Table 5.1 Categories of land ownership in Fiji

	Per cent of total area
Native land	83
Crown land	10
Freehold	7
Total	100

Source: Nayacakalou, R., 1971. 'Fiji: manipulating the system', in R. Crocombe (ed.), *Land Tenure in the Pacific*, Oxford University Press, Melbourne.

called *mataqali*, which is called 'native land'; owned by the state, which is called 'crown land'; or can be privately owned, which is called 'freehold' land. Whilst the figures in Table 5.1 underestimate the distribution of native land, in that some crown land has reverted to native land (Ward 1995), they are broadly accurate. As is demonstrated in Table 5.1, 83 per cent of land in Fiji is classified as native land. Some 10 per cent of land in Fiji is owned by the state. This land is subdivided into two categories: crown land schedule A; and crown land schedule B. Schedule A is native land that reverted to the state after the demise of the *mataqali*. Schedule B is state land over which there are no *mataqali* claims. Finally, 7 per cent of the land is classified as freehold. The majority of this land was acquired during the late 1800s. While a small percentage of the overall land area, it should be noted that this land covers a large proportion of the arable area, and often includes better quality land.

Table 5.2 classifies land according to its suitability for agricultural purposes for the years 1965 and 1978. Significant changes took place in the thirteen-year period. In 1965 Twyford and Wright found that 40 per cent of Fiji's land area was unsuitable for agriculture, as it consisted of undulating to steep mountains covered with forests. In 1978, using slightly different but broadly comparable definitions, the Ministry of Agriculture and Fisheries found that only 6 per cent of the land area was wholly unsuitable for agriculture. Twyford and Wright found that only 20 per cent of the land area could be used for agriculture without any improvements being made. In 1978 this figure had dropped to only 16 per cent. In 1965 some 10 per cent of the land area could have become available for agriculture if appropriate improvements had been made. In 1978 this category had dramatically increased, to constitute 43 per cent of the land area. Finally, whereas in

Table 5.2 Land use classification in per cent, 1965 and 1978

Land classification	1965	1978
Suitable for agriculture ('First Class')	20	16
Suitable for agriculture only after advanced improvement ('Second Class')	10	43
Suitable for agriculture only after advanced drainage and soil conservation work ('Third Class')	30	35
Unsuitable for agriculture ('Fourth Class')	40	6
Total	100	100

Source: Fiji Ministry of Agriculture and Fisheries, 1978. *Census of Agriculture*, Ministry of Agriculture and Fisheries, Suva.

1965 some 30 per cent of the land area needed drainage and soil conservation work in order to make it available for agricultural purposes, by 1978 this figure had increased to 35 per cent.

Native land dominates the distribution of land in Fiji. It also dominates the distribution of arable land. This gives rise to a complex ethnic dimension in access to scarce arable land in Fiji. Currently, some 75 per cent of sugarcane farmers are Indo-Fijian. They are responsible for about 88 per cent of sugarcane production. By way of contrast, about 25 per cent of sugarcane farmers are indigenous Fijian. They are responsible for about 12 per cent of total sugarcane production. Clearly, with the majority of agricultural land controlled by one community, the indigenous Fijian community, and with the majority of sugarcane farmers coming from a second community, the Indo-Fijian community, ethnicity is a major factor in agricultural production in Fiji.

Moreover, ethnicity may also be a major factor in agricultural productivity in Fiji. The figures just quoted demonstrate that indigenous Fijian sugarcane farmers are comparatively less productive than Indo-Fijian sugarcane farmers. The cause of comparatively poor performance amongst indigenous Fijians is often put down to a lack of experience in sugarcane farming within the indigenous Fijian community, 'Fijian tradition', and institutional constraints of the type which will be discussed later in the chapter. Efforts have been made however to try and increase both the participation and the productivity of indigenous Fijians in sugarcane production in Fiji. One such effort has been the Seaqaqa cane project on Vanua Levu.

Table 5.3 Sugarcane production in the Labasa mill area, 1986–95

Years	Production area (hectares)	Tonnes per hectare	Total production (tonnes)
1986	19,757.6	51.5	1,017,372
1987	19,369.6	45.3	877,652
1988	19,353.7	53.5	1,034,787
1989	20,083.7	49.3	989,847
1990	19,990.6	58.5	1,168,824
1991	21,560.5	47.7	1,029,223
1992	22,624.0	51.3	1,161,245
1993	23,043.9	48.8	1,124,357
1994	23,346.7	55.6	1,298,285
1995	236,861.1	54.1	1,216,291

Source: Fiji Sugar Corporation, 1996. *Labasa Mill Database*, Fiji Sugar Corporation, Labasa.

A World Bank assessment of the Seaqaqa project argued that efforts to boost indigenous Fijian participation and productivity in sugarcane farming could be successful if such efforts both boosted the output of cane and witnessed improved performance by those indigenous Fijian farmers who had come from outside the district and were thus new to sugarcane farming (World Bank 1995a). Table 5.3 gives details of sugarcane production in the Labasa mill area, encompassing the Seaqaqa project area, between 1986 and 1995. Table 5.3 demonstrates the increase in productivity, from 51.5 tonnes per hectare in 1986 to 54.1 tonnes per hectare in 1995, an arithmetic trend rate of growth of 1.37 per cent per annum over the period.

However, it can be debated whether there is a relationship between improved productivity in the Seaqaqa project and increased indigenous Fijian participation. The project sought to maintain a minimum 50 per cent farmer participation rate from the indigenous Fijian community. Table 5.4 details the ethnic origin of farmers in the Seaqaqa project between 1981 and 1993. Table 5.4 illustrates that by 1993 indigenous Fijians comprised only 45.7 per cent of all farmers in the project, a decline of 11.4 per cent over a 13 year period.

Clearly, indigenous Fijian farm productivity remains at the very least a contentious issue. Notwithstanding this issue though there is a widespread movement in Fiji amongst the indigenous Fijian community which seeks to increase the participation of indigenous

Table 5.4 Percentage of Indo-Fijian and indigenous Fijian farmers in the Seaqaqa project, 1981–93

Years	Indigenous Fijians (%)	Indo-Fijians (%)	Others (%)
1981	56.1	42.3	1.6
1982	55.8	42.7	1.5
1983	55.0	43.4	1.6
1984	53.5	44.9	1.6
1985	51.7	46.7	1.6
1986	50.7	47.7	1.6
1987	50.4	48.0	1.6
1988	49.1	49.5	1.4
1989	47.7	50.8	1.5
1990	47.4	51.3	1.3
1991	47.1	51.3	1.6
1992	46.9	51.6	1.5
1993	45.7	53.0	1.3

Source: Fiji Sugar Corporation, 1996. *Labasa Mill Database*, Fiji Sugar Corporation, Labasa.

Fijians in farming, and particularly in sugarcane production. This would, as a first step, require that some land that is currently worked by Indo-Fijians revert to indigenous Fijian farmers. In order to understand how this might occur, and the possible consequences of such a development, it is necessary to examine land tenure institutions in Fiji.

Land tenure institutions

Access to native land is regulated by the Native Lands Trust Board (NLTB), which was created by the colonial government in 1940. The creation of the NLTB as the primary agricultural institution dealing with land tenure can be traced back to the needs of the sugar industry during the colonial period. According to Moynagh (1981), the Colonial Sugar Refinery pushed for the formation of smallhold farms. This required the division of native land into small units, under some kind of tenancy arrangement. However, dealing with individual and often undefined indigenous Fijian land-owning units was cumbersome. The establishment of the NLTB provided tenants with a single institutional body with which to deal. As will be seen, it did not remove the element of insecurity from tenurial relations in rural Fiji.

Table 5.5 shows the distribution of native land in Fiji. Section 15 of the Native Lands Trust Act (NLTA) provides that land may be 'reserved' for the exclusive use of indigenous Fijians. Such land may not be leased out to non-indigenous Fijians unless it is not being used. Unreserved land may be used by indigenous Fijians or may be leased out. As demonstrated in Table 5.5, some 63 per cent of native land is unreserved, while some 37 per cent of native land is reserved. Of that land which is unreserved, just under 41 per cent is leased out. Of that land which is reserved, fewer than 15 per cent is leased out.

Thus, the main institutional duty carried out by the NLTB, as specified by Section 8 of the NLTA, is the granting of leases to work native land and to consider the renewal or non-renewal of such leases. Section 9 of the NLTA gives a very specific condition that governs land leasing (Government of Fiji 1985:6):

> No native land shall be dealt with by way of lease or licence under the provisions of this act unless the Board is satisfied that the land proposed to be made the subject of such lease or licence is not being beneficially occupied by the Fijian owners, and is not likely during the currency of such lease or licence to be required by the Fijian owners for their use, maintenance or support.

Section 9 of the Act thus provides the NLTB with the power to determine the granting of leases on land that is not being used by indigenous Fijians. Indeed, any rental agreement that does not have the consent of the NLTB is null and void. Granted, informal

Table 5.5 Classification of native land in Fiji

	Area (km²)	Per cent of total native land
Unreserved	9528.15	63.37
Reserved	5508.47	36.63
Total	16036.62	100.00
of which:		Per cent of unreserved/reserved land
Unreserved native land leased	3869.31	40.61
Reserved native land leased	816.43	14.82

Source: Ward, M., 1995. 'Land, law and custom: diverging realities in Fiji', in R.G. Ward and E. Kingdon (eds), *Land, Custom and Practice in the South Pacific*, Cambridge University Press, Cambridge:199.

arrangements between local *mataqalis* and tenants do occur. However, there is no legal basis for these arrangements. Thus, the NLTB dominates the supply of rentable agricultural land.

In supplying land for rent, the NLTB must abide by provisions that regulate the leasing of agricultural land in Fiji. These regulations provide a framework within which the NLTB operates. As such, they could be considered a second agricultural institution dealing with land tenure. In 1966 comprehensive legislation called the Agricultural Landlord and Tenants Ordinance (ALTO) was put in place to formalise the leasing of agricultural land. The ALTO provided that leases be a minimum of ten-years and offer the possibility of two ten year renewals. The ALTO thus effectively provided maximum leases of thirty years, a degree of tenurial security that had not previously existed in rural Fiji. Nonetheless, in that there was not an automatic renewal of a lease after the initial ten-year period, an element of insecurity remained. This insecurity will no doubt have had an effect on economic incentives and, thus, long-term growth.

In 1976, the ALTO was amended by Parliament, in the form of the Agricultural Landlord and Tenants Act (ALTA). Like the ALTO before it, the ALTA was intended to harmonise landlord-tenant relationships so that agricultural productivity could be increased. However, unlike earlier provisions both under the NLTA and the ALTO, the ALTA offered better protection for tenants seeking to exercise their right to use the land. This was particularly the case for tenants on freehold land. The ALTA thus provides the legal framework under which land leases are granted on all agricultural land in Fiji. The ALTA is therefore, after the NLTB, the second key institutional structure dealing with property rights and land tenure in rural Fiji.

Sections 4 through 15 of the ALTA deal with issues around security of tenure. Under these sections, the ALTA provides a minimum thirty-year period for all newly agreed leases. Moreover, for leases agreed under the ALTO regulations, a twenty-year renewal is stipulated. The tenant is required to pay a rent to the NLTB, which is set at 6 per cent of the unimproved capital value of the land. The unimproved capital value of the land is in theory determined every five years. Rents as a proportion of crop value vary tremendously. For example, conflicting data from the World Bank (1995a) and local research (Prasad 1995) suggests that rents for sugarcane land may vary from a low of F\$50 per hectare to a high of F\$350 per hectare.

The NLTB distributes the rents it receives to the indigenous land-owning unit, through its chiefs. Table 5.6 presents the distribution of rents collected by the NLTB. The figures provided in Table 5.6 differ from those used by many authors, including Nayacakalou (1971), Eaton (1988), Overton (1987), Rutz (1987) and Spate (1959). This is because, as Ward (1995) points out, there has been some scholarly confusion regarding the distribution of rents. The figures in Table 5.6 follow Kamikamica and Davey (1988) and the NLTA itself, which is quite clear.

> After deduction of any sums in accordance with section 14 of the Act, the balance of any monies received by the Board by way of rents and premiums in respect of native land shall be distributed by the Board as follows: (a) to the proprietary unit, seventy per cent; (b) to the *turaga ni mataqali*, fifteen per cent; (c) to the *turaga ni yavusa*, ten per cent; (d) to the *turaga I taukei*, five per cent (NLTB Act, Section 11 (1), Cap134:28).

As is seen in Table 5.6, 25 per cent of the total rent goes to the NLTB. This is used to cover its own administrative costs. It is a matter of some debate as to whether this allocation represents value for money. The NLTB has been running at a loss for some years, requiring additional transfers from the state, and has not produced an audited financial statement since 1989. Its management of resources thus lacks transparency. This may have created opportunities for rent seeking behaviour on the part of its bureaucrats. Moreover, the introduction of positive discrimination into the civil service created a 'culture of mediocrity' which may have also affected the NLTB and which may have also contributed to the pursuit of directly unproductive profit-seeking activities on the part of bureaucrats.

Table 5.6 Distribution of rents collected by the NLTB

Recipient	Per cent of rent
Native Land Trust Board	25
Head of *vanua* (Turaga ni Taukei)	3.75
Head of *yavusa* (Turaga ni Qali)	7.5
Head of *mataqali* (Turaga ni Mataqali)	11.25
Members of *mataqali*	52.5
Total	100

Source: Kamikamica, J. and Davey, T., 1988. 'Trust on trial: the development of the customary land trust concept in Fiji', in Y. Ghai (ed.), *Land, Government and Politics in the Pacific Island States,* Institute of Pacific Studies, Suva.

Of the remaining 75 per cent of the rent, three chiefs, that is the head of the *vanua*, the *yavusa* and the *mataqali*, receive a total of 22.5 per cent. The remainder goes to the members of the *mataqali*. It can be questioned whether the distribution of the 75 per cent of the rent that does not go to the NLTB is equitable, in that three members of one proprietary unit receive 22.5 per cent of the rent and all other members of the proprietary unit together receive 52.5 per cent. Moreover, just as the role of the NLTB may distort the operation of the land rental 'market', so too does the unequal distribution of land rents, in that the unequal distribution of land rents may act as an incentive for rent seeking behaviour (Prasad and Tisdell 1996a). Certainly, there can be little doubt that the designer of the institutional structure, the colonial power, did not mean it to be equitable; rather, it was meant to integrate chiefs into the hierarchy of colonial rule and thus remove a possible source of opposition to colonial power (Akram-Lodhi 1997).

In exchange for the payment of rent, the NLTB is required to allow the peaceful occupation and cultivation of the land during the tenancy, provided the tenant adopts 'proper' husbandry techniques in using the land. At the same time, the tenant has the right to harvest any standing crop on the land within 12 months of the expiry of the lease. Any improvements to the land or construction of dwellings on the land must have the consent of the NLTB. Finally, in the event of a dispute between the tenant and the NLTB the ALTA provides for the establishment of a tribunal to arbitrate the dispute.

The ALTA appears, on the surface, to provide considerable security of tenure for tenants. However, the element of insecurity remains. This insecurity arises because the NLTB is functionally if not formally powerless to stop informal demands being made by the local land-owning units. Such informal demands are very common: the local *mataqalis* claim to be the rightful owners of the land and often seek to negotiate directly with tenants over a range of issues, particularly rents and leases. These arrangements are known as *vakavanua* (Ward 1995; Overton 1987; Eaton 1988; Prasad 1984). These informal demands have, at times, been translated into forceful and violent action designed to achieve a particular claim. Indeed, it has been recently noted by the *Fiji Times* (16 February 1996) that

> land disputes have reached new heights in Fiji. Across the nation, landowners with a gripe against tenants are adopting a forceful and, in a few instances, violent methods to make their complaint known. They are resorting to vigilante-style roadblocks.

Conflicts between *mataqalis* and tenants often evolve into conflicts between landowners and the NLTB when the NLTB does not accede to landowner demands. In such circumstances, landowners, faced with opposition from both tenants and the NLTB, often threaten eviction.

Conceptually, the NLTB can be understood as an institutional monopoly designed to manage common property in the land rental market. In Africa, the World Bank has argued that institutional monopolies designed to manage common property in land create unnecessary economic costs. The World Bank has made a similar argument in Fiji, claiming that the NLTB is a costly and inefficient economic institution (World Bank 1995a). Moreover, as an institutional monopoly which distorts the operation of a key factor market, that of agricultural land, the NLTB has the capacity to distort economic signals on a national scale by affecting relative prices, production and distribution.

Institutional rigidities and the future of land tenure arrangements

As already noted, the ALTA came into effect in 1976. Pre-existing tenancy contracts were extended by 20 years, which meant that in 1997 leases began to expire. The expiry of land leases creates a major institutional rigidity that constrains growth in Fiji. Moreover, the long-term survival of the NLTB as a land tenure institution depends on how land lease problems are resolved, if for no other reason than the fact that the NLTB depends on rents to provide its income. The land lease problem in turn reflects a lack of flexibility within both the NLTB and the ALTA: despite being a pivotal land tenure institution, the NLTB cannot solve the land lease problem. This demonstrates that the NLTB and the ALTA (which regulates it) are inefficient economic institutions. The inefficiencies caused by such rigidities within land tenure institutions must be resolved if an economic environment within which growth can be facilitated is to be established.

With an awareness that land leases were going to eventually expire, a number of reports have been produced since 1992 which consider the future of legislation governing agricultural land in Fiji, and in particular whether land leases should be renewed. These have been written within a context of declining land availability: it is clear that the availability of agricultural land will continue to decline as demand for residential, commercial and tourism development continues to increase. Moreover, they have been written in light of the aforementioned movement within the indigenous Fijian community to encourage a reversion of agricultural land to farmers within the indigenous Fijian community. Finally, the reports have been written in light of the apparent productivity differences that exist between indigenous Fijian and Indo-Fijian farmers. Prasad and Tisdell (1996b) have estimated that if 30 per cent of the leases currently held by Indo-Fijians were not renewed and the production on such land reverted to farmers from the indigenous Fijian community, there would be a production loss of 15.7 per cent of total sugarcane production. The estimate is based on the assumption that the productivity ratio between indigenous Fijian and Indo-Fijian farmers does not change.

In 1992 the NLTB considered the land lease issue. In 1993 the Sugar Cane Growers Council considered the same issue, and in 1996 the government set up the Agricultural Landlord and Tenant Review Research Unit to recommend changes to the ALTA. Even the World Bank, which has traditionally refrained from commenting on land leases and the structure of property rights in land, has now identified it as a major problem (World Bank 1995a). These reports highlight five issues that must be considered. The first issue is the duration of the leases that are to be renewed. Surveys into this issue have invariably found that tenants want leases with duration of more than 50 years, while landowners prefer leases with duration considerably shorter than the current 30 years. The second issue is the conditions attached to the awarding of a lease, including landlord-tenant relations and issues around compensation for land degradation and land improvements. The third issue is the compensation that is to be paid to tenants whose leases are not renewed. The fourth issue is the need for more land to be made available to members of the land-owning units. The fifth issue is the need to further develop dispute settlement mechanisms.

A widely canvassed solution to the land lease issue is that of a simple renewal of leases under the ALTA. However, this only provides a temporary solution to what is an institutional problem. So too does an alternative suggested by some in the NLTB: that leases be automatically renewed while at the same time the provisions of the ALTA are amended to restrict the rights of tenants. Therefore, the NLTB has recently issued a report on the ALTA which seeks to offer solutions to the land lease problem (NLTB 1997). In this report, the

NLTB considers the practicality of increasing the use of sharecropping and fixed wage contracts in sugarcane farming. This strategy is based on the assumption that ultimately leases will expire and land will revert to indigenous Fijian owners. Not all of these landowners will want to directly engage in production; therefore, they will enter into sharecropping arrangements with former leaseholders or they will hire Indo-Fijian wage labour to work on the land. To support an expansion of sharecropping or an increased use of wage labour, the strategy suggests that the leases of tenants be extended, but only for that area of their land on which their dwellings are located. Some leaders within the Indo-Fijian community have argued that this strategy represents a return to the *girmit* era, during which time indentured South Asian labourers worked in Fiji under 5 year contracts.

The strategy contained within the NLTB report does not however understand the mechanics of sharecropping or wage labour contracts. Sharecroppers and wage labourers have no incentive to increase the intensity of their effort, as they do not receive rewards commensurate with production risk (Stiglitz 1986; Newbery 1979). Furthermore, the cost of monitoring and supervising sharecroppers and wage labourers is high, representing an extra cost that must be borne. As a consequence, a shift towards sharecropping or wage labour may result in a decline in net income. The productivity implications of such a strategy would be reinforced by the reversion of a substantial proportion of cultivated land to comparatively less-productive indigenous Fijian farmers. This strategy could therefore have extremely detrimental economic implications for Fiji as a whole.

Contrary to a strategy designed to increase sharecropping and waged labour, there are some who believe that farms should be amalgamated and the industry mechanised in an effort to enhance productive efficiency (NLTB 1996). It is true that amalgamation might result in economies of scale. Nonetheless, the financial cost of mechanisation could be very high and indeed might outweigh any efficiency gain for a considerable period of time. Furthermore, mechanisation would reduce the number of seasonal workers employed in farming, and particularly the large numbers involved in harvesting. The social cost of the loss of income could be significant.

A problem with these proposed 'solutions' is that they fail to recognise that the institutional structure governing tenure relations in rural Fiji results in a lack of well-defined property rights in land and limits the extent of private property. From a theoretical point of view, this is likely to have a detrimental affect on economic performance, if for no other reason than the creation of what are in all likelihood substantial transactions costs in sorting out the existing leasing arrangements. Solving this problem, from the point of view of neoclassical economics, is reasonably straightforward: extend the development of private property rights in land. This implies two steps. The first step would be to convert all crown land into freehold property and allow any lease holders to buy the land they work at a market-determined price. This could have several benefits. The first would be to initiate an increase in agricultural productivity. The second would be to bring in revenue for the government. The third would be to boost public support for government economic policy, and in particular privatisation policy. However, as already demonstrated, crown land represents only a small percentage of total agricultural land.

Therefore, a second, more radical, step would be necessary. This step would be the sale of all native land under lease. As demonstrated in Table 5.3, some 29 per cent of total native land is under lease to indigenous Fijians, Indo-Fijians and members of other communities. This means that the sale of native land under lease would involve more than a quarter of all native land. This land could be sold to the leaseholder at a market-determined price. However, the sale of native land does not necessarily imply the ownership of all such land leaving the indigenous Fijian community. There is no doubt that some of the land would be bought by individuals from within the land-owning unit; indeed, population growth requires that some land revert to the *mataqalis*.

The cessation of communal ownership would of course be controversial. However, as pointed out by Ward (1995), the indigenous Fijian chiefs of Ba, Bua and Lau advocated individual ownership before the first native land ordinance in 1880. Indeed, Ward (1995) argues that the colonial rulers may have imposed communal ownership in Fiji. Moreover, the NLTB was created in an era where both the international and the domestic political and economic environment were very different. It was, as has already been argued, created by the British to serve specific political purposes. In this light, private property in land is not necessarily alien to indigenous Fijian political thinking.

Nonetheless, the privatisation of Crown land and the sale of native land would mean that some farmers would lose their leases. The impact of this could however be obviated to a degree by the sale of unleased land in a different location to those who had lost their land. This should, of course, apply to both Indo-Fijian and indigenous Fijian leaseholders. It could also be obviated by carefully planned resettlement and compensation packages for displaced tenants.

There are however problems with the neoclassical solution. Obviously, even if one accepts that the sale of land to individuals would increase efficiency, the actual transaction would take place in a relatively new market in which prices would be unlikely to reflect opportunity costs; this could distort the incentives usually associated with the private ownership of property. At the same time, there are reasons to doubt that land privatisation would in fact increase efficiency. Certainly, in Africa, where efforts at land privatisation have gone quite far, there is little evidence to support the argument that land privatisation has increased agricultural productivity and hence agricultural efficiency (Bassett 1993:14).

The reason why land privatisation has not improved agricultural efficiency is because, in the language of economics, land privatisation is a partial equilibrium solution to a general equilibrium problem: the theory of 'second best' must be taken into account. The theory of second best demonstrates that when markets are subject to a series of distortions the removal of one distortion need not necessarily improve economic performance and can indeed lead to a deterioration in economic performance (Lipsey and Lancaster 1956).

The theory of second best is relevant to the circumstances in rural Fiji. Clearly, the operation of the NLTB and the ALTA has affected the process by which land transactions in Fiji take place: the inflexibility of both institutions has undoubtedly created inefficiencies. These inefficiencies will have had effects on other, related markets, and most notably labour and product markets, as the impact of distortions filter through the economy. This then is where the theory of second best can be applied. Even though the NLTB and the ALTA have created inefficiencies in land transactions in Fiji, labour and product markets have undoubtedly adjusted in light of these inefficiencies. In such circumstances, removing the influence of the NLTB and the ALTA from land transactions—through, for example, privatisation—can have no predictable effect because it is not possible to know how labour and product markets, having adjusted to take account of existing inefficiencies, would readjust in light of privatisation. Indeed, it is quite possible that privatisation would result in labour and product market adjustments that would further weaken economic performance. Thus, even though it is land transactions that are the source of economic inflexibilities, it is the overall institutional structure within which rural markets in Fiji operate which has been compromised. In such circumstances, there is no reason to believe that the removal of distortions in one market, the land market, no matter how inefficient, will in fact improve economic efficiency.

It has already been argued that institutional rigidities in rural Fiji are likely to have had an effect on production, investment and distribution. These rigidities require imaginative solutions, the details of which are beyond the scope of this chapter. What is clear however is that further work is urgently needed. Out of a total of 134 native land leases that have expired at the time of writing, 102 have been renewed for a further term of 30 years. While such a development is to welcomed, albeit as a temporary solution, this does means that 32 leases have not been renewed. The ongoing expiry of land leases suggests that land will revert back to farmers from within the indigenous Fijian community even though such farmers are less productive than their Indo-Fijian counterparts. The implications of such a development for economic performance are nothing less than a particularly vicious cycle: less productivity implies less investment, less growth and economic stagnation. There can be little doubt that Fiji is confronting a major challenge.

Conclusion

Mainstream economics has long been criticised for not taking seriously the role of institutional factors in determining the economic performance of countries. However, renewed interest in institutional economics has firmly put the role of institutional factors on the economic policy agenda for many developing countries. One pivotal institutional factor is the nature of property rights. According to North (1990), explaining disparities in the performance of economies requires consideration of, amongst other institutional factors, the nature of property rights. In many developing countries the nature of property rights are not well defined. Uncertainty over property rights has implications for investment, production and distribution.

In the case of Fiji, uncertainty over property rights in land is clear. The indigenous Fijian community controls the bulk of the arable land in Fiji. This land is managed on behalf of the land-owning units by the NLTB, which negotiates land leases and collects rents within the framework of the ALTA. The bulk of the tenants dealt with by the NLTB are from the Indo-Fijian community. However, both the NLTB and the ALTA, as land tenure institutions, lack flexibility: they are not 'efficient' institutions. The ongoing expiry of land leases has led to renewed examination of alternatives to the current, inflexible institutional structure. This chapter has critically reviewed the alternatives, and has found them lacking. Yet the need for an alternative is clear if Fiji is to avoid a vicious cycle of less agricultural productivity, less investment and less growth. The new government which emerged following the 1999 general elections will therefore have to address the important task of finding a viable alternative to the current institutional structure and restoring confidence amongst the agricultural community in Fiji.

Endnote

1. This subsection is based directly on Prasad and Akram-Lodhi (1998) and is used with their permission.

CHAPTER 6

Confronting social policy challenges in Fiji

John Cameron

Introduction

Every society has ways of distributing social and economic uncertainty and insecurity within and between individuals, groups of individuals and institutions. The basis of this distribution is not random but rather is a result of a set of historically constituted processes that shape a society's institutions and its people's beliefs, motivations and aspirations. Social policy is an intervention by the state designed in general to alter this distribution and, more specifically, to redistribute and ultimately reduce the experience of uncertainty and insecurity. A critically important way by which social policy can reduce the experience of uncertainty and insecurity is through a reduction in the degree of inequality found within a society. In fostering socioeconomic security through a greater degree of equality within a society, state social policy represents an investment in the trust which underpins 'social wealth' and which builds an inclusive polity.

Fiji had a per capita GNP of over US$2,000 in the mid 1990s (World Bank 1995a). Further, with a comparatively long life expectancy, comparatively low infant mortality, and comparatively high adult literacy, Fiji had a reasonably satisfactory level of social development relative to its income. Despite this, however, Fiji did not have a socially inclusive polity. Notwithstanding a rich history of strong civil society actors and institutions, for most of the post-independence period state policy has been shaped by an élite which has used ethnic identity as the basis for political mobilisation (Sutherland, this volume). The 'politics of ethnicity' have not been able to foster trust between the archipelago's two major ethnic groups, in large part because state social policy has sought to redistribute social and economic uncertainty and insecurity between ethnic groups, to the detriment of one group, the Indo-Fijian community, in an effort to deliberately maintain the pre-independence policy framework of 'separate development'. A major consequence of such a policy framework has been to foster inequality and social exclusion, both between and within the indigenous Fijian and the Indo-Fijian communities.

It was only for a brief period during the mid 1980s that the policy framework that fostered inequality and social exclusion was challenged. During a period of multidimensional crisis, social demands based upon regional, class, gender and environmental conditions led to the formation of the Fiji Labour Party (FLP) and the call from those who had been excluded from élite politics for the construction of a less unequal, socially-inclusionary, multicultural polity which systematically confronted the deeper problems of ethnic tension, developmental values and dysfunctional economic tendencies. This call was however cut off by the 1987 military coups, which violently reasserted the primacy of the politics of ethnicity.

Despite this, the call for a more inclusive polity did not disappear. Indeed, at the end of the 1990s it is being reactivated. The new constitutional settlement explicitly recognises the need to construct a less unequal, socially inclusionary multicultural polity in Fiji (Ghai, this volume). The overwhelming victory of the FLP in the 1999 general elections demonstrates the extent to which the call for a more inclusive polity has deep roots within Fiji society. This is because ethnic tension and contradictory development processes have not disappeared; neither have claims based upon regional, class, gender and environmental conditions. In the construction of such a polity, the social policy of the state has a pivotal role to play. The redistribution of social and economic uncertainty and insecurity by the state must be done in a way which complements and augments the strengths of a diverse civil society, and in so doing develops the trust—and most particularly the inter-ethnic trust—which can improve the quality of people's lives in Fiji.

This chapter examines some of the major strategic issues in Fiji confronting social policy. A fundamental proposition of the chapter is that Fiji society was diverted from important debates about the fundamentals of social policy by the coups of 1987. Confronting the future of social policy would thus benefit from looking to the past. Looking back, it is clear that there remains a major challenge confronting civil society and the state in seeking to redistribute social and economic uncertainty and improve the degree of equality within society, and in so doing build social wealth in Fiji. In the next section, the neoliberal approach to social inequality and hence social policy is critically assessed and the new institutional economics (NIE) introduced as a countervailing approach rooted in distinctive moral and political perspectives which emphasise the interaction between civil society, state institutions and imperfect markets in facilitating improvements in the degree of equality within a society. In light of this framework, the third section examines the material reality of social inequality in post-colonial Fiji. It is argued that the challenge confronting the state is not in the detail of policy design but rather in the need to build on and invest in existing social wealth so as to institutionalise positive socioeconomic processes. The fourth section illustrates how this might be done by briefly examining three possible fields of policy which require the institutionalisation of positive socioeconomic processes, namely health and nutrition, education and community relations. The final section offers some conclusions.

Neoliberal ideology, social policy and the NIE

For most of the past two decades socioeconomic development thinking has been fundamentally neoliberal in outlook. From a neoliberal perspective, inequality between individuals in both potential and outcome is the natural condition of humanity. The primary cause for this innate inequality may be either genetic potential or the mysterious ways of a divine creator. In either instance, as members of the species are observed to be different they will therefore be doomed to be unequal in socioeconomic experience.

This view of society is found in Western liberal philosophy. It is consistent with the theorems of neoclassical economics concerning efficiency, equity and stability. The conclusions from such analysis, stressing a condition of 'natural' inequality, is that societies are best organised for the social good on the basis of equal rights to individual voluntary contracts negotiated in free markets. The resulting allocation of resources, including inequality in control over resources between individuals, households and nations, will reflect unequal abilities and efforts in contributing to meeting others' desires, and the strength of one's own preferences for possessing scarce goods and services. The resulting distribution may thus be said to be equitable, albeit in a limited sense. Granted, some neoliberals go further, recognising that equality of contract requires equality of opportunity. They thus become advocates of equality in access to education, health and recruitment through merit-based procedures. Some may also show concern on the question of the right to inherit material wealth. Nonetheless, the argument that any form of deprivation rooted in social inequality demands collective action, in the shape of allocating resources towards the deprived, is marginalised by most neoliberal thinkers. The neoliberal view does not rule out individual altruistic, charitable actions as the philosophical basis for social policy: indeed, it highlights them.

Recent emphasis in the development literature on the need to encourage growth in 'human capital' demonstrates the dominance of neoliberal thinking. Human capital is most easily applied to individuals; thinking about relationships between individuals and between groups of individuals is peripheral. Thus, inequality is not relational; it is the outcome of inadequate 'investment' by the individual or the individual's 'agent' in developing their own capacities. Human capital is thus, in its emphasis on the isolated individual, very much a product of neoliberal thinking.

The introduction of the concept of 'social capital' recognises this deficiency, highlighting as it does the importance of both the quantities and qualities of relationships in the development process. However, social capital also has problems: in particular, the implicit application of quantification to non-material phenomena betrays its neoliberal origin. Therefore, an alternative concept can be proposed: social wealth. Social wealth is centrally concerned with the degree of trust in a society, a trust which is established on the frontier where culture, politics and economics intersect. Social wealth is the outcome of 'the form of norms of reciprocity and networks of civic engagement' (Putman 1993:167) which facilitate the coordination of action within societies. Clearly, in order to be able to coordinate action, such norms must build trust. This concern with trust can lead to an analysis of the distribution of insecurity as a social phenomenon restricting trust and, in so doing, fostering a degree of inequality within a society. Indeed, although every society has ways of distributing social and economic insecurity, it is rare for the distribution to be egalitarian. Thus, inequality is a social phenomenon. Social policy can then, as already noted, be broadly conceptualised as being centrally concerned with how the state acts to reduce and redistribute uncertainty and insecurity and in so doing reduce the degree of inequality within a society.

The all too apparent failure of neoliberalism to remove uncertainty, insecurity and inequality from the lives of people means that there is a need to develop a new policy agenda. This policy agenda should be based upon a countervailing philosophy rooted in distinctive moral and political perspectives and yet qualified by an element of hardheaded, rather than hard-hearted, economics. It can be suggested that the NIE could provide the basis of such a countervailing philosophy. The essential aspects of NIE which have attracted development economists can be summarised as being: an assumption that the operation of market forces has to be understood in a long term, institutional context; an assumption that changing civil society institutions can have high transitional costs; and a profound doubt regarding neoliberal claims that open markets guarantee efficiency, equity and stability, in large part because of bounded rationality, public goods, risk and uncertainty, and moral hazard, all of which facilitate the emergence in open markets of informational deficiencies.

The NIE generates an economics that emphasises the interaction between civil society, state institutions and markets (Harriss, Hunter and Lewis 1995). Moreover, in this interaction, state institutions are critical. State institutions can, by investing in social wealth, reduce inequality, strengthen civil society, and in so doing facilitate better outcomes from imperfect markets. Using the NIE and an emphasis on social wealth as the theoretical basis for state intervention thus requires understanding the historically-constituted processes shaping a society's institutions, its pattern of inequality, and its social wealth: the beliefs, motivations and aspirations of its people. The details of such an account are clearly beyond the scope of this chapter. Nonetheless, it can act as an organising framework to guide the analysis that follows.

The material reality of inequality in Fiji

Fiji came to political independence in 1970 with a discriminatory
pattern of policy priorities that had been set by the colonial regime.
However, both major ethnic groups had, to an extent, sought to bypass
the policy priorities of the colonial state. Within both the indigenous
Fijian and the Indo-Fijian communities there was a long history of
active civil societies fostering the development of non-market
socioeconomic relationships and in so doing deepening the formation
of social wealth. This social wealth facilitated self-provisioning in the
areas of health care, education and social security. Thus, an extensive
network of self-provisioning in health, education and social security
was maintained and indeed deepened during the colonial period. This
self-provisioning was crucial to the quality of lives of the most
vulnerable people in Fiji prior to independence.

The 1970s can be characterised as a decade of progress in
equalising the terms and conditions under which the forms of state
social provision inherited from the colonial period could be accessed.
State institutions, particularly those delivering social policy
interventions, were reformed and expanded, and much space was left
to civil society and its institutions, which utilised the strong social
wealth within both of Fiji's two main communities. This was
accompanied by significant investment in infrastructure and the
reform of taxation structures, which, along with institutional reform,
removed some of the worst elements of the colonial inheritance.

Nonetheless, by the start of the 1980s significant inequalities
remained. Income inequalities between the indigenous Fijian and
Indo-Fijian communities, to the benefit of the latter, were well
documented (Sutherland 1992). So too were the income inequalities
between men and women. However, as in other societies, the
experience of inequality went beyond the monetary. The impact of
state and civil society-led efforts to address non-monetary inequality
were indirectly assessed in the early 1980s, when a program of
research was undertaken to assess the adequacy of using 'active life
profiles' (Seers 1977) as a means of integrating social analysis and
planning under varying national conditions. As part of this program, a
country study was carried out in Fiji (Cameron 1987a).

Active life profiles are non-monetary indicators of social
development. They seek to show how, for a specific group of people at
a point in time, life expectancy can be broken down into a set of

activities that will be conducted over a life. In order to do this, life is first broken down into a set of mutually exclusive activities, or 'states of life'. The states of life considered in this chapter are those generally collected in national population censuses under the three headings of education, forms of economic activity and forms of economic inactivity. Demographic data provide links between these states of life. The proportion of people in a particular state of life are subdivided by age and then each age weighted by the average chance at birth of a person being alive at that age. Such weighting enforces consistency in the calculation. The results allocate a number of years to each state of life, and because the states of life are mutually exclusive the weighted sums will add up to life expectancy at birth. The expected duration in any state thus depends on the frequency of other states and a hidden state, that of being dead. A comparison of states of life across different groups can then be used to assess socioeconomic patterns and the general development status of a group of people.

By way of example, Table 6.1 presents the active life profiles for men in Fiji's two main ethnic groups around 1980. Table 6.1 demonstrates that around 1980 out of a life expectancy of 65.83 years for indigenous Fijian males, some 19.67 years would, on average, be spent as a villager or as a family worker. By way of contrast, amongst

Table 6.1 Active life profiles in years for men in Fiji around 1980

State of life	All Fiji males	Indigenous Fijian	Indo-Fijian
Pre-school and in education	16.35	16.10	16.36
Villager and family worker	10.54	19.67	2.64
Own business, including sugar cane farming	9.73	5.42	14.42
Employed by private employer	12.13	9.13	13.52
Employed by government	7.10	7.70	6.31
Inactive, unemployed, retired, unknown	8.01	7.33	8.04
Life expectancy at birth	63.86	65.83	61.61

Source: Cameron, J., 1987b. 'Fiji: the political economy of recent events', *Capital and Class*, 33:32.

Indo-Fijian males, out of a life expectancy of 61.61 years, some 14.42 years would be spent, on average, engaged in their own business, including sugar cane farming.

The research carried out in Fiji documented the material reality of social inequality between the two main ethnic groups in the early 1980s. The research found that Fiji possessed the demographic and educational characteristics of a relatively developed country. This applied to the population as a whole, both major ethnic groups, and sexes. At the same time, the research found that the difference in the relative position of the two major ethnic groups in terms of average money-equivalent incomes was offset by differences in their relative position in terms of active life profiles. Thus, inequality between the ethnic groups in active life profiles ran against inequality in monetary terms, to the benefit of the indigenous Fijian community. A complacent conclusion might have been that the socioeconomic positions of the two main ethnic groups in Fiji were merely different, and not fundamentally unequal. However, the reality was more complex: while income was only one factor in inequality, the impact of other factors which might have been thought to offset monetary inequality, were in fact differentiated along clear lines.

The research therefore considered in detail the components of the active life profiles, as indicators of inequality amongst groups in Fiji. Considering first data on education and economic activity for indigenous Fijians and Indo-Fijians, it appeared that both groups had a similar expected duration of education. This is demonstrated, for example, in Table 6.1 for males. This equality was however offset by dissimilarity when life cycles in patterns of economic activity were considered. A key difference existed between the communities in terms of their involvement in rural economic activities. Indigenous Fijians could expect a longer duration in rural economic activities where the individual exercised some explicitly recognised control over their life. Moreover, indigenous Fijians could expect a shorter duration of economic inactivity. Both are demonstrated in Table 6.1 for males. In large part, this dissimilarity might have been due to the term 'villager' being exclusively applied to indigenous Fijians in the census data that formed the basis of the construction of the active life profiles. The exclusive assignation of this category did capture some important attributes of indigenous Fijian rural life, in terms of strong communal rights and obligations involving agricultural and non-agricultural production and the distribution of produce. Indigenous Fijian life, by combining virtually equal access to education when compared to that obtained by Indo-Fijians, a longer expected duration in economic activities where the individual exercised some explicitly recognised control over their life, a shorter expected duration of economic inactivity, and a longer life expectancy, might have appeared to have had a higher quality of life and less inequality than that experienced by Indo-Fijians. This apparently higher quality of life amongst indigenous Fijians could be clearly contrasted with that of Indo-Fijians, many of whom, having been involved in monocultural sugar cane production, homestead production for self-provision, or being economically inactive in agriculture, faced different relationships in agriculture as well as in private sector non-agricultural activity.

In terms of gender-based differentials, the research on education and economic activity demonstrated that the expected duration of schooling for males and females in Fiji during the 1970s was virtually identical (Cameron 1987b). At the same time, women in Fiji had a life expectancy at birth seven years greater than men in the early 1980s. Lower infant mortality rates for females were important in explaining part of this difference; however, lower age-specific death rates were found for women at most ages when compared to men. Nonetheless, women faced a disadvantaged position. In terms of economic activity, including declared unemployment, women had an expected duration of economic activity which was only a fraction of that for men, although indigenous Fijian women had a higher expected duration of economic activity than Indo-Fijian women. Clearly, men stood between women and economic activity. This difference was reflected in the very large variation in the expected duration of economic inactivity between men and women; women could expect substantially longer periods of inactivity. It is however worth reinforcing the point that ethnic differences existed within women. Indo-Fijian women were disadvantaged in comparison with indigenous Fijian women, through having shorter lives, less control over their economic activities, and lower money-equivalent incomes.

Gender-based differences in economic activity and inactivity in part reflected the way in which the census data collected in the 1970s, which formed the basis of the information used in the construction of the active life profiles, 'pushed' women into the economically inactive category. As elsewhere, women in Fiji have multiple economic roles.

Census questions in the past tended to seek to find a unique role. In these circumstances, when a person was asked whether their single role was looking after children, tending livestock, maintaining crops, selling vegetables, participating in community projects, going fishing or seeking waged work, it was not surprising that priority was attached to childcare—a category deemed in most censuses to reflect economic inactivity. However, for women, economic inactivity did not mean leisure but rather repetitive unremunerated domestic work in the service of others, including husbands, children and kin networks. The small number of women credited in the census as family workers and villagers compared with men supports the suggestion that women's work was inadequately recognised in the censuses of the 1970s. Thus, the long expected duration of economic inactivity for women did not reflect freedom to choose.

Inequality in Fiji in the post-independence period was thus multifaceted. It could exist in monetary or non-monetary dimensions. The way in which it existed in these two dimensions could be either mutually reinforcing or offsetting. The pattern of inequality also differed on the basis of certain group characteristics: whether someone was male or female, rural or urban, indigenous Fijian or Indo-Fijian. The research had clear implications for social policy: there was an obvious need to be sensitive to differences in patterns of life between Fiji's two main ethnic groups while at the same time using common principles to be even-handed in resourcing the differing needs of indigenous and Indo-Fijians.

This pattern of inequality did not significantly change during the 1980s. During the early 1980s Fiji underwent a multidimensional crisis. Economic indicators were moving violently as a consequence of the second major oil price rise and major fluctuations in the world market price of sugar. Environmentally, the impact of a year of drought was compounded by cyclone Oscar early in 1983; both had mutually reinforcing negative consequences for the sugar crop, the economy and thus for inequality.

The multidimensional crisis damaged the process of social development in Fiji. Studies of poverty in the early 1980s suggested that there were roughly equal proportions of vulnerable people in both ethnic groups, though the risk of deep poverty may have differed between the two groups (United Nations Development Programme/Government of Fiji 1997). Thus, both major ethnic groups had, as in the 1970s, broadly comparable experiences of socioeconomic deprivation and inequality, although this must be qualified by the recognition that specific differences in monetary income, economic activity, economic inactivity and non-monetary indicators were, as in the 1970s, real.

The crisis demanded confident leadership; however, the Fiji government was unable to provide such leadership. In 1982 Fiji's socioeconomic development started to be governed by the dictates of neoliberalism. The failure of the government to provide confident leadership signalled the end of the independence 'honeymoon', exposed the ideological bankruptcy of the 'Pacific Way' as an innovative development strategy and facilitated the emergence of claims based upon regional, class, gender and environmental conditions. At the heart of these claims lay a common set of demands: for an end to an élite-dominated, socially exclusionary politics based upon ethnic mobilisation; and for the construction of a less unequal, socially-inclusionary multicultural polity in Fiji.

The 1985 Fiji Trades Union Congress annual conference was a vital event in the process of the formation of the FLP as an organised expression of such demands. The FLP was not only needed to halt the erosion of the hard-earned rights of organised labour, but also to represent the demands of wider interests seeking to challenge the dominant status quo. This challenge had strong social policy implications: the emergence of the FLP helped to initiate a society-wide debate on the future of multicultural relations in Fiji, and, more particularly, the way in which social policy could be configured so as to facilitate a less unequal, socially-inclusionary multiculturalism in Fiji.

The previously predominant politics of ethnicity offered a fundamental challenge to those who sought to justify broad-based interventionist social policies designed to reduce inequalities in wealth, income and consumption, and to encourage the full expression of the capabilities of all citizens. The politics of ethnicity were however violently reasserted in 1987. It is not surprising that neoliberalism in Fiji was solidified during a period when the politics of ethnicity were being violently reasserted. With its explicit acceptance of 'natural' difference, neoliberalism is consistent with any politics that emphasises difference; thus, neoliberalism has clear affinities to the politics of ethnicity.

While both major ethnic groups could draw on histories of non-market socioeconomic relationships rooted in active civil societies and deploying strong social wealth to provide education, health care and social security, neoliberal development strategies since the early 1980s may have undermined those aspects of civil society and social wealth that emphasised non-market relationships and guaranteed access to basic needs (Barr 1990; United Nations Development Programme/ Government of Fiji 1997). At the same time, anti-poverty social policy was very weak in the 1980s, in large part because neoliberal ideology both 'naturalises' difference and questions the efficacy of intervention. Thus, neoliberal development strategies since the early 1980s increased inequality and poverty between and within both ethnic groups.

The challenge for social policy

The 1990s have witnessed a sharp intensification of the politics of identity around the world. In many cases, greater sensitivity to the politics of diversity has been beneficial by increasing awareness of the need for socially inclusive policies: for example, increased consciousness concerning the social impact of gender relations. However, this need not be the case. The increasing politicisation of ethnicity within Fiji during the 1980s has meant that dissent and conflict are commonly rooted in the identity politics of ethnicity. The politicisation of ethnicity cannot produce uniform and predictable outcomes. It is therefore clear that the management of ethnic diversity in Fiji remains the major challenge for the next millennium. Social policy has a major role to play here. In that social policy is an intervention by the state designed in general to alter the distribution of social and economic insecurity, a critically important way by which social policy can reduce the experience of economic insecurity is through a reduction in the degree of inequality found within Fiji. In fostering socioeconomic security, social policy can build trust which can in turn help create the foundations of a new pattern of multicultural relations—one which recognises difference while noting common ground. Moreover, social policy can provide, or not provide, resources to challenge and change already-existing patterns of multicultural relationships.

The challenges that the state in Fiji confronts in social policy are not those of detail. Social policy must confront the deeper problems of ethnic tension and contradictory developmental values. The challenge now is thus to develop a social policy that complements and augments the strengths of those civil society institutions which remain strong despite more than a decade of neoliberalism. The state needs to institutionalise positive socioeconomic processes which build upon existing social wealth in order to develop a less unequal, socially-inclusive society with higher levels of trust and an improved quality of life for the people of both ethnic groups. Meeting this fundamental challenge will contribute to eradicating poverty, ill health, and insecurity. This challenge demands much of the state in terms of creating an atmosphere for new interventions. Clearly, the agenda facing the new government is large. Space precludes detailed consideration of the breadth of interventions that could contribute to eradicating insecurity and building a socially inclusive society. Rather, three areas where new interventions would be welcome can be briefly discussed. These three areas are health and nutrition, schooling and community relations.

Health and nutrition

The relationship between undernutrition and poor health status has been emphasised in international conferences and is widely accepted as a 'stylised fact' (Asian Productivity Organisation 1991). However, the availability of sufficient calories is neither a necessary nor a sufficient condition to break the link between diet and ill health. This is because the way in which diets change in the process of development can be a major cause of ill-health (Bonnemaison 1978; Thaman 1983; Cameron 1991). This has been the case in the South Pacific in general, and Fiji in particular, since the late 1970s.

Fiji's Eighth Development Plan was the first plan to highlight the 'promotion of proper nutrition' (Fiji Central Planning Office 1980:267) as the first priority of health policy. The 1980s saw some efforts in nutritional education as part of health policy. In practice, however, health policy in general and nutritional policy in particular has been uneven, primarily in terms of its spatial distribution, but also in terms of its impact on lower income households, as under neoliberalism market forces have been used increasingly to allocate access to nutritional and health care resources.

The increasing resort to market forces, particularly in the allocation of access to nutritional resources in Fiji, has resulted in a dietary and lifestyle revolution over the past 20 years. This revolution has brought with it a number of health problems that resemble those of richer economies, and particularly the significant increase in vulnerability to diseases linked to diet. The source of these problems is not however undernutrition. Rather, it is the contradictory articulation of unbalanced diets and overnutrition as the allocation of access to nutritional resources has become market-led. Unbalanced diets and overnutrition imply a different set of issues than those conventionally found in developing countries. In particular, it implies that poor nutritional status can exist side by side with good nutritional status, and that different policies are required to deal with the two sets of issues.

In the case of poor nutritional status, an association between high food imports and low status can be observed and positively links economic policies, health policies and nutritional policies. A cross-section of the overall level of Fiji's food imports in the 1980s showed a relatively high level of food imports, expressed in US dollars per capita per year. Under neoliberalism, the ratio of food imports per capita has increased. More imported food generally means a diet consisting of greatly increased proportions of refined sugar and saturated fats from both fatty meat and dairy products, with an associated higher energy intake. But more energy and less dietary fibre, in conjunction with the reduced physical activity associated with urbanisation, places stress on the body and can produce ill health, lower productivity and, in general, a lower quality of life.

Granted, if diets prior to the increase in the intake of imported food had contained little animal-derived protein or were highly restricted in the variety of foods on which they were based, then the 'gastronomic transition' might have had some desirable nutritional effects, which may in turn have offset some of the undesirable ones. However, except in the extreme conditions of natural disaster, there is no reason to believe that people living in such a biodiverse environment as that found in Fiji were regularly deprived of energy or protein. In these circumstances, few food imports are in any sense nutritionally 'essential'. An argument can therefore be made in favour of reducing food imports. Health and nutrition policy would then have a trade impact, by discouraging the use of low quality imported food and returning to greater self-provisioning, a return that would be predicated upon deepening investment in social wealth. Indeed, the peoples of Fiji, of both major ethnic groups and all income levels, have, by not making full use of the capacity of their environments to provide healthy diets, unnecessarily high risks of ill health. However, self-provisioning should not be taken to mean exclusively community-based production. Self-provisioning can also have a regional and a national dimension; indeed, it must have this dimension if it is to foster the development of social wealth between the two major communities in Fiji.

Two possible policy options exist which would increase the ratio of self-provisioned food. The first would be to ban or impose quotas on imported items which were judged to be actually harmful nutritionally; this should not be ruled out, although it is up to nutritionists to make the case in Fiji. The second would be to raise duties differentially over time in a manner that took account of food consumption, nutritional status and agricultural production. Either policy option implies that decisions in the agricultural sector, and macroeconomic policy more generally, will impact upon the nutritional choices available and thus the overall health of the population.

The problem of unbalanced diets has a health impact. In Fiji there has been some evidence of various forms of child malnutrition, notably around weaning, indicating the need to buttress nutrition policy with the promotion of breast feeding and adequately resourced, easily accessed, primary health programs (Barr 1990). There has been much useful experience in innovative primary health care in the public and non-governmental sectors within the South Pacific region. Best practices need to be examined and assessed for their transferability. At the same time, the nutritional well being of adults in both the indigenous Fijian and the Indo-Fijian communities is also a concern. Adult malnutrition may be associated with a number of disorders, such as diabetes, hypertension, cardio-vascular disease and gout (Barr 1990).

Some of these adult diseases are, it must be admitted, also a function of overnutrition. In part, overnutrition has occurred because the peoples of Fiji have not been making full use of the capacity of their environment to provide healthy diets suitable to their cultural, and possibly physiological, potential. At the same time however the social and political upheavals of the last decade may have contributed to self-induced ill health. The possibility of self-induced ill health and its related health care costs suggests a peculiar variation on the syndrome described by Illich in the 1970s (Illich 1976). In this view, changes in diet can be a reflection of more general cultural, economic and ecological pressures. These pressures have an impact on nutritional status, giving rise to phenomena such as alcohol abuse, the early cessation of breast-feeding, and other problems associated with 'modernisation'. These pressures are recognisable in many societies. The policy response has to be multidimensional, involving agricultural, macroeconomic, health, education and social policy. The response also raises global issues involving the regulation of transnationals involved in the agro-food sector.

Nutrition has in general not been a resource priority for the public sector. This must change. Health and nutrition policies in the complex mix of environments of Fiji will only be effective when the objectives, targets and strategies of such policies are adjusted to the conditions and needs at the country, regional, provincial, island, municipality and village level. This in turn requires a continuous dialogue between the various levels of government on all aspects of food production, distribution and consumption. There are international models of interactive, community based approaches to social policy formation which might be relevant to the country in this regard.

Dialogue has not been the rule in the past. Specific policy development for nutrition was in the past largely allocated to the Food and Nutrition Committee, which brought together civil servants from various ministries plus representatives of non-governmental organisations and academics with interest in the health field. It can be argued that Fiji's Food and Nutrition Committee needs to be relaunched in order for it to take greater responsibility for coordinating nutrition interventions. For this to work, it is crucial that there are opportunities for people to comment systematically on program and project proposals, not only in the health field but also in the broader sphere of agricultural and marine resource development. In part, this is because in the longer term sustaining access to a nutritious diet means sustaining the environment within which that diet is produced.

Education

In order to foster the emergence of a less unequal, socially inclusive polity, there is a need to develop new approaches to Fiji's school curriculum. Four concepts should be integrated as core principles into Fiji's school curriculum: anti-racism, multiculturalism, global citizenship and sustainable development education. In terms of the first two concepts, a lively debate has been conducted in the education field over the philosophical relationship between anti-racist and multicultural education (Foster 1990; Troyna and Hatcher 1992). This debate can be understood to have been centered on the challenge of presenting anti-racism as a universal, moral obligation for everyone, alongside a multicultural approach emphasising an element of moral relativism within a society. Anti-racism and multiculturalism can be considered to be consistent with the concept of global citizenship, which stresses universal political equality and thus has clear affinities with anti-racism and multiculturalism. Sustainable development education as a concept stresses the role of structural economic factors in fostering social inequality, as well as the impact of choices of technology in contributing to or restricting ecological degradation.

Putting these issues into a formal curriculum context involves differing disciplinary emphases. The demands of multicultural education in schools can be understood as falling primarily upon the arts and humanities, while anti-racist education looks to politics and an element of biology. Global citizenship education requires a basis in environmental science and peace studies, while sustainable development education puts a stress on economics with an element of geography. Experience suggests that multicultural and global citizenship issues as wholly positive, universal concepts may be well understood by younger children. Anti-racism and sustainable development education are more complex concepts. Their more subtle relativistic considerations may be best handled from more local, immediate, experiential starting points which look towards older children and adult education.

Despite the fact there are clear practical problems with handling the four concepts in one consistent framework, the shared values of all the concepts suggests that integrating them into one framework suitable to the specificities of Fiji offers an important challenge to Fiji's educationalists. However, the need to raise the profile of anti-racist, multicultural, sustainable development and global citizenship education within an integrated school curriculum in Fiji can only yield full benefits if even the most committed school staff are adequately resourced and supported by a multicultural, anti-racist ethic in social policy at national government level.

Community relations

Community relations in Fiji turned violent in the 1980s, in part because of a growing criminalisation of urban young men who demonstrated especially violent individual behaviour. Moreover, since 1987 there was a marked increase in the risk of collective violence. The major contributory factor to this deterioration in community relations was the increase in the social acceptability of violence, primarily as a result of the activities of the state in legitimising arbitrary violence. The increased politicisation of ethnicity meant that the potential for violence increased, and powerful interests sought to promote inter-communal hostility. However, it should be stressed that while the potential for violence has increased in the last decade, Fiji has been atypical in that there has been only a limited recourse to the use of violence in civil society. Nonetheless, it remains the fact that there are now larger numbers of men who are ideologically and technologically equipped to engage in violent action. Positive action to reduce the potential for violence is needed as a social policy priority.

In order to reduce the potential for violence, social policy in Fiji needs to be pro-active in building bridges between the two major communities. There is much that can be done in Fiji in developing means of communication and indicators that allow patterns of whole lives, including experiences of coercion and deception, to be understood sensitively at all levels of aggregation and in a way which omits no sub-group of people. Communicating the patterns of the lives of others to people remote from that experience is needed if community relations are to improve. Facilitating unstructured, mutually reflective cultural contact has a role to play in this regard.

Conclusion

Neoliberalism has been dominant in Fiji since 1982. This approach to development 'naturalises' inequality and fosters a degree of social exclusion which, in a divided society, can serve to maintain the status quo. Fiji, both prior to and during the period of neoliberalism, had at best limited success in reducing inequality. This limited success can be easily understood: civil society, social wealth and the NIE constitute a framework that asks questions about the effectiveness of market forces as guarantors of socioeconomic development. At the same time, from the mid 1980s up to and including the 1999 general elections, there have been challenges to inequality and social exclusion in Fiji. Granted, Fiji's history of strong civil society institutions in both major ethnic groups has facilitated social wealth formation and a good quality of life for many of Fiji's people. Nonetheless, challenges remain. The construction of a less unequal, more socially-inclusive, multicultural polity requires that state social policy actively support civil society institutions in both major communities involved in the self-provisioning of healthcare, education and social security, while at the same time augmenting those institutions in a manner conducive to reducing inter-community inequalities and increasing trust. Social policy in health and nutrition, education and community relations can help in this regard.

The people of Fiji still have exceptional room for maneuver with respect to their stocks of social wealth and natural capital. A future, progressive social policy could seek to ensure that all people in Fiji have sufficient knowledge and trust in each other to forego the possibility of inter-community violence. This requires that all people derive sufficient income to sustain themselves in good health, that the degree of equality within the country be increased, while at the same time bequeathing sufficient natural capital to future generations to meet the objectives of both local and global sustainability. Fiji was an example to the world in the 1970s, produced a promising indigenous socio-political movement in the 1980s, has stepped back from the brink of breakdown in the 1990s, and could become a leader in the construction of a more equal, socially-inclusive, multicultural polity. To do this requires a major rethink of the strategic objectives of state social policy, to which this chapter has been addressed.

CHAPTER 7

Labour market deregulation in Fiji

Ganesh Chand

Introduction

In 1991, the military-backed Interim Government in Fiji promulgated numerous decrees that substantially amended the labour legislation of the country. The decrees were a part of a wider set of policies designed to deregulate the labour market, which in turn formed a component of a package of structural adjustment policies. The overall objective of these policies was to reassert the role of an unhindered market mechanism in allocating resources. In Fiji, this objective was to be achieved in various areas. In the public sector, the role of the government was to be reduced; towards this objective, all publicly owned ventures were to be gradually corporatised and eventually privatised. To provide incentives to the private sector, an indirect tax system was to take over from reliance on direct, and particularly income, taxes. In trade, protective policies were to be eliminated and the international market was to determine the prices of imports and exports. In the labour market, the free play of the forces of supply and demand was to determine labour utilisation and remuneration.

While the policy shift towards structural adjustment had begun to be gradually implemented in Fiji in the mid 1980s, it was the military coup of 1987 and the subsequent collapse of the economy that provided the impetus for a rapid implementation of these policies. By the end of 1988, the Interim Government had announced that it was escalating the pace of implementing these policies, in order to revive economic growth. The cornerstone of the revival was to be export-oriented industrialisation. For this to succeed, the government emphasised the need to foster a wage-competitive economy. It was from this perspective that labour market deregulation policies were developed.

For many years prior to the military coups national wage guidelines had been established, either through tripartite negotiations, through government initiative, or through semi-autonomous wages councils. However, within the new economic environment which followed the coups the government began to view such processes of wage determination as being 'not consistent with the flexibility and commercial realism required in different industries to retain a competitive position' (Government of the Republic of Fiji 1993:6). A new agenda was thus developed, a cornerstone of which was labour market deregulation.

Labour market deregulation is an attempt by the state to free the determination of workers' wages from the influence of 'distortionary' institutions like trade unions. A totally deregulated labour market is one where only the worker and the employer determine the wages of the worker, through a process of decentralised bargaining. Wage levels are set through the interplay of labour market demand and labour market supply, which establish an 'equilibrium' wage which 'clears' the labour market. In principle, the equilibrium wage should reflect productivity of the workers. This theoretical perspective informed policy. When delivering his 1991 budget address, the Finance Minister announced that the regime was deregulating the wage settlement process. He argued that a primary cause of distortions in the labour market was 'excessive and uncontrolled union intervention' (Ministry of Finance 1991:21). Policies announced in the budget were followed up, during 1991 and 1992 in particular. The essence of the changes in the policy framework was to limit the influence of trade unions on the functioning of the labour market.

This chapter examines what labour market deregulation has entailed, the reasons for the reforms, and the impact of the reforms on the functioning of the labour market. It demonstrates that labour market deregulation has had a significant effect upon the rate of unionisation, upon strikes and industrial disputes, upon employee remuneration, and upon the structure of employment. The chapter recognises that the new Constitutional settlement has repealed many of the amendments to labour law, which were responsible for these changes. The new government may also move to repeal some of changes to labour law enacted in the early 1990s. Nonetheless, in that the operation of the labour market has fundamentally changed, the impact of deregulation will continue to be felt.

The post-independence labour market

At independence in 1970 the labour market in Fiji was regulated by a set of laws which were inherited from the colonial power, Britain. The key acts regulating the labour market were the Wages Council Act of 1960, the Trade Unions Act of 1964, the Employment Act of 1965, the Workmen's Compensation Act of 1965, and the Shop (Regulations of Hours and Employment) Act of 1965. In the immediate post-independence period, the scope of this legislative framework was considerably enlarged, as state intervention in the labour market deepened.

In part, expanded state intervention in the labour market was designed to offset increased labour militancy. The inflation rate rose from 4.1 per cent in 1970 to 6.5 per cent in 1972, 9.1 per cent in 1973, 11.2 per cent in 1974 and a peak of 14.4 per cent in 1975 (Fiji Bureau of Statistics, various issues (a)). The increase in inflation coincided with growth in formal employment outstripping growth in the labour force (Chand 1996). In a situation of an increasingly tight labour market, worker solidarity increased and the unionisation rate rose in successive years following independence. In large part, worker solidarity increased because most of the post-1959 ethnically based unions had already collapsed by the late 1960s. The trade union movement was increasingly cutting across ethnic barriers, and worker solidarity was on the rise. Unions, with increasing success, militantly pressed the case for improvements in the terms and conditions governing the employment of labour. In 1971 a record number of strikes took place, and a record number of workdays were lost. In subsequent years, strike activity and lost workdays increased so that by 1975, 46 strikes took place involving 12,180 workers and resulting in 57,373 lost working days (Chand 1997). To a large extent, organised labour was successful in pressing its case for improved living standards. The average annual increase in daily wages for the years 1966 to 1970 had been 6.2 per cent. For the years 1971 to 1975, this jumped to 19.5 per cent (Chand 1996).

In that price rises played a pivotal role in sustaining increased labour militancy, the post-colonial state rapidly sought to intervene to limit price rises. In April 1971, under Price Control Legislation, the Government placed certain commodities under price controls. While the range of controls was not very broad, it indicated the beginning of a deeper intervention into both product and labour markets. In 1972 the Prime Minister's working party on unemployment recommended that a Prices and Incomes Board be formed to monitor prices in Fiji and, where necessary, set price controls. The Prices and Incomes Board was established in 1973. It was accompanied by a Counter Inflation Act, which imposed a wage and salary freeze for the year. At the same time, a Trade Disputes Act was passed. Its stated objectives were to provide an 'efficient' system for resolving industrial disputes through conciliation, voluntary mediation, and arbitration; to encourage the voluntary use of third parties by unions and employers so that solutions to differences that they could not solve between themselves might be found; and to provide powers to both the Minister and the Permanent Secretary for Labour and Industrial Relations to intervene in trade disputes, in order to facilitate an early settlement. Clearly, the state rapidly sought to regulate the activities of organised labour. In this light, it is not surprising that the Fiji Trades Union Congress (FTUC), the umbrella body of trade unions in the country, opposed the Trade Disputes Act: it placed limits on the use of industrial action as a tool for workers to improve their terms and conditions of employment. The FTUC held that the Act would 'result in a virtual stranglehold on trade unions. It will lead to reducing the free collective bargaining system to a farcical exercise' (FTUC 1976:9)[1].

Soon after the legislative barrage of 1973, an Industrial Relations Code of Practice was drawn up. Receiving support from the Labour Advisory Board, the Code, though not a legally binding document, aimed at introducing a 'reasonable' and constructive environment for collective bargaining (Leckie 1988:140). Then, in 1976, a Trade Union (Recognition) Act was enacted, which laid down the procedure for the recognition of trade unions.

However, state efforts to regulate organised labour were not working. Workers in general, and public sector workers in particular, were not satisfied with the mechanisms developed by the state between 1971 and 1976. In response to increasing industrial disputes, growing unionisation, and a tense industrial relations climate, in 1976 the Prime Minister, representatives of the FTUC and employers established a Tripartite Forum, in which all three stakeholders were represented. In a sense, attempts by the state to unilaterally regulate the labour market were abandoned and organised labour was formally recognised as a social partner. From 1977 until 1984 the Forum was the single most important institution for wage negotiations in Fiji, developing in particular an institutional framework for the determination of national wage guidelines. The establishment of Wages Councils for various industrial sectors, and the setting of minimum wage guidelines complimented the Forum; both served to strengthen the institutional framework for determining labour incomes in Fiji.

Why reform?

Following the 1979 oil price shock, unstable international prices for Fiji's main export, sugar, and a series of natural disasters, the early 1980s witnessed visible signs of economic stagnation. As economic performance deteriorated, union organisation deepened. In the mid 1970s, the unionisation rate was about 44 per cent. The unionisation rate increased to a peak of 49 per cent in 1982 (Chand 1996). When, in the early 1980s, and following advice from international consultants and multilateral organisations, the government began re-examining the role of the state in light of poor economic performance, the labour market came under particular scrutiny. In line with an emerging neoliberal consensus in the developed market economies, trade unions came to be increasingly viewed in official circles as institutions that create distortions in what would otherwise be a reasonably 'efficient' labour market. Such distortions, it was argued, were primarily responsible for inflation and poor economic performance. In this context, and with a sluggish economy, it came as little surprise when the Government in November 1984 unilaterally imposed a wage freeze and effectively terminated the Tripartite Forum. The 1984 wage freeze heralded the beginning of a new era in economic policy in Fiji: that of structural adjustment.

As a consequence of the wage freeze, the trade union movement announced plans for the launching of a political organisation to safeguard its interests in the legislature. The Fiji Labour Party (FLP), organised and formally launched by the FTUC in 1986, went on to win the 1987 national elections in coalition with the National Federation

Party (NFP). When a military coup deposed the newly elected
government in May 1987, most of the trade union leaders behind the
FLP and the FTUC began to play an active role in opposing the coup,
through the promotion of a movement for the restoration of
democracy. International union solidarity also became a useful tool in
pressuring the military-backed regime to return power to a
democratically elected government.

The coups led to the collapse of the national economy (Sepehri and
Akram-Lodhi, this volume). Given this, a new economic policy
package designed to revive the economy was put in place in 1989. The
structural adjustment process, which had begun prior to the coups,
was accelerated, with the aim of transforming Fiji from an inward
looking economy into one that relied on export processing. The most
important ingredient in the proposed transformation of the economy
was to be the creation of wage-competitiveness with respect to other
export processing economies around the Pacific Rim.

To this end, labour law amendments were promulgated in 1991
and 1992. These sought to address two concerns simultaneously. First,
by weakening trade unionism, the military-backed regime thought it
would weaken opposition to its rule. Second, by weakening trade
unionism, union induced upward pressure on wages would be
weakened, promoting greater wage competitiveness with respect to
other export processing economies.

Ingredients of the reforms

In 1991 and 1992 the Industrial Associations Act, the Trade Union
(Recognition) Act, the Trade Unions (Collection of Union Dues)
Regulations, the Trade Unions Act, the Trade Unions Regulations and
the Trade Disputes Act were all amended so that the substance of each
were substantially changed. The changes in each of these areas are
examined in turn.

Industrial Associations Act

Trade unions usually represent employees of a single employer.
However, employees can have more than one employer: workers may
be seasonally employed, while workers in agriculture may be engaged
by different employers at different periods of the production cycle,
making it impossible to identify a single employer over the entire

production period. In a similar vein, it may be difficult to clearly draw the line between employer and employee. For example, sugarcane farmers produce commodities that are sold to a central purchasing authority. While the central purchasing authority does not employ sugarcane farmers, they clearly have a hierarchical contractual relationship. In these sorts of circumstances, trade unions of the usual definition cannot be formed. Prior to 1991, in circumstances where a trade union was difficult to form, an industrial organisation could be formed to represent collective interests. The 1991 amendments to the Industrial Associations Act barred an industrial association registered under the Act from engaging in any trade dispute or matters connected with the regulation of relations between employees and employees, between employees and employers, or between employers and employers. The change thus restricted, if not eliminated, the capacity of an industrial association to represent collective interests.

As a consequence of this amendment, industrial associations could no longer register industrial disputes. This provision effectively eliminated the power of industrial associations in the sugar industry. These associations were amongst the most powerful of the groups supporting democracy that emerged after the 1987 coups; the amendment thus restricted dissent. The amendment also restricted the capacity of the Fiji Garment Workers Association to represent collective interests. According to a Ministry of Labour official, this 'ensured the garment industry complete freedom from interference by its workers. The effect has been a continuation of individual bargaining in an industry where possible unionisation of approximately 10,000 workers could pose a big threat to a comparatively new industry' (Khan 1994:8).

The amendments to the Industrial Associations Act were also designed to weaken the leadership of industrial associations. Under the amendments, an officer of an industrial association was prohibited from being an officer of another industrial association or of a trade union. This amendment was effectively intended to limit the power of particular trade union leaders who also held official positions in industrial associations. Commonly, these leaders were also active in the democracy movement. In a related amendment, the Registrar of Trade Unions was empowered to declare the election of a Secretary or a Treasurer as null and void on the grounds of the elected official lacking a formal education. A prohibition could also be placed on any person convicted of fraud, dishonesty or extortion. Such individuals were banned for 5 years from holding the position of an officer in an industrial association. While this latter amendment might at first glance appear appropriate, it must be seen within the context of the amendments as a whole; it could be used to bar officials who had breached the amended laws—such as holding dual offices—and who in so doing were found to be 'dishonest'.

Trade Union (Recognition) Act

The amendments to the Trade Union (Recognition) Act dealt with the provisions by which new trade unions could gain recognition. Prior to 1991, when 50 per cent of eligible employees joined a trade union and when there was no rival union a Compulsory Recognition Order could be obtained. This legally entrenched the position of the trade union. Under the amendments, when applying for a Compulsory Recognition Order the percentage of employees who had joined the union had to be based on the number of employees on the date of the application for recognition. The only exception was for those employees who left of their own accord. This amendment thus prevented employers from manipulating the 50 per cent requirement by either firing union members or hiring more non-union workers after the application for recognition had been made. This amendment was obviously to the benefit of trade unions. Many others, however, were not.

One amendment allowed the Permanent Secretary for Labour to exclude from recognition those employees who acted in a confidential capacity or in matters relating to industrial relations. Through this provision the government substantially reduced the number of potential union members in the labour force. Many categories of workers, including administrative and secretarial workers and supervisory and managerial workers, could be excluded from collective bargaining on the basis that they had to maintain confidentiality or that they dealt with staff matters.

A further amendment repealed provisions relating to the compulsory 'check-off' of trade union dues from members of recognised trade unions. Under the check-off provision, employers deducted union dues from pay packets and transferred the dues directly to the union. The repeal thus substantially weakened the financial base of trade unions, as it required financial officers of unions to collect dues from members individually on a weekly, fortnightly or monthly basis, a task which was cumbersome, in part because the fees charged by banks to deduct dues directly from bank accounts was more than the cost of union membership. While the amendment to the Trade Unions (Collection of Union Dues) Regulations allowed unions and employers to enter into agreements to allow for union dues to be deducted 'at source', the provision clearly favoured employers, in that employers could charge heavy fees for this facility.

Numerous unions and industrial associations felt the effect of the repeal of the check-off provision. A case in point is the Fiji Public Service Association (PSA), whose membership fell from approximately 4,500 in 1990 to about 2,800 by late 1992; the fall was to a large extent because of the repeal of the check-off provision. In its capacity as employer, the government negotiated with the PSA over the re-introduction of the check-off system. However, the government sought to drive a hard bargain. It sought a written undertaking from the PSA to acknowledge, support and endorse the labour reform decrees; abrogate the right to strike; cease seeking international solidarity for the trade union and democracy movement in Fiji; and bear the costs of the deduction. That the Government finally agreed in 1992 to maintain the check-off system without condition reflects the efforts of the PSA in the face of attempts clearly intended to severely limit the effectiveness of public sector unions.

In the private sector, following negotiations with employers many unions continued to use the check-off system. But 'the threat of withdrawal...hung over their heads' and 'could force them to compromise their demands' (Khan 1994:10). Indeed, refusal to agree to the maintenance of the check-off system effectively killed some private sector unions. An example was the Fiji Garment, Textile and Allied Workers Union. This was registered in 1992 but was unable to survive as the garment manufacturers refused to provide a check-off system (Khan 1994:10).

Yet another amendment empowered the Minister for Labour to declare as unlawful a strike or lockout over trade union recognition when, in the Minister's view, all procedures governing recognition had not been followed. The Minister was thus provided with discretionary power in declaring strikes concerning recognition unlawful. The effect of this was the elimination of strikes and lockouts over the issue of trade union recognition. The implication of this amendment went beyond recognition, however; in a dispute over wages or conditions an employer could challenge recognition as a means of restricting recourse to industrial action (International Labour Organization (ILO) 1992:161).

Amendments regarding 'unlawful' strikes criminalised certain union activity. Thus, causing, procuring or counseling, or in any way encouraging, persuading or influencing others to take part in any strike, lock-out or boycott which had been declared unlawful were made criminal offences. Similarly, a cessation of work or a refusal to continue work in circumstances which gave rise to 'reasonable suspicion' that the worker was taking part in or acting in furtherance of an unlawful strike was made a criminal offence. A person found guilty of an offence relating to an unlawful strike was also barred from holding any post as an officer of a trade union for a period of two years from the date of committing the offence.

Finally, an amendment gave Ministry of Labour officials the power to demand employers' employment records and from trade unions trade union membership records. In the wake of the coups, and the political environment they created, such an amendment might be considered an infringement of freedom of association. In summary then, these amendments weakened union membership, union solidarity, and union leadership.

Trade Unions Act

Amendments to the Trade Unions Act brought about substantive changes in the industrial relations climate. A starting point was the redefinition of 'strike'. 'Strike' had previously been defined as a cessation of work. This definition was expanded to include go-slows, work-to-rule, the withdrawal of goodwill, breaches of contract of service, and refusing to accept engagement for any work in which the workers were usually employed. A parallel amendment to the Trade Disputes Act similarly extended the definition of strikes. These amendments eliminated the use of 'non-strike' tools as a means of pursuing industrial action.

A second change to the Trade Unions Act repealed the provision for disallowing the registration of unions where a union already existed. According to the Administrator General, Government policy had previously been to encourage horizontal industrial and sector-based unions rather than 'in-house', plant-based, vertical unions. The result had been the rise of some very large unions which, according to the Administrator General, were 'too politically powerful and aligned so that quite often the interests of many of their members get forgotten...[I]n their internal workings, principles and etiquette's (*sic*) of democratic practices do not get observed' (FTUC files 1998). While the Administrator General stressed that the amendment was in line with the advice of the ILO's Committee of Experts and the ILO's Convention 87, this amendment, together with a provision enabling a group of five or more workers to form a trade union, encouraged the formation of 'new' trade unions. This was clearly the purpose behind the amendment. Some of the 'new' unions were ethnically based, while others were management-sponsored. Thus, whereas between 1990 and 1991 only five new unions were registered, between 1992 and 1994, 14 new unions were registered (Chand 1996). Of the newly registered unions, nine were the result of splits within existing larger unions. The amendment thus reduced the power of large unions, and, according to the Administrator General, were expected to 'lead to the formation of a new union federation rival to FTUC' (FTUC files 1998). It comes as little surprise then that according to its General Secretary the provision—by allowing a gold mining company to sponsor a rival workers' council—aided the collapse of the Fiji Mine Workers Union (personal communication 1995).[2]

In a third change to the Trade Unions Act, the section covering immunity from civil prosecution as a consequence of trade union activities was repealed, with the exception of activities which had been endorsed in a secret ballot of union members conducted under the provisions of the labour legislation. As a consequence of this change, unions, officials and members could be sued for loss of output or damage to materials on account of 'illegal' strikes. The immediate impact of this amendment was that it reduced the number of 'wild-cat' strikes from 25 in 1990 and 11 in 1991 to three in 1992 and six in 1993 (Khan 1994:12).

A fourth change was a new provision that required unions seeking international solidarity to get a mandate from their members through a secret ballot. The effect of this was to reduce, through delay, efforts designed to mobilise international support for workers' struggles in Fiji.

Trade Unions Regulations

The Trade Unions Regulations were amended to allow the government to supervise union ballots. The amendments allowed the government to report on the regularity of ballots and to intervene to prevent any irregularity in connection with ballots. An associated amendment required that unions seeking a ballot had to notify the

Registrar of Trade Unions at least 21 days before the date of the ballot. Moreover, proxy voting was disallowed in any ballot concerning executive positions in a union. The amendments also placed a time restriction on the use of the ballot: once balloting concerning industrial action had been completed, the validity of a strike mandate was limited to six weeks. In addition, the amendments allowed the government, in its role as an employer, to directly supervise ballots in civil service unions.

The amendments thus served to limit the right of workers to conduct their affairs according to rules that they had drawn up. They also restricted the capacity of unions to immediately resort to industrial action when seeking to rectify grievances. In so doing, they violated workers' rights to freedom of assembly and organisation. Moreover, they also introduced a degree of arbitrariness into the industrial relations system: pro-regime unions which went on strike without fulfilling the necessary procedural requirements—like the Port Workers and Seafarers Union and the National Union of Factory and Commercial Workers Pacific Fishing Corporation branch—were not charged with violating trade union regulations, while anti-regime unions such as the Fiji Aviation Workers Association were charged with violating the law (Khan 1994:12).

Trade Disputes Act

There have been numerous smaller amendments to the Trades Disputes Act, which together constitute a significant rewriting of the Act. A first set of amendments served to distinguish between disputes of interests, which deal with the procurement of a collective agreement, and disputes of rights, which cover all other disputes. Separate procedural machinery for dealing with disputes of interests and disputes of rights were set up. This provision reduced the number of strikes on disputes of interests from an average of 7 per year between 1988 and 1990 to 2 per year for the years 1993 and 1994 (Khan 1994).

A second set of amendments disallowed individuals or groups of workers or unions who were unrecognised by the Registrar of Trade Unions from reporting trade disputes. As a consequence of this amendment, the Garment Workers Union could not file a trade dispute concerning check-off because it remained unrecognised. Similarly, the government did not recognise a dispute between Emperor Gold Mines and the Fiji Mine Workers Union because the employer had successfully challenged a compulsory recognition order from the Ministry of Labour.

A further amendment repealed the provision of representation by a lawyer in dispute and conciliation proceedings except those before the Arbitration Tribunal. The rationale was to reduce the involvement of outside parties such as lawyers, in order to resolve disputes more quickly. This had a possible benefit for unions because employers had a greater financial capacity to hire lawyers. However, this benefit was muted by the fact that employers could still obtain leave from the authorities to be represented by lawyers.

A key amendment of the Trade Unions Act was an expansion of the list of essential services. Essential services require a forty-nine day notice to the Ministry of Labour before any strike action; strikes thus become a more difficult tool for unions dealing with essential services. Indeed, since the Minister of Labour is empowered to order compulsory arbitration for disputes in essential services, the range of activities in which strikes become effectively redundant has increased as a result of the enlargement of the list of essential services.

The impact of labour market reforms

There can be little doubt that the labour market reforms of the early 1990s have had an impact on the functioning of the labour market. This section discusses this impact. In what follows, attention will be paid to unionisation rates, strikes and industrial disputes, wages and employee remuneration, and the structure of employment. The discussion is largely confined to the trends in these variables; no attempt is made to find a correlation between the reforms and the variables as this would require more detailed econometric testing.

Unionisation

A specific aim of the government when undertaking labour market deregulation was to weaken the influence of trade unions. The unionisation rate can be used as one indicator of the influence of unions. If used in this way, it is clear that deregulation has had significant success. First, union membership has plunged. Table 7.1 shows the unionisation rate in per cent between 1985 and 1995 for different economic sectors.

In the period 1985–86 the overall unionisation rate was 45 per cent. This compares to a peak unionisation rate of 49 per cent in 1982. The rate declined to 37 per cent by 1995, a decline of 25 per cent (Chand 1996). It is of interest to note that the decline from 1985–86 followed the imposition of the wage freeze in 1984, when structural adjustment policies began to be implemented in earnest, and when the capacity of unions to produce a key benefit—wage increments—was directly inhibited by government. Moreover, the decline in the unionisation rate has been systematic in all industrial sectors except mining, transport and finance. Indeed, even in mining union power has been reduced: a management-sponsored 'in-house' union has been created, weakening union autonomy.

The National Union of Factory and Commercial Workers (NUFCW) demonstrates the impact of labour market reforms on a large union. From a peak of 5,021 members in 1972, its membership declined to 2,270 by 1995, a decline of about 50 per cent (Chand 1996). Most of this decline occurred during the structural adjustment period. The decline in the membership of the NUFCW was due to job reclassifications, which has resulted in a higher proportion of 'casual' workers; the formation of new plant-based unions; the collapse of certain branches in factories affected by trade liberalisation; and specific efforts at union busting by management. Labour law amendments empowered management further, thereby creating greater job uncertainty and fear amongst the workers of job losses if they resorted to trade unionism.

Table 7.1 Unionisation rate by sector, per cent

	1985–86	1988–91	1992–95
Agriculture	14.6	12.9	12.5
Mining	12.4	26.7	65.8
Manufacturing	48.8	27.7	24.2
Electricity	32.8	25.5	25.5
Construction	54.2	64.1	45.2
Wholesale/Retail	15.8	18.5	17.6
Transport	33.2	30.5	32.4
Finance	35.3	31.6	42.3
Services	64.8	58.8	54.9
Overall	45.2	38.4	36.6

Source: Chand, G., 1996. 'The labour market and labour institutions in Fiji in an era of globalisation and economic liberalisation', Fiji Trades Union Congress, Suva.

Unionisation rates have also been affected by the already-noted changes in the Industrial Associations Act. One impact of the changes in the Act was to reclassify certain unions as associations, with the consequent 'loss' of thousands of union members. An example is the National Farmers Union: with the reclassification of the union as an association, statistics on unionisation dropped by about 3,000.

A significant aspect of unionisation in the era of labour reforms is that while the rate of unionisation has declined the number of trade unions has increased. In the years 1965 to 1990, 84 trade unions were registered; of these, 25 were cancelled, abandoned or amalgamated with other unions, leaving 59 registered unions. Of these, a maximum of 45 could be considered 'operational' in that they were active, and of these, 36 were affiliated to the FTUC. However, between 1991 and 1997 a total of 36 new unions were registered. Of these, at least 6 were breakaways from existing unions.

The increase is largely due to two factors. The first factor is management-sponsored workers' councils or plant-based unions encouraging sections of the workforce to splinter from existing unions in order to form a new collective bargaining unit. The second factor is turbulence within the FTUC during the period 1991–94. A group within the FTUC sought to gain control of it by actively forming new unions in order to weaken existing unions and, as a corollary, create a potential 'vote bank' for itself within the FTUC. This second factor ceased after 1994, when peace returned to the FTUC and union-sponsored breakaways ceased.

Strikes and industrial disputes

A central objective of the government in introducing changes to the labour laws was to reduce strikes and industrial disputes. Table 7.2 reports strike activity between 1970 and 1997. As Table 7.2 demonstrates, the average annual number of strikes during the period 1970–75 was 51; during the period 1978–84 it was 41; during the period 1988–90 it was 17; and during the period 1991–97, a mere 9. The decline from the 'Tripartite era' of 1978–84 to the era of labour reform of 1991–97 was 78 per cent; in the manufacturing sector the decline was 50 per cent. Table 7.2 also shows that the number of workers involved in strikes declined between the two periods. The number of working days lost, however, rose. The rise in the number of working days lost is explained by three specific strikes: the Fiji Bank

Table 7.2 Strike activity, 1970–97

	Overall strike activity			In manufacturing		
	Number	Workers	Work Days	Number	Workers	Work Days
1970–75	51	7765	47846	6	1465	9938
1978–84	41	3721	20970	6	1126	4283
1988–90	17	1640	50433	9	826	40699
1991–97	9	1763	36399	3	1009	11934

Source: Ministry of Labour records/Unpublished data held at Ministry of Labour, Suva.

Employees Union strike in 1996, involving 656 workers and 11 days; and the 1995 and 1997 Fiji Sugar and General Workers Union strikes, involving around 800 workers over 10 and 16 days respectively.

In terms of industrial disputes, Table 7.3 provides data on the number and nature of industrial disputes between 1980 and 1997. Table 7.3 demonstrates that disputes reported rose from 63 per year during the period 1980–86 to 102 per year during the labour reform era of 1991–97—an increase of 62 per cent. The basis of this increase is a jump in disputes relating to the dismissal of workers and the log of claims. Those relating to dismissals rose from 19 per year during the period 1980–86 to 34 per year during the labour reform era of 1991–97 —an increase of 79 per cent. The number of disputes relating to either a refusal to negotiate log of claims or disputes over the application of log of claims rose from 9 per year in the period 1980–86 to 30 per year in the period 1991–97—a jump of over 230 per cent. The jump in disputes on refusal to negotiate unions' log of claims can be explained in terms of the attitude of employers towards trade unions in the era of labour market reform, which re-asserted the philosophy that it is management's prerogative to exclusively determine the terms and conditions of employment, as well as a more aggressive approach by trade union leaders who had become discouraged over the lack of consultation about labour market deregulation at the firm as well as at the national level.

Table 7.4 provides evidence on modes of dispute resolution between 1980 and 1997. Table 7.4 demonstrates that in the period 1980–86 and 1991–97, there was a 48 per cent decline in the incidence of settlement through the conciliation machinery provided by the Ministry of Labour. At the same time, there was a 68 per cent increase in the resort to arbitration. Thus, reliance on conciliation mechanisms has declined significantly during the era of labour market reforms.

Table 7.3 Number, nature and composition of disputes

	1980–86			1991–97		
	Total	%	Yearly	Total	%	Yearly
Dismissal of workers	135	31	19	239	33	34
Log of claims negotiation	62	14	9	212	30	30
Conditions of employment	61	14	9	40	6	6
Non-payment	63	14	9	4	0	1
Breach-collective agreement	50	11	8	162	23	23
Job evaluation	7	2	1	1	0	0
Others	62	14	9	55	0	8
TOTAL	439	100	63	713	100	102

Note: From 1993, job evaluation related disputes were merged with others, while non-payment was merged with breaches of collective agreements. 'Others' include disputes over redundancies.
Source: Ministry of Labour records/Unpublished data held at Ministry of Labour, Suva.

The effect of labour market reform has therefore been to increase reliance on arbitration to settle industrial disputes. The arbitration mechanism for the settlement of disputes was established by the Trade Disputes Act, which provided for one or more arbitrators to resolve disputes. A key reason for the increasing reliance on arbitration procedure in the era of labour market reform is that the incidence of non-agreement has increased. With the rapid rise of a professional cadre of unionists seeking to justify their positions and pay, with the establishment of a new generation of management asserting its right to make decisions, and with an inability of the government to keep pace with the negotiation and analytical skills of employers and unions, seeking a binding solution from an arbitrator often seems preferable to conciliation. As a past Arbitration Tribunal put it, the 'process has made an excuse for avoiding or evading extensive negotiations and conciliation' (Madraiwiwi 1994:6).

Wage and salary trends

Table 7.5 provides evidence on trends in real wages between 1972 and 1996, using the wage settlements of the 1977–84 Tripartite era as the basis of a comparative index. Table 7.5 demonstrates that while the mining sector did particularly well during the labour reform era of

Table 7.4 Dispute resolution

	1980–86			1991–97		
	Total	%	Yearly	Total	%	Yearly
Voluntary arbitration	95	23	14	41	6	6
Compulsory arbitration	3	1	0.4	124	17	18
Industrial Relations Committee	13	3	2	106	15	15
Conciliation Machinery	240	58	34	124	17	18
Pending	38	9	5	72	10	10
Withdrawn	11	3	2	74	10	10
Dead Locked	17	4	2	21	3	3
Rejected	0	0	0	97	14	14
Sent back to parties	0	0	0	44	6	6
Other	0	0	0	14	2	2
Total	417	100	60	717	100	102

Sources: Chand, G., 1996. 'The labour market and labour institutions in Fiji in an era of globalisation and economic liberalisation', Fiji Trades Union Congress, Suva; Ministry of Labour records/Unpublished data held at Ministry of Labour, Suva.

1992–96, so too did electricity, commerce and agriculture. However, with the exception of commerce, the sectors where the private sector predominates—manufacturing, construction, and transport—fared badly during the labour reform era. The manufacturing sector showed a marked decline; its average real wages were only 68 per cent of the 1977–84 level in the period 1992–96. Overall, Table 7.5 shows that there was a decline in real wages during the era of labour market reform between 1992 and 1996.

Table 7.6 displays salary data for the period 1970–96. It shows that, in general, the era of labour market reform from 1992 to 1996 has produced gains for salaried workers when compared to the immediate post-coup period. This is particularly the case for private sector workers with scarce skills, such as professional and technical workers. The trend away from national-level salary setting through Tripartite mechanisms and towards enterprise-based bargaining could be one reason for the improvement in relative salaries. However, the key finding of Table 7.6 is that real salaries in the era of labour market reform have, in general, declined when compared to those in of the Tripartite era salaries. The exceptions to this trend are the agriculture, mining and transport sectors.

Table 7.5 Real wage ratios

	1972–76	1977–84	1985–86	1987–91	1992–96
Agriculture	102	100	87	86	91
Mining	102	100	92	92	114
Manufacturing	90	100	90	72	68
Electricity	83	100	100	89	94
Construction	92	100	91	84	83
Commerce	94	100	91	79	84
Transport	91	100	95	86	84
Services	91	100	92	81	81
Overall	91	100	92	80	79

Note: The data expresses real wages as a percentage of the average 1977–84 real wage.
Real wage data is the average daily wage rate deflated by the consumer prices index.
The base year is 1972.
Source: Fiji Bureau of Statistics, (various issues). *Current Economic Statistics,*
Government Printer, Suva; *Annual Employment Survey*, Government Printer, Suva.

Table 7.6 Real salary ratios

	1970–76	1977–84	1985–86	1987–91	1992–96
Agriculture	92	100	97	95	118
Mining	124	100	87	125	141
Manufacturing	94	100	98	92	94
Electricity	92	100	87	80	89
Construction	99	100	78	72	83
Commerce	103	100	98	92	96
Transport	85	100	105	91	105
Finance	94	100	98	92	98
Services	84	100	112	91	95
Overall	88	100	105	90	96

Note: The data expresses real salaries as a percentage of the average real salary for the
period 1977–84. Real salary data is the average annual salary deflated by the consumer
prices index. The base year is 1970.
Source: Fiji Bureau of Statistics, (various issues). *Current Economic Statistics,*
Government Printer, Suva; *Annual Employment Survey*, Government Printer, Suva.

Employment structure and gender differentials

It can be hypothesised that the deregulation of the labour market
might have had an impact on the structure of employment in Fiji.
Moreover, it might be hypothesised that the increasing
commercialisation of the economy under adjustment might have led to
an increasing proportion of females in the labour force: the increased

availability of jobs perceived to be predominantly for females and the decline in the relative number of 'traditional male jobs', like those in commercial agriculture, would tend to attract more females into the labour market. These propositions are examined in Tables 7.7 and 7.8. Table 7.7 gives the sectoral composition of employment by gender for the period 1980–93. Table 7.8 gives the structure of wage and salary remuneration by gender for the period 1980–93.

Table 7.7 shows that the female share of formal employment has increased from 20 per cent of total employment in 1980 to 31 per cent of total employment in 1993. Within the increasing 'feminisation' of the labour force, there has been a particularly sharp jump in the proportion of females working in the manufacturing sector (Table 7.7). In 1986 the share of females in total manufacturing sector employment was 16 per cent. By 1993, the female share of total manufacturing employment had doubled, to stand at 32 per cent. This dramatic increase is the result of economic policy. The shift to export-oriented industrialisation in Fiji under structural adjustment was largely based on garment and footwear processing in 'tax-free' manufacturing sites which were actively promoted by government policy; both these industries grew rapidly following the coups, just as both these industries relied predominantly on female labour.

Table 7.7 The sectoral composition of employment by gender

Year	% of females in manufacturing	% of females in distribution	Total females in employment	Female labour force (% of total)
1980	10.3	24.7	14402	20.29
1981	11.1	22.2	15516	22.04
1982	10.7	23.3	14613	21.81
1983	13.0	24.3	15814	22.42
1984	13.3	23.7	17117	22.91
1985	13.8	22.0	19027	24.60
1986	15.6	20.8	18999	25.09
1987	18.9	18.3	19563	26.14
1988	20.2	18.9	19655	26.94
1989	28.7	18.4	24725	29.35
1993	32.3	18.8	31126	30.50

Source: Devi, P. and Chand, G., 1997. 'Female employment and earnings' in G. Chand and V. Naidu (eds), *Fiji: coups, crises, and reconciliation, 1987–1997*, Fiji Institute of Applied Studies, Suva.

The increasing feminisation of the workforce is essentially taking place in the private sector. Indeed, there has been a decline in the share of females employed in the public sector, from 45 per cent of total employment in 1986 to 29 per cent of total employment in 1993 (Devi and Chand 1997). Public sector jobs are, comparatively speaking, more secure than private sector jobs; thus, the feminisation of the workforce and the predominance of females in the private sector also suggests increasing employment insecurity.

In addition to a possible increase in employment insecurity, the feminisation of the labour force has not been accompanied by a shift into the 'salariat' by females. Salaried jobs carry relatively greater stability, greater job-related benefits, better fringe benefits, better prospects of upward mobility, greater authority, and more social prominence. They are, in short, more 'desirable'. Table 7.8 shows the female share of total wage employees rose from 14 per cent in 1980 to 28 per cent in 1993. By way of contrast, in salaried employment the female share of total employment rose from only 31 per cent in 1980 to 34 per cent in 1993. Moreover, this trend peaked in 1985, and remained reasonably unchanged thereafter. Thus, while female employment over the period has increased, the concentration of female workers in

Table 7.8 Wage and salary structure by gender

	Wage employment		Salaried employment	
	% females	% males	% females	% males
1980	13.9	86.1	30.5	69.5
1981	15.4	84.6	31.2	68.8
1982	16.6	83.4	28.6	71.4
1983	16.7	83.3	30.2	69.8
1984	17.1	82.9	30.4	69.6
1985	17.1	82.9	34.7	65.3
1986	18.1	81.9	34.3	65.7
1987	20.7	79.3	33.2	66.8
1988	22.2	77.8	32.6	67.4
1989	27.2	72.8	32.3	67.7
1993	28.1	71.9	34.1	65.9
Averages:				
1980–86	16.4	83.6	31.4	68.6
1887–93	24.6	75.5	33.1	67.0

Source: Devi, P. and Chand, G., 1997. 'Female employment and earnings' in G. Chand and V. Naidu (eds), *Fiji: coups, crises, and reconciliation, 1987–1997*, Fiji Institute of Applied Studies, Suva.

relatively more desirable jobs has stabilised. Moreover, in terms of earnings, female earnings as a proportion of national income have increased by only 0.7 per cent between the 1980–86 and 1987–93 periods (Devi and Chand 1997). Almost the entirety of this minimal rise has been due to the rise in the female wage earnings component of national income. In summary, it is clear that in Fiji women are increasingly becoming a cornerstone of the working class, and that in part the reason for this structural change is, simply, that women are paid less than men.

Ethnic differentials

It can be hypothesised that labour market reforms would also have had an impact on ethnic differentials in the labour market. Concrete evidence of ethnic differentials requires employment and earnings data by ethnic categories, but these are not available. Nonetheless, three comments can be made.

The first comment is that, as noted earlier, the reforms were brought in following the coups; one purpose behind the weakening of what were predominantly multiethnic trade unions was to increase the role of ethnicity in Fiji society, and thereby weaken anti-regime forces. As a consequence, it might be expected that labour market reform would have had an impact on ethnic differentials. It is in part for this reason that unions with a predominantly Indo-Fijian membership base—like the National Farmers Union—were specifically targeted by the amendments. However, in most instances the expected outcome did not materialise. In the case of the National Farmers Union, the union remained strong, vibrant and multiethnic, largely because of its strength in the sugar industry.

The second comment is that despite ongoing centers of trade union strength, the reforms have succeeded in creating labour market conditions in which individual workers have become relatively vulnerable, and this may have had an ethnic dimension. In its 1998 Country Report on Human Rights Practices, the US Department of State (1999:15) noted that 'Indo-Fijians, who generally require a cash income to survive, are more vulnerable to pressure to work long hours than are ethnic Fijians. Many ethnic Fijians can and do return to their villages rather than work what they consider excessive hours'. In a sense then, the greater reliance on the cash economy found within the Indo-Fijian community may, in the context of labour market reforms, have increased the vulnerability of the Indo-Fijian community.

The third comment supports this point. Public sector jobs in Fiji are dominated by indigenous Fijians, while private sector jobs are dominated by Indo-Fijians. Given that labour market reforms negatively affected private sector employment and earnings more than they affected the public sector, Indo-Fijian workers have possibly been subject to a more severe impact than indigenous Fijians.

In summary, while definitive evidence on the ethnic impact of labour market reforms has yet to emerge, there is reason to believe that the reforms have had a larger impact upon the Indo-Fijian labour force.

The new constitutional settlement

The operation of the labour market has changed significantly since the labour legislation amendments of the early 1990s. Expecting a significant deterioration in the state of trade unionism, the trade union movement launched an intensive campaign against the amendments. Internationally, the FTUC, through the International Confederation of Free Trade Unions and the Public Services International, lodged complaints to the ILO. The ILO rejected many of the FTUC's complaints; these included the administrative restrictions on recognition, the exclusion of certain categories of workers from recognition, the notice and secrecy requirement governing strike action, and the removal of compulsory check-off facilities. The ILO accepted the other complaints of the FTUC and asked the Government to amend the amendments 'so as to leave the necessary autonomy to worker's organisations' (ILO 1992:174).

The government did not take any serious step to meet any of the ILO's recommendations on amending the labour law amendments until July 1997, when the Constitution (Amendment) Act was passed by Parliament. The resulting new Constitution has already had a significant effect upon the industrial relations framework in Fiji. This is because of the fact that under Section 195 all decrees relating to labour legislation, except those amending the Trade Disputes Act, the Trade Unions Act, and the Trade Unions (Recognition) Regulations, have been repealed. The amendments that were not repealed concern trade disputes, voting and union dues.

At the same time, the Constitution (Amendment) Act represents a significant advance for labour when compared to other constitutions. In previous constitutions, labour relations were covered under the 'Protection of Freedom of Assembly and Association' provisions of the chapter on the 'Protection of Fundamental Rights and Freedoms of the Individual'. For example, the specific provision in Section 14(1) of the 1990 Constitution was

> Except with his own consent, no person shall be hindered in the enjoyment of his freedom of assembly and association, that is to say, his right to assemble freely and associate with other persons and in particular to form or belong to trade unions or other associations for the protection of his interests.

Under the 1997 Constitution a specific section is devoted to labour relations. Section 33 of the new Constitution specifically provides for the right to collectively organise and bargain. It states

(1)   Workers have the right to form and join trade unions, and employers have the right to form and join employers' organisations.

(2)   Workers and employers have the right to organise and bargain collectively.

(3)   Every person has the right to fair labour practices, including humane treatment and proper working conditions.

The provision of these rights is a major achievement for labour in Fiji, in that legislation must be consistent with the Constitution. The right to bargain collectively presupposes union recognition. The latter presupposes the existence of a union. Moreover, it is possible, even likely, that those 1991 and 1992 amendments which were not repealed under the new constitutional settlement may eventually be deemed to be inconsistent with the provisions of the Constitution.

Nonetheless, the optimism engendered by the new constitutional settlement must be tempered. The 1997 Constitution will affect a labour market that operates in a very different way from that which existed prior to the amendments of the early 1990s. It remains to be seen whether the 'success' of the labour market reforms of the early 1990s will effectively reduce or indeed negate the impact of the new Constitution on the operation of the labour market.

Conclusion

This chapter has examined labour market deregulation in Fiji. Tracing the background to the deregulation policies, the chapter has documented the objectives of the deregulation drive, the key mechanisms for deregulating the labour market, and some consequences of the deregulation. It has been argued that the deregulation of the labour market was a central part of the wider structural adjustment policies that Fiji began adopting in the mid 1980s. The military coups and the subsequent collapse of the economy provided the opportunity for Fiji to push ahead with the adjustment program. Since the basis of the adjustment program was export-oriented industrialisation, and this required, in the view of the government, a wage-competitive economy, the government attempted to restructure the operation of labour market in order to foster wage competitiveness. A second central objective was to reduce the power of trade unions, since many trade union leaders were leading the democratic movement in Fiji.

To this end, labour laws were amended by decrees and national wage settlement mechanisms terminated. Deregulation had, in broad terms, four consequences. The first was that the decline in the unionisation rate, which had begun in the early 1980s, rapidly accelerated, particularly in the manufacturing and construction sectors. The second consequence was that while both the number and intensity of strikes fell significantly, industrial disputes increased as the conciliation machinery provided by the Ministry of Labour fell into disuse, being replaced by the resort to arbitration. The third consequence has been an overall decline in real wages, particularly in the manufacturing, construction and transport sectors—sectors where the private sector dominates. The fourth consequence has been a change in the employment structure, where there has been a significant increase in the number of women employed in low-paid jobs, particularly in the manufacturing sector, and specifically in the garment and footwear industries.

The new Constitution has repealed some of the decrees that were promulgated during 1991 and 1992. However, this has occurred after a significant transformation in Fiji's labour market. Despite the already apparent consequences of this transformation, the long-term impact is not clear. What is clear, however, is that labour markets have never operated according to the principles of neoclassical economics. Even if 'distortions', in the form of trade unions, were not present, the mere fact that the agents entering into the bargaining process do so with vastly unequal economic strength implies that the terms and conditions of negotiation are affected by the economic strength of the agents who are undertaking the negotiation. Power hierarchies thus structure the operation of the labour market, and it is for this reason that there is a role for the state. The state provides the institutional framework within which the labour market operates, and thus within which negotiations between unequally endowed agents occur. When the institutional framework reflects the collective will of the citizenry, labour market outcomes will usually be regarded by the various participants as 'just'. When the institutional framework does not reflect the will of the people, labour market outcomes will not be regarded as just. There can be little doubt that the new Constitution, in repealing many of the labour legislation amendments of the early 1990s, suggests that the institutional framework structuring labour market outcomes in the early 1990s was regarded, by many of the peoples of Fiji, as unjust. This may in turn help in part explain the outcome of the 1999 general elections. The past can be undone; but whether the peoples of Fiji continue to choose to do so remains to be seen.

Endnotes

1. Fiji Trades Union Congress files held at the FTUC Building, Suva.
2. Transcribed interview with the General Secretary of the Fiji Mine Workers Union, 1995.

CHAPTER 8

Women in post-coup Fiji: negotiating work through old and new realities

Jacqueline Leckie

Introduction

The political economy of post-coup Fiji has profoundly shaped women's lives, expectations and identities. Changes in gender relations were evident by 1987, but the unprecedented upheavals of the coups and subsequent political and economic restructuring accelerated change for Fiji's women. Initially, many bore the negative consequences of the coups as silent individuals; a few celebrated new opportunities as role models for their gender and ethnic group. Women have increasingly recognised, to varying degrees, a commonality behind the changes that have taken place. Change is a reflection of their cultures, the legacy of colonialism, the education system, the impact of the post-coup regime, and globalisation. For women, gender is the central thread through these changes; but they are also linked to other identities and hierarchies, and especially those of ethnicity and class. In part, this sheds light on the contradictory responses to change from women. Even the most progressive women eventually confront 'old realities', not just from the past but as a daily reality in the present. Similarly, women identified as traditionalists can rarely ignore local and global cultural, economic and political challenges. For most women these extremes are not polarised choices but rather represent what may seem to be a never-ending balancing act between old and new realities, in which personal and collective identities are negotiated to varying degrees. This chapter[1] explores these issues primarily through women's work in Fiji. However, it is predicated on the recognition that it is futile to separate work from other components of women's lives.

Women and work, past and present

Women's labour was essential, providing food and services, during Fiji's initial participation in the global economy, before and after cession to Britain in 1874, when Fiji became dependant on the export of sugar, copra and gold. The plantation-dominated economy was responsible not only for Fiji's distinctive ethnic composition, it also shaped gender relations. For example, from 1879 to 1920 sugarcane was produced on plantations that relied upon indentured South Asian workers. However, regulations stipulated that forty per cent of indentured labourers should be female. Thus, the plantation system utilised women's cheap labour. After the last indenture in 1920, sugar production shifted to small family farms. Cane contracts were only issued to married men, but farms were too small to support extended families. Men therefore worked in sugar mills, harvesting gangs and other forms of off-farm agricultural work. Women and children's unpaid labour was vital for on-farm production.

Colonial policies also sought to regulate indigenous Fijian participation in the paid workforce. Indigenous Fijians were predominantly subsistence workers, but many also took up cash cropping and paid work to meet taxes and buy commodities (Emberson-Bain 1994b:7). However, customary controls on women's geographical and occupational mobility, which effectively restricted entry into paid work, were strengthened by colonial regulations. Nonetheless, women's village, fishing and horticultural activities, while not recognised as 'work' within colonial society, were essential for economic survival, financial resources and community obligations. Thus, I suggest that in common with other societies, women's work in Fiji's villages subsidised the costs, resources and care of the workforce.

Women's constricted involvement in Fiji's paid workforce continued after political independence. Although their participation in paid work expanded, these activities—casual or unregulated, as domestic workers, market vendors, in family businesses, or on farms—were largely unrecorded. Thus, by independence only 14 per cent of women workers were recorded as participating in the cash

economy. This increased to 30.5 per cent by 1992 (Fiji Bureau of
Statistics 1996), representing over 55 per cent of Fiji's 'economically
active' female workforce. There can be little doubt though that these
figures severely underestimate the contribution of women. For
example, only 4,857 women, 5.2 per cent of all, were classified as
farmers in Fiji's 1991 agricultural census (Department for Women and
Culture 1995). Women's farming roles are much greater, however, as
subsistence and unpaid agricultural labour. Much of this work though
is categorised as domestic work, and is thus statistically unrecognised,
because it results in no direct renumeration. Labour force participation
rates therefore reflect the gender bias of official statistics (Cameron,
this volume). The assumptions, terminology and categorisation, and
public identification by women of their working contribution to
society can all lead to gaps in measurement (Waring 1990).

Women's formal employment opportunities are mainly in the
public, retailing, financial, manufacturing and tourism sectors. Today,
two-thirds of women in paid labour in Fiji are employed in
government and manufacturing (International Labour Organisation/
South East Asia and the Pacific Multidisciplinary Advisory Team
(ILO/SEAPAT) 1997:15). Public sector workers may appear to be
comparatively well paid, but their salaries were cut by fifteen per cent
after the coups. Subsequent restructuring, through fiscal cuts,
privatisation, and the corporatisation of government departments, has
had major implications for the high proportion of women working in
the public sector, most of whom are employed at lower levels than
men (ILO/SEAPAT 1997). Thus, while by 1996 women accounted for
45 per cent of civil servants, females represented only 8 per cent of
senior positions, 20 per cent of middle posts, and 48 per cent of lower-
level positions (Booth 1994:18). Moreover, the gendered segmentation
of the public sector labour market was indicated by female
concentration in health and education. In 1996, 48 per cent of female
civil servants worked in the Ministry of Education, Women and
Culture, primarily as lower-level teachers. Even when women are
appointed as head teachers they tend to remain in smaller schools.
Similarly, 75 per cent of civil servants in the Ministry of Health were
women, mostly employed as nurses (Public Service Commission
1996). The gender segmentation of the public sector labour market is
blamed by unionists on management boards. For example, in teaching
'they say women aren't capable, they can't attend evening meetings,

or would feel uncomfortable with a mainly male management committee, but these are lame excuses' (*Fiji Times*, 13 February 1997).

Following global trends, much of the growth in new employment in Fiji is concentrated in an increasingly feminised manufacturing sector. Manufacturing became the main growth area of employment since the coups, accounting for about a quarter of formal employment (Fallon and King 1995:7; Sepehri and Akram-Lodhi, this volume). This work is generally poorly paid, insecure, usually non-unionised, and with low levels of responsibility. Undoubtedly, the garment industry has attracted the most attention in post-coup Fiji. This has become Fiji's main employment growth area and the biggest export after sugar. Garment production was integral to the post-coup government's drive towards a foreign investment-based export-driven economy. State support was delivered through tax-free factories and labour legislation outlined below. Structural adjustment policies, including currency devaluation, external trade liberalisation and internal deregulation, were designed to promote internationally competitive industries such as garments. The impact on female employment was rapid. In 1986 women comprised only 9.7 per cent of the manufacturing labour force. They now account for 50 per cent, equating to 14 per cent of formal sector employment (Forsyth 1996:8). By 1996 the garment industry had an estimated 14,000 workers, the majority of whom were women.

Women's work in garment production aroused controversy because of poor wages, poor working conditions, and little or no union protection. Reports revealed 60 hour work weeks without payment for overtime. They noted inadequate health and safety protection. They spoke of harassment of workers. They demonstrated no paid holidays, no leave for illness, and no maternity leave (Harrington 1996:3; Ram 1994:246). These reports, however, had a limited impact. Pay had been very poor, with many workers earning only F$20 to F$40 per week. In 1997 a new Wages Council Order set minimum rates at 90 cents an hour for beginners and F$1.10 an hour for trained workers. The order introduced five days of sick leave for workers with three months employment. Garment workers also became entitled to annual leave, paid public holidays and national provident fund contributions. However, at F$1.10 an hour, pay remains very low. Moreover, qualifying for sick leave is more stringent: other manufacturing workers are entitled to ten days leave with no qualifying period.

The focus on the garment industry has spurred awareness of poor remuneration and employment conditions elsewhere. For example, it is argued that the Pacific Fishing Company (PAFCO), a government owned tuna cannery, has tapped into a 'captive labour market' (Emberson-Bain 1994a) of women from villages on Ovalau and nearby islands. Critics have condemned the exploitation of women through poor pay and working conditions. In 1994 these workers earned between F$65 and F$70 a week before taxation and other deductions. However, many women had costly loan repayments to Westpac Bank, so that cash-in-hand might, at the end of the week, be only F$10. At the same time, because of the seasonality of the tuna industry many workers were casually employed, even if they had worked at PAFCO for several years. Emberson-Bain's report also considered the controls and inspection of health and safety for women inferior to that of men.

The position of women workers on Ovalau indicates the conflicting pressures faced by the majority of Fiji's women, who live in comparatively small rural settlements. Farming continues to be the biggest source of livelihood security for all indigenous Fijians, and women's participation in both subsistence and cash farming is essential. A recent study found that women did not regard farm work as 'the sole responsibility of males or that it was secondary to women's roles as wives and mothers. Farm work was perceived and defined as an integral part of women's work' (Fiji Association of Women Graduates (FAWG) 1994:51). Those who took part in the study worked up to five hours daily on family farms, except on Sundays or when selling produce at the market. Researchers throughout the Pacific (for example, Fairbairn-Dunlop 1994) suggest that women's workloads are burgeoning as rural communities become more integrated into market relations. This increased work manifests itself through not only the double shift of farm and domestic work but also through the multiplicity of often contiguous tasks in cash cropping, informal trading, subsistence and community activities. Similarly, women's role in fishing is widening to include not only subsistence activities but also collecting and processing fish and shellfish for the market.

Female farmers, compared to men, have less access to state and financial support. Women's labour has been essential to subsistence farming and cash cropping but there is little recognition, external advice or access to new machinery. Many women still have considerable difficulty in securing loans, lacking not only collateral and deposits but

also confidence. Thus, during 1993, 56 per cent of Fiji Development
Bank loans went to agriculture but only 11 per cent were exclusively
secured by women (Department for Women and Culture 1995:5).
Similarly, Sue Carswell found that agricultural extension officers rarely
consult women on farms. Overall, this 'affects not only the subsistence
situation of rural families but also employability of women in
agricultural activities' (Department for Women and Culture 1995:10).

Opportunities for off-farm labour are also gendered throughout
Fiji, depending on access to industrial or tourist centres. Negative
attitudes continue to persist about Indo-Fijian women in rural
communities participating in formal work. Single women migrating to
towns are considered morally vulnerable in some Indo-Fijian families.
However, economic necessity and individual choice are pushing an
increasing number into seeking off-farm employment. This has
occurred though during the post-coup period, when Indo-Fijian
women were susceptible to employment discrimination. As a
consequence, in many regions off-farm work opportunities for women
are limited to informal sector cash and exchange opportunities, such
as producing crafts or providing services such as sewing. At the same
time, migration depletes the availability of domestic and farm labour.

Rabuka promised better opportunities for indigenous Fijians but
many have experienced greater economic hardship. Rising post-coup
unemployment[2] and retrenchment in the public and private sectors led
to many men being unable to support their families. As the financial
onus fell on women, many could only turn to the informal sector. A
survey of market vendors in Suva revealed ethnic disparity, with 44
per cent of Indo-Fijians supporting unemployed husbands, compared
to only 12.5 per cent of female indigenous Fijian vendors (FAWG
1994:61–2). Ethnic occupational discrimination in the formal sector in
however refracted through gender relations: obtaining work requires
migration from villages, and this has implications for childcare which
many women are reluctant to accept.

Education and gender

The education system, consciously and indirectly, has a key role in
reproducing gender stereotypes. As elaborated below, these are being
challenged, but gendered assumptions within Fiji's communities
channel women into sectors of the labour market and hamper their

ability to negotiate gender and work (Leckie 1997a). Hindu, Muslim and Christian cultures, and ethnic, gender and class stereotypes, structured partly through colonialism, have mediated gender and work through education.

Christian ideals of femininity (Ralston 1990:74–5) and appropriate education, long ago introduced by missionaries, remain prominent in Fiji. Many young women are encouraged or choose to pursue 'caring' or service occupations. The origin of these choices can be traced back to the colonial period: the colonial authorities fostered ethnically and gender-segregated education, which in turn was also segmented by traditional hierarchies and class. The élite attended boarding schools, but most indigenous Fijians had more limited village education, which in turn offered fewer occupational possibilities.

For many years Indo-Fijian women had less access to formal education than their indigenous sisters. In a sample of market vendors (FAWG 1994:21–5, 61), 44 per cent of Indo-Fijians had no education compared to only 2 per cent of indigenous Fijian women. Reasons for such disparities in education and the correlation with occupation are complex. Indo-Fijian communities have preferred to educate male children but the persistence of gender ideology needs also to be considered against economic constraints and family labour requirements. Moreover, expectations of early marriage and gender roles within families have been considerably disrupted by the realities of economic and social change during the past decade. Nevertheless, in 1996 Carswell was reminded of dominant attitudes among Indo-Fijian farming families: 'the girls should be only educated up to class eight [age 13], then keep two or three years home, stay home, just get some education in cooking food and how to put their houses and then seventeen, eighteen they marry' (Carswell 1996, personal communication). According to the Director of Fiji's Council of Social Services, investment in education still favours boys rather than girls (*Balance*, September–October 1997:1). Economic pressures and increasing poverty influence gender choices in allocating money and time for education. Young women's labour may also be needed, especially for childcare, if the mother is working within the family farm, business or elsewhere.

Having said that, education levels for all women in Fiji have increased during the past decade, with high levels of females attending primary and secondary school. Women comprise 45 per cent of students at the University of the South Pacific (ILO/SEAPAT 1997:24)[3]. 'Whatever other aspects of Fiji culture limit the economic advancement of women, it seems clear that existing attitudes about gender have not stopped girls from attending and completing school in large numbers' (ILO/SEAPAT 1997:23). However, these impressive educational achievements are inadequately developed in the workplace, indicating that gender bias still channels women's employment. For example, unpaid farm work is acceptable for women in most cane farming localities but pursuing it as paid employment is frequently considered inappropriate. Community constraints are replicated at the wider state level, with little acknowledgment of women's farming skills in educational and agricultural extension programs. Before 1983 the intake of women at the Fiji College of Agriculture was restricted to two and in 1988 no females were enrolled there (Department for Women and Culture 1995:10). According to Carswell, some change is now evident, with the Ministry of Agriculture, Forestry and Fisheries and the Agricultural Landlords and Tenants Act extension services beginning to recruit female officers, conduct gender awareness staff courses, and incorporate women into programs.

Significant gender disparities remain in technical training. In 1993 women were still concentrated in 'traditional' programs at the Fiji Institute of Technology: business studies, secretarial studies, hotel and catering services. Participation in all courses—which cover management, marketing, and business, with the exception of accounting and secretarial work, offered by the Fiji National Training Council—is mostly by males (ILO/SEAPAT 1997:20). Employers reproduce gendered training opportunities through their selection of sponsorship candidates. Teaching and nursing trainees are predominantly women. Women may comprise over half of the undergraduates at the University of the South Pacific but there is a marked drop in female participation in postgraduate and advanced professional studies.

The introduction of compulsory education in 1997 brought the promise of greater equity, but this was offset by rising educational costs for families and schools, a trend which was accentuated by currency devaluation in early 1998. Books, uniforms and equipment are imported and school fees continue to increase. The impact may however have been mediated by ethnicity. Some researchers argue that Indo-Fijians have less access to a 'community safety net' (ILO/ SEAPAT 1997) compared to many indigenous Fijian families living in villages. Indo-Fijian families are likely to bear educational costs as individual families, while indigenous Fijians usually have more communal and state support. However, as the joint United Nations/ Fiji Government *Fiji Poverty Report* revealed, such assumptions no longer apply to all indigenous Fijians. Indeed, community care may have been lacking for some destitute women in the past (United Nations Development Programme/Government of Fiji 1997:90).

Ethnicity and gender

As this volume reiterates, Fiji's contemporary political economy bears the legacies of colonial practices. These established Fiji's ethnic population; current census figures indicate that 51 per cent are indigenous Fijian, 44 per cent trace South Asian ancestry, and 5 per cent identify with other ethnic backgrounds. This is a reversal from earlier patterns, when Indo-Fijians numerically exceeded indigenous Fijians.

Colonial and racially-bounded hierarchies reinforced ethnic and gender stereotypes and inequalities through both ideology and more visible structures. Ethnic divisions appear to have been cast in stone but in practice were undoubtedly flexible and negotiated (Robertson, this volume). Tensions between essentialised ethnic and gender constructions and their constituencies, and the increasing irrelevance of such categorisation and identity, evoke contradictory dynamics within Fiji society. The implications for women in the contemporary political economy of work are explored here.

Women's identities are more fractured than the seemingly rigid ethnic and gender boundaries moulded by colonisation and tradition. This disruption reflects changes of the past decade, including political upheavals, economic hardship, structural adjustment, changing gender relations, and changing expectations from women. Many progressive women acknowledge the 'messy realities' (Chhachhi and Pittin 1996) of balancing and challenging the gender expectations of their cultures. Despite this, representations of ethnic gender stereotypes are too often simplistic. These idealised qualities may have some purchase on reality; however, they intersect with newer pressures, exacerbated by the coups and late 20th century globalisation. As noted, gender stereotypes are manifested in paid and unpaid work, sometimes confined to ethnicity, but more often cross-cutting these boundaries.

In the Indo-Fijian community, Shireen Lateef has emphasised the reproduction of aspects of South Asian gender ideology in Fiji, most notably the cultural and spatial constraints of *purdah* (Lateef 1990b:44–8)[4]. This stresses gender segregation, male protection of women, and male responsibility for the material welfare of the family. An Indo-Fijian farming woman told Carswell that although she had impressive school qualifications and intended to pursue a career, her father blocked this by arranging her marriage so that most of her activities were confined to the family space. Her husband also prohibited her working outside the farm even when she was offered employment as an assistant teaching in a nearby school.

Limits over women's occupational and spatial mobility are reinforced through personal ties of love and loyalty, fear of non-acceptance in the local community, and bringing shame to the family. Control is also maintained through psychological and physical abuse. Lateef (1990b:43) identified the 'threat and use of physical violence against wives as a powerful and effective mechanism for ensuring the maintenance and reproduction of traditional gender relations among Indo-Fijians'. This is by no means specific to this ethnic community. Women can face violence when their paid work appears to be interfering with domestic work. Some men become angry over disruption to domestic routines, or when their role as family 'provider' reverses to that of dependent. Women can also reinforce gendered expectations and controls, both over themselves and other women.

Although violence against women features in all ethnicities, the wider context of fear in post-coup Fiji did have specific implications for Indo-Fijians. As targets of violence, many families tightened controls on women's mobility: 'for Indo-Fijian women the coups represent a retrogressive step in their struggle for greater freedom' (Lateef 1990a:121).

Not all indigenous Fijian women consider the coups to have enhanced their lives. Rabuka declared that he seized power in 1987 to protect and advance indigenous control of power and resources in Fiji. Colonial structures had incorporated these goals, provided they remained within precise ethnic boundaries. Indigenous Fijian paramountcy was bolstered through the strengthening of chiefly authority and European guardianship (Lawson 1991:81–123). Colonial and native administrations and traditional structures and values specified roles that limited women's access to land, monetary resources and political authority. This has been challenged in the post-coup years, but Pauline McKenzie Aucoin's observations of life in the interior of western Viti Levu remains pertinent in the understanding of contemporary gender roles within indigenous Fijian communities.

> Men exercise authority over women. Their authority derives from a number of sources. First, the fact that they are leaders at the societal level—the district, village and clan heads are always male—justifies extension of 'male authority' over family members. In addition, men have control over religious practices that center on the clans' men's houses (*na beto*). Finally, they are considered stronger than women, and strength is valued in Fijian society. These factors allow them to lead society and to be leaders within the clan and the household (McKenzie Aucoin 1990:26; see also Ravuvu 1987:261–80).

Indigenous Fijian customary and hierarchical links of authority and respect are not confined to traditional spheres but permeate gender relations in paid and professional work. For example, nurses have encountered political and family interference in the health sector with irregular appointments to top nursing posts, selection for post-basic training, scholarships and workshops. One nurse noted that 'clan favouritism and nepotism within nursing at CWM Hospital had overruled the power of wisdom and merit' (Fiji Nursing Association (FNA) archives, member to General Secretary FNA, 3 February 1993). Indigenous Fijian nurses complain about the influence of customary status in the workplace. Some tutors are appointed on 'qualifications of blue blood' which 'makes nurses quite passive'. Chiefly rank and state political connections have particularly controlled women's post-coup political and union activities. At the same time, victimisation was common after a major nurses' strike in 1990. Favourable duties, promotions, training and leave were allocated to non-striking wives and relatives of senior health officials (*Fiji Times*, 3 October 1990; FNA, nd).

Clearly, while the specifics of gendered roles in Indo-Fijian and indigenous Fijian cultures are significant, restrictive gender representations are common to women of all cultures in Fiji. These have proved convenient in hiring practices, low pay and gendered skill differentials, particularly in the garment industry, but also in other paid manufacturing work as well. Clichéd stereotypes include women's 'nimble fingers', passivity and the assumption they should be grateful for any paid work as 'half a loaf is better than none' (Slatter 1987). This is because women are perceived by employers as supplementary wage earners, choosing to work for personal motives: 'lipstick', 'pin money', self-fulfilment or social interaction (Grynberg and Osei 1996:15). As a general rule, gendered stereotypes over skills and divisions of labour are carried over into factories. Men's and women's tasks tend to be segmented according to different classifications of skill and remuneration. In many factories men occupy most of the managerial and supervisory roles, work on fully automated machines and in the 'skilled' cutting sections.

Women also repeatedly identify how gendered stereotypes are reinforced by tradition to shape their working predicaments. For example,

> [a]ttitudes about gender provide, first, the immediate motivation and a ready rationale for discrimination. Also, aside from direct discrimination and male actions that discourage them from advancing economically, many women themselves make choices about their lives—about family responsibilities, about training, about career options—that work to maintain the economic differences between themselves and men (ILO/SEAPAT 1997:3).

Imrana Jalal and Wadan Narsey have labelled this a 'culture of silence' that condemns women's assertiveness as disrespectful to those with traditional power. They stress that

> why women remain silent is neither about being inferior, being less knowledgeable nor economically disadvantaged. It is a combination of many factors such as religion, culture, upbringing, the fear of retaliation, the lack of protection—dynamics which attribute to people's expectations of an ideal female in a patriarchal society such as Fiji (*Balance,* September–October 1997:8–9).

Health activist Mridula Sainath (1997:3) found restrictions still applied to business women who were attempting to break out of traditional gender moulds. Although discrimination in accessing loans and credit appeared to be declining, 'what women were really up against were the hostile cultural and traditional environment which does not encourage women to own property and assets. In most families, the purse strings and investment strategies are men's domain'.

Women in Business was founded by Nur Ali Bano to counteract women being ostracised and stereotyped as weak in business dealings (*Fiji Times*, 25 April 1998). Indigenous Fijian representations of men as *qwaqwa*—'hard, strong, tough and resistant'—and women as *malumaluma*—'soft, weak, gentle and easygoing' (McKenzie Aucoin 1990:27)—can apply to women of any ethnicity. Such stereotypes affect professional women. For example, women may numerically dominate teaching but, as already noted, promotion to higher levels can be constrained by culture and tradition (*Fiji Times*, 1 April 1996). This also reinforces the concentration of women in primary teaching (Booth 1994:42–6).

Likewise, nursing (Leckie 1997a) illustrates how multiple hierarchies of gender, family, politics, colonialism and ethnicity overlay one another. The 'Nightingale tradition' of nursing (Bradley 1989:193–4) as an autonomous female space has shaped nursing discourse and practices in Fiji. This fitted into indigenous female healing roles and missionary ideals of feminity, which together resulted in chiefly women being considered as suitable nursing trainees (Fiji National Archives, F48/168 1936). By way of contrast, although Indo-Fijian communities formerly considered nursing to below status, today it is an acceptable career for women and can be valuable when seeking work abroad. Pay and working conditions for nurses in Fiji do not though match this positive status. Many nurses explicitly attribute such discrepancies to the gender inequalities within Fiji's cultures. As one has said,

> customs and traditions have continued to place women in an inferior position. This cultural background colours the attitude of the Ministry of Health, male society as a whole, in regard to nurses and their problems. From time immemorial, therefore, nurses in Fiji have generally accepted their inferior role as an integral part of their existence (FNA archives, FNA General Secretary to Minister, Women's Affairs and Social Welfare, 9 August 1988).

Since the coups, ethnicity and politics have further cut into workplace relations and added to gender discrimination in promotion and training for Indo-Fijian women in the public sector. Some indigenous Fijian women have also found that favours based on regional, kinship and political ties increased during this period. Family relationships are evident in the health sector, where many female nurses are married to male doctors. These ties were invoked to break the 1990 strike. Some nurses kept their strike participation a secret from their husbands in order to avoid conflict with his political identity. Those women who defied their husbands' censure of strike participation were challenging his authority as household head. Contradictions among attitudes to the nurses' strike were reflected in Rabuka's support of their cause while his government declared it illegal.

The coups ushered in a resurgence of indigenous Fijian traditionalism and nationalism but this representation, particularly over gender, was highly contested. Fiji appears progressive at a global level, through the ratification of the United Nations Convention on the Elimination of All Forms of Discrimination Against Women (CEDAW). However, cultural and traditional values supersede gender equality, as Fiji has entered a reservation to two CEDAW articles[5]. This diluted acceptance of the CEDAW is at odds with the declaration of gender equality in Fiji's 1997 constitution.

While some Hindus and Muslims have advocated the maintenance of traditional gender roles to strengthen religious identity, conservative gender roles have been particularly reinforced by post-coup Christian fundamentalism. Christian morality is linked with indigenous identity. A spokesperson for the Methodist Church regarded any differing gender roles or sexualities as a threat to indigenous Fijian values when they stated that

> Fiji must also be cautious of Western influences. Not all good things come from Western civilisation. We must base our future with sound Christian doctrine...we should treasure family values and teach our people to live a healthy moral standard (*Fiji Times*, 13 July 1994).

Christianity remains the religion that is invoked to control labour in Fiji. In the aftermath of industrial unrest at PAFCO during 1993, management encouraged prayer meetings that preached obedience, non-confrontation, love, unity and 'family togetherness' in the factory. Christian values were also reinforced through a company prohibition on adultery, which could illegally result in instant dismissal (Emberson-Bain 1994a:160).

Christianity has also been central to nursing discourse in Fiji, with the nursing establishment encouraging nurses to seek solace through the Nurses' Christian Fellowship rather than engaging in militant or activities. A nursing unionist was frustrated by some members accepting their poor pay because 'nursing is seen as a vocation...[A] real calling...[with] healing hands in place of Jesus. The Lord will reward you' (field notes 1996). The applicability of Christian discourse in the caring professions is however contested not only by non-Christians but also by committed Christians. Biblical texts have been invoked to rationalise rebellious behaviour and to challenge the status quo (Leckie 1997b:135). A prominent FNA official resolved any incapability between her religious beliefs and taking strike action when she said

> the message was loud and clear to me, see the message I was given was Romans 13, I still remember that, it says that we have to honour the government, the government of the day is the one that god, the interpretation that was given to me that the government of the day has set out the strategies to follow in this time of crisis and that we had followed...industrial action was also within government strategies for such a situation which we have done...So that was really clear in my mind, God had chosen this government, this government had given this provision and we were working within that provision. That to me was enough (field notes 1996).

Women and poverty

If subjective gendered stereotyping has few ethnic boundaries in Fiji, so too does the harsh reality of poverty. The gendered impact of poverty reflects women's inferior position in the labour market and changing family structures. Between 1989 and 1991 the percentage of poor urban households doubled from 20 to 40, while in 1993 one in three rural households were estimated to live below the poverty line (Bryant 1993:74). More recent estimates of Fiji's poor vary from the *Fiji Poverty Report's* quarter of the population (UNDP 1997:39) to the Fiji Council of Social Services's half of the population (*Fiji Times*, 28 January 1998). Estimates of the poverty line in 1995 ranged from a low of F$45 per week to a high of F$94.20 per week (UNDP 1997:32–40). The 'economic miracle' of export manufacturing created jobs for women, but the low levels of pay documented above mean that wages, particularly in tax-free factories, fall short of minimum household weekly income levels, trapping many in poverty. One survey found 55.5 per cent of Fiji's female-headed households lived in poverty and among all poor households, 20 per cent were headed by women (Bryant 1993:79). Eighty per cent of very poor families housed by the Housing Assistance and Relief Trust have a female head (Booth 1994:59).

Women's vulnerability to poverty is associated with shifting family structures over the past decade. Accurate figures are not available but it appears there has been an increase in the number of nuclear households, an increase in the number of female-headed households, and an increase in the number of sole parent households (UNDP 1997:76–7). Of 260 female garment workers surveyed in 1993, one-third were sole income earners (Harrington 1994:90). Up to 70 per cent of the mostly female casual vendors at Suva market are sole family income earners (FAWG 1994:27–8, 62). The poverty position of female-headed households has been documented, but given the overlap between female-headed and sole parent households, it is worth noting that conservative estimates derived from the 1990–1 Household Income and Employment Survey of the very poor suggest at least four out of five widowed household heads and two-thirds of separated and divorced household heads are women (UNDP 1997:52). Separated or divorced women are more likely to live in urban areas, where they are dependent on a cash income. However, older and widowed women also may lack support. That

> almost 40 per cent of women heads who are over 60 years of age are economically active is quite remarkable and demonstrates the degree of economic need they experience. In other words, if their families were supporting them, as the stereotypical view of family support nets proposes they do, then this pattern would not be seen. Women are disadvantaged by the job market and must often seek menial jobs, such as domestic workers (UNDP 1997:57).

The economic pressures faced by sole mothers were compounded when maintenance support for divorced women was sliced from between F$10 and F$15 a week to between F$5 and F$7.50 after the coups. To compound this, only 19 per cent of maintenance orders are regularly paid and almost half are defaulted on by ex-husbands (UNDP 1997:64). The meagre resources of welfare agencies, such as the Bayly Clinic, have been under unprecedented pressure since 1987. During 1997 Fiji's Department of Social Welfare exhausted funds to assist the very poor.

Agency and resistance: contradictions and gender

The post coup decade appears to have cast a gloomy despondency over Fiji's women. In many ways economic pressures and political and cultural discrimination have sharpened women's subordination. Yet during these years there have been strong visible actions by women to redress not only their circumstances but also those of others in Fiji. Political contestation, albeit focused on indigenous and ethnic issues, has accentuated concern over women's rights in Fiji.

Although many women are self-congratulatory over their more public assertiveness, this is usually tinged with caution. The contradictions of women's agency were summed up to me by a young nurse who protested about pay and conditions but shrugged her shoulders in defeat and said 'we are women, can't fight' (field notes 1996). This does not mean that women passively accept the status quo but that gender identities and stereotypes override or reinforce other hurdles women encounter in the home, community, workplace, and at national and global levels. Despite these parameters, women do individually and collectively resist the limitations of gender, ethnicity, tradition and poverty, but often covertly. Within both the home and workplace this can be, for example, through sickness or absenteeism. For example, the Indo-Fijian woman described earlier became anorexic after her father forbade her to pursue nursing as a career. She says that she 'really cried for the work and still I don't go well now. I didn't eat food for I think about a week' (field notes 1996). Industrial sabotage and low productivity may also indicate resistance to the labour process. Christy Harrington (1999) reported women protesting by smearing lipstick on clothes or shoddily sewing garment pieces together. David Forsyth (1996:16) attributed the high labour turnover in factories to 'an adversarial and unhappy environment'. This equally reflected employer tactics of keeping costs low by dismissing employees qualifying for full pay rates.

When women publicly negotiate their roles, it is often through established community structures such as religious groups, women's village committees or service organisations. However, beginning in the 1970s, and particularly in recent years, increasing numbers of women have been dissatisfied with 'silent resistance' and conventional 'ladies' organisations. This mirrors global shifts, where women have become more proactive through new feminist movements and within existing organisations, notably trade unions, to confront worsening economic realities. These two strands of collective activism have coalesced over common issues in post-coup Fiji but also diverged over methods, aims and ideals.

Women's networks, involvement and solidarity were vital in workers' protests and achieving union representation. Women in Fiji are active as unionists in occupations where they numerically dominate: nursing and teaching in the public sector, and banking in the private sector. However, overall there has been limited female involvement in Fiji's paid, unionised workforce, and in some service sectors such as tourism representation is seriously lacking. According to a 1993 South Pacific and Oceanic Council of Trade Unions survey, female union membership in Fiji is, at 22 per cent, much lower than in Western Samoa, the Solomon Islands, Vanuatu, the Cook Islands and Kiribati (South Pacific and Oceanic Council of Trade Unions (SPOCTU) 1993).

Initially, the military-backed government banned unions in Fiji's tax-free factories. However, in 1989 the Fiji Association of Garment Workers (FAGW) gained registration as an industrial association. When employers opposed this, workers took strike action (Leckie 1992). In 1990, for example, an international ban loomed when government rejected a dispute over the dismissal of three union activists from Lotus Garments (*Fiji Times*, 2 November 1990). Workers struck for a month over 'appalling working conditions and extremely long hours'. Wages and conditions have improved in some factories, but discontent remains. Despite initial optimism, the FAGW has not been able to maintain this momentum, with membership plummeting from around 2000 in 1992 to less than 700 in 1996 (Forsyth 1996:15). This is due to obstacles from employers—only 2 among 200 firms recognise the union—labour laws, the state, and, admittedly, internal problems within the FAGW.

In contrast, nurses are strongly unionised with around three-quarters belonging to the FNA. There is considerable contestation within the FNA about the association's methods and its identity as a union and as an organisation representing primarily women. Contradictory views on unionism and industrial action were evident during the 1990 strike. The key issue of demands for safe night transport for nurses highlighted deeper labour discontent in the health sector over salaries, understaffing, inadequate promotions and arbitrary transfers. Nonetheless, some nurses who went on strike experienced guilt, describing the strike as a 'sad occasion.....It's unprofessional to go on strike.....the ministry should look after nurses and their welfare' (field notes 1996). One nursing activist was frustrated over divided solidarity within Fiji's wider union movement for the FNA, in part because of its status as an association, and in part because of the FNA's identity as a mainstream women's organisation. Frustration focused around affiliation to the Fiji Trades Union Congress (FTUC). She said of affiliation that

It's still a main issue that comes up in the AGM of the FNA, every year
we have to vote to stay in. I have always maintained when we are out
on our own we will never be able to do anything, if we stick with our
other brothers and sisters especially the ones in the public service then
hand in hand we could fight issues together. Out on our own the Fiji
government could do whatever they want to do and I have always
maintained this issue is religious because that most of the people want
us to get out of [F]TUC. They see it as a satanic organisation, this is the
way they think...There is one argument that says that it [the FNA] was
a women's organisation and the Fiji Nurses Association is one of the
most popular women's organisations in Fiji. I said that only because
we are together with our other brothers and sisters. If we went out on
our own we are nothing, that's what I maintained, we fight it, we fight
it together (field notes 1996).

The ability of unions to represent women workers has been tested
by labour legislation introduced in 1991 to tighten control over unions
and to shape the labour market to meet the need to be globally
competitive. Amendments to the Industrial Associations, Trade
Unions (Recognition) and the Trade Unions Acts (*Fiji Republic Gazette*
1991; Chand, this volume) had specific implications for women
workers, as many were unorganised and new to the labour market.
During 1990 and 1991 garment workers had organised under the
FAGW and taken strike action (Leckie 1992). Local and overseas unions
were lobbied to provide solidarity but the new labour laws impeded
this. Industrial associations, which technically deal with relations
between members rather than between employers and employees, and
which include the FAGW, could no longer engage in labour disputes.
It became illegal to take direct action to achieve union recognition.
One of the biggest changes in the legislation was the registration of
enterprise and employer-dominated unions. This widened the scope
for ethnic fragmentation within organised labour. It also reinforced the
isolation of many women workers in small enterprises, especially
waitresses, retail workers and domestic workers.

The newer women's organisations have been confronting the
realities of women's agency and choices with Fiji's traditions and
economic and political pressures. The two spearheads of feminist
organisation in Fiji are the Fiji Women's Crisis Centre (FWCC) and the
Fiji Women's Rights Movement (FWRM), both founded in the mid
1980s. The FWCC intervenes in situations of sexual assault and
violence against women and children. It educates about these

problems, and lobbies for law reform in these and associated areas. It is based in Suva but in response to an increase in demand since 1987 centres have been opened in Labasa, Lautoka and Ba.

The FWRM also has its roots in responses to violence against women and to economic exploitation, as became visible in the garment industry. Its constitution states that it aims 'to improve women's domestic, social, legal, economic and political status in Fiji and to promote the equality of women in Fiji'. Workplace discrimination heads FWRM's objectives, as outlined in its constitution: 'to remove discrimination against women in the work force such as discriminatory wages, sub-standard working environments, unequal opportunity, restricted access to jobs and promotions, discriminatory and inadequate terms and conditions of employment and sexual harassment'. Linkages between women's economic vulnerability, workplace exploitation, violence and poverty converged in FWRM's Women, Employment and Economic Rights Project. Like the FWCC, the FWRM has extended its activities outside the capital. Its legal literacy, anti-violence and wages for housework campaigns now focus on farming localities.

The FWRM has concentrated its efforts in seeking to change labour laws by removing discriminatory employment legislation which works against women (Emberson-Bain and Slatter 1995), by introducing protection for non-unionised workers, and by enforcing employment equity. To date Fiji has not ratified ILO Convention 100, covering equal pay for work of equal value, and ILO Convention 111, which provides for equal treatment regarding employment.

The debate over women doing paid night work highlighted differing interests over women's rights in post-coup Fiji. Pressures to remove legislative prohibitions on female night employment came from both employers and women's activist groups, notably FWRM and the FWCC (Sharma 1996:1). Garment employers sought an extension of women's working hours to further secure cheap labour and boost production. In practice, women have been doing evening work in Fiji, both legally—for instance as health and hospitality workers—and illegally—for instance as garment workers. Feminists pushed for legislative change, as existing laws were discriminatory. They sought legal sanction for women's right to choose or refuse night work.

They also rejected arguments that had stressed the protection of the 'weaker sex'. Protectionist laws had excluded women from categories of employment, such as underground mining, and could be conveniently invoked when women's labour was not required. Women's restricted mobility was tied to cultural and moralistic strictures which equated the 'breakdown of the family' with women working outside the home. Union voices in post-coup Fiji queried these latter views, but still opposed women's entry into night employment on the basis that it would increase the scope of women's exploitation and increase women's workloads in both paid and unpaid work. The ban on women working at night was lifted in 1996.

Conclusion: old and new realities and women's working futures

For many women in Fiji, questions about the impact of the coups may be difficult to isolate from personal changes during the past twelve years, including gendered expectations from family, community and state. The meaning of the coups varied for women of diverging ethnicity, class, region and religion. These are not easily quantified allegiances, as women sharing such identities may still have diametrically opposed views on the coups and Fiji's post-coup political economy. This has been evident within the FNA.

Women's working lives in Fiji highlight the need for caution in reductionist arguments that attribute gendered changes purely to the coups. The baggage of culture and colonialism is persistent, while globalisation both reinforces past and new pressures. Women in Fiji, as elsewhere, are increasingly in paid work, are household heads, are making significant gains in education, and are active in existing and new political and social structures and movements. Women are also vulnerable to economic exploitation, sexual discrimination, poverty, violence and inadequate political representation.

What of the specifics for the future of women in Fiji, especially within the workplace? Fiji ranks relatively low on the UNDP's gender empowerment index, reflecting women's small share of earned income (ILO/SEAPAT 1997:4). Moreover, the instability of Fiji's political economy does not bode well for women. In many households women experience the direct effects of a faltering economy and a higher cost of living. Economists disagree over the impact of the 1997–98 East Asian economic crisis on Fiji. Nonetheless, the Fiji dollar was devalued by twenty per cent in early 1998, ostensibly to attract foreign investment and tourists. This means little to consumers, for whom the price of imports, including many basic household items, have increased. Fiji long ago ceased to be a tropical idyll of self sufficiency. Dependence on cash income embraces almost all families, including those in very remote villages as well as recent migrants to urban areas.

Garment manufacturing was heralded as a panacea for the economic gloom of the 1980s. Despite low wages, many women welcomed this as an attractive option to work in the informal or domestic sectors. Exporters have relied upon not only cheap labour but also protective trade agreements, which are due to be lifted or renegotiated. These include the South Pacific Regional Trade and Economic Cooperation Agreement (SPARTECA) and the Multi-Fibre Arrangement. The percentage of Fiji's garment exports destined for New Zealand declined from 55 in 1989 to just eight in 1994 (Chandra 1996:56). Fiji now faces competition from lower cost suppliers in Asia in the wake of the East Asian crisis. Government economist *Ratu* Sakuisa Tuisolia predicts that 7,000 garment workers may face redundancies because of the increased costs of importing raw materials under SPARTECA and because of sharper competition in markets flooded by cheaper Asian exports (*Fiji Times,* 5 February 1998). There seems now little chance that wages in Fiji's garment industry will improve. Indeed, even with relatively cheap female labour, employers have resorted to recruiting foreigners. In 1996 approximately 2,000 garment workers were hired, some illegally, from China, Taiwan and the Philippines (International Confederation of Free Trade Unions 1997).

Women who remain on sugar farms also have an insecure future, with the possible renegotiation of sugar quotas to the European Union as a consequence of the end of the fifth Lomé Convention. This has coincided with sugar growers facing the renewals of leases from state or indigenously-owned land. A severe drought has caused the most recent rural crisis. Such transitions and upheavals cast uncertainties over family security in Indo Fijian sugar communities. Occupational diversification is trumpeted as an answer to dependency on the sugar industry, but women's options remain circumscribed. It seems however that many Indo-Fijian farming families have abandoned strictures for daughters to remain on farms. Education for girls has greater urgency, while young women may be encouraged to leave families for employment or to marry abroad.

Education can open greater employment diversity and personal choices but Fiji's healthy statistics concerning female scholastic achievements have not been commensurate with professional and personal advancement. The public sector continues to attract many well-educated women, but into familiar territory: nursing, teaching and clerical work. Gender stereotypes have not disappeared with a more educated workforce. The FWRM's 1997 campaign against sexual harassment was greeted by some with amusement or disbelief. Public sector unions condemned the removal of employment appeals legislation in 1987, although gender was never recognised as grounds for appeal. The reconstitution of the appeals system under the 1997 constitution recognises appeals against discrimination based on gender. Structural safeguards are an important step in dislodging more subtle forms of discrimination and women's resignation to the status quo.

The acceptance of gender stereotypes and discrimination inside and outside the home is being challenged by women. The ability to negotiate work reflects wider cultural values. Proactive groups, including the Women's Coalition for Women's Citizenship Rights, recognise that traditions are not fixed and as interpretations of tradition sharpened gender divisions and inequalities in the past, so can thorny issues be renegotiated in the future, without condemning important cultural identities. Such processes are never easy but contestation over tradition, culture and political rights has been ongoing since the coups, although not given legitimate public space until the review of the 1990 Constitution. As the implementation of Fiji's new constitution unfolds over time, it remains to be seen how this will translate into women's rights, given the cultural and economic realities of the present.

Endnotes

1. *Vinaka vakalevu* to Fiji's Ministries of Health and Labour, the Public Service Commission, the Fiji Nursing Association, the Fiji National Archives, and the nurses who shared their life histories with me. Most interviewees must, however, remain anonymous. This chapter gratefully includes insights from Sue Carswell and Christy Harrington. Our research was assisted by an Otago Research Grant and was affiliated to the Development Studies Programme, University of the South Pacific. This chapter is based on a paper

presented at the International Conference on Women in the Asia-Pacific Region: Persons, Powers, and Politics, Singapore, 11–13 August 1997, which was initially revised and published as Leckie (1997a).

2. Ganesh Chand (1996:28–31) queries official unemployment rates of 10.2 per cent in 1987 and 6 per cent in 1995. His revised 'back of the envelope' figures suggest 10.6 per cent and 19.3 per cent respectively.

3. University figures are not broken down by nationality so the proportion of female students from Fiji is unclear.

4. Chandra Talpade Mohanty (1988:66) deconstructs the universalist applicability of *purdah* and the negative implications of this for Muslim women.

5. These are: article 5(a), which aims to achieve the elimination of prejudices, customary and all other practices which are based on the idea of the inferiority or the superiority of either of the sexes or on stereotyped roles for men and women; and article 9, covering the equal rights of nationality and the nationality of children.

Part II

The 'Fijian' question

The problematics of reform and the 'Fijian' question

William Sutherland

Introduction

Following the coups of 1987 the indigenous Fijian-dominated state mapped out an economic reform program which by the early 1990s had lost much of its steam but regained momentum in the second half of the decade. This pattern was mirrored in political reforms. Three years after overthrow of the democratically-elected coalition government of the Fiji Labour Party (FLP) and the National Federation Party (NFP) came the racist and undemocratic constitution of 1990, which lay the foundation for the huge electoral victory in 1992 of the indigenous Fijian political party, the *Soqosoqo Vakavulewa ni Taukei* (SVT). By the mid 1990s, however, the tide had begun to turn as internal struggles for democratic reform intensified. In 1995 the process of reviewing the 1990 Constitution began and in July 1997 the Constitution (Amendment) Act was passed. With that came fresh hopes for political stability and heightened expectations of economic growth but whether these hopes and expectations will be realised remains to be seen, even in light of the outcome of the 1999 general elections. In the twists and turns of Fiji's lost decade lie grounds for cautious optimism; on the other hand, while the democratic space is now much wider than before, as is evident in the huge victory of the FLP in the 1999 general elections, the key issue of indigenous Fijian discontent remains unresolved and therein lies a major threat to Fiji's future stability.

The argument in this chapter is that from 1987 to about the mid 1990s the reforms pursued by the post-coup state were driven primarily by the demands of nationalist indigenous Fijians. However, this project became increasingly problematic as the contradictions between the demands of economic reform on the one hand, and economic affirmative action in favour of indigenous Fijians on the other, intensified. From the mid 1990s the state increasingly moved away from its nationalist agenda and, driven now by stronger and more persistent external pressures for greater economic liberalisation, increased the pace and scope of economic reforms. In so doing, however, its capacity to deliver on the 'Fijian' question became even more limited; and the more it distanced itself from its nationalist agenda, the higher the level of indigenous Fijian disaffection became. By the second half of 1998, with the 'Fijian' question still unresolved, indigenous Fijian dissatisfaction with the SVT-dominated state had grown and a range of new indigenous Fijian political parties had emerged, which jockeyed amongst themselves for electoral advantage. In the aftermath of the 1999 general elections, the viability of the new FLP-led government will depend to a very large extent on how it manages the 'Fijian' question, and its performance in that regard will shape the country's prospects for growth and stability.

The 'Fijian' question

At the heart of the 'Fijian' question is a longstanding indigenous Fijian concern about their 'economic backwardness'. As early as 1959 an inquiry into the 'economic problems and prospects facing the indigenous Fijian people' identified the root causes as the indigenous Fijian communal way of life and the system of 'Fijian Administration' instituted by the colonial state. One year later another report concurred and indigenous Fijian economic disadvantage came to be explained in terms of their 'subsistence affluence', their preference for a 'leisurely' village lifestyle, a lack of entrepreneurship and capitalist discipline, communalistic as opposed to individualistic values, and a strong sense of traditional obligation (Sutherland 1992:112–13). Educational underachievement was later added to the list, as was also a lack of capital.

The other key dimension of the Fijian question is the highly sensitive matter of native land leases, most of which are held by Indo-Fijians, especially sugarcane farmers (Prasad and Kumar, this volume). The origins of the problem here lie in the shift from plantation to small holder production in the colonial sugar economy. Native land leases are regulated by the Agricultural Landlord and Tenant Act of 1976 (ALTA) and in 1976 the indigenous Fijian-dominated Alliance government granted lease extensions of up to 30 years. This decision was strongly opposed by indigenous Fijian nationalists and was a key reason for the Alliance's electoral defeat in April 1977. Twenty-one years later the leases began to expire, the first 47 in 1997, and by 2005 more than 5000 will have expired. Many indigenous Fijian landowners want the land back and leaseholders, understandably, are anxious. Up to 1998, attempts to come up with an arrangement which broadly satisfied the stakeholders had failed and the ruling SVT, clearly with an eye to the upcoming elections, effectively put the matter on hold by referring the whole matter to a parliamentary committee. For the new government, there are rocky times ahead. But it is not only the land issue that remains unresolved.

At independence in 1970 indigenous Fijian hopes for improvement were pinned on the Alliance government but its early failure to fulfil these hopes led in 1973 to a stinging attack by Sakeasi Butadroka, an indigenous Fijian and Assistant Minister for Commerce and Industry. Soon afterwards Butadroka formed the Fijian Nationalist Party, which became the political spearhead of indigenous Fijian nationalist aspirations. The Alliance response was its policy of economic affirmative action, which had three key elements: preferential access for indigenous Fijians to state-funded scholarships; state-funded soft loans to assist indigenous Fijians in business; and state assistance to various indigenous Fijian business ventures. These initiatives had only limited success (Sutherland 1992:142–51; Ratuva, this volume). The 1987 coups renewed indigenous Fijian hopes that their fortunes might finally change.

In the area of education, a key response of the post-coup state was to increase funding for indigenous Fijian scholarships. In addition to the existing policy of reserving 50 per cent of Public Service Commission scholarships for indigenous Fijians, the annual allocation to a special education fund administered by the Fijian Affairs Board was increased from F$3.5 million to F$4.5 million. While this helped a larger number of indigenous Fijians, it did little to improve the poor and longstanding record of indigenous Fijian educational achievement. At the time of the coups indigenous Fijians were still performing poorly compared to the other ethnic communities; by 1995 the situation had not changed (Sharma 1997).

Against this history of comparative underachievement in
education, indigenous Fijian underrepresentation in the professional
classes is not surprising. Figures from the 1986 census reveal, for
example, that indigenous Fijians held 39 per cent of lower level
professional and managerial jobs, 35 per cent of middle level ones, and
only 17 per cent at the senior level (Sutherland 1992:153). The
increased 'Fijianisation' of the public sector that followed in the wake
of the coups is therefore not surprising. In May 1987, indigenous
Fijians held 47.6 per cent of public service positions; Indo-Fijians held
47.8 per cent. Two months later, the figures were 53 per cent and 43
per cent respectively (Leckie 1991:67). By then, increasing numbers of
Indo-Fijians, especially professionals, were emigrating—with the
result that even more public service opportunities were created for
indigenous Fijians. In 1991, for example, indigenous Fijians accounted
for 61 per cent of public service appointments and 57 per cent of
promotions. Five years later the figures were still high, at 58 per cent
and 53 per cent respectively. Also, in 1996 indigenous Fijians
accounted for only 23 per cent of public service resignations, while
Indo-Fijians accounted for 70 per cent (Kumar 1997:87).

Successful 'Fijianisation' of the public service was not matched in
the private sector. Seventeen years of indigenous Fijian state power
under successive Alliance governments had failed to produce a
successful indigenous Fijian capitalist class and the much better record
of Indo-Fijians strengthened the widely-held but false view that Indo-
Fijians dominated the economy, a perception that fuelled anti-Indo-
Fijian sentiment. The coups were supposedly meant to change this and
the state, now commanding much greater political control than
previous Alliance governments, appeared much better placed to
deliver on the promise of ensuring the 'paramountcy of indigenous
Fijian interests' (Durutalo 1986). For the challenging task of increasing
indigenous Fijian economic power, the state mapped out an ambitious
plan which dovetailed with the goal of the Viti Chamber of Commerce,
an indigenous Fijian organisation formed in late 1987, to 'promote and
encourage meaningful participation by indigenous Fijians in business'
(Sutherland 1992:193).

A key element of the plan was to strengthen the executive
capability of the Fijian Affairs Board in order to enable it to formulate
and implement specific policies and strategies. Another was the
provision of a F$20 million interest-free loan to the Fijian Affairs Board
to buy shares in the Fijian Holdings Company Limited (FHC), which

was 'the holding company for Fijians at the national level'. The FHC would in turn acquire shares in 'profitable companies in the industrial and commercial sectors' (Ratuva, this volume). The objective was for indigenous Fijians to own 15 per cent of the corporate sector by 1995 and not less than 30 per cent by the year 2000. Other initiatives included the reservation of certain lines of industrial and commercial activity for indigenous Fijians; a minimum level of indigenous Fijian ownership of at least one English daily newspaper; the introduction of an indigenous Fijian retail store scheme, later called the Eimcol scheme, to help 'selected indigenous Fijians with the necessary talent to successfully manage retail businesses'; and increased funding to the state-owned Fiji Development Bank (FDB) to allow greater preferential access for indigenous Fijians to soft loans for commercial purposes (Sutherland 1992:93).

Ten years after the coups, however, this grand design remained largely that; for the vast majority of indigenous Fijians it meant little. Certainly, the FHC grew, and there were marginally more indigenous Fijian businesses than before, including one indigenous Fijian-owned English daily newspaper. On the other hand, the Eimcol store scheme had collapsed and the number of public notices of receiverships and mortgagee sales underscored the continuing high level of indigenous Fijian business failure. To be sure, a small indigenous Fijian élite did well, as Ratuva discusses more fully in his contribution to this volume, but it can hardly be said that there was anything like a successful indigenous Fijian business class which remotely rivaled the dominance of established foreign and local, including Indo-Fijian, capital. Indigenous Fijian political power clearly had not translated into indigenous Fijian economic power. Much of the explanation for this lies in the contradictions between the post-coup state's nationalist agenda and its wider economic reforms.

The contradictions of reform and the indigenous Fijian nationalist agenda

Since independence in 1970 sugar and tourism have been the mainstay of the economy and the manufacturing sector remained relatively small until after the coups. At the center of the post-coup economic reforms, therefore, was the shift in industrial policy away from import-substitution towards export-promotion. Such a shift had been mooted as early as 1970 but it had 'an extremely long gestation period'

(Akram-Lodhi 1996:263). Why was this so? Why was the Alliance government 'tentative' about shifting away from its import-substitution strategy? The limited level of industrial development between 1970 and 1987, Akram-Lodhi correctly explains, was 'largely based on import substitution, and the economy was subject to a regulatory regime deploying quota, license, and tariff protection' (Akram-Lodhi 1996:263). The telling point about this regime, however, is that the major beneficiaries were a few local Indo-Fijian businessmen who, importantly, had close links with the Alliance government and who were financial backers of the Alliance party. With this kind of support, therefore, the Alliance's longstanding reluctance to change its industrial policy is not surprising. From the early 1980s, however, there was external pressure to effect such a shift.

A employment mission undertaken by the Institute of Development Studies of the University of Sussex in the United Kingdom argued in 1982 that Fiji's labour costs were uncompetitive by international standards and had to be reduced to enhance the country's export potential. In 1986 the World Bank did the same (Akram-Lodhi 1996:265). By then the Alliance government had sought to cut labour costs by announcing retrenchments in the public service as well as a freeze on all wages, salaries and increments (Sutherland 1992:173–74). What followed was widespread opposition, the birth of the FLP and, in April 1987, the Alliance's second electoral defeat. The coups that followed created the political space that made a decisive shift towards export-oriented industrialisation possible. To be sure, the shift was also a response to international trends towards economic liberalisation and export-oriented industrialisation, as well as specific advice from consultants and international agencies (Akram-Lodhi 1996:265). Without the coups, however, it is unlikely that the shift would have been as swift and wide-ranging as it was. But the change brought its own tensions. Having promised to deliver on indigenous Fijian economic aspirations, the post-coup state was now faced with the task of managing the inherent contradictions between the imperatives of economic liberalisation on the one hand and the demands of economic affirmative action on the other (Sepehri and Akram-Lodhi, this volume).

The showpiece of the post-coup economic reform agenda was the spectacular growth of the manufacturing sector and central to this success was the establishment of tax-free factories, most especially for garment production. Underpinning this shift towards export-oriented industrialisation was the policy of deregulation and the provision of highly attractive tax and other concessions. International competitiveness, however, required more than this, and in 1991 the push for labour market reforms began with the promulgation of draconian anti-labour legislation (Chand, this volume). In 1992 a value-added tax was introduced and plans for further tax reforms were flagged. Financial sector reforms were also planned, and so too key public sector reforms, including downsizing, performance-based remuneration, administrative reorganisation, and financial and budgeting reforms. In addition, state enterprises were earmarked for corporatisation or privatisation and a Public Enterprises Unit was established within the Ministry of Finance to oversee the process.

For the state these reforms were necessary to rescue the economy from the severe downturn that followed the coups and lay the foundation of longer-term economic growth. In terms of the task of delivering on indigenous Fijian economic aspirations, however, the reforms were problematic because they impacted negatively on large numbers of indigenous Fijians. Labour market reforms affected them as workers; the value-added tax did not discriminate between ethnic groups; the pain of public sector reforms increasingly fell on indigenous Fijians the more that the public service was 'Fijianised'; and divestiture of state assets hurt the many indigenous Fijians employed in state-owned enterprises. In the face of such negative impacts, the significant level of indigenous Fijian support for wider worker struggles—for example, against the value-added tax and the labour reforms—is not surprising. For the state this was a major concern, for the very political support on which it depended most critically was being eroded.

Worried by this the state began to waver in its commitment to implement economic reform and investors, of course, complained about a lack of leadership, prevarication and backpedalling. The state had hoped that with the reforms would come greater opportunities for indigenous Fijian economic advancement, especially in the burgeoning garment industry. Economic liberalisation, however, meant open competition and a 'level playing field', and economic affirmative action ran counter to this. Nowhere was the contradiction demonstrated more clearly than in the state's changing position on deregulation.

Early in 1989 the regulation of imports was relaxed and the number of items subject to import licensing was reduced to 48 (Parliament of Fiji 1997a:63). Restrictions on the import of one of these items, white polished rice, was eased and of the 17,000 tons to be imported that year 3,000 tons were set aside for importation by indigenous Fijians (*The Review*, May 1995:28–29). Hari Punja, a leading Indo-Fijian importer and industrialist, whose business empire was then estimated at F$180 million, cried foul (Sutherland 1992:194) but the state stood its ground and indigenous Fijians rushed for import licenses. Significantly, FDB loans to indigenous Fijians for 'commercial/ business services' suddenly leapt, accounting for 43.5 per cent of the total value of all its commercial loans to indigenous Fijians. But this spurt of enthusiasm soon waned and, as Table 9.1 shows, the pattern of indigenous Fijian borrowing changed markedly. Borrowing for investment in real estate now became the preference and the value of FDB loans to indigenous Fijians for 'commercial/business services' fell to a mere 4.5 per cent in 1993, temporarily increased to 25.4 per cent in 1994 but then dropped back to a low of 3.7 per cent in 1995. Indigenous Fijians soon realised that it was one thing to go into business, but quite another to be viable and successful. The harsh reality was that established competitors would not yield easily.

Table 9.1 **Distribution of Fiji Development Bank commercial loans to indigenous Fijians by sector, 1989–96, per cent**

	1989	1990	1991	1992	1993	1994	1995	1996
Service Sectors								
Transport and Communication	30.4	25.8	37.7	21.8	34.1	16.4	9.2	4.6
Real Estate	-	31.5	36.2	25.8	22.6	36.7	61.6	58.1
Wholesale/Retail	-	-	-	-	14.8	11.3	7.6	2.8
Commercial and Business Services	43.5	28.9	13.4	17.6	4.5	25.4	3.7	31.5
Investment/Finance	-	-	-	10.9	16.3	2.9	7.5	1.8
Tourism	10.0	1.0	0.7	3.4	1.9	3.7	3.2	0.5
Productive Sectors								
Manufacturing	7.7	3.6	8.0	15.6	1.5	1.9	3.6	0.5
Construction	0.4	2.4	1.7	0.6	0.5	0.8	-	-
Timber/Agro-Industry	8.0	6.8	2.3	4.3	3.8	1.7	3.6	0.2

Source: Fiji Development Bank 1992/93:8; 1994/95:13; 1995/96:19.

Nevertheless, over this period indigenous Fijian nationalists complained increasingly that the government was not doing enough to help indigenous Fijians in business. They again pressed the point about Indo-Fijian economic power and reminded the government that deregulation undermined the policy of economic affirmative action. In the lead up to the 1995 National Economic Summit, the Subcommittee on Indigenous Fijian Participation in Business bemoaned, yet again, the lack of indigenous Fijian business success and argued that state support had to include softening the policy of deregulation.

> The government's deregulation policy runs contrary to its policy of enhancing indigenous Fijian business participation because most Fijians are involved in small enterprises which are in their infancy and cannot compete in terms of economies of scale and product quality with more established (and mostly Indian) companies which developed during Fiji's import-substitution era. Therefore, Fijian entrepreneurs should be protected...Because of the need to replace market entry barriers for Fijians, they should get equal opportunities in government services that will be contracted out [as well as in] government entities and services to be privatised. Apart from a 50 per cent opportunity [for] Fijian business participation in the economy...tenders by Fijian suppliers should enjoy a 15 per cent preference margin (*The Review*, May 1995:28–29).

The Subcommittee had an ally in the Finance Minister, Berenado Vunibobo. Although widely perceived as a hardheaded economic rationalist, Vunibobo was also a nationalist and he was clear about where the major threat to the nationalist agenda lay. For him the business community 'essentially belong[ed] to the Indian community' and affirmative action was necessary.

> The Fijians seem to have developed the feeling that by having political control, they are the master of the house. It doesn't work that way. You have to have a significant say in influencing the economy...but at the end of the day the Indian business community could squeeze the country dry if they choose to do so because of their hold on the economic levers. The Fijians realise that now. That is why there is so much input, so much concern, about helping and encouraging Fijians to get into the economic mainstream (*The Review*, May 1995:29).

With the Finance Minister taking this line it is not surprising that in the following year the value of FDB loans to indigenous Fijians for 'commercial/business services' increased markedly. From a mere 3.7 per cent of the total value of all commercial loans to indigenous Fijians in 1995, it jumped to 31.5 per cent. On the other hand, the

Subcommittee's plea for the state to go soft on deregulation and give indigenous Fijians more preferential treatment did not elicit a positive response. Here was evidence that the state was willing to go only so far, and further evidence that it was now distancing itself from the nationalist agenda would soon emerge.

Other, more influential sections of the private sector, especially several key Indo-Fijian companies, were also opposed to deregulation and in the following year the state's class bias towards them was revealed. In August Isimeli Bose, the Minister for Trade, Industry, Commerce and Public Utilities, announced a qualified softening of the deregulation policy. Competition would continue to be encouraged but there would also be limits. Certain interests, in his view, were much too important and had to be protected. Those interests, however, were not indigenous Fijian ones, as the following report on an interview with the Minister revealed:

> He is keen on protecting the interests of local entrepreneurs—the Hari Punjas, the Vinod Patels and Mahendra Patels—and long established businesses such as Shell, Carlton Brewery and Morris Hedstrom. 'They have put their money where their mouth is'...Already the minister has advised the [Fiji Trade and Investment Board] to take special care of these local investors and make sure that they receive support...And he is going to 'fight very hard' to protect the big local investors. 'I will run to their help whenever they need me'. While the Minister is aware of the World Trade Organisation rules promoting a freer trading environment, Bose insists that at the end of the day, it's the national interest that 'must come first' (*The Review*, August 1995:38).

Bose's explicit privileging of the national interest, together with the conspicuous absence of indigenous Fijians from the list of local entrepreneurs whose interests were to be protected, underscored the state's increasing abandonment of its nationalist agenda.

Indo-Fijian entrepreneurs and 'long-established' foreign companies were the 'pillars of the economy' and it was they who would best advance the 'national interest'. They therefore required 'special care' and the state duly obliged. One month after Bose's announcement, 55.6 per cent of the businesses surveyed identified deregulation as the 'most critical' issue facing them (*The Review*, November 1996:58). Eight months later the figure was just 27 per cent (*The Review*, June 1997:21). The state had moved further away from the nationalist agenda and indigenous Fijian entrepreneurs, whose performance continued to be generally poor and showed little sign of improving, now had a minor place in the state's economic agenda. The prospect of this changing was further reduced in the following year, when indigenous Fijian economic performance and the whole policy of economic affirmative action were again publicly scrutinised. A well-known indigenous Fijian journalist brought to public attention yet again the continuing poor record of indigenous Fijians in business (*Fiji Business Magazine*, October 1996:20–21). Earlier, the policy of economic affirmative action had again been publicly questioned, this time by Don Aidney, a local Euro-Fijian and an influential economic figure of long standing (*Fiji Business Magazine*, July 1996:40–41).

By the end of 1996, then, with its nationalist agenda now giving way to a national one, the state began pursuing with renewed vigour the wider economic reform program mapped out in the immediate post-coup years but which had been frustrated by the requirements of its nationalist project. But this new resolve was not entirely of the state's own making. It was also a consequence of growing external pressures to adjust to the imperatives of globalisation.

Global imperatives and the new reform agenda

By the early 1990s global pressures for economic liberalisation had intensified. The Cold War was over, the Uruguay Round was nearing completion, and neoliberalism had swept the industrialised world and become even more firmly entrenched as orthodoxy in the International Monetary Fund, the World Bank, the Asian Development Bank, and other international organisations with which Fiji had close links. Increasing competition for shrinking aid budgets strengthened the hand of donors in pressing the case for economic reform, which the World Bank did in 1991 1993 and 1995 in three reports on the Pacific island economies, including Fiji (World Bank 1991; 1993; 1995b). The Bank also urged other donors to be more forthright in their policy advice to Pacific island governments (Sutherland 1998:5–6). Closer to home, Australia and New Zealand pushed for reform and the key regional site for intervention was the South Pacific Forum (referred to hereafter as the Forum). Wearing two hats—as Forum members and as major donors—they were uniquely well-placed to use the Forum to urge reforms on the island countries, and in the early 1990s the regional reform agenda which they were highly instrumental in developing began to emerge.

In 1990 the Forum 'took cognisance of the rapid changes in the international political and economic situation' and in the following year 'endorsed the view that although many issues, such as programs of economic structural adjustment, required action at the national level, there was also a key role for regional action' (South Pacific Forum 1990; 1991). Such action was to begin in 1994 but in the meantime the general message about the need for adjustment and reform needed to be made more concrete. In 1992, therefore, Forum members agreed to put in place 'effective' domestic policies, give recognition to the vital role of the private sector, and develop a sound investment strategy (South Pacific Forum 1992). For Fiji, this was particularly significant. Investment was low and foreign investors, like many of their domestic, and especially Indo-Fijian, counterparts, were not enamoured of the government's policy of economic affirmative action.

In 1993 the Forum again reiterated the need for policy adequacy and private sector development (South Pacific Forum 1993) and in the following year Australia, as host of the Forum, put regional reform at the top of the agenda. Also at Australia's suggestion, the 1994 Forum established the Forum Finance Ministers' Meeting to begin the task of developing regional reform initiatives. The first meeting of the Forum Finance Ministers, which was funded by Australia, sought to 'improve overall economic management' and 'identified structural reform as a vital element in improving...competitiveness and efficiency' (Forum Finance Ministers, 21 February 1995). The second meeting agreed that member countries 'should not delay implementing necessary reforms until...forced to do so by economic crises or external pressures' (Forum Finance Ministers, 8 December, 1995).

The 1996 Forum noted the Ministers' 'progress towards defining a practical, regionally-focussed, economic reform agenda' and, to allow their agenda 'to cover the breadth of economic issues', agreed to expand membership of the ministers' meeting to include 'Forum Ministers with appropriate economic portfolios' (South Pacific Forum 1996). The meeting thus became known as the Forum Economic Ministers Meeting (FEMM) and met as such for the first time in Cairns in July 1997. There the ministers 'agreed that private sector development [was] central to ensuring sustained economic growth, and that governments should provide a policy environment to encourage this' (Forum Economic Ministers 1997).

In an address to the Fiji Australia Business Council in the following month Australian Foreign Minister Alexander Downer warned against 'rely[ing] on inward policies of protectionism and import substitution to the exclusion of more outward-looking policies'. He noted the efforts of the FEMM in advancing the regional reform agenda and that Fiji, along with other Pacific island economies, was 'already well down the path of reforms', although he then added that the world was 'moving on quickly' and there was 'no room for a slackening of the pace of reform' (Downer 1997). One month earlier, at a joint conference of the New Zealand and Fiji Business Councils, Sir Roger Douglas, the architect of economic liberalisation in New Zealand in the 1980s, proposed a comprehensive package of reforms for Fiji which, he stressed, should be implemented in its entirety and not on a piecemeal basis. The conference gave its backing to Roger's package. In the audience was Fiji's indigenous Fijian Prime Minister, Sitiveni Rabuka (*National Business Review*, 20 June 1997). The key message from interventions such as these was clear: reforms were necessary and the momentum had to be maintained. For Fiji it was particularly apposite. Although there had been some progress, on the whole its record on reform was patchy.

By this time, Fiji had responded to other external pressures. The Mid-term Review of the Lomé Convention cast doubt over the future of Fiji's sugar exports and forced the government to draw up plans to restructure the industry. In relation to the manufacturing sector, continued pleas by Fiji to Australia to relax the rules of origin for preferential access of its manufactured goods, especially garments, under the South Pacific Regional Trade and Economic Cooperation Agreement (SPARTECA) met not only with refusal but strong urgings to become more competitive. Then, in April 1996, Fiji faced the World Trade Organization's (WTO) Trade Review Panel.

The Panel highlighted Fiji's relatively slow economic growth and raised questions about fiscal balance; progress on public enterprise reforms; the promotion of greater competition; exchange and price controls; and land tenure issues, including changes to the ALTA. Attention was drawn to 'the slowing pace of tariff reform and liberalisation'; Fiji was 'encouraged...to continue progress on this front and in relation to deregulation' and questions were posed about 'measures to encourage greater competitiveness in the clothing sector'. In relation to the service sector, the Panel sought further information on the 'scope and timing' of the 'new policy statement on services [being developed] by the Fijian Government'. A whole range of other issues was also brought to scrutiny. The Panel welcomed answers given by Fiji to questions and 'looked forward to written replies on outstanding issues' (World Trade Organization 1997:2–5).

In November 1996 the Finance Minister presented his budget for 1997. The title of his budget address is revealing: 'Confidence through clear policy'. That the Minister was concerned about the confidence of external actors, especially Australia, the European Union and the WTO, is suggested by this remark:

> We would be very short-sighted to retreat from the policies of liberalisation...For too long we have relied solely on preferential trade agreements...[but] this is a dangerous strategy, as continued benefits from SPARTECA...and the Lomé Convention are beyond our control. As a step in the right direction and away from relying on [such] trade agreements, Fiji has...[joined] the World Trade Organization. WTO membership greatly assists Fiji's integration into the global economy. But it also places an obligation to comply with its requirements (Ministry of Finance and Economic Development 1996a:12).

The subtitle of the Minister's address, 'A commitment to Fiji's future', is also telling. The government's commitment was to Fiji's future, not indigenous Fijians' future. In his speech there was not a single mention of indigenous Fijian interests or of the policy of economic affirmative action, let alone any suggestion that these might be boosted. Economic affirmative action did not cease, of course, but clearly the government's agenda was now a national one. As the Minister put it, 'since 1987, a new economic strategy has been formulated and implemented. The new approach seeks to encourage the economy to grow for the benefit of *all* our people' (emphasis added) (Ministry of Finance and Economic Development 1996a:2). The nationalist agenda was weakening and in the face of growing external pressure the wider economic reform program gathered speed.

The record until then was uneven at best. There had been some deregulation but some backtracking as well: the anti-labour laws introduced in 1991 had been repealed; progress on public sector reform was minimal; only two state-owned enterprises had been corporatised, the Department of Post and Telecommunications and IKA Corporation; and only two had been partly privatised, the Fiji Pine Commission and the Marketing Authority (Ministry of Finance and Ministry of National Planning 1996b:54). But things were about to change and the Minister of Finance signaled the government's renewed resolve in November 1997 when he presented to the parliament the budget for the following year.

Six more government enterprises were earmarked for corporatisation. The telecommunications sector, which had recently been reviewed, would be opened up to competition. Further tax reform would be implemented following completion of two studies on company and income tax then underway and, in line with the recently announced Investment Policy Statement, the investment regime would be streamlined to make it more workable and transparent. The domestic capital market would be boosted by the creation of a Capital Market Development Authority. Foreign exchange regulations would be further relaxed and the whole financial sector reviewed. Greater effort would be applied to initiatives already underway in the public sector, including corporate and strategic planning, performance-based remuneration, performance-based contract employment for senior officials, improved financial systems and management, more effective budgeting, and increased devolution of financial and human resource management responsibility (Ministry of Finance and Ministry of National Planning 1997a; 1997b).

Although not as speedy and thoroughgoing as some would have liked, the progressive implementation of these reforms in the course of 1997 showed that the state was now more serious about its reform program. By late 1997 the Public Enterprise Act had been passed; the Government Shipyard was privatised and the Fiji Broadcasting Commission corporatised; the process of corporatising the Civil Aviation Authority of Fiji was well underway; further steps had been taken to sell 49 per cent of the Government's share of the national carrier, Air Pacific; the Capital Market Development Authority had been established; some foreign exchange controls relaxed; and significant progress had been made on public sector reform (Ministry of Finance and Ministry of National Planning 1997b; *Fiji Times*, 23 September and 7 October 1997). In the area of industrial relations, the Health and Safety at Work Act of 1996 was passed and, significantly, the Tripartite Forum, which brings together employers, employees and government representatives, was reconvened for the first time in two years (*Fiji Times*, 26 September and 7 October 1997). There was also a proposal to merge the Departments of Inland Revenue and Customs into a single 'revenue authority' (*Fiji Times*, 3 October 1997). Presented as a means of streamlining revenue collection, the proposal was also seen, however, as partly a response to the release the previous June of a report on an investigation into corruption in the Customs Department (Parliament of Fiji 1997b).

Reporting on this progress in November 1997, Jim Ah Koy, the new Finance Minister and one of Fiji's leading businessmen, announced yet more reforms, including further streamlining of investment approval procedures, greater liberalisation of foreign exchange controls, financial market reforms and various measures to achieve a 'large reduction' in the budget deficit, which in 1997 stood at 9.2 per cent of GDP. To 'speed up the public enterprise reform process', which was 'now very high on the Government's agenda', over F$10 million was allocated to the Public Enterprise Unit over the next two years—an enormous increase over the F$0.5 million allocated one year earlier. In the area of public sector reform, some earlier initiatives such as employment contracts for Departmental Heads had not yet been implemented; but Ah Koy reaffirmed the government's commitment to push ahead with the reform program.

Reactions to the 1998 budget were mixed. Some saw it as an electoral sweetener; for others it did not go far enough and the government's softer position on deregulation was especially worrying. Just four months earlier a five-member panel drawn from the private sector had tabled its report on deregulation and had strongly argued for more wide-ranging reforms (Parliament of Fiji 1997a). But the various criticisms notwithstanding, it was clear that the government was committed to pressing ahead with its expanded reform program. That it was now being driven increasingly by global pressures was made clear by Ah Koy: 'our survival rests on how well we adjust to these daunting challenges. We cannot run away from these developments and isolate ourselves from the rest of the world' (Ministry of Finance and Ministry of National Planning 1997a:27). By then the deepening Asian crisis was increasingly taking its toll on the Fiji economy and further evidence that state policy was indeed being shaped by the logic of globalisation came in January 1998 when the Fiji dollar was devalued by 20 per cent.

With that the state's ability to resolve the Fijian question became even more limited. As it was, the nationalist agenda had already been severely compromised by the growing pace and expanded scope of the economic reforms, and the 1998 budget contained nothing to suggest an about-turn. As was the case with the budget address in the previous year, the 1997 address made no mention of indigenous Fijian interests and Josefata Kamikamica, leader of the Fijian Association Party (FAP), was quick to point this out. Section 44 of the 1997 Constitution, he reminded the government, explicitly required parliament to make provision for programs designed to help those that were disadvantaged. The 1998 budget, he complained, contained no specific program for this purpose. More specifically, the Fijian Affairs Ministry had not been provided with resources to develop an effective program and indigenous Fijian participation in business had not been adequately addressed (*Pacnews*, 10 November 1997). Kamikamica was, in effect, charging the government with doing a great deal less than before to resolve the Fijian question.

In the second half of the 1990s, then, the state increasingly distanced itself from its earlier nationalist agenda. In the first half of decade the contradictions between the needs of that agenda and those of economic liberalisation intensified and, pushed along by growing external pressures, the state shifted increasingly towards the latter. Driven now by global imperatives, it pressed ahead on the reform path and in so doing further limited its capacity to deliver on the Fijian question. The change of tack alienated the very political support on which the government depended for its survival. What, then, of the future?

The Fijian question and Fiji's prospects

The new constitution makes power-sharing mandatory and for some time after its enactment in July 1997 the general expectation was that the most likely outcome of the next general elections would be a coalition government of the two major political parties, the SVT and the NFP. Two factors, however, made this rather less certain. One was the growing political fragmentation amongst indigenous Fijians, as evidenced by the increase in the number of indigenous Fijian political parties; the other was the electoral coalition between the FLP, the indigenous Fijian FAP, and the Party of National Unity (PANU).

At the party level, one of the earliest signs of cracks within the indigenous Fijian community came in 1991. Less than one year after the promulgation of the racist and undemocratic constitution of 1990, Apisai Tora, then a Cabinet Minister, joined the recently-formed,

western-based, multiracial All National Congress (ANC). As a
westerner, he was concerned about eastern chiefly dominance, and
believed that 'it [was] time western Fijians challenged the convention
that eastern Fijians [were] the country's naturally-born leaders'
(Sutherland 1992:203). He criticised the formation of the SVT and was
promptly sacked. Over the next eight months intra-indigenous Fijian
tensions intensified and by February 1992 there were no less than six
indigenous Fijian political parties opposed to the SVT. Their small size
and lack of resources, however, made them no match for the SVT and
it easily won the general elections later that year. But a major split
within the SVT beckoned. Disgruntled party members engineered the
defeat of the 1994 budget and broke away to form the FAP. But it too
could not match the resources of the SVT and in the snap elections
held in 1995 won only five seats compared to the SVT's thirty-one.

By then, as shown above, the tide was turning against the
indigenous Fijian nationalist agenda and later in 1995 the review of
the 1990 Constitution got underway. In the course of the review,
nationalist sentiment again came to the fore, including from within the
SVT, and continued well after the Constitutional Review Commission
presented its report in September 1996. With the adoption of a new,
more democratic constitution in July 1997, however, the nationalist
cause was dealt a severe blow. But the extremists would not give up
easily and their cause was bolstered in the following October when
Kavekini Navuso, a former member of the FLP and trade union leader,
won a by-election under the banner of the recently-formed and
Nationalist *Vanua Takolavo* Party. His objective, he announced, was to
change the new constitution that had overturned indigenous Fijian
political dominance and in his maiden speech in November he
attacked the SVT government for selling out on indigenous Fijian
rights (*Pacnews*, 25 November 1997).

In the same month, disgruntled members of the recently-formed
Viti Levu Multiracial Democratic Dynamic Party broke away to form
the Viti Levu, Kubuna, Burebasaga Multiracial Democratic Party.
Headed by two chiefs, one from Ra and the other from Rewa, the
party's main concern was to ensure an equal distribution of wealth
between indigenous Fijians, especially those they saw as having been
'forgotten by the SVT and FAP' (*Pacnews*, 13 November 1997). By this
time the SVT and the FAP had formed a coalition but negotiations for
a merger were floundering and an FAP spokesman predicted that

coalition with SVT would be over by Christmas. The main reason for this was the lack of consultation by the SVT, especially over the new constitution (*Pacnews*, 29 November 1997). In December the parliamentary coalition between the two parties collapsed and the FAP began to discuss with the FLP the possibility of jointly contesting upcoming elections (*Pacnews*, 31 December 1997).

By early 1998 rumours were circulating that an indigenous Fijian movement known as *Cadra Mai*, which means to rise up, was planning to topple the government and in February Prime Minister Rabuka challenged its members to come out into the open. He said he knew who they were and described them as a group of clergymen and senior military and police officers that had supported him in the coups of 1987 (*Pacnews*, 16 February 1998). The group was opposed to the new constitution and the government's moves to deal with the issue of native land leases through a Joint Parliamentary Select Committee (*Pacnews*, 18 February 1998). A few days after Rabuka's statement the head of the Methodist Church distanced the church from 'moves by some senior clergy to form a political party to rival the SVT' (*Pacnews*, 20 February 1998). Soon afterwards a new indigenous Fijian party, the *Soqosoqo Vakakarisito Party* (SVP) or Fijian Christian Party, was formed. Its leader, the Reverend Manasa Lasaro, was an extremist nationalist who had figured prominently in the events of 1987. There were thus in early 1998 five indigenous Fijian parties opposed to the SVT.

However, yet another indigenous Fijian party was in the offing. At a meeting in March 1998 the Ba Provincial Council unanimously agreed to form the PANU. Launched by no less a figure than the High Chief of Ba, the Party appointed Apisai Tora as its general secretary. The PANU was the latest political expression of the longstanding regional cleavage between eastern and western indigenous Fijians. As a senior party official, echoing Tora's earlier expression of western indigenous Fijian resentment of eastern indigenous Fijian political dominance, put it, 'although [Ba] province controls 60 per cent of the country's resources, it does not have much say in the political arena' (*Pacnews*, 15 January 1998).

The threat from the new indigenous Fijian political parties was not lost on the SVT. Prime Minister Rabuka claimed that this was simply an indication of indigenous Fijians becoming more aware of politics (*Pacnews*, 2 April 1998). The uncomfortable reality, however, was that by the time the 1999 general elections took place the SVT was opposed by a number of rival indigenous Fijian parties, albeit with varying degrees of credibility. The threat to the SVT became even more real when an electoral coalition between the FAP, PANU and FLP was announced. In August 1998 the attractiveness of this coalition as an alternative to one between the SVT and the NFP was boosted by the election of Adi Kuini Bavadra to the leadership of the FAP following the death of Kamikamica earlier that month. Previously the wife of the late Dr Timoci Bavadra, former leader of the FLP and Prime Minister in the FLP-NFP Coalition government that was overthrown in 1987, Adi Kuini was a western chief but also had close family connections to the eastern chiefly establishment. Sharp, articulate and finely attuned to traditional indigenous Fijian politics, she also made a mark within the Great Council of Chiefs. Moreover, in September 1998, 27 per cent of people surveyed in a public opinion poll ranked her second as preferred Prime Minister, just one percentage point behind Prime Minister Rabuka (*Pacific Islands Report*, 28 September 1998). Advantages such as these no doubt figured prominently both in her election to the leadership of the FAP as well as in the eventual success of the FLP/FAP/PANU coalition in the 1999 general elections.

Conclusion

In the latter half of 1998, then, the evidence was becoming increasingly clear that SVT rule was unlikely to continue. The new electoral system could not guarantee indigenous Fijian political dominance, increasing indigenous Fijian disaffection had thrown up some credible indigenous Fijian rivals, and the new constitution required power sharing between electorally successful political parties. In this light, the outcome of the 1999 general elections is perhaps not as surprising as some have thought it to be.

However, the new government still faces the thorny Fijian question, a question that the SVT was unable to resolve. The highly sensitive matter of native land leases has not been settled and the stand-off between the government and landowners over compensation for land taken over for the hydroelectric power station in Monasavu will undoubtedly have long term effects. In the area of education, indigenous Fijian underperformance continues to be a problem. As recently as January 1998 poor indigenous Fijian performance in external examinations caused the government to commission yet another an investigation (*Pacnews*, 15 January 1998). On the economic front, ten years since its formulation, the grand design for greater indigenous Fijian control of the economy remains largely that—although, it is true, a small minority has prospered.

In the elections the failure of the indigenous Fijian-dominated post-coup state to resolve the Fijian question figured prominently. How the new government deals with it will be crucial for the country's prospects for economic growth and political stability. The danger is that for some indigenous Fijians there remains unfinished business. Against this stands the hope is that the greater democratic space that now prevails in Fiji will allow more sensitive and effective management of the problematics of reform and the Fijian question.

Addressing inequality? Economic affirmative action and communal capitalism in post-coup Fiji

Steven Ratuva

Introduction

Economic affirmative action, defined as '*government*-mandated preferential policies toward *government*-designated groups' (Sowell 1990:10), became an important state policy in Fiji after independence in 1970. Economic affirmative action emerged as a result of growing concern about imbalances between Fiji's two principal ethnic groups, which was the result of the unequal process of capitalist development in the colonial economy in general, and the agricultural sector in particular (Narayan 1984; Overton 1988). However, it was not until after the 1987 military coups that the term 'affirmative action' began to be widely used in government circles. In the period since 1987, economic affirmative action has come to occupy a prominent place in Fiji's political discourse, being seen as an imperative for post-coup national reconstruction. Moreover, economic affirmative action is now commonly seen as an embodiment of 'progressive' ethnic Fijian thinking. This represents a change in perspective. Previously, economic affirmative action was associated with the more conservative 'paramountcy of Fijian interests' perspective (Durutalo 1986). This latter approach to economic affirmative action was embedded in the abrogated 1970 Constitution, as well as in colonial and post-colonial legislation relating to both land and aspects of ethnic Fijian culture. Given its pre-independence origins, it was concerned with preserving the hegemony of essentially colonial values. This conservatism may appear to stand in contradiction with the progressivity currently associated with economic affirmative action, but, as we shall see later, the seemingly contradictory nature of the two perspectives can be synthesised into what I propose to call in this chapter 'communal capitalism'.

Economic affirmative action has been an integral component of conflict resolution, sustainable and equitable development, democratisation and human rights in many societies. This is because it purports to address the phenomenon of equality—or rather, its absence. At the level of abstraction, the term equality seems to be a simple one. However, when used to examine concrete phenomena in their social context it has been the target of semantic manipulation. It thus continues to be elusive (Faundez 1994:1). In the US, for example, conservatives oppose economic affirmative action, and especially the use of quotas, on the grounds that it is a form of 'reverse discrimination' with the potential to create a new 'victim class'. American advocates of economic affirmative action on the other hand argue that it helps to redress the historically determined disadvantaged position of marginalised groups like African-Americans. However, advocates are divided as to whether economic affirmative action should be based on class, using 'the poor' as the designated social category, or based on ethnicity (Kahlenberg 1996). Notwithstanding this division though it remains the case that in the US economic affirmative action is official policy in some states. A similar debate has been witnessed in South Africa, where economic affirmative action has become part of the broad post-apartheid process of national reconstruction and reconciliation (Adam 1997). As in parts of the US, in South Africa economic affirmative action is mandatory, under the Employment Equity Bill. A third example can be found in Malaysia, where economic affirmative action was an integral component of the New Economic Policy (NEP) of 1970. It was imposed by a regime with authoritarian tendencies, and was aimed at alleviating the poverty within the *bumiputeras*—ethnic Malays—which was a critical source of income inequality between ethnic groups in Malaysia (Emsley 1996).

Key aspects of economic affirmative action debates found in the US, South Africa and Malaysia can be found in Fiji. There are two main strands to the debate on economic affirmative action in Fiji. The first is the nationalist position, which pushes for economic affirmative action policies to be specific to the indigenous people of the archipelago. This position has both conservative and progressive adherents, as noted above, and is embodied in the 1990 Constitution. The second is the liberal position, which opts for the application of economic affirmative action for those deemed to be disadvantaged, regardless of ethnicity (Citizens Constitutional Forum 1995). This position is reflected in the 1997 Constitution (Amendment) Act.

The nationalist position has dominated attempts to introduce economic affirmative action in Fiji. However, despite an increasingly ambitious expression of political will, especially during the immediate post-coup period, there is still no coherent economic affirmative action blueprint in Fiji. Instead, there are a number of individual state-sponsored programs implemented by a number of institutions. In part, the lack of a coherent blueprint in Fiji for economic affirmative action may be because it cannot be justified on the grounds of political powerlessness. Like South Africa and Malaysia, but unlike the US, the ethnic Fijians who have been designated as the intended beneficiaries of economic affirmative action constitute both the demographic majority and the politically dominant ethnic and social group. The overriding objective of economic affirmative action when it has been designed to benefit a designated group which is politically dominant has been to address historically-determined socioeconomic disparities. This is the case in Fiji. Economic affirmative action in Fiji has been designed to redress socioeconomic imbalances between ethnic Fijians and other ethnic groups found in the country. This justification has however been increasingly called into question in South Africa and Malaysia, as well as in the US, because many economic affirmative action programs have in fact largely benefited those who least need them: the middle class of the designated ethnic categories.

This chapter will similarly call into question the benefits of economic affirmative action in Fiji. The chapter begins by examining the origins of what I term communal capitalism. It continues by providing an analysis of the economic affirmative action intended to benefit ethnic Fijians in the wake of the 1987 coups. The chapter will then offer a case study of communal capitalism, using the Fijian

Holdings Company Limited (FHC) as its source material. The reason for choosing the FHC is because, as the flagship for ethnic Fijian communal investment, it has been seen by many in Fiji as a success story in as far as communal capitalism is concerned. Be that as it may, it manifests some fundamental contradictions, which I will explore in this chapter.

Economic affirmative action and communal capitalism

Before and immediately after independence two seemingly contradictory positions were articulated in relation to the protection and enhancement of ethnic Fijian rights. The first was the protection of colonially inherited neotraditional institutions. This focused on preserving the vestiges of the colonial Native Policy, which was responsible for the marginalisation of ethnic Fijians from mainstream economic transactions. The second was the encouragement of ethnic Fijian participation in commerce. This focused on creating institutions that would be the guardians of ethnic Fijian commercial endeavours.

The 1970 Constitution contained provision for the protection of ethnic Fijian rights, but this was limited to preserving existing institutional arrangements such as the Native Lands Trust Board (NLTB), the Fijian Affairs Board (FAB), the Great Council of Chiefs, the Fijian Development Fund, the Native Land and Fisheries Commission, and the Agricultural Landlord and Tenants Ordinance of 1967, which was transformed into the Agricultural Landlord and Tenants Act in 1977. In that these institutions had originally been set up to sustain the communalistic 'divide and rule' philosophies of the colonial Native Policy, which excluded most ethnic Fijians from wider politics, the maintenance of these institutions in the immediate post-independence period had the direct role of consolidating and legitimising the postcolonial state–chiefly class alliance. This alliance constructed a new form of hegemony that continued to keep most ethnic Fijians within a constricted, 'protected' political space, and served, to use Gramsci's (1971) terminology, as a 'historic bloc' in Fiji (Durutalo 1986; Akram-Lodhi 1997).

Paradoxically, this institutionalised neo-colonial hegemony was to be the facilitating mechanism and guardian for ethnic Fijian participation in commerce. In the early post-independence period, an institution of neo-colonial hegemony—the Provincial Councils—

served to promote economic affirmative action in Fiji. The Provincial Councils are a semi-state and semi-traditional administrative system with direct links to the FAB and the Great Council of Chiefs. The Provinces themselves are largely subsistence rural economies. Beginning in the 1970s Provincial Councils formed companies and invested in local or foreign corporations. As a form of economic affirmative action, the entry of the Provinces into capital and product markets was based on the neoclassical theory of 'trickle-down': that with sound investment and good businesses, the benefits of development would filter down to ordinary ethnic Fijians. In order to be able to pursue economic affirmative action, however, the Provincial Councils had to bridge the divide between the capitalist logic of accumulation and the need to maintain the hegemony of the state–chiefly class alliance. In order to do this, resources for investment were mobilised through an appeal to a communal sense of obligation to the *vanua*.

Vanua refers to the relationship between the land and the people indigenous to the land. Critically, this relationship is symbolised by chiefly power: the chief 'owns' the land and 'owns' the people. The relationship has both political and spiritual dimensions, and is thus intensely ideological. It can however have a material impact. In making an appeal for investable resources to a communal sense of obligation to the *vanua*, capital is ideologically conceptualised as a collective entity belonging to the *vanua*. It is this conceptualisation which inspires the altruism witnessed in *soli vakavanua*, or community collection: money is mobilised through neotraditional festivals in which various tribal units compete. Indeed, tribal competition becomes an end in itself, because winning, and the publicity generated by winning, becomes a source of pride for the *vanua*. As a result, Provinces are continually engaged in competition over their *soli vakavanua*.

However, for the members of the *vanua* competition is a rivalry over the accumulation of social assets such as prestige, rather than the accrual of capital for investment in the market. Similarly, the ownership of a company that can result from *soli vakavanua* is not seen as a means towards accumulation but as an expression of political prestige for the *vanua* and its symbolic representation, the chief. Indeed, there is a painful psychological sanction in a failure to mobilise resources: it is an insult to the *vanua*, the chief and to ethnic

Fijians themselves. The significance of capital as an accumulative factor of production is thus subsumed within a communal obligation to the *vanua*, and capital becomes an expression of a hegemonic collective identity rather than individual enrichment. Recall however that the *vanua* is symbolised by chiefly power. Capital may be ideologically conceptualised as belonging to the *vanua*, but the chiefs symbolise the *vanua*, 'owning' the land and the people. Therefore, in the various investments made by the Provincial Councils, chiefs were often made the legal holders of shares, the legal holders of company titles, and the directors any companies that were created. The result was the creation of a hybrid form of capitalist relations, based on the communal mobilisation of resources to collect capital for investment in enterprises, but often with the chiefs in formal legal control of that which has been invested: primordial servitude had been adapted to modern commercial exploitation. This is communal capitalism.

This form of communal resource mobilisation has contributed to the failure of many commercial enterprises organised on behalf of ethnic Fijians. Simply put, investments have not been based on commercial principles, and thus many of the enterprises arising out of such investments have been unable to compete in market relationships. Moreover, even when enterprises have been able to compete, the downside of such investment has been significant and perhaps unacceptable risk. As an example, in the 1970s the three Provincial Councils of Cakaudrove, Bua and Macuata formed a company called CBM Holdings, which operated a diverse investment portfolio. CBM Holdings bought shares worth 2.5 per cent of a major local company, Stinson and Pearce Limited, owned by a Euro-Fijian who was a former Alliance Party Minister of Finance. CBM Holdings' large investment left it exposed to significant risk, and when Stinson and Pearce was eventually closed, leaving behind a F$12 million debt to the National Bank of Fiji, CBM Holdings lost a lot of money. This was not the only case in which CBM Holdings' exposure to risk resulted in losses: its investment of F$150,000 in the Ferry Freights Company was lost. Cakaudrove, Bau and Macuata were not alone in making such investments. Tailevu, Rewa, Lau, and Kadavu all had investment arms. Many of these investments were in areas that were highly competitive, such as retailing, commercial agriculture, transport and shipping, and where, as a result, rivalry was fierce and the risks involved were great. Moreover, the investments were often in activities that tended to be dominated by Indo-Fijian business. The failure of many of these investments has been translated by some into an inappropriate ethnic stereotype: namely, that ethnic Fijian culture is not conducive to free enterprise. This stereotype has served to undermine the genuine efforts of many ethnic Fijian entrepreneurs.

Ethnic Fijian entrepreneurship grew in the post-independence period. Over the three decades preceding 1986 the number of ethnic Fijians in business increased dramatically (Hailey 1986:4). Most of these were small-scale businesses in the informal sector that survived without state subsidy on a day-to-day basis and which generated income for a family unit. Despite this increase in informal small-scale entrepreneurship however there was a marked absence of ethnic Fijians from the formal and the large-scale business sector. In June 1987, for example, of the 700 companies listed by the Registrar of Companies, the ethnic ownership pattern was 50 per cent Indo-Fijian; 15 per cent ethnic Fijian; 20 per cent other; and 15 per cent joint venture between ethnic groups (Fiji Office of the Registrar of Companies 1987). Little appears to have changed in the decade since 1987. In 1997, of the 101 local companies registered under the Tax Free Zones policy, less than 10 per cent were owned by ethnic Fijians (Fiji Trade and Investment Board 1997).

Moreover, most ethnic Fijian businesses have been concentrated in the urban areas. Rural areas remain largely untouched. Thus, a survey done in 1995 by the Ministry of Fijian Affairs (MFA) showed that some 62 per cent of rural ethnic Fijians survived by participating in subsistence agriculture. Of those who earnt wages, 22 per cent relied upon agriculture as the source of their income and some 10.6 per cent were in non-agricultural paid employment. Only 4 per cent earnt their livelihood in retail trade and services (MFA 1995:64). Indeed, part of the reason for the perpetual underdevelopment of the rural economy may have to do with the drain of valuable family resources, as a result of the material impact of the *soli vakavanua*, to sustain an exploitative communal capitalist system.

The system was exploitative in the sense that the revenues generated from these businesses were not equitably distributed. The institutionalisation of communal resource extraction reproduced the poverty and perpetual marginalisation of many ethnic Fijians: there was no 'trickle down'. The contradiction is that personal and family savings that could have been used for daily sustenance and local investment were controlled by dominant state and chiefly élites to sustain an agenda which formally fulfilled the imperative of economic affirmative action but which in reality fulfilled the economic aspirations of élite ethnic Fijians. Thus, the resources mobilised through *soli vakavanua* were passed on through chiefs to Provincial bureaucrats and then on to Provincial companies, which then worked out the investment technicalities with the relevant financial institutions and authorities 'on behalf' of the people of the provinces. In the case of the business activities of the Provincial Councils, a substantial amount of any surplus that was generated was used to finance the administrative operation of the Provincial Councils: it thus served to sustain an ethnic Fijian bureaucratic strata. It was not distributed as dividends to individual ethnic Fijians, which would be normal investment practice, and which might have assisted in the alleviation of rural poverty. Moreover, many of these Provincial Council companies over the years formed partnerships, based on political cronyism and economic expediency, with foreign companies with interests in logging, hotels, and other resource-based sectors. I have already noted however that within these companies the chiefs were usually the legal holders of shares and company titles. Thus, using Provincial Council companies, some chiefs were able to acquire considerable personal benefit through the accumulation of wealth, while foreign and local non-ethnic Fijian companies benefited through political security and ready access to natural resources. The results were clear: during the 1970s and early 1980s communal capitalism clearly benefited the ethnic Fijian élite, whether it was entrenched within the state or the *vanua*. Moreover, the logic of communal capitalism served to reproduce the conditions of the colonial Native Policy; ethnic Fijians remained locked into a communal existence predicated upon chiefly hegemony.

In light of the widespread failure of many ethnic Fijian enterprises other than those operating in the informal sector through the 1970s and the 1980s, and the state's inability to create an institutional framework which would foster profitability amongst ethnic Fijian business, the need to consolidate an ethnic Fijian bourgeois class to complement both the chiefly élite and the ethnic Fijian bureaucratic strata since the military coups of 1987 became an increasingly urgent political priority. The Minister for Trade and Commerce suggested that 'Fijian society must be prepared to accept changes if our people are to

become part of the mainstream of the economic life of our country'
(*Fiji Times*, 11 January 1990). This advice was consistent with post-
coup plans that sought to promote economic affirmative action
amongst ethnic Fijians. These plans had two general characteristics.
The first was to enable ethnic Fijians to engage in a wider and deeper
range of market activities. The second was to dispel the stereotypic
myth, reproduced over the years, that ethnic Fijians were not
culturally induced towards private enterprise. Thus, economic
affirmative action was tied to an expression of a modernist,
'progressive' ethnic Fijian identity.

The *Nine Points Plan* was drawn up in 1988 by a group of ethnic
Fijian intellectuals, professionals and bureaucrats who came together
in an umbrella body called the Fijian Initiative Group. Its explicit
purpose was to promote economic affirmative action in favour of
ethnic Fijians. It recommended: that F$20 million in equity be injected
from the FAB to the FHC; that a unit trust for ethnic Fijians be
established; that a compulsory savings scheme for ethnic Fijians be
created; that government concessions to ethnic Fijian businesses be
enhanced; that a Management Advisory Services Department be
established within the FAB; that ethnic Fijians be allocated a minimum
ownership of resource-based industries; that certain sectors of the
economy be reserved for ethnic Fijian investment; that a daily
newspaper be owned by ethnic Fijians; and that the FAB be
restructured and strengthened (Fijian Initiative Group 1988).

Clearly, the proposals were far-reaching. In response to the
proposals, the government allocated a F$20 million grant to the FHC
from the FAB. The Fiji Development Bank (FDB), a parastatal, bought
shares in an ethnic Fijian-owned daily newspaper. A review of the
structure of the FAB made recommendations to make it both more
independent of the MFA and make it more responsive to changes
within the ethnic Fijian community. Finally, the Interim Government
also approved the compulsory savings concept, although it has yet to
be implemented.

However, the *Nine Points Plan* failed to deal with two key issues
that have surrounded attempts to promote economic affirmative
action within the ethnic Fijian community. The first issue has to do
with the failure to systematically and objectively identify what
constituted the 'designated group' to benefit from economic
affirmative action. The new 1997 Constitution is vague, referring to 'all

groups or categories of persons who are disadvantaged'. Even Section 21 of the 1990 Constitution, the strongest articulation of the nationalist view on economic affirmation action, vaguely designated 'Fijians and Rotumans' to be the designated group, stating that

> parliament shall, with the object of promoting and safeguarding the economic, social, educational, cultural, traditional and other interests of the Fijian and Rotuman people, enact laws for those objects and shall direct the Government to adopt any program or activity for the attainment of the said objects and the government shall duly comply with such direction.

Section 21 was based on Article 153 of the Malaysian Constitution, which vests power in the *Yang di-Pertuan* (President), acting on behalf of the Cabinet, to safeguard 'the special position of the Malays'. What Section 21 clearly fails to do is to engage with the complicated constitutional debate concerning who exactly is a 'Fijian' (Robertson, this volume).

The second issue concerns the continuing inability of advisory reports and policy makers to institute relevant and appropriate programs which ensure an efficient return on the capital invested as a result of economic affirmative action. In post-independence Fiji attempts at economic affirmative action in favour of ethnic Fijians has resulted in unsustainable waste. Two examples will suffice: the Commercial Loans to Fijian Scheme (CLFS); and the Equity Investment Management Company Limited (EIMCOL) general store scheme of the FDB. The CLFS was specifically designed to create a class of indigenous Fijian entrepreneurs. However, failure to repay both interest and principal was so common that a number of loan portfolios within the CLFS were suspended, including loans for real estate and transport. By 1996 some F$70 million worth of CLFS loans remained outstanding (FDB 1996). The EIMCOL scheme was established to train general store managers, who were also to be provided with loans for the purchase of a general store by the FDB. However, the performance of the EIMCOL general stores was very poor; all the EIMCOL general stores have either been closed or sold.

These failures were not addressed in the follow-up to the *Nine Points Plan*. Laisenia Qarase, the former Managing Director of the FDB, and a leading proponent of 'progressive' ethnic Fijian economic affirmative action, suggested that the objective of such action 'should be the achievement of overall parity between Fijians and other communities in all spheres of activities within the shortest period of time possible' (Qarase 1995:4). In a proposal entitled *Ten Year Plan for Fijian Participation in Business*, carried out under the auspices of the United Nations Economic and Social Commission for Asia and the Pacific, Qarase put forward five proposals to be carried out by the government to 'ensure that indigenous Fijians achieve 50 per cent ownership of the corporate sector and other business sectors by the year 2005' (Qarase 1995:2). The five proposals were: the enactment of appropriate legislation with the object of promoting and safeguarding the interest of ethnic Fijians; the reorganisation and strengthening of the ethnic Fijian administration; the accumulation of savings by ethnic Fijians to provide investment capital; the encouragement of ethnic Fijian investment; and the development of ethnic Fijian entrepreneurship, business education and training.

Both the *Ten-Year Plan for Fijian Participation* and the *Nine Points Plan* heavily drew upon the Malaysian NEP. This is especially apparent in relation to the proposal to establish a definitive timetable within which 50 per cent of the economy would come under ethnic Fijian ownership. As such, like the Malaysian policy, the plans represented attempts at social engineering. However, the uncritical introduction of the Malaysian model into the Fiji context can be questioned. The NEP has had some unfavourable consequences that must be acknowledged, as they could be replicated. Economic affirmative action in Malaysia has reinforced ethnic segregation; consolidated a small but disproportionately powerful indigenous bourgeoisie which operates in conjunction with foreign capital and which survives on state patronage; worsened disparities in the distribution of wealth amongst ethnic Malays; and created unhealthy competition within the designated group itself (Gometz 1994). It can also be noted that the provision of a timetable in Malaysia has not worked (Emsley 1996).

Both plans can also be questioned for what they attempt to do. In their emphasis on enhancing the size of investments made within the ethnic Fijian community, they sought to foster large-scale, capital-intensive growth directed by ethnic Fijians. In part, this was probably due to the marked absence of ethnic Fijians from high profile corporate activity, as we have seen. However, in following such a strategy, embourgeoisement was the centripetal focus of the government's economic affirmative action—as in Malaysia. The economic leverage of the ethnic Fijian chiefly and bureaucratic strata were thus to be enhanced.

This can clearly be seen by some of the criteria that were used to judge the effectiveness of economic affirmative action. The FDB, one of the sponsors of the two plans, has, during the early 1990s, been using the size of loans disbursed to ethnic Fijians as a criteria to measure the 'success' of its economic affirmative action programs (FDB, various issues). As in the past, the rate of return on the investment was not a critical variable in judging success. In that the FDB is a parastatal, such an approach to lending demonstrates state intervention to carve out an economic space for élite ethnic Fijians within the economy. The number of ethnic Fijians eligible for large loans was obviously limited; the scope for patronage is thus clear. Indeed, ethnic Fijian élites made it a point to be seen to be actively promoting large ethnic Fijian businesses, in an effort to win political legitimacy. Ironically, such a policy, in not letting resource allocation take place through the market, ran counter to the economic liberalisation policies of the state (Sutherland, this volume).

The pursuit of large investment by the ethnic Fijian élite that benefited from communal capitalism paradoxically undermined and marginalised

> very small informally-operated (ethnic Fijian) businesses, including people who sold cordial and home-made sweets outside urban schools, prepared cooked food for wharf and factory workers, operated grass-cutting contracts and sold in the municipal markets (Chung 1989:193).

So too did the failure of the two plans to make recommendations designed to assist the development of ethnic Fijian entrepreneurial skills. Indeed, a critical area where the plans departed from the Malaysian NEP was the failure to couple embourgeoisement with poverty alleviation. The two plans did not present an alternative development paradigm suitable to the socioeconomic conditions and limited resources of the majority of ethnic Fijians, and especially the economically marginalised. This is not surprising. Economic affirmative action through communal capitalism merely served to reproduce the conditions of the colonial Native Policy, in which ethnic Fijians were locked into a communal existence under chiefly hegemony. It is not 'progressive', it is conservative, and this helps explain why a key role of economic affirmative action has been its use as an instrument of ethnically based political mobilisation by ethnic nationalists and the traditional aristocracy seeking to defend of the status quo (Prasad, this volume). However, the ethnic Fijian élite was not the only beneficiary in this structure. By endorsing, in the guise of economic affirmative action for ethnic Fijians, orthodox investment strategies that had proven wasteful and unsustainable in the past, the non-ethnic Fijian bourgeoisie—both local and foreign—had their economic dominance within the economy reinforced.

Although it appears to be a particular—and peculiar—kind of entrepreneurial strategy, communal capitalism is more: it has a deeper structural form which incorporates ethnic Fijian communal obligations, chiefly authority, and collective investment. It is thus an adaptation of ethnic Fijian 'tradition' to the demands of the market that simultaneously serves to reinvent what had been colonial paternalism. It is perhaps this adaptation which serves to give it such clear ideological power. Moreover, despite the entrepreneurial failures of communal capitalism, it has continued to be the only economic strategy that enables the continued enrichment of the ethnic Fijian élite. It is in this that it is possible to witness the fundamental contradiction of communal capitalism: communal capitalism has retarded the development of a vibrant ethnic Fijian bourgeoisie because a lot of the capital available for investment and the energy needed for individual entrepreneurship has been 'collectivised' through communal investment, to the benefit of an élite bureaucratic and chiefly strata. That this is so in practice will be demonstrated in the next section, where a case study of the flagship of communal capitalism, the FHC, is presented.

The FHC and communal capitalism

As already noted, the *Nine Points Plan* argued in favour of enhancing the equity of the FHC. Although it pre-dates the coups, and thus the deepening of the discourse around economic affirmative action, the FHC is nonetheless modelled on the Malaysian *bumiputera* investment body, Permodalan National Berhad. However, the principle underlying the FHC is that of communal capitalism. The FHC was incorporated in December 1984, and was a creation of the Great Council of Chiefs. Under the hegemonic guardianship of the Great Council of Chiefs the FHC was to symbolically represent the interests of ethnic Fijians. Thus, the investment mandate of the FHC, as outlined in its corporate plan, was 'to increase Fijian participation in the commercial economy...through acquisition of equity in established, well-managed, profitable companies with excellent prospects for growth'. Moreover, the FHC was to ensure that the 'benefits spread as widely as possible among the Fijian people' (FHC 1994:1).

In keeping with communal capitalism, share holding was communal, being mobilised through the Provinces, through the NLTB, and through the FAB. When the FHC was incorporated resources worth F$1,145,145 were mobilised from the ethnic Fijian community for investment in it. Of this, F$1 million came from the Provinces, the NLTB and the FAB, who in turn received shares in the FHC. The FHC then used the same quantity of resources, F$1million, to purchase 1,000,000 higher dividend 'A' class shares in its first major investment, Basic Industries Limited. Proposals were then made for the FHC to expand its investment portfolio. The first proposal was that the FHC buy a majority holding in two companies, Fiji Industries Limited and Standard Concrete Industries Limited; both were owned by Basic Industries Limited. Thus, this implied increasing the share ownership of the FHC in Basic Industries Limited. The second proposal was that the FHC invest in Carlton Brewery (Fiji) Limited, an Australian transnational which produced Fiji Bitter, the market leader in the country. The FHC however lacked the resources needed to fund either proposal.

One possibility that was suggested was that the FDB act as a middleman, buying shares which would later be sold to the FHC. In the event, the Great Council of Chiefs agreed that the proposals represented a good way by which to expand the FHC. An action plan was drawn up by the board of the FHC, in response to the agreement of the Great Council of Chiefs. A key part of this action plan was the proposal to increase the share capital received from the Provincial Councils, the FAB, and the NLTB, in order to finance the acquisition of shares from both Basic Industries Limited and Carlton Brewery. It was proposed that F$2 million be raised to buy more shares in Basic Industries Limited, and that a further F$4 million be raised to purchase a stake in Carlton Brewery. Thus, the capital invested in the FHC rapidly increased from F$1 million to F$5 million.

With an expanded capital base, the FHC increased its portfolio of investments. For example, one of its early commercial ventures was to buy 50 per cent of the shares in Burns Philp, an Australian company with investments in shipping, brewing, agricultural production and agro-processing, and wholesale and retail trade. As a result the FHC grew quickly. In 1985, only a year after its creation, it paid its first dividend to its shareholders. Moreover, as the portfolio of investments held by the FHC expanded, so too did the dividends it paid out to its shareholders, barring the disruptions of the 1987 coups. By 1992, profit after tax had reached F$2,752,554.

In 1992, the FHC underwent a corporate restructuring when it went from being a public limited company to being a private limited company. By changing its status to that of a private company, the FHC hoped to facilitate an expansion of individual and private group investment through it, in the form of managed funds, and in so doing expand its investment portfolio. The FHC thus began to manage individual and group investment funds to a maximum limit of F$10,000, to ensure that the 'benefits of Fijian Holdings' shareholdings are spread as widely as possible' (FHC 1993:7–8). To ensure that only ethnic Fijians were able to buy into these managed funds, individual purchasers were confined to those registered in the *Vola ni Kawa Bula*, the kinship and land ownership register which determines who exactly is an ethnic Fijian (Robertson, this volume). This shift in company status was significant: it indicated a recognition of the fact that economic affirmative action had to generate, in addition to communal benefits, benefits for individual ethnic Fijians. Given, however, that few individual ethnic Fijians had access to F$10,000 it was in reality a recognition of the principle of embourgeoisement which, behind the rhetoric, underpinned much of the economic affirmative action taking place on behalf of the ethnic Fijian community.

The dramatic expansion of the FHC in the 1990 to 1994 period was not only a result of corporate restructuring; it was also a result of the F$20 million interest-free loan provided by the government through the FAB in 1989 under the *Nine Points Plan*. In the wake of both this loan and the receipt of funds from individual and groups of ethnic Fijians, paid up capital grew from F$1.2 million in 1985 to F$27.5 million in 1994. Total assets rose from F$1.3 million in 1985 to F$36.3 million in 1994. The net value of assets increased from $170,248 in 1985 to $3.2 million in 1994. During the 1990s, the dividend paid to FHC shareholders was 20 per cent for those with 'A' shares and 5 per cent for those with 'B' shares. However, in keeping with corporate practice, the 'B' share dividend was paid into a sinking fund to meet the repayment obligations of the F$20 million loan received from the government through the FAB.

In 1994 the FHC had interests in nine major companies in Fiji, worth F$27,111,948. These were: Basic Industries Limited, which was 100 per cent owned by FHC; the Fiji Sugar Corporation, in which the FHC had a 13.2 per cent stake; the Fijian Property Trust, in which the FHC had an 89.7 per cent stake; Carlton Brewery (Fiji) Limited, in which the FHC had a 30 per cent stake; the Unit Trust of Fiji, in which the FHC had an 8.9 per cent stake; Motibhai and Company Limited, in which the FHC had 100 per cent of all preference shares; the Merchant Bank of Fiji Limited, in which the FHC had a 50 per cent stake; Carpenters Properties Limited, in which the FHC had a 50 per cent stake; and Goodman Fielder Watties, in which the FHC had 100 per cent of all preference shares. In 1995 these companies had profits of between F$0.9 million and F$4 million (FHC 1994; 1995).

Clearly, as an investment company equipped with an astute young management, the FHC has done relatively well, especially in comparison to the overall performance of the Fiji economy (Sepehri and Akram-Lodhi, this volume). However, as an institution created to economically advance the interests of ethnic Fijians, it is necessary to deconstruct the actual interests it represents by examining the distribution of share holdings in the FHC. Shareholders' names were last published in the 1992 Annual Report. That report shows the distribution of the outstanding 4,647,934 'A' class shares of the FHC to comprise: the NLTB (500,000 shares); the FAB (100,000 shares); the Provinces (713,650 shares); and private shareholders (3,384,034 shares). Each share is worth one Fiji dollar. Shares held by the NLTB, the FAB and the Provinces thus amount to about 27 per cent of FHC equity. The following sections examine each of these shareholders in turn.

The NLTB

The biggest single FHC shareholder, the NLTB was founded in 1940 to administer 'native land' which is communally owned by ethnic Fijians. Such land cannot be bought or sold; it can only be leased, for agricultural, commercial or residential purposes. Today, the NLTB administers about 83 per cent of the country's land. Of this, 420,000 hectares is leased out to 24,700 tenants in agriculture, commerce, industry, tourism, and public and civil projects. Royalties and lease monies from land are distributed by the NLTB in a way that reproduces socioeconomic inequality. The NLTB takes 25 per cent of land revenues for institutional maintenance, which in essence benefits the ethnic Fijian bureaucracy. Some 75 per cent is distributed to the landowners through the chiefs (Prasad and Kumar, this volume). It is common for the chiefs to receive the bulk of the money. The rest trickles down the ethnic Fijian social hierarchy, with individuals receiving amounts compatible with their social position.

As an investor and guardian of ethnic Fijian land, the NLTB's record leaves a lot to be desired. Over the years it has been rocked by financial scandals, charges of nepotism, cronyism and corruption (*Fiji Times*, 15 April 1996). Moreover, despite a 25 per cent charge for administering lease monies from a fixed asset and despite an annual government subsidy of F$1 million, the NLTB has recorded losses since 1986 and the accounts have not been audited since 1991. The unaudited figures showed an operating deficit of F$1.6million in 1992, a figure that seemed reasonably consistent over the previous few years (*The Review*, June 1997:19). At the end of 1993 the NLTB had an overdraft of F$16.1 million, with some F$4.4 million worth of cheques still pending presentation to the bank. By 1997 the NLTB was on the verge of bankruptcy.

The difficulties faced by NLTB are in part due to the extremely complex relationship between the state and the chiefs in financial affairs. This complexity can be illustrated by an example. In the 1980s F$1.7 million of Australian overseas development cooperation money designed to enable ethnic Fijian landowners to participate in the timber industry was used to finance a company, Kubuna/Fiji Forest Industry (FFI) (*The Review*, June 1997). The FFI was a joint venture between CBM Holdings and Westralian Forest Industries, an Australian company. As we have already seen, CBM Holdings was an ethnic Fijian company 'owned' by the landowners of the three provinces of Cakaudrove, Bua and Macuata, but in reality controlled and run by chiefs and, in this instance, their foreign business counterparts. The company belonged to the *lewe ni vanua*, or people, of the Kabuna Confederacy,[1] operating through their paramount chief, *Ratu* Sir George Cakobau, who was also both the highest traditional chief in Fiji and Fiji's Governor General. Moreover, in his capacity as Governor General, Cakobau was not only Head of State, he was also Chairman of the NLTB. In charge of the financial operations of the company was the General Manager of the NLTB, Josevata Kamikamica, a member of the Kubuna Confederacy and a subject of

Cakobau. The Chairman of CBM Holdings was *Ratu* Sir Penaia
Ganilau, the paramount chief of three provinces within the
Confederacy, who would be the successor to Cakobau as both Fiji's
Governor General and Chairman of the NLTB.

Clearly, huge potential conflicts of interest were witnessed in this
business arrangement. Power to grant logging licences and
concessions[2] on all native land is vested in the NLTB under the Native
Land Trust Act. The FFI 'belonged' to the Confederacy of which the
Head of State and the Chairman of the NLTB was the chief. The General
Manager of the NLTB was a subject of the chief. The Chairman of CBM
Holdings was the paramount chief of a component part of the
Confederacy to which the Head of State and the Chairman of the
NLTB was the chief. Thus, the power vested in the NLTB could give
rise to a potential conflict of interest, as in the case of CBM and FFI.
This is not to say that it did; merely to strongly stress that the complex
political, communal and bureaucratic entanglement witnessed in the
establishment of FFI is symptomatic of an NLTB corporate culture that
makes it difficult to distinguish between purely market, purely
communal, and purely personal interests. There are many other
examples to support the premise that, under the guise of *vanua* or
vakaturaga, interpersonal relationships can be the basis of decisions
that are then legitimised within institutional structures. As a
consequence, economic affirmative action for ethnic Fijian landowners
has the potential to become a vehicle for the enrichment of companies
acting in collaboration with strategically located chiefs, self-appointed
ethnic Fijian leaders, and influential bureaucrats.

Given such an example, the NLTB's communal investment in the
FHC needs serious scrutiny. The NLTB, given its history of financial
scandals, does not have the institutional capacity to be able to
appropriately scrutinise entrepreneurial investment, especially on
behalf of ethnic Fijians, who themselves constitute a heterogeneous
diffusion of class, tribal and political loyalties. Thus, the NLTB does
not represent a homogeneous ethnic Fijian interest, despite official
claims to the contrary. It represents a narrow parastatal, bureaucratic
and private institutional interest, propagated as universally ethnic
Fijian. The NLTB's shares in the FHC are an entrepreneurial
engagement that advances this narrow interest. In so doing, the NLTB
not only administers land, it also legitimises communal capitalism and

chiefly hegemony. This will only be deepened if NLTB investments in the FHC are ploughed back into the institution. Such a strategy will reproduce the cycle of impotent investment that could instead be creatively deployed for poverty alleviation amongst ethnic Fijians.

The FAB

Established under the Fijian Affairs Act of 1940, the FAB has institutional and political control over the MFA, in order to ensure that the MFA promotes the well-being and proper government of ethnic Fijians. The MFA, which is directly accountable to the Cabinet and the FAB, and thus the Great Council of Chiefs, is, as a consequence of this line of authority, still anchored to chiefly authority and the political norms necessary to preserve that authority. In turn, the FAB is accountable to the Great Council of Chiefs. Thus, despite radical changes in the national and international political climate, both the MFA and the FAB are extremely conservative institutions. Nonetheless, both are important institutions in the lives of ethnic Fijians. The MFA is an important institution in promoting economic affirmative action, especially through its scholarship scheme which, despite problems, has been hailed as a success in creating a large group of educated ethnic Fijians.

In addition to the 100,000 'A' class shares already mentioned, the FAB has 20 million 'B' class shares in the FHC. As noted above, each share is worth one Fiji dollar. The government provided the F$20 million needed to make the investment under the *Nine Points Plan*. This is the largest single amount of money that has been disbursed for economic affirmative action. It was envisaged that being sold to ethnic Fijians over time would disperse the amount. However, this has not taken place. In this light, it can be argued that ordinary ethnic Fijians have not benefited. The FAB, by receiving dividends, has been a major beneficiary; this though serves the interests of the ethnic Fijian bureaucracy. There have been two other major beneficiaries of this investment. First, there have been those who already have shares in the FHC: the investment of the FAB serves to enhance the value of their holding. Second, there have been local and foreign corporations like Carlton Brewery and Motibhai and Company Limited, in which the FHC heavily invests, and which stand to gain from the FHC having a larger market capitalisation. In both cases, ordinary ethnic

Fijians at best stand to make only a peripheral gain. Moreover, in that the investment of the FAB in the FHC came from the government, FHC investors and investments are in fact being indirectly subsidised by the state through its efforts to promote economic affirmative action.

The Provincial Councils

As has already been discussed, the Provinces are a mixture of state and traditional administration. Investible resources are extracted as a consequence of the obligation of ethnic Fijians to the *vanua* and to the chief. Chiefly authority is usually used to collect quotas such as F$1,000 per *tokatoka*, or extended family, or F$15,000 per village. The quotas are however arbitrarily imposed by Provincial bureaucrats using the authority of the chiefs. With minimal sources of income, villagers expend labour and time collecting money in an effort to accrue social assets, even at the price of their own domestic poverty.

All fourteen Provinces have shares in the FHC. If we crudely allocate the distribution of shares equally amongst the Provinces, there would be about 50,000 per province. If we crudely allocate the distribution of shares equally amongst ethnic Fijians, there would be 1.68 shares per ethnic Fijian. Even if we crudely allocate the distribution of shares equally amongst the rural ethnic Fijian population, there would still only be 2.84 shares per rural ethnic Fijian. These are very low allocations, given that each share is worth one Fiji dollar and given that individual donations to communal collections are often larger by a factor of ten. The figures don't add up, and from the point of view of the return on the investment, undoubtedly individual ethnic Fijians would have been better off keeping their donations to communal collection and investing it themselves. The meagre return from the investment of the Provinces is because the dividends paid by the FHC have been used mostly to sustain the Provincial institutions and the privileges of individuals and groups who have direct access to Provincial institutions. Such is the degree of absurdity of communal capitalism.

Private companies and small groups

Private companies and small groups such as *tikina*, or districts, and *mataqali*, or land-owning units, possess about 72 per cent of the shares of the FHC. However, most of the private companies who own shares in the FHC are owned by individuals or groups of individuals who are established business people, professionals or bureaucrats. Given ethnic restrictions on the ownership of shares in the FHC, they are clearly owned by the ethnic Fijian élite. In 1992 only about 30 companies which were kin or community-based owned shares in the FHC (FHC 1992).

It has already been noted that the change in status of the FHC from a public company to a private company was officially justified on the basis that the change in status would extend the benefits of the FHC to as wide a group of ethnic Fijians as possible. This justification was disingenuous. The change in the status of the FHC was primarily a result of lobbying by the ethnic Fijian élite who dominate its private company share ownership, and who wanted greater control over their investment and the dividends that it paid. Moreover, this emerging ethnic Fijian bourgeois class has found a new ally: with the foreign and local non-ethnic Fijian bourgeoisie in whose companies the FHC has purchased equity. Thus, the new ethnic Fijian bourgeoisie has been able to use economic affirmative action policies in order to promote its own interests through state-subsidised capital accumulation. This is consistent with a long-standing aim of post-coup governments in Fiji to create an ethnic Fijian bourgeois class rooted in the market-driven logic of capital accumulation.

This aim has not gone uncontested. There has, for example, been growing criticism that economic affirmative action has favoured certain individuals from certain Provinces. Most of the private company and small group shares in the FHC are from the Provinces of Kadavu, Lau and Lomaiviti, all outlying archipelagos (FHC 1992). Thus, many of the Provinces are not represented in the emerging ethnic Fijian bourgeoisie. This is a potential cause of inter-provincial dispute. Moreover, there has been public controversy about whether some of the individuals who have invested in the FHC have been engaged in insider trading. Some individuals have shareholdings that exceed those of their Province. Given the influence and professional skills of some within the emerging ethnic Fijian bourgeoisie, it is possible that they have been able to monopolise access to information about the FHC, and this has raised questions about commercial ethics and personal credibility (Korovulavula 1994). However, these criticisms have not extended to the implicit principle underlying much government action to promote economic affirmative action since the coups: the need to create an ethnic Fijian bourgeoisie.

Conclusion

The FHC is undoubtedly a successful private company. However, it does not represent a successful example of either the entry of ethnic Fijians into business or of economic affirmative action. Capital accumulation in market economies is ultimately determined by the forces of market, even if those forces are regulated by the state, and not by the ethnic identity of the market participant. Economic affirmative action interacts with this dynamic. In Fiji, the interaction between economic affirmative action and accumulation has been problematic. Part of the problem has been an inability to precisely define the group designated to receive economic affirmative action: who exactly is an ethnic Fijian? Part of the problem has been the unimaginative and uncritical way in which economic affirmative action strategies were imported from Malaysia and not based upon the socioeconomic position of ethnic Fijians.

More fundamentally, economic affirmative action through the activities of institutions such as the FHC has had a questionable impact upon the majority of ethnic Fijians. The FHC is an example of economic affirmative action that serves to reproduce what has been termed in this chapter communal capitalism. Communal capitalism has resulted in institutions such as the NLTB, the FAB and the Provincial Councils all becoming directly involved in commerce and investment, with often poor economic results. Communal capitalism has however served to reproduce the exploitative hegemony of a minority of ethnic Fijians within the state–chiefly alliance, and in so doing maintained the broad outlines of colonial Native Policy. Communal capitalism, and the need for resources that it entails, becomes an arena for economic and political mobilisation of ordinary ethnic Fijians by an élite concerned with sustaining its own economic and political hegemony. Meanwhile, poverty amongst ethnic Fijians deepens (Sepehri and Akram-Lodhi, this volume). Such an outcome is a consequence of the fact that the benefits of economic affirmative action have been concentrated in the hands of a few: state bureaucrats, chiefs, the foreign and local non-ethnic bourgeoisie, and the emerging ethnic Fijian bourgeois class.

The future of economic affirmative action in Fiji had come increasingly into conflict with the economic liberalisation policies of the previous government. The reason was obvious: liberalisation must ultimately threaten state policies that seek to grant ethnically based preferences. In this light, the state in the post-election period faces two clear challenges. The first is that the state will need to respond to the climate of globalisation. Despite the clear victory of the Fiji Labour Party in the 1999 general elections, it is entirely possible that as a result of multiparty government the state will do this by maintaining as close an affinity as possible to the policies of the International Monetary Fund and the World Trade Organization. The second challenge faced by the state is that it will need to try and accommodate the political impact of the nationalist constituency, which policies of economic affirmative action have sustained. Given the contradictions of economic affirmative action discussed in this chapter, and the limited capacity of the state apparatus in Fiji, whether these two challenges can be met is an open question.

Endnotes

1. A number of Provinces make up a Confederacy (*matanitu*). There are three main Confederacies in Fiji: Kubuna, Tovata and Burebasaga. These Confederacies are based upon traditional alliances between tribal polities, and have their roots in precolonial attempts to form centralised governments in Fiji by early European settlers and chiefs. Presently, Confederacies act as means of ceremonial and traditional mobilisation. In a way, the political loyalty of ethnic Fijians is diverse: they have loyalty to various levels of tribal categories, loyalty to the Confederacy and loyalty to the state.
2. The granting of logging licences by the NLTB does not require the consent of the members of the landowning unit, but, if deemed necessary, the NLTB will carry out consultation with the landowners. A concession, on the other hand, is also a licence but is 'granted over a large area, usually to a major logging company, and over land owned by many owning units, and for a longer period than a standard licence' (NLTB, nd:2).

CHAPTER 11

Ecotourism and the politics of representation in Fiji

Holger Korth

Introduction

Development initiatives in the South Pacific have intruded in often harmful ways on indigenous people's lives. Indeed, many projects have become examples of 'maldevelopment' (Emberson-Bain 1994c). This has led to the search for alternative development options. In recent years this search has fostered the emergence of the discourse of sustainable development. In essence, sustainable development promises holistic solutions to maldevelopment, solutions that are guided by sociocultural and environmental considerations. In the South Pacific, this discourse has in particular been articulated as the solution to the diverse range of economic, social and environmental problems associated with the tourism sector.

Since the mid 1980s development assistance programs in Fiji have sponsored sustainability-based ventures in the tourism industry. These ventures are now commonly called 'ecotourism'. Major donors have included multilateral aid agencies such as the United Nations Development Programme (UNDP) and the South Pacific Regional Environmental Programme, as well as the official development assistance of regional industrialised countries. For example, the New Zealand Official Development Assistance program (NZODA) has sponsored ecotourism projects in Fiji's rural tourism periphery. The rationale for such support is clear. According to NZODA, ecotourism offers a sustainable alternative that not only helps combat environmental degradation and achieve economic growth but also provides an alternative to capital-intensive, large-scale mass tourism development by creating business opportunities for rural communities (New Zealand Ministry of Foreign Affairs and Trade 1995). With such overseas economic assistance, it is perhaps not surprising that tourism planners in the Fiji government have shown a growing enthusiasm for ecotourism. It is also not surprising that indigenous Fijian landowners have welcomed ecotourism, predicated as it is supposed to be on the principle of sustainability, as an attractive development option (Cabaniuk 1989; Wakelin 1991).

However, despite widespread and growing support for ecotourism in Fiji, the belief that ecotourism is a clearly delineated development alternative is erroneous. While ecotourism ideally denotes nature and culture-based tourism that involves active appreciation, education or interpretation (Backman 1994), in practice it is not the panacea for maldevelopment that many purport it to be. Moreover, it has in reality often been applied to virtually any kind of tourism which has even the vaguest connection with nature (Harrison and Brandt 1997) or with culture (Helu-Thaman 1992). This chapter[1] will illustrate that both of these propositions apply to Fiji.

The chapter begins by offering a brief outline of the impact of 'traditional' mass tourism in Fiji, in order to contextualise the evolution of ecotourism. It will be argued that the negative aspects associated with mass tourism led to a search for innovative solutions, which then acted as catalysts for the emergence of an alternative tourism planning discourse in Fiji. This is witnessed in planning documents that sought to incorporate Fiji's natural and cultural heritage as tourism assets. This process led to the establishment of the so-called 'secondary tourism' sector, which laid the foundation for the emergence of ecotourism.

The principal government institutions involved in the establishment and development of ecotourism in Fiji have been the Native Lands Trust Board (NLTB) and the Ministry of Tourism (MOT). As will be seen in the chapter, the NLTB has become increasingly concerned with policy development and implementation, while the MOT has utilised ecotourism as a marketing tool in order to remodel the image associated with the secondary tourism sector. However, ecotourism representations have not only remodelled the images associated with the culture and natural heritage of Fiji, but have also remodelled more traditional tourist attractions. This demonstrates the problematic status of the ecotourism label. At the same time, despite these remodelling efforts the economic returns to ecotourism have been low. As will be shown, rural initiatives have not become commercially self-sufficient, nor have they met financial expectations, even though the ecotourism label has been part of mainstream tourism promotions[2].

Finally, in order to complement the analysis of ecotourism's conception, gradual implementation and economic performance, the chapter will evaluate its cultural impact on post-coup Fiji. It will be argued that compared to ecotourism's limited economic role, its cultural significance has been disproportionate. While ostensibly seeking to provide resources to rural communities as a means of promoting localised nature conservation, ecotourism has in fact reflected communalist divisions. Representations of ecotourism have been politically motivated and ethnically biased towards the indigenous Fijian population. Ecotourism discourse has thus become tied into a wider discourse, that of communalism.

Mass tourism in Fiji

Since the 1950s, intercontinental air travel has enabled fast and relatively affordable access to Fiji, leading to rapid growth in the tourism industry. Air travel to Fiji increased by about 20 per cent annually between 1965 and 1973; in 1973 186,000 visitors arrived by air. Apart from temporary slumps as a result of the oil crisis in 1974 and cyclones in 1983 and 1985, visitor arrivals continued to increase by nearly 4 per cent a year up to 1986. After the military coup in 1987 arrivals temporarily fell to 189,900, a drop of 26.3 per cent. However, by 1995 numbers had almost doubled to 359,400. By the mid 1990s tourism was, at 18.3 per cent of GDP, more important to the economy than sugar, which generated 11.4 per cent of GDP (Fiji Visitors Bureau 1995; Fiji Bureau of Statistics 1997).

Tourist expansion concentrated notably on western Viti Levu, the Coral Coast, and the Yasawas and Mamanucas; the spatial integration of remoter islands into the tourism industry only partially took place. Thus, the Nadi area attracted 31 per cent of hotel visitor bed nights in 1995, while the Coral Coast and the Mamanucas and Yasawas attracted 31 per cent and 20 per cent respectively. In contrast to these flows to Fiji's tourism 'centre', the frequency of visitation by tourists to the more 'peripheral' outer islands was, at 4 per cent of visitor bed nights, much lower (Ministry of Tourism and Civil Aviation 1995b).

Growing visitor numbers encouraged the colonial administration to provide legislative support for tourism development, in the form of the Hotel Aids Bill of 1958 and the Hotel Aid Ordinance of 1958, which was rewritten in 1964. The legislation respectively liberalised duty free trading and offered substantial economic incentives to encourage the construction of new hotels. Foreign consultants meanwhile advised successive Fiji administrations to focus on large-scale tourism development as an alternative development option designed to reduce the economy's dependence on the production of sugar.

Ambitious tourism development initiatives sought to capture economies of scale; in practice this meant that proposed projects were frequently too capital-intensive to be locally funded. State policy was thus strongly biased in favor of attracting international capital to supplement any investment made by the expatriate business community that had come to dominate the local economy. As a result, Fiji's tourism industry was an early site of contestation between local investors who received token concessions from the state, and foreign interests, who sought to consolidate their control of the tourism sector (Britton 1983; Britton and Clarke 1987; Plange 1996). Over time, many local entrepreneurs were pushed to the margins of the industry.

By the 1970s, the predominance of foreign capital in the tourism sector led some to argue that it was a new form of colonialism that reinforced relations of dependency on metropolitan core capital (Britton 1980). In large part, this was because of the fact that as the tourism industry became predominantly foreign owned, increases in tourism receipts were offset by revenue leakages. Retention of earnings from prepaid tour packages by expatriate agencies, as well as the need to import fuel, food, construction materials and expertise, contributed to the substantial leakage of tourism revenues out of the economy. In 1975 the leakage of earnings amounted to 70 per cent of total revenues (Britton 1980:148). Indeed, even in 1996 revenue leakages remained around 44 per cent of tourism earnings (Tabua 1996). There can be little doubt that the leakage of tourism revenues slowed the pace of socioeconomic development in Fiji.

Large-scale tourism has increasingly drawn Fiji into a globalised modernity, and rapidly growing numbers of visitor arrivals have continued to accelerate this process. However, mass tourism development in the postcolonial period has to some extent been dependent on Fiji's pre-existing colonial infrastructure (Britton 1980);

it has thus brought less economic development of benefit to wider Fiji society than might be supposed. Moreover, mass tourism's human development impact on both the indigenous and the Indo-Fijian communities has remained limited (UNDP 1994). These shortcomings have not gone unnoticed. A growing concern in Fiji has been how to redress the flaws of conventional tourism development. These concerns have found expression in planning discourse and policy development, at both the regional and local level.

Ecotourism, planning discourse and policy development

Given the flaws of mass tourism, ecotourism initiatives have developed in Fiji in the period since 1986. These initiatives emerged through a succession of policy planning documents that increasingly noted the possibilities of rural ecotourism as a means of combatting uneven development, enhancing autonomy in the tourism industry, and promoting community involvement. In this section four such plans are examined. These plans demonstrate how ecotourism came to be incorporated within planning discourse in Fiji, in large part because of a rising awareness within the NLTB of the possible importance of Fiji's unique natural environment and indigenous culture in sustaining localised tourism initiatives in the rural economy, an awareness that found expression in NLTB policy.

The Belt Collins Report

The 1973 Belt Collins Report was jointly commissioned by UNDP, the International Bank for Reconstruction and Development, and the Government of Fiji. The purpose of the Report was to establish Fiji's first comprehensive tourism development program and, at face value, the report did indeed maintain a conventional expansionist perspective towards the development of Fiji's traditional mass tourism market. Promotions were to focus on 'sun, sand, sea and smiles', while economic incentives were to be geared towards attracting inward investment from foreign capital. According to the Report

> the obvious solution [to tourism development] is to attract capital from overseas, but it is equally obvious that overseas capital will remain in its own region unless there is sufficient incentive to motivate its own movement (Belt Collins and Associates 1973:184).

However, although understated, the Report did contain a skeleton of ideas and criteria, including concern for the community, the environment, and education, which, as we will see, became central to landowner-operated ecotourism initiatives during the 1990s. Thus, the Report noted that a balance needed to be developed so that the potentially substantial economic benefits of tourism could go hand in hand with maintaining Fiji's cultural integrity. It was in this context that the section on 'visitor attraction' urged that attention be paid to the cultural impact of tourism, in order to mitigate any possible social conflict. Moreover, a growing cultural and environmental awareness was expressed in recommendations for the preservation of significant archaeological and historic features. At the same time, and of particular significance for the future development of ecotourism, the Report urged that national parks be designated as 'tourism assets'. Finally, and more generally, the Report argued that tourism development should encourage

> the spreading of the economic benefits of tourism throughout the society, providing the opportunity for Fiji citizens to participate in and control the industry...[T]ourism...[is] a means of residents learning from visitors as well as visitors learning from residents...[and] a means of cultural and environmental conservation...[V]isitor facilities [should be] based on the local environment and culture so that residents can relate to the facilities and have a sense of pride in their heritage...[E]ducation and training of residents to work in tourism...[should provide] for adequate housing and community facilities for persons employed in tourism (Belt Collins and Associates 1973:17).

There can be little doubt that these ideas contributed to the evolution of the concept of ecotourism in Fiji. Nonetheless, while over the course of the late 1970s and early 1980s the tourism sector started to diversify, much remained to be done. For example, in 1986 a visitor's survey carried out in Nadi revealed that visitors felt Fiji holidays offered little in the way of diversion and few places to visit (cited in Sawailau 1996). Clearly, shifting consumer needs and perceptions indicated a need for change. However, the conceptual roots of later ecotourism initiatives still needed to be fully elaborated.

Fiji's Ninth Development Plan

Until 1986, government economic policy was based on five-year development plans. The last of these was the Ninth National Development Plan (DP9), designed to cover the period between 1986 and 1990. The strategy of this last five-year plan was neoliberal, emphasising the promotion of export-led growth, the phasing out of tariffs and trade restrictions, the corporatisation of the state-owned enterprises, labour market reforms, and the deregulation of the financial and service sectors (Government of Fiji 1986; Chandra 1988).

The objectives for the tourism sector in DP9 were decidedly economistic: the maximisation of the net value of tourism earnings was emphasised. Nonetheless, in DP9 one of the nine separate tourism sector programs that was elaborated was dedicated explicitly to the promotion and development of so-called 'secondary tourism' activities by local entrepreneurs, through the provision of basic infrastructure, physical resources and credit facilities. This was to encourage 'local people to establish rest homes and long distance cross-country walking trails...[and] the provision of facilities for horse riding, river rafting, diving and other secondary activities' (Government of Fiji 1986:87). The plan explicitly noted that 'to encourage...local participation, the entry of expatriate operators in these [secondary tourism] areas will be discouraged'. The plan further set out the government's intention to maintain the 'judicious' utilisation of resources, which, according to Weaver (1994), allowed environmental management to form an integral part of development planning.

Thus, DP9 contained two elements of future ecotourism initiatives: one, its promotion of greater 'local', by which is meant indigenous Fijian, participation in all sectors of the tourism industry; and two, its advocacy concerning the need to protect and conserve the natural environment. Thus, environmental conservation and the provision of business opportunities for indigenous Fijians in the tourism industry, concerns which had been present, if understated, in the Belt Collins Report, became legitimate parts of Fiji's planning discourse. In the years following the coups, these aspects increasingly came to the fore.

The Cleverdon and Brook Report

In 1986 and 1987 a comprehensive review of alternative tourism in Fiji was comissioned by UNDP, under the auspices of the World Tourism Organisation. This review culminated in the publication of the Cleverdon and Brook Report (1988). The Report provided a thorough assessment of what was then conceptualised as the 'fledgling field' of secondary tourism. Secondary tourism was used

> to refer to all activities in which tourists and recreating Fijians may engage, and for which facilities may be provided on a commercial basis, which are not 'mainstream' resort accommodation or transport operations, either in respect of their style, or location/area of operations.

It argued that

> Secondary tourism activities typically take place in rural regions where there is little, or no, previous tourism development (ie off-the-beaten-track) and the tourism operations catering for such activities are operated and controlled by Fijians, in line with recommendations outlined in DP9 that such operations are to be reserved for Fijian interests (Cleverdon and Brook 1988:4).

The Report went on to more precisely define secondary tourism as: water-based activities, including scuba diving, surfing, and boating; land-based activities, including trekking, secondary accommodation and village tourism and entertainment; and 'general possibilities', including plantation and farm visits, anthropology, archaeology, forests, landscapes, mountain climbing, and ornithology (Cleverdon and Brook 1988:28–80).

The contents of the Report had implications for the emerging discourse of ecotourism. For a start, the Report displays the bias of expatriate discourse. In particular, references to local cultural idiosyncrasies are minimal. Thus, the discussion of the role of local communities and their need to mediate the social and cultural impacts of secondary tourism is very brief, pointing towards a lack of acquaintance with local knowledge and sensitivities. At the same time, the Report's definition of secondary tourism identified a vast range of activities. As will be seen, the broad definition of secondary tourism has had a direct impact on ecotourism, in that it has become an imprecise classification which eludes clear definition.

The Coopers and Lybrand Tourism Masterplan

In 1989 the Coopers and Lybrand Tourism Masterplan was published. The Masterplan called for higher levels of public sector support in the tourism sector, recommended implementation of social monitoring and public awareness programs, and explicitly advocated the provision of safeguards for the natural environment through the creation of nature reserves and recreation areas, as had been called for in the Belt Collins report (Coopers and Lybrand Associates 1989). At the same time, the Masterplan recognised the potential of secondary tourism. The Masterplan's chapter on secondary tourism proposed the development of culture and environment-based activities. It called for the identification of avenues to promote greater local community participation, including the recommendation that effective training programs be implemented in order to increase local participation in secondary tourism. Finally, like DP9 the Masterplan endorsed discouraging foreign involvement in secondary tourism, in part because of the supposition that it had low capital and technology requirements.

The Masterplan's elaboration of the concept of secondary tourism demonstrated the extent to which environmental conservation, the provision of entreprenurial alternatives for indigenous Fijians in the tourism industry, and the opportunities provided by indigenous Fijian culture were becoming part of 'mainstream' discourse in the tourist industry. Clearly, policy advice for Fiji's tourism industry was moving closer towards what would later be regarded as ecotourism. Aspects of each of the four documents just discussed therefore contributed to the formation of the concept of an environmentally-based, sustainable tourism.

The NLTB and tourism policy

Alongside the documents just discussed a fifth intervention should be seen as having contributed to the formation of the concept of ecotourism and its entry into Fiji's planning discourse: the NLTB's tourism policy. Whereas each of the four documents elaborate possibilities, the NLTB has formulated and implemented tourism policies which have facilitated the beginning of experimental tourism initiatives and which moreover point to possible ways in which an environmentally-based, sustainable ecotourism may develop in the future.

Since 1946 the NLTB has had the responsibility of administering the 83 per cent of Fiji's total land area which is classified as 'native land'. This has been done on behalf of the indigenous Fijian landowning groups who were assigned title (Prasad and Kumar, this volume). As the most important institution designed to administer land in Fiji, the NLTB has emerged as a powerful leader in sustainable resource management. The sustainable land management policies of the NLTB have evolved over time through a series of documents: the NLTB (1985) Policy on the Logging of Indigenous Forests; the Policy for Tourism Development on Native Land 1990–95 (NLTB 1990); the Environmental Charter (NLTB 1992); and the Tourism Policy for Native Land 1997–2000 (NLTB 1996; see also Cabaniuk 1996). These documents, and the policies which they have produced, have developed a greater clarity concerning the need to ensure that Fiji's natural environment is safeguarded, that indigenous Fijian lands are developed and used in a sustainable fashion, and that the cultural heritage of indigenous Fijians is preserved.

It is the Board's Landuse Planning Section which is the local leader in current ecotourism development efforts. In so doing, the NLTB is following the medium-term policy direction envisaged in the government's 1993 economic strategy, which included the promotion of ecotourism in order to enhance an awareness of Fiji's ecology and cultural heritage while at the same time ensuring enhanced indigenous Fijian participation, particularly in rural areas (Government of Fiji 1993). As a consequence, in partnership with indigenous Fijian landowners the Landuse Planning Section seeks to link ecotourism development with the conservation of nature, the protection of Fiji's heritage, and community development. In order to do this, the Section chairs and provides the secretariat for the inter-departmental Native Lands Conservation and Preservation Projects Steering Committee (NLCPPSC). The NLCPPSC was founded in 1991 to provide input into NZODA projects and is a multi-sector advisory panel including representatives from the Ministry of Tourism and Civil Aviation, the Ministry of the Environment, the Department of Forestry, the Fijian Affairs Board, the Fiji Development Bank, the Fiji Museum, the National Trust for Fiji, and Fiji Pine Ltd. The group meets irregularly to discuss environmental conservation projects. The Section has also prepared an enviromental policy statement; it has worked directly with landowners to promote ecotourism around forest conservation; and it has been working with the Fiji Museum on an integrated educatational ecotourism package tour (Matararaba and Cabaniuk 1996).

The Landuse Planning Section is currently seeking to facilitate enhanced coordination and management of tourism development across the regions, by working towards the establishment of a nation wide system of forest conservation areas, reflective of recommendations in the government's National Environment Strategy (Watling and Chape 1993). These forest conservation areas will be community-based, and should form a keystone for both rural ecotourism initiatives and the protection of Fiji's natural environment.

It is thus reasonably clear that over the last two decades planning discourse and policy interventions in Fiji have started to incorporate concerns regarding the impact of tourism on the natural environment and on indigenous culture. Ecotourism has as a result become conceptually embedded within the dominant planning discourse. This has been particularly the case since the late 1980s, when the need to mitigate the negative economic, sociocultural and environmental impact of conventional mass tourism became increasingly apparent. In recent years interventions by the NLTB in the field of secondary tourism perhaps demonstrate most clearly the growing conceptual power of ecotourism.

Thus far this chapter has emphasised the development of the concept of ecotourism in Fiji through an interpretation of planning and policy texts. However, the development of ecotourism in Fiji warrants a wider reading. In particular, it is necessary to take account of the evolution of the concept as a reflection of political agency within the MOT. By changing the angle of observation in this direction, the polysemy of ecotourism representations and terminology will become apparent.

The MOT, ecotourism and changing significations

The use of ecotourism as a label in Fiji can be traced back to the early 1990s, when concern grew within government and industry over secondary tourism's negative image as 'second best' tourism. Institutions involved in travel promotion and tourism marketing were weary of this negative connotation, prompting MOT officials to seek to replace the label with a more positive term (Schuller 1996: personal communication; Sawailau 1996: personal communication). As a result, during the early 1990s ecotourism began to replace secondary tourism as a marker for sustainable tourism initiatives. Of course, ecotourism is not a hermetically sealed concept. It is however a convenient rhetorical device.

The reinvention of secondary tourism as ecotourism coincided with the establishment of the MOT's small Ecotourism Unit in 1993, which was given a brief to further the understanding of ecotourism and advance the perceived benefits of it through the establishment of education and training programs. The Unit was to coordinate the development of Fiji's cultural, natural and historical resources as tourist attractions (Fiji Ministry of Tourism and Civil Aviation 1995a). Furthermore, it was to render advisory assistance to the private sector, support ecotourism marketing initiatives, and develop policy directives. Finally, it was to strengthen relationships between various government departments with a stake in either tourism or the environment (Francis 1994).

In so doing, the Ecotourism Unit had to deal with intra-governmental contestation concerning the development, classification and implementation of ecotourism: without doubt, at times, only nominal cooperation between departments occured. For example, despite regular meetings that were held under the umbrella of the NLCPPSC, members claim that feedback from individual departments for its initiatives, recommendations and development strategies remained extremely low. In part, this was due to certain sections in the civil service which were too conservative in their attitude to change. Innovation has often been stifled by a public service ethos in Fiji that sanctions adherence to hegemonic power structures. Influenced by the prominence of the chiefly system, an established culture of tradition, especially among non-unionised sections of the public service, has been perpetuated (Leckie 1997b). At the same time, the Ecotourism Unit has had to deal with diverse and at times conflicting interests amongst those with a stake in ecotourism. In addition to the members of the NLCPPSC, players with a stake in ecotourism include the Department of Town and Country Planning, the Lands Department, the Fiji Trade and Investment Board, the Fiji Ecotourism Association, the Fiji Hotel Association, the Tourism Council of the South Pacific, the Foundation for the Peoples of the South Pacific, NZODA, and UNDP.

In a bureaucratic environment that is averse to change, the Ecotourism Unit had the difficult brief of implementing an innovative concept. One of its first objectives was to raise ecotourism's public profile. Promotional articles were compiled and stronger liaising between various government departments with a stake in tourism and the environment advocated. More directly, in 1993 a series of Fiji National Heritage Posters was launched as the result of successful collaborative efforts between the Ecotourism Unit, the Ministry of State for the Environment, and to a lesser degree various other departments, including the NLTB and the Fiji Museum. Conceived as a linchpin in the development of ecotourism (Francis 1994), the posters vividly expressed a move away from Fiji's 'sun, sand, sea and smiles' image by fostering an appreciation of both the environment and of culture while at the same time conveying linkages between conservation and heritage.

The heritage poster series depicts particular aspects of selected landowner-operated ecotourism ventures such as the waterfalls at Bouma and archaeological features of the Tavuni Hill Fort. It also included images of native fauna such as the crested iguana, along with more surreptitious features such as World War II sites and depictions of Fiji's Parliament. Thus, under the heritage umbrella, themes were used to rightly or wrongly identify, define, and represent ecotourism. The selection of themes and images is consistent, with a bias towards those aspects of the environment and culture that lend themselves to commodification as tourism assets, thus selectively prioritising the preservation of reified places, environmental features and cultural artefacts.

Ecotourism classifications and definitions

As a new marker that replaced the label of secondary tourism, ecotourism offers an alternative mediation of reality. Its image allows for the invention of a hyperreality in which its products appear more authentic, more real, and more traditional than conventional tourism products. Over the last five years, the MOT has harnessed this image to denote innovative tourism ventures as well as reinvent selected traditional mass tourism attractions. This can be witnessed in the eclectic ecotourism classification system produced by the MOT. Listed ecotourism ventures include privately run hotel accommodation, tribally operated nature trails and tourist lodges, as well as mainstream cultural attractions such as the Fiji Museum and the Pacific Harbour Cultural Centre. Indeed, even general public transport operators such as Air Fiji are included (Fiji Ministry of Tourism and Civil Aviation 1996). It thus becomes apparent that the branding of ventures with the label 'ecotourism' has occurred on an *ad hoc* basis, comprising a diverse selection of tourism projects and operators. The heterogenous character of registered ecotourism ventures reflects not only on the success of the label and the image as a marketing tool, but is also the result of differing definitions of what constitutes ecotourism amongst diverse groups—definitions that have at the same time been subject to change.

There are two explanations as to why ecotourism has attracted such a diverse range of groups. On the one hand, ventures may have been deliberately incorporated in order to become associated with an attractive image that enhances commercial possibilities. On the other hand, the *ad hoc* fashion in which the terminology has been applied suggests that definitions have lacked clear direction and have thus allowed for the identification of a wide range of very different ventures.

Indeed, the definition of ecotourism used by the MOT has been variable. At one time, two different definitions were published by MOT employees within a single year (Sawailau 1994; Francis 1994). However, while precise definitions have changed, over a two-year period in the mid 1990s the general meaning of ecotourism contained three common themes: ecotourism should supplement the subsistence economy of indigenous Fijian landowners by providing opportunities for employment and the enhancement of communal resources; it should conserve the environment by minimising the negative impact of tourism; and it should sustain traditional cultural identities by promoting two-way interactive experiences which educate visitors in the cultural and environmental activities of indigenous Fijians. A concern with nature is thus arrayed with culturally essentialist notions of tradition and identity and articulated within a terrain dominated by economic logic.

The latest policy draft of the MOT on ecotourism is more comprehensive than previous efforts, indicating that ecotourism should be small scale, labour intensive, locally owned and operated, and involve fewer leakages than mass tourism (Harrison 1997). Nonetheless, the draft continues to perpetuate bounded and functionalist concepts that value yet at the same time seal the environment and culture in a seemingly timeless shell. For example, the draft defines ecotourism as

> a form of nature-based tourism which involves responsible travel to relatively undeveloped areas to foster an appreciation of nature and local cultures, while conserving the physical and social environment, respecting the aspirations and traditions of those who are visited, and improving the welfare of local communities (Harrison 1997:5).

The definition continues to perpetuate, if ever so slightly, a particularistic vision of indigenous Fijian identity. Of course, any attempt to classify or essentialise ecotourism, as is attempted in the draft, is inevitably reductionist. Ecotourism's definitional transience resists closure, and it is quite possibly an unworkable task to create a comprehensive classification system based on a term that is subject to constant change.

The economic significance of ecotourism

Despite the continued emphasis within Fiji ecotourism on the importance of indigenous Fijian culture, very few of the projects listed as ecotourism by the MOT are run on communal principles, which form the basis of many indigenous Fijian social institutions; private sector ventures predominate. These private sector enterprises are however caught in a sharp contradiction. For ecotourism to maintain its distinctiveness from mass tourism, it will have to remain a fringe activity. However, with only a limited number of tourists participating in ecotourist activities, activities which are predominantly small in scale, the income generated has remained marginal within the tourist industry as a whole. For example, the income generated by two of Fiji's foremost landowner-operated ecotourism projects—in Bouma and Abaca—barely reached F$12,000 annually by 1996.[3] Thus, that which is unique about ecotourism may also render it economically unviable. Indeed, in common with many landowner-operated ecotourism projects, substantial funding for the two projects mentioned above had to come from official development assistance. For Bouma and Abaca, establishment costs were almost entirely funded by official development assistance from NZODA. Thus, by 30 June 1996 total NZODA expenditure for ecotourism in Fiji stood at NZ$797,953, according to officials at the New Zealand Embassy in Suva.

The economic performance of ecotourism in Fiji is questionable, especially to the consultants and policy makers who frequently assess ecotourist initiatives. At the same time, in a society that implicitly sanctions nepotism the distribution of the revenues from ecotourism will continue to lack transparency. This is especially true for landowner-operated ecotourism projects. Thus, in the Bouma project, between 1991 and January 1996 only F$5,123 had apparently been accumulated[4]. The wider Bouma community enjoyed few tangible returns, and real income distribution apparently centered on the kin group associated with project management.

This indicates the continuing marginalisation of the subaltern majority of rural people involved in ecotourism in Fiji. Fringe benefits to communities are negligible, while low revenue structures keep wage levels at a minimum in the ecotourist service sector. For example, the main benefit from ecotourism for Abaca village was a foreign-funded truck. Little money has been made available to maintain it; in 1996 the driver, working standby, received as little as F$50 for up to 80 hours work.

In part, the poor economic performance of ecotourism is not surprising. Donor pressures continue to influence its pace of development. A good example of this was the controversial appointment of a consultant from the parastatal Fiji Pine Limited (Harrison and Brandt 1997) for rural ecotourism projects in Bouma and Koroyanitu. Since Fiji Pine is a quasi-autonomous agency, it fell outside established channels of communication between government departments. Information flows were subsequently limited and at times failed. Moreover, since the appointment was driven by NZODA both government and the private sector withdrew their support, albeit informally, from the projects, thus laying the groundwork for disappointing economic returns. As is demonstrated in the example, poor communication strategies often mean that donor-driven initiatives in ecotourism negatively affect relations between government departments, the private sector and other bilateral, multilateral and non-governmental donors. They also can fuel the civil service conservatism previously noted.

The cultural significance of ecotourism

Indigenous culture has been a major feature in the spread of ecotourism. The perceived exoticism of the culture and people who are indigenous provides the context for a cultural tourism experience. According to Din (1997), the association with 'indigenous' ensures product differentiation in the face of homogenising forces associated with the internationalisation of destinations and economies. However, in order to turn culture into a commodity that tourists can consume, its complex processes and features have to be abstracted and refined so as to become embedded as a consumer product. Li and Butler (1997) argue that commodification may protect a cultural resource, as its maintenance is vital to secure the flow of financial returns that are generated in exchange for cultural experience. Whether this has been or will be the case in Fiji is an open question: the cultural significance of ecotourism is only starting to become clear.

Ecotourism in Fiji has a strong yet relatively little studied ethnic component. In the recent past, the culture of Fiji has been perceived by visitors only as a bonus and not a primary reason for a visit. Thus, in a 1992 international visitor survey 86 per cent of visitors holidaying in Fiji sought 'rest and relaxation'; only 1.88 per cent sought 'Fiji culture' (Fiji Ministry of Tourism and Civil Aviation 1992:B15). For these resort-based visitors, the 'culture' that has been integrated into mass-based tourist experiences has been represented as staged events which occur within the overarching infrastructure of the resort. These versions of staged indigenous elements for the tourist gaze (Urry 1990) cannot replace authentic and inimitable indigenous products and elements. The staged event as a literal frontstage spectacle (Goffman 1963) does not meet the need to become acquainted at a more intimate level, where the authentic is spontaneous, unpredictable and unprovoked, and thus allows for the possibility of liminality (Turner 1978). Staged events do not appeal to a desire for escape, but ecotourism does, in promising transcendence.

Similar to the experience of other countries, yet with its own idiosyncratic features, the indigenous tourism components of ecotourism in Fiji are geared towards the desire of many tourists to learn about, witness and experience indigenous cultures (Li and Butler 1997). Ideally they foster mutually beneficial exchanges between hosts and guests. However, for the visitor, the focus of acquaintance rests on

the inwardly gazing private definition of a rediscovered postcolonial—
and increasingly post-coup—indigenous Fijian self. At the same time
though the apparent reciprocal intimacy of the ecotourism
experience—for example, overnight stays in villages or participation
in kava sessions—is mediated by indigenous hosts. Trajecting their
post-independence experience, hosts appear reflexive, and mindful of
their different identities during the encounter. Thus, breaches of
cultural protocol are met with enormous tolerance. During kava
sessions it is common to witness ecotourists getting up to spit the kava
out. The insult to the host is usually disguised by their laughter. After
all, the host needs to mediate advertised promotional representations
that construct them as culturally exotic with non-advertised
representations that reveal their economic disadvantage in relation to
the affluent who partake of these experiences.

In the wake of the coups, there has been a self-conscious
celebration of indigenousness and a growing nostalgia amongst many
indigenous Fijians for an illusive past. Post-coup sentiment has
become sharply associated with the politics of difference and an
exacerbation of communalism (Durutalo 1986). Conflict has emerged
between the advancement of a cosmopolitan liberalism, which can be
tied to an environmentalist ethos, and the conservation of a rigid and
essentialist traditional ethos, which is constructed around an
indigenous identity. Ecotourism is positioned at the intersection of this
conflict, as it seeks to encompass both the environmental and the
cultural.

The experience of culture in post-coup Fiji has been characterised
by the widespread fragmentation of traditional sociocultural norms. It
has been expressed distinctly along both a geographical rural–urban
divide, as well as along ethnic divides, between Indo-Fijian and
indigenous Fijian communities. By focusing on indigenous Fijian
culture, ecotourism has become an involuntary ally in power struggles
that centre around ethnicity. The monopolised domination of a
projected ecotourism image focuses singularly on the indigenous
ethnie and thus enhances the experience of alienation amongst the non-
indigenous population. The tourist gaze marginalises Indo-Fijian
experiences and accentuates ethnic divisions.

Thus, the voyeuristic perspective of the tourist in cultural
ecotourism unconsciously witnesses and participates in the private
struggle to redefine post-independence and post-coup social space
that has been prominently associated with communalist identity

politics. The coercive stifling of the formerly pluralist political
landscape has ensured that post-coup identification focused on a
unilateral valorisation of ethnic difference. The ecotourism process
reflects and contributes to this process. This is a disappointing
outcome. Fiji's incorporation into the global economy provides ample
opportunities for ethnic barriers to be reduced. In that tourism has not
been used to promote an image of emerging cosmopolitan
heterogeneity, a chance to reconstitute a national image that would
reduce ethnic tension—even if within the context of a re-awakening
political pluralism—has so far been missed.

Confronting futures

Ecotourism neither alleviates the ethnic tensions created as a result of
indigenous Fijian identity politics nor does it fulfil the modernist
promise of providing socioeconomic returns that can ensure sustained
environmental conservation. Thus, as a sustainable development
initiative ecotourism has so far failed to counterbalance growing
ethnic and financial inequalities in Fiji. Yet the development of a
successful ecotourism sector in Fiji faces an even greater challenge. At
the core of the development paradox lies a premise of sustainability.
That premise promises the recognition and maintenance of tradition
and heritage, while simultaneously striving for community
development through the establishment of a conservation ethic,
democratic decision-making processes, equitable resource distribution,
and equal opportunities across the age and gender divide.

However, as has been shown in this chapter, much of the focus of
ecotourist initiatives in Fiji has been on the preservation of cultural
integrity and the conservation of nature. The conservation of the
social, cultural and natural ecology suggests stasis. Thus, ecotourism
development in Fiji has not dealt with the promises of the
sustainability premise. Indeed, in many ways those promises stand in
sharp contradiction to ecotourist initiatives in Fiji. At a time when the
indigenous and non-indigenous peoples of Fiji are invariably
integrating into the world economy, global imperatives are becoming
all the more apparent. If ecotourism is to deal with the paradox of
sustainability, the old dichotomies between modernity and tradition
and between indigenous and non-indigenous will have to give way to
a more syncretistic relationship. If not, ecotourism will become just
another doomed sustainable development initiative.

Endnotes

1. The research for this chapter is based on fieldwork that was carried out throughout 1996 and 1997. It is part of a larger study of ecotourism development in Fiji, and will form the basis of a PhD thesis. The research results are currently being written up in the Department of Anthropology at the University of Otago, Dunedin, New Zealand. I would like to acknowledge helpful comments on this chapter from Ian Fraser, Trisha Korth, Jacqui Leckie and Peter Wilson.
2. The Fiji Visitors Bureau hosts an ecotourism site on the World Wide Web: <http://www.fijifvb.gov.fj/ecotour/ecotour.htm>.
3. These figures come from the confidential monthly revenue summaries of the Bouma and Abaca ecotourism projects for the period between 1994 and 1996. They have been confirmed as authentic by the author.
4. Personal communication with members of the landowning unit.

CHAPTER 12

Retreat from exclusion? Identities in post-coup Fiji

Robbie Robertson

Introduction

For many in Fiji, the coups of 1987 represented an attempt to dismiss Fiji's postcolonial policies of multiracial accommodation and to determine much more exclusive identities for its peoples. Aboriginal Fijians—in the vernacular *i Taukei*—stood to gain most from post-coup changes, which promised to grant them, through the economic affirmative action policies of the state, preferential access to jobs, contracts and resources (Ratuva, this volume). While the coups created opportunities to 'sever the apron strings which tied us to inherited colonial characteristics' (*Fiji Times*, 3 June 1989), the harshness of what was required was 'payment for the ease with which we got independence' (*The Age*, 9 September 1991). Indeed, many people in Fiji believed this was Fiji's belated but nonetheless real struggle for independence. However, far from severing 'the apron strings' the coups prompted a massive reassertion of colonial power structures. A new constitution in 1990 gave political power to chiefly and provincial *Taukei* authorities, and foreshadowed a separate justice system for aboriginal Fijians. It was as if the restoration of colonial controls would allow the *Taukei* to bestow upon the future all the certainties the past now represented but which the present so obviously and manifestly lacked.

These contradictions owed much to the differing objectives of classes in Fiji. The nascent *Taukei* middle class expanded after 1987, engaging the chauvinistic rhetoric of the coups in order to gain both space and benefit for itself. At the same time it employed the rhetoric of deregulation in order to weaken the advantages Indo-Fijians were said to have gained under the pre-coup postcolonial accord. However, the long-term viability of this nascent middle class could not be sustained solely by access to cheap state resources. Only a thriving economy promised long term viability. Unfortunately, policies of ethnic exclusion did not inspire business confidence; consequently, the very investment upon which the economy depended for growth shrank drastically (Sepehri and Akram-Lodhi, this volume).

The small but powerful bureaucratic and chiefly classes within the *Taukei* also had agendas. The coups provided them with opportunities to re-establish control over the political system and to refashion the economic base so as to make it less dependent upon already weakened and potentially unstable traditional structures. The Fijian Holdings Company Limited and other state-financed Provincial investment companies expanded rapidly in the decade following the coups (Ratuva, this volume). So too did the fortunes of well-placed bureaucrats, who used access to cheap loans to reconstitute themselves as a strong faction of the country's bourgeoisie. However, in doing so they simultaneously reduced opportunities for others. Indeed, the massive costs associated with the National Bank of Fiji's loan losses so weakened the economy that Fiji may be unable to reap any of the anticipated economic dividends that constitutional reform promises (Robertson 1998:192).

Ultimately, the inability of Fiji's coup leaders to deliver on their promises of a new era for the *Taukei* forced a partial retreat from the goals of 1987. A new constitution ten years later permitted a fairer electoral system and created space in which to develop the interests of civil society. Both goals have been widely praised and accepted by Fiji's peoples, as is manifest in the outcome of the 1999 general elections (Prasad, this volume). However, despite these important concessions, the new 1997 Constitution also symbolises Fiji's continued failure to confront its history, and in particular the way in which colonial and postcolonial élites have fostered and exploited ethnic divisions in order to maintain power and wealth. The 1987 coups were but an extreme consequence of those strategies.

Taukei identity: accommodation or exclusion?

Rhetoric implied that the coups were for the benefit of the *Taukei*. It quickly became apparent however that not all *Taukei* would be allowed to call themselves 'Fijian', the common English language description for the *Taukei*, and so gain from changes in state policy designed to promote *Taukei* economic affirmative action. The 1990 Constitution determined that only people registered on the *Vula ni Kawa Bula* (VKB) could be deemed to be 'Fijian'. Appropriately enough, this colonial register, begun eighty years earlier to record landowners, was housed with the Native Land Commission. However, the VKB mocks the traditions of Fiji. For the past 3000 years Fiji has absorbed—no doubt not always easily—many peoples from the Pacific, resulting in a unique society with both Melanesian and Polynesian characteristics. Paul Geraghty, in *Islands Business*, has argued that there has been no tradition of exclusivity in becoming 'Fijian'. 'Ancestry had very little to do with' qualifying 'as a Fijian in a traditional sense', he claimed (*Islands Business*, February 1992:19). For example, earlier this century Tongan warriors at Sawana were given tribal status equivalent to that found within *Taukei* tribes. The tribe was given the name Toga, and the *Tui Lau* title, associated with a nineteenth century Tongan leader, was resurrected for its head. Similarly, in Rewa one group of Tongans took the name '*Vulagi*', which means outsiders or visitors, and became a dominant family.

Much of this flexibility was lost in a British drive to standardise and regulate relationships after Fiji became a British colony in 1874. More than one hundred years later, coup leader Sitiveni Rabuka continued this trend with his 1990 Constitution. Thus, people whose ancestors came from the Solomon Islands, Vanuatu, Banaba and Tuvalu, at one time all accepted as 'Fijian', became 'others'. Of course, the *Taukei* had always made decisions about who would be accepted into their communities and who would not. Accordingly, most that came from outside the South Pacific region were excluded. To some extent the different relationships that those who were excluded experienced with their former colonial overlords, the British, combined with their own different cultural inheritances to create new postcolonial Fiji identities. Not surprisingly, these identities were also sustained by reference to one another, including the identity of aboriginal Fijians. As parliamentarian Mesake Baisagale argued, 'the

presence of the Hindi-speaking community is like a covering that
keeps the indigenous people together' (*Fiji Times*, 24 March 1995).
There was though a cost: in the process the aboriginal peoples of Fiji
over time became far more selective in applying the values of sharing
and reciprocity which they argued lay at the heart of *Taukei* culture.
The unintended consequence of exclusion festered destructively.

Exclusion did not just apply to non-aboriginal Fijians. *Vasu* had both
aboriginal and non-aboriginal parents. They were however excluded.
Taukei were not untouched by this perversity. *Ratu* Jo Nacola declared

> my wife is a part Fijian, a *vasu*, and my children are of mixed ancestry
> but they are every bit as Fijian as the offspring of a woman from my
> own *mataqali* who marries into another community and her children
> are accepted as members of my *mataqali* in accordance with our
> customs (*Daily Post*, 11 February 1994).

Similarly, businessman and politician Jim Ah Koy, whose *Taukei*
registration had been challenged in the courts during 1992, argued
that 'irrespective of whether I got into the VKB does not alter the
Fijianness in me. I can't help the fact that two bloods run through my
veins' (*Fiji Times*, 14 October 1994).

A final point can be made about the *Vula ni Kawa Bula*. Its
significance within contemporary *Taukei* culture can perhaps be
gauged by the fact that many *Taukei* have never bothered to register
with the VKB. If 1993 estimates are correct, some 66000 *Taukei*—just
under one fifth of the aboriginal Fijian population—have failed to
register. As a consequence of this technicality, 20,000 *Taukei* were
excluded from voting in 1992 (*Daily Post*, 8 October 1993).

A second restriction on the definition of 'Fijian' has much older
roots than the 1990 Constitution. A rigid fixation with patrilineal
descent reflects historical disadvantages faced by women (Leckie, this
volume). It also fosters exclusion. Any concessions to women have
invariably been seen as gestures of goodwill or favour; they were
certainly not those of equal rights. Consequently, the state's definition
of 'Fijian' came to rest solely upon a father's ethnic classification. No
offspring could be recognised as *Taukei* if the father was non-aboriginal,
even if the mother's *mataqali* (clan) accepted the child. The marital
status of the child's parents was irrelevant. Ironically, there are
Taukei—even *Taukeists*, members of the extremist *Taukei* Movement
which claimed responsibility for the first coup in 1987—whose fathers
or grandfathers were not aboriginal Fijians. That did not deter them

from arguing that the *Bose Levu Vakaturaga* (BLV), the Great Council of Chiefs, had ruled in favour of patrilineal descent in 1962 in order to 'save the Fijian people from being swamped by others and reduced to a pitiful race of beggars' (*Fiji Times*, 9 October 1993). That the ruling has been largely ignored by aboriginal Fijian people themselves reflects its departure from reality. As in the past, *mataqalis* simply decided for themselves whom they would accept and whom they would not.

The coups' supporters took the BLV's ruling seriously however, and began to quietly review all registrations of aboriginal Fijians since 1962. In 1992 a committee recommended cleansing from the VKB thirty-six *mataqali*-approved *Taukei*, including Jim Ah Koy, former Reserve Bank Governor Savenaca Siwatibau, and Colonel Pio Wong (*Fiji Times*, 10 July 1996). Its recommendations were chauvinistic and sent 'out a sad message for the future of the country', noted the *Fiji Times* (12 July 1996), adding that the heritage of those enforcing it might not bear too close a scrutiny. Certainly, the committee's recommendations contained uncomfortable shades of a 'master race' concept, which had always lain uneasily behind the *Taukei* Movement. Indeed, one of the founders of the *Taukei* Movement declared that *Taukeists* shared the same dedication to their people as the Nazis did to Germans (*Auckland Star*, 24 August 1987).

These attempts to redefine identity assumed that identities are static, homogeneous, and can be measured against an idealised norm. In Fiji this has never been the case. For example, Indo-Fijians are far from homogeneous. At the very least, they came from geographically distinct regions of South Asia. They left at a time when the concept of India as a nation was in its infancy and there was no fully articulated vision of independence. Consequently, the South Asians who came to Fiji were not a singular or united people. They were divided by gender, religion, caste, place of origin and language. They were also divided by their status: indentured or free settler. Ironically, what transcended these divisions were their colonial and postcolonial experiences of ethnic chauvinism and communalism. The Fiji experience created, united and 'indigenised' the Indo-Fijian community.

Aboriginal Fijians too are far from homogeneous. They are divided by commoner and chiefly status, by gender, origin, language, and the geography of east and west. Such divisions assumed new characteristics under colonialism and postcolonialism, much as they did amongst descendants of South Asian migrants. These combined with the consequences of a monetised economy and urbanisation to provide both threats and opportunities for hereditary chiefs struggling to maintain communal leadership and relevance. Under such circumstances the colonial communal divide provided too strong a possibility for chiefs and politicians to resist. Using communalism, they locked themselves and their people into the rhetoric of ethnic difference and conflict, with all its consequences. Communalism transcended class—or so they believed—and bestowed new meaning on the socioeconomic consequences of change amongst the *Taukei*. Indo-Fijians became the cause of *Taukei* disadvantage, creating a scapegoat that empowered a crusade to draw aboriginal Fijians back into the communal fold.

Divide and rule: colonialism, class and exclusion

The postcolonial party of government until 1987, the Alliance, began by presenting itself as a multiethnic party, despite being dominated by aboriginal Fijians and being controlled by one of Fiji's highest chiefs, *Ratu* Kamisese Mara. When rural *Taukei* deserted the party in droves in 1977, the Alliance successfully wooed them back by pursuing an election campaign that chauvinistically appealed to ethnic identity. Communalism gave the Alliance unity, stability and purpose in the face of division and confusion until 1987. However, these tactics divided Fiji ethnically, frustrated national unity and purpose, diminished the benefits of development, and ultimately produced political instability and economic stagnation. This occurred because Fiji failed to transcend the strategy of divide and rule that had been devised by Britain to sustain colonialism as cheaply and as comfortably as possible. The failure to transcend the strategy of divide and rule was not a recipe for postcolonial development and cooperation; it was a recipe for neocolonial stagnation.

In the wake of the use of communalism by the Alliance, *Taukei* leaders began to rewrite history, portraying Indo-Fijians as colonisers— wealthy, greedy and ungrateful. This occurred despite the fact that those South Asian migrants and their descendants had not been and were not privileged. In fact, the majority of Indo-Fijians in the late 1980s were little better off than *Taukei*. The commonly held image of wealthy Indo-Fijians was highly selective. In 1986 Indo-Fijians held 58.5 per cent of all white-collar jobs; *Taukei* held 30.9 per cent. Indo-Fijians held 69.1 per cent of professional and managerial jobs; *Taukei* held 17.4 per cent. Yet the vast majority of Indo-Fijians—89 per cent—and the vast majority of *Taukei*—79 per cent—belonged to disadvantaged classes: farmers, wage earners, peasants, unpaid family workers and the unemployed (Sutherland 1992:153–59). These facts though were not allowed to get in the way of political goals. The *Taukei* Movement's spokesperson histrionically observed that Indo-Fijians 'can't leave us for dead socially, they can't leave us for dead economically, and then think that they can take over the political leadership of this country without Fijians fighting back' (Radio Australia, 5 October 1987). Such abuse worked because ethnic chauvinism had long permeated Fiji society as a consequence of divide and rule. Ethnic chauvinism inverted the meaning of the thriftiness and education upon which Indo-Fijians, the Jews of the South Pacific, relied for their security and from which they benefited. As the Leader of the Opposition noted, 'in this country Indians have a lot now which they did not have fifty years ago...The most powerful thing we have today is our education' (*Fiji Times*, 8 April 1996).

Yet it was Britain that had segregated the peoples of Fiji. It developed the best schools for Europeans and for the sons of chiefs. Separate suburbs existed for different ethnic groups. Unions were ethnically segregated, often mirroring different patterns of ethnic employment. Different laws existed for the different peoples of Fiji. Ethnic differences were explained by reference to grand narratives on civilisation and children were raised on the resultant stereotypes. Although postcolonial policies of multiculturalism in education and employment weakened many stereotypes, politically motivated ethnic scapegoating during the late 1970s and 1980s served to maintain them. Moreover, migrants from monocultural rural areas brought with them their own regional variations, and passed these on to their offspring as well. They also retained their provincial identities and loyalties, sometimes grouping together in urban village settlements, sometimes maintaining social links through provincially oriented churches. In the short term at least, urbanisation exerted a conservative influence in stressing difference and fostering exclusivity.

In Larry Thomas's play, *Men, Women and Insanity*, a young woman reflects

> The problem is we are all frightened. We like each other, but we don't like each other. If we like each other, then there's something wrong. You see we are not supposed to like each other. That's the way we are

brought up. For the Fijian kid they are told not to like the Indian kid because he is cunning and has no manners. For the Indian kid, he is told the Fijian kid is lazy and good for nothing and you will never learn anything from him. So even if an Indian kid and a Fijian kid grow up together, they will still be an Indian and a Fijian, not people who are friends (Thomas 1995:201–2).

However, behind these 'everyday' stereotypes lay a material basis, Sutherland argues.

With Indians being so visibly dominant in high paid professional, managerial and other white-collar occupations, the deepening sense of Fijian disadvantage is even more understandable. For not only did they dominate those economic activities which impacted daily and most directly on Fijian lives, they also commanded the most sought after jobs (Sutherland 1992:153).

Grievances may, over time, have come to be seen in 'everyday' stereotypical terms: 'Indian success, Fijian failure'. Sutherland stresses though, that the basis of these 'everyday' stereotypes is actually class.

When, for example, Fijians sneer at an Indian businessman, it is out of resentment and envy. He is resented because he is an Indian (as opposed to say a European). But he is certainly not envied for being Indian. Rather he is envied because he is a businessman. The envy has to do primarily with class not race, even if the resentment might spring from both. Unfortunately, the racial form of the problem invariably hides its class content. And this helps sustain the myth of Indian domination (Sutherland 1992:153).

Grounds for envy based on ethnicity are indeed problematic. They are a myth, and a very convenient one, in a country in which transnational control, with or without local collaboration, is massive.

In the early postcolonial years foreign companies retained their dominance of the Fiji economy, particularly sectors such as utilities, mining, and finance, and controlled 65 per cent of Fiji's total turnover in 1980. In the tourist retail sector Indo-Fijians dominated the non-hotel retail infrastructure, controlling 91 per cent of it, but accounted for only 26 per cent of retail turnover. The greatest share—some 72 per cent—went to foreign companies (Sutherland 1992:147–50). However, for political mythmakers only the visible infrastructure mattered—the number of Indo-Fijian owned shops, buses and taxis. 'One of the greatest causes of dissatisfaction that caused the coup', explained *Ratu* Mara, 'was the fact that Fijians didn't think that they have a fair share of the cake' (*Pacific Islands Monthly*, October 1991).

Ethnic envy was a dangerous weapon for the Alliance to employ politically. It created unrealistic expectations and poisoned communal relations at a time when economic development began to challenge old colonial barriers. As a consequence, it backfired on its propagandists. Sakeasi Butadroka, the leader of the extremist Fijian Nationalist Party, a long time opponent of Mara and his Alliance government, and a staunch advocate of Indo-Fijian expulsion, stood outside Parliament within hours of the first coup on 14 May 1987 and shouted to the crowds that had gathered 'Where is Kamisese Mara? Don't blame Bavadra, don't blame anybody, blame Kamisese Mara who sold Fiji. Where is he? Where is he now? Mara, the bloody Judas Iscariot?' (Robertson and Tamanisau 1988:70). Mara believed the rejection of the Alliance government in 1987 to be cross-communal. Nonetheless, he reserved his greatest condemnation for Indo-Fijians. In any country in which overseas South Asians are 'almost a majority, you have problems', he declared (*Fiji Times*, 4 December 1991). Mara painted a striking picture: a disloyal and ungrateful Indo-Fijian majority avariciously grabbing power and bringing down upon itself and the postcolonial leadership the wrath of an enraged aboriginal Fijian people. His traditional superior and former political colleague, Governor General and later President *Ratu* Sir Penaia Ganilau, was blunter. 'The migrant races in the country have complete control— except for political leadership'. A new constitution, he asserted, would guarantee the *Taukei* the fulfillment of their aspirations (*Fiji Times*, 11 January 1989).

Constitutions, chiefs and communalism

A founder of the *Taukei* Movement and later government minister *Ratu* Inoke Kubuabola claimed that Indo-Fijians did not acknowledge that aboriginal Fijians had 'made their heritage available for others to share. It is time they come to terms with the reality of the situation that exists today' (*Fiji Times*, 27 September 1989). However, this was not true. The 1970 Constitution, not the *Taukei*, gave equality to all citizens of Fiji, including Indo-Fijians. In 1970 Fiji declared that it would abandon the ethnically divisive policies of colonialism and promote instead a new sense of national unity based upon respect for ethnic differences. Multiculturalism did not deny communalism; it just did not accord it precedence over respect for equal peoples. It was an

important symbol of difference for a new postcolonial era, even if it
was increasingly honoured only in the breach. However, in 1987 new
communal moguls dismissed multiculturalism as a facade. An
unwritten agreement, they claimed, made aboriginal Fijian
paramountcy the reality. It became convenient to deny that Indo-
Fijians were citizens. Aboriginal Fijians were the hosts; Indo-Fijians
mere guests. The problems involved in regarding fourth or fifth
generation citizens as guests, not equals, and implicitly giving them
the same status as immigrants on short term work permits, are
obvious. Mara 'lamented on his failure to create a truly multiracial
Fiji', Rabuka declared. 'I think he was too cruel on himself, he was
trying to achieve something that was impossible' (*The Age*, 21 July
1990). Following the coups no space existed for multiculturalism.

Or for democracy. Democracy meant equality according to
members of the *Taukei* Movement. It respected that which
communalism had to destroy in order to dominate. The *Taukei* called
democracy 'demon-crazy', claimed it to be alien to *Taukei* culture,
argued that it was a conspiracy to deprive aboriginal Fijians of the
leadership of their own country, and saw it as a means to drive a
wedge between commoners and chiefs. *Taukeist*, unionist and
government minister Taniela Veitata distributed 10,000 letters to *Taukei*
households in 1988 declaring that 'he who is not proud of his race has
no right to live and should go hurrying with that crazy demon
democracy to bloody hell' (*Daily Post*, 12 December 1992).

In 1988 Rabuka told a provincial council that 'the chiefs are the
mainstay of the Fijian race and it is important that the chiefly system
be maintained if the Fijian race is to remain united' (*Fiji Times*, 31
October 1988). However, there was no consensus amongst aboriginal
Fijians as to whether the chiefs should assume complete political
leadership. Politician Kolinio Qiqiwaqa noted that chiefs sold Fiji to
Britain in 1874 to liquidate a debt owed by the *Vunivalu* of Bau (*Fiji
Times*, 7 August 1987). By way of contrast, the commoner Rabuka
justified his first coup by claiming that personal attacks made by
politicians against Mara—a high chief—were too much for
commoners to bear (*New Zealand Herald*, 19 May 1987). By the time of
the second coup, though, his views had changed. 'A lot of people say
that chiefs should not participate in politics because in politics you
might be subjected to some adverse comments that are unbecoming to
your status', he claimed (*Islands Business*, October 1987). Mara

disagreed, retorting that chiefs had always been involved in politics and could not remain aloof as they provided stability and moderation (*Fiji Times*, 3 October 1991). Both men did however recognise that 'for the last 20 years [*Taukei*] have failed to distinguish between culture and politics, between chiefs as chiefs and chiefs as part of the political structure' (Vesikula 1989:12).

The nature of relations between chiefs and commoners was also a subject for disagreement. Leading *Taukeist* and later government minister Filipe Bole regarded chiefs and their people as indivisible (*Fiji Times*, 5 August 1991). Yet for much of Fiji's history, both before and after colonisation, chiefs and 'their' people had been divisible. Indeed, one of the most striking class struggles of twentieth century Fiji is that of chiefs struggling against the social and political consequences of change and the not inconsiderable antipathy of some colonialists to the retention of their roles within society. Britain benefited from the chiefly struggle—it enabled a conservative alliance of chiefs and locally based Europeans to emerge, reducing pressures for decolonisation. It was only on the eve of its departure that Britain, not wanting to be seen internationally as condoning the communalism it had fostered, sought to dismantle the structures of communalism in Fiji by introducing a new power sharing constitution which, while marginally biased towards aboriginal Fijians, was purportedly designed to break down communalism. It is not very surprising that within seventeen years both legacies of the last years of British colonialism in Fiji—power sharing and multiculturalism—were overthrown: the chiefs had to ensure that the communal project remained under their effective control in order to maintain their own social and economic position. At first there seemed no doubt. 'We want the chiefs to hold leadership', Rabuka stated late in 1987 (*Islands Business*, December 1987).

Twenty-one months later Rabuka's position had changed. He was out of the army and had become a politician. He could afford a touch of defiance. While 'chiefs have the final say', 'when it comes to politics these chiefs do not have the mandate of their people' (*The Age*, 17 August 1991). Rabuka wanted chiefs to assume a symbolic role and to modernise by being trained to use 'modern systems of leadership, rather than relying on total loyalty, traditional blood-ties and so on; you make them effective managers' (*Fiji Times*, 29 August 1991). There was a need to slow down the process of totally making ineffective the chiefly system and hopefully we can introduce certain policies and systems in which we can work at getting our chiefs into an effective ruling group, not to the extent that they rule the politics of the nation, but they rule their own little *vanuas* (territories) and the divisions of the *vanua* effectively, capable of understanding the modern democratic systems that we now live in (*Islands Business*, July 1991).

Any alternative, he believed, eroded the chiefly system and produced a new élite based on competition, education and personal initiative. While Rabuka did not endorse that 'kind of democracy' (*The Age*, 21 July 1990), it was clear that his views concerning the political role of the chiefs had dramatically changed. Many chiefs had expected something different after 1987.

Certainly the Fiji Labour Party's leader, Dr Timoci Bavadra, had promised the chiefs nothing when he upset the postcolonial cocoon by winning the 1987 election. His new deal had been for commoners. He wanted to return to them the management and wealth of their own lands. Bavadra's Minister of Labour and Immigration was unequivocal when he said 'the days of the old leaders club are coming to an end. In the modern world, it is democratic rights that give the commoner Fijian their best chance in life' (*Dominion Sunday Times*, 17 April 1988). Nationalist Butadroka had similarly promised little for the chiefs. 'The time for chiefly leadership had long gone' (*Fiji Times*, 6 December 1988), he declared.

The assumption of such a view had not been expected from Rabuka. He was the chiefs' 'brave hearted champion', as *Ro* Lady Lala Mara reportedly called him at the first BLV meeting after the coup which toppled Bavadra (*Fiji Times*, 2 November 1995). They anticipated using post-coup circumstances to secure their own status. Indeed, they succeeded in gaining paramountcy in the 1990 Constitution by restoring the political role of their provincial bases and by winning a new role for a much more concentrated BLV, which now became a *de facto* parliament, closed to the public and media. Rabuka accepted that the BLV was 'the supreme constitutional body' (*Fiji Times*, 16 January 1989).

The chiefs saw their post-coup consolidation within the Fiji polity as essential in order to achieve a central goal of the coups: maintaining the unity and self-reliance of *Taukei* culture. For the chiefs, achieving this goal meant restoring to themselves control over many *Taukei* institutions, which were increasingly influenced by commoners. Moreover, the chiefs saw themselves as moderates and regarded their

own self-interest as altruism. Not all *Taukei* agreed. Bavadra for one
was dismayed, seeing it as 'the manipulation of Fijian institutions for
advantage of a particular proposition shared by the military leader
and some members of the interim administration' (*Far Eastern
Economic Review*, 28 June 1990). Similarly, the dissident Bauan chief
Ratu Jone Madraiwiwi argued that the actions of the chiefs were 'the
result of an attempt to shore up a system that is being eroded by
change' (Griffen 1997:231). Such actions, he believed, would
encourage tribalism and provincialism at the expense of nation
building. Butadroka too dismissed the BLV, although this did not stop
him from creating his own rival Viti Levu Council of Chiefs in 1992
(*Fiji Times*, 6 December 1988).

The chiefs viewed their critics suspiciously. The Bavadras,
Butadrokas, Vesikulas, and perhaps even now the Rabukas of this
world sought to upset chiefly power bases inherited from the
nineteenth century and frozen by colonialism. They would throw
these bases into confusion. They wanted a western fourth confederacy,
which might become the revenge of old Colo, once the first casualty of
colonialism but now, with western Viti Levu, the backbone of the
economy. They would, as Rabuka himself proposed, keep the chiefs
one level removed from politics by harmlessly confining them to the
Senate, a kind of House of Lords. A Senate of Chiefs might enable
chiefs to be involved in politics, Rabuka speculated, while not 'getting
down to the level of politics where, look, I can say this against the
prime minister, regardless of who he is' (*Islands Business*, July 1991).
This was not what the chiefs had wanted. Nonetheless, as time went
on, Rabuka—his goal now firmly on succession to Mara once the
Interim Government's term ended—identified himself more and more
with those calling for reform of the role of chiefs in the governance of
Fiji. The coup leader now staked his claim both as a commoner and as
a moderate in arguing that

> Sakeasi Butadroka, Jolame Uludole, Isireli Vuibau and the *Soqosoqo ni
> Vakavulewa ni Taukei* are all fighting for the same cause—ensuring
> Fijian political dominance and protection of indigenous rights. The
> only difference in our style is that we're following different channels
> to achieve such ends (*Fiji Times*, 11 November 1991).

Nonetheless, Rabuka's emergence as a moderate was relative. He
wanted to help 'Fijians live with the threat [from Indo-Fijians]; and not
only living and surviving but overcoming it' (*Fiji Times*, 16 July 1991).

His views were the same as nationalists such as Butadroka, except that he promised not to expel Indo-Fijians. Rabuka made no promise of equality or a return to multiculturalism.

Exclusionary economics

When Mara retired as Prime Minister in 1992, he told President Ganilau that 'if our people are misled into believing that economic manna will simply fall from heaven because there is a Fijian government, then those responsible will have to answer to the country when the truth becomes evident' (*Fiji Times*, 30 May 1992). Yet the Interim Government which Mara headed had been created specifically to secure aboriginal Fijian political paramountcy as the necessary precondition of Fiji's economic growth. As a leading technocrat noted, 'businessmen don't care about the voting structure' (*Islands Business*, February 1989). That might have been true for short-term foreign investors, but Fiji in the early 1990s depended to a large extent on internal investment; and many internal investors sought evidence of the government's commitment to an acceptable constitution and to a resolution of land lease negotiations before they committed resources. Indeed, as early as 1988 Westpac Pacific's General Manager had put the case very directly: growth would remain frustrated until such time as people saw 'a democratically elected government in place' (*Financial Review*, 30 November 1988).

The understandable failure of many Indo-Fijian businesses to invest following the coups sent an important message to politicians. As Mary-Louise O'Callaghan wrote, 'if Fiji is really only for Fijians with Indians as guests...not much long term commitment can be expected from non-Fijians or as equal but different citizens (*The Age*, 1 June 1991). Exclusion thus fostered a form of economic apartheid that could not work in Fiji. Mara too seemed on occasion to accept the fallacy of apartheid. In 1989 he told the National Economic Summit that 'the major challenge on the road to economic progress at this time, and no doubt we will face it in the next 11 years, is national unity' (*Pacific Islands Monthly*, July 1989). Two years later a senior government minister told a Fiji Trade and Investment Forum that 'the welfare of the country takes precedence over the rights of any specialised group' (*Fiji Times*, 16 November 1991). Jai Ram Reddy, the leader of the opposition National Federation Party, also recognised the impact of economic apartheid, stating that 'the success of my community depends on the success of every other community in Fiji' (*Fiji Times*, 8 April 1996).

Despite widespread agreement about the negative economic consequences of exclusion, *Taukei* leaders did not act to dismantle economic apartheid in Fiji. In 1988 Sir Shridath Ramphal, then Secretary General of the British Commonwealth, could not 'see much evidence of even a will to forge a political settlement'(*The Age*, 17 September 1988). Accommodation was indeed slow in coming. In 1992 Rabuka succeeded Mara as Prime Minister, but he regarded himself first and foremost as a *Taukei* prime minister, not as a prime minister for all Fiji's peoples (*Fiji Times*, 4 August 1994). Only in early 1997 did Rabuka appear to concede that government must serve the interests of other communities and that the *Taukei* would have to learn to accept that there were other communities which belonged to Fiji (*Fiji Times*, 28 February 1997).

'Throughout history, when a state has taken an exclusive and intolerant idea such as religion and ethnicity as its cornerstone', wrote former Canadian Prime Minister Pierre Trudeau, 'this idea more often than not has been the very mainspring of violence and war'.

[A] state that defines its function essentially in terms of ethnic or religious attributes inevitably becomes chauvinistic and intolerant...[A] truly democratic government...cannot be nationalist because it must pursue the good of all citizens, regardless of their sex, colour, race, religious belief or ethnic origin. Democratic government stands for good citizenship, never nationalism (*Australian*, 2 July 1990).

Identity in post-coup Fiji

Fiji, of course, is a modern creation. Prior to colonisation the nation of Fiji did not exist, although parts of the country were known as *Viti*, from which the British corruption derived. The British came to call its aboriginal peoples 'Fijians', but they could just as easily have called them *kai Viti* or *i Taukei*. Over time, the use of 'Fijian' to describe the aboriginal peoples of Fiji has become natural. However, it makes finding a common name to describe the citizens of Fiji very difficult. Sixty-three per cent of the people of Fiji polled in 1995 favoured a common name, but aboriginal Fijians were almost equally divided on the issue. Less than forty per cent recognised 'Fijian' as the logical national name (*Fiji Times*, 28 March 1995). Clearly, a society in which one community takes for itself exclusive ownership of the country's name will have difficulties making other communities welcome. As a former Deputy Leader of the Opposition lamented, 'I, being a third generation and my children being a fourth generation in this country, born and bred here, are still called Indians...In Fiji, after living together for more than 100 years, we do not yet have a common name' (*Weekender*, 2 April 1994).

For a long time some descendants of South Asian migrants have attempted to overcome this dilemma by explicitly referring to themselves as 'Indo-Fijian'. Indeed, for convenience this term has been used in this chapter. However, this term is highly problematic because it maintains a focus on ethnicity. National identity, not ethnicity, must be the focus for identity in a multicultural country, especially when the variety of relationships between peoples increasingly contradicts rigid definitions and when a substantial proportion of the population is saying in effect 'we believe that our lives here have produced a culture peculiar to Fiji, that is, indigenous to Fiji, and often transcultural. We want to belong'. Unfortunately, many *Taukei* do not believe this or deliberately choose not to acknowledge this publicly. They argue instead, against all evidence, that Indo-Fijians regard India and not Fiji as their homeland (*Fiji Times*, 12 July 1995). Indeed, it is important to recall that ethnic diversity in Fiji extends beyond the two principal communities. Non-aboriginal Fijians and non-Indo-Fijians also regard Fiji as their home, 'the country of their roots, their citizenship and their heritage. They are not strangers and outsiders here. They belong here' (*Fiji Times*, 11 July 1995). They too require a national identity.

Unfortunately, this has not happened. Ethnic identities in the 1990 Constitution were so 'boxed [in] that national identity [was] virtually nonexistent', claimed Yash Ghai in 1993. People might be *Taukei* or Indo-Fijian, but 'in fact we're all of those things and many more; there are many points of intersection'. What the country needed was to start seeing problems as national problems, rather than as communal problems, he concluded (*Fiji Times*, 25 April 1994). President Mara expressed a similar view when told the BLV in 1996 that ethnic integration was the only way forward.

> While each race may possibly find solutions to its own problems, it has to be understood that such solutions will react on other races. And therefore, it is only when the races get together to discuss problems, that solid and lasting progress can be achieved (*Fiji Times*, 16 August 1996).

Yet, as former *Taukeist* Filipe Bole noted, aboriginal Fijian paramountcy was 'deeply entrenched' and would be 'difficult to erase' (*The Review*, November 1994).

The role of Rabuka in the growing recognition of the need to retreat from exclusion is contradictory. In his 1995 New Year address Rabuka tried to move beyond exclusivity, just as Bavadra had ten years earlier, when he stated that

> for too long we have kept our society fragmented by concentrating too much on our racial origins. We look upon ourselves as Fijians, as Indians, part-Europeans, Chinese, Pacific Islanders. A country that does not have an encompassing identity for its citizens will always be incomplete. I have concluded, after much searching of my conscience, that it is time for us to become 'Fijians'. I will repeat that—all citizens of Fiji should be known as Fijian (*Fiji Times*, 2 January 1995).

In 1996 Rabuka condemned his old soul mates, the *Taukei* Movement, arguing that 'the stance of Fiji for Fijians won't work. We need others. People have to change their attitude. I am for Fiji and I am pro-Fijian. That doesn't mean that I'm anti-Indian. Indians are good for Fiji. Other communities are good for Fiji. What's good for Fiji is good for Fijians' (*Fiji Times*, 6 September 1996).

In 1997 Rabuka welcomed the Fiji Sevens home by referring to 'Fijians of all races' (*Fiji Times*, 5 April 1997). Later, when addressing Commonwealth leaders in Edinburgh on the occasion of Fiji's re-admission to the British Commonwealth, he described the peoples of Fiji as 'the family of Fiji': 'we are all bound together by the reality that we need each other, that we can't do without each other and that we are indeed a family' (*Fiji Times*, 25 October 1997). However, remarkable as these public utterances are by the two-time coup leader, they did not necessarily represent a significant change in attitude. Rabuka acknowledged the continuing strength of 'us' and 'them' perspectives when referring to his days in exclusively aboriginal Fijian schools and in the military, stressing that

> my tolerance level of other races was very low. But since coming out of that cocoon I have managed very well to accept that I have to compete with them, I have to look after them, and I have to devise policies and programmes that will be good for them as well as being good for us (*Fiji Times*, 17 January 1997) .

For Rabuka to be credible, there is a need to acknowledge that past actions have been misguided. This he has consistently refused to do. In 1994 he declared that 'apartheid here in Fiji...[is] a necessary evil'

(*The Review*, April 1994) and that 'the interests of indigenous people come first' (*The Review*, September 1994). 'I will not and will never apologise for the coups of 1987' (*Australian*, 17 June 1994). He was though prepared to make some concessions. A stagnant economy and growing popular disenchantment with corruption and cronyism left him little choice. A clause within the 1990 Constitution stipulating regular constitutional reviews provided a means by which to make concessions. Moreover, he received unexpected support from Jai Ram Reddy, who had declared dead the multicultural goals that his party had previously pursued while in coalition with the Fiji Labour Party (*Daily Post*, 19 March 1993).

With the majority of parliamentary seats still communally defined, the compromise Constitution that emerged in 1997 retained much of its former communalist orientation (Ghai, this volume). However, it did promise to bring Indo-Fijians into government through the mechanism of a government of national unity. Some small concessions were also made to urban *Taukei*; their proportion of the aboriginal Fijian population rose from 33 per cent to 41 per cent between 1987 and 1997, and they were underrepresented in parliament (*Statistical News*, 1997:4). Rural *Taukei* seats were also adjusted to better reflect population distribution rather than that of provincial authority. One third of lower house seats were no longer communally reserved. Concessions were made to enable greater Parliamentary accountability and to remove the strict definitions of race imposed by the 1990 Constitution. The Constitution gave equal status to the country's three main languages—Fijian, Hindi and English—for the first time, although with local language usage increasing at work places and on the air waves, and with a new emphasis on teaching local languages to all students at school, one colonial legacy might be about to pass. In other matters though the Constitution did not mark a clear transition. 'Besides broad references to equality [and] citizenship rights, Fiji essentially remain[s] a nation of separate identities', sociologist Satendra Prasad wrote at the end of 1997. 'Its political structures and institutions emphasise and feed off the separateness of those identities' (Griffen 1997:317). 'The "us" and "them" mind set...is still in our midst', lawyer Imrana Jalal concurred (*Fiji Times*, 19 June 1997).

Indeed, Rabuka made it very clear that despite the potential of these changes to restore much of the emphasis on multiculturalism eroded by the coups, as far as he was concerned most of the measures were symbolic. He intended to pursue the goal of *Taukei* communal unity. However, given the huge migration of Indo-Fijians from Fiji since the coups, the *Taukei* no longer feared Indo-Fijian numerical domination. They could afford to retreat a little from 1987. Consequently, clauses stressing ethnic exclusivity were no longer required; their damage to Fiji's reputation internationally was deemed now to outweigh their usefulness nationally. Nonetheless, the communal emphasis remained entrenched. The Constitution sidestepped the issue of 'Fijian' as the national name by adopting 'Fiji Islander' as a common name. In this way the communal divide remains. Singular ethnic perspectives and zero-sum relations between communities remain, defining identity and shaping the nation's future. 'It shows that while policies steeped in racism and based on racial supremacy can be instilled into the system almost overnight', the *Fiji Times* lamented, 'any changes towards multiracialism can only be achieved in small doses' (15 April 1997).

Before being adopted as the inclusive national name, the description 'New Zealander' described only Maoris. Today *Pakeha* is the term used to describe the descendants of European settlers. Both *Pakehas* and Maoris are New Zealanders. Some change of that order is required in Fiji. As early as 1969 *Ratu* Mara suggested 'Fijian' as the logical common name, but the BLV insisted on preserving the national name for aboriginal Fijians. 'Fijian' has thus remained, a little uneasily, the name used to describe only the *Taukei*. This must change. 'If we cannot come together to agree on a common name for ourselves, something that effects each of us equally', the *Fiji Times* editorialised in 1994, 'how can we ever hope to agree on anything more difficult...[which] demand[s] even greater sacrifice and understanding from each other' (*Fiji Times*, 15 October 1994). All Fiji citizens should be Fijians, because the name of the country is Fiji. Those derived from the aboriginal peoples of Fiji—no matter their specific heritage— should be *kai Viti* or *i Taukei*, if they personally wish to be so described. All others should be known by some non-ethnic and inclusive term such as *vasu*. Such an accommodation better reflects the values of sharing, hospitality and respect at the center of the way of life of Fiji.

Conclusion

Even in light of the results of the 1999 general elections, Fiji's retreat from exclusion remains qualified. Powerful interests have too much to lose by conceding to change, while at the same time one of the most important stumbling blocks remains the nation's failure to address adequately issues of identity. Fiji needs to use its official resources to overcome the chauvinistic rhetoric that has been encouraged during the last twelve years. Much of this, as political philosopher Richard Mulgan wrote concerning New Zealand, is due to oversimplifying abstract theories of societies (Mulgan 1989:71). Generalisations and stereotypes not only reinforce distrust and division, they rebound on their advocates by generating a belief in collective failure, cultural backwardness, and a loss of control. A 'victim syndrome' is re-established, as Fiji's most persistent public nationalist, Sakeasi Butadroka, demonstrated when he translated ethnic antagonism into genetic backwardness. 'Indians and Asians have civilised blood in them because when they were civilised we were still cannibals', he said. The *Taukei* need more 'time to develop a better sense of the Western World' (*Fiji Times*, 6 October 1996).

No one has yet been able to adapt in a manner and pace directed solely by themselves. The notion though that Indo-Fijians are 'naturally' better than aboriginal Fijians in education and business is not new, despite flying in the face of logic and causing the infrastructural basis for educational and business success to be neglected. Nor is there evidence for such assertions. The 1996 Fiji Poverty Report demonstrated that while *Taukei* households in general had the lowest incomes, lower income Indo-Fijians were worse off than lower income *Taukei* households. Half of the poor were Indo-Fijian, with incomes fourteen per cent lower than *Taukei* households. Taukei dominated middle income groups. Only in the small proportion of high income households were Indo-Fijian households 42 per cent better off than high income *Taukei* (*Fiji Times* 19 March 1997).

These matters are rarely commented on by politicians. Public debate and official assistance to get the picture right is rare. Instead, myths are perpetuated. Even the former managing director of the Fiji Development Bank, Laisenia Qarase, sees *Taukei* development in these terms. '[W]hat we must always keep in mind', he contended, 'is that we are dealing with a problem which has its origins in thousands of years of culture and tradition' (*Weekender*, 25 June 1993). Such beliefs fit well with the siege mentality Imrana Jalal believes many of Fiji's leaders have adopted, making 'ceaseless calls for ethnic unity and the preservation of tradition and custom, even as they personally discard them to make their own compromises with the modern world'. Blaming someone else might be politically useful for survival in communal electorates, but it is misdirected, she argued. Indo-Fijians do not threaten the so-called 'Fijian system'. Equal opportunity, education, and nuclear families do (*Fiji Times*, 24 October 1996). The late sociologist Simione Durutalo said the same thing in 1993. Indo-Fijians had become the scapegoat even though 'it is not [they] who are the threat to Fijian culture, but the modern way of life' (Durutalo 1993:7).

At the heart of ethnocentrism lies a series of misconceptions about the world and ethnic identity. In many ways race and ethnicity are imperial artifacts. The ideas of race and ethnicity spread as industrialisation fragmented societies across the world. They remain today socially constructed concepts, with no biological basis except in terms of superficial appearances (Jones 1996:172–6). Genes have nothing to do with business acumen; 'success', senator Francis Hong Tiy noted, is 'based on the acquisition of skills', not race or cultural heritage (*Fiji Times*, 13 August 1992). Aboriginal Fijian nationalists are mistaken when they regard their cultural heritage as an inhibitor; they perform a great disservice to their own communities. Not only do they foster a victim mentality, but they also hide from their people a very important truth: that all societies are dynamic and that they themselves have already survived great changes. As anthropologist Nicholas Thomas wrote, the British may not have dispossessed the *Taukei* as they did Aborigines in Australia or Maoris in New Zealand, but they certainly did not preserve village society in Fiji. In fact, whole villages were relocated or broken up. New health and gardening regulations dramatically changed their appearance, as did the transformation of *bures* and the ending of male and female segregation. Land tenure practices in the country were homogenised, religious practices and authorities changed, the language of Bau became the national standard, and kava drinking became democratised. Even *Taukei* values such as respect, kinship and sharing underwent change, sometimes gaining exaggerated importance as they confronted British efforts to transform them. Consequently, these values are not 'those of timeless tradition'. Nor is the role of chiefs a timeless one. Their reciprocal obligations have been reduced while the removal of traditional priests made chiefs more central than they had once been (Thomas 1992:17–8).

Fiji was and is a dynamic and inclusive society, not the exclusive patrilineal one of the colonial VKB or the master race of the *Taukei* Movement. *Taukeism*, in all its manifestations, produces a victim mentality from which it is difficult to escape. Under the umbrella of aboriginal Fijian nationalism it raised a false notion of indigenousness and a false concept of chiefly protection which served to disguise abuse. Too often, lamented the former head of the Methodist Church, Reverend Josateki Koroi, 'the chiefly dictatorship system is promoted as the ultimate good as though the mastery and exploitation of other races were the high road to the new world order' (*Fiji Times*, 1 May 1992). 'The main culprits are people who have gone to monoethnic schools and see themselves as the select race to run this country', argued Vijay Naidu. '[T]his orchestration takes place not only at the level of political leaders but through the Methodist Church, community leaders, school teachers and the public service' (*The Review*, April 1997).

The *Soqosoqo ni Vakavulewa ni Taukei* (SVT), the 1992 replacement for the Alliance Party, told the Constitutional Review Commission that political control 'is the collective right of self determination of the indigenous people' (*Fiji Times*, 11 October 1995). However, contrary to SVT belief, it is not a right promoted by the Draft United Nations Declaration on the Rights of Indigenous Peoples. The Draft Declaration is designed to encourage special protection and privileges for threatened groups. Disadvantage, not indigenousness, is the criteria for assistance. 'Otherwise the result of special protection is not to achieve equality', Mulgan commented, 'but to offer the possibility of entrenching an unequal position of superiority' (Mulgan 1989:85).

The word 'indigenous' has been hijacked in recent years and given connotations it should not enjoy. In 1990 at a United Nations Development Programme regional workshop on environmental management and sustainable development, a senior government minister claimed that 'the environmental perceptions of their cultural heritage' had served Pacific peoples well before 'the arrival of white men'. Perhaps, he mused, island nations should return to these. Although evidence to the contrary abounds, the image of aboriginal people as noble custodians of the environment is a powerful one. Ironically though the real message to the workshop was the opposite: that 'developing countries could not afford to bend to environmental concern' (*Fiji Times*, 18 April 1990).

Rabuka also believed that 'indigenousness' created a special bond, particularly among the peoples of the Pacific (*Fiji Times*, 26 April 1997). Yet his 1990 Constitution meant that all descendants of Europeans, Indians, Solomon Islanders, ni Vanuatu, Tuvalu, i-Kiribati and others could never regard Fiji as their home, no matter whether they and past generations had been born and raised in the country or were in fact indistinguishable from most 'indigenous peoples'. Indo-Fijians are certainly different from the *Taukei*, but their culture is a branch of South Asian culture now indigenous to Fiji. After 120 years the mix of many different peoples descended from South Asia living in the Fiji environment has produced something different, something unique to Fiji, evolving within Fiji and therefore indigenous to Fiji. The same is true of all other peoples. *Taukei* culture is likewise indigenous to Fiji, even though today it is very different from what it was 100 years ago, and has been greatly influenced by British, Australasian and South Asian cultures (Mulgan 1989:20–1). Moreover, Fiji and its peoples—like peoples in most countries—are integrated into and influenced by a growing global culture that is experienced through the media, professional organisations, business and political organisations, and education.

As one nation, with at least two main peoples and many cultures, Fiji needs to treat identity carefully. Mulgan argues that flexible ethnic identity is an essential lubricant for any ethnically tolerant society. The dangers and injustices inherent in exclusive definitions of ethnicity have already been pointed out. They are not only historically wrong, but they also retard the growth of the nation (Mulgan 1989:132). Some *Taukei* have been dismissive of attempts to forge a stronger, more inclusive, Fiji identity, especially by means of the word 'Fijian'. However, inclusive symbols and language are very important for social and national development. According to one Australian commentator it 'helps create spaces of temporary equality, working tolerance in which every one has a good chance to participate' (Morris 1997:13). If Fiji is to prosper, it will do so only as one nation, with all cultures and backgrounds working together to create a transformed and vibrant society. Calling everybody by the name of the country is such a small thing to do, and yet its consequences are vast. Certainly, it is the first step in overcoming the legacies of colonialism and moving forward. It tells everybody they belong, that they are equal and valued as people and as individuals.

'It is not enough that we should accept our collective presence in Fiji as simply one of coexistence', Rabuka conceded when introducing his constitutional amendments in 1997. 'We should accept each other as belonging together as one people and one nation' (*Fiji Times*, 21 April 1997). Nonetheless, the question remains: is this clear to the country's leaders? Have they conceded the problems of the past and moved forward? Or will they once more fall victim to their own power and greed and—as conflicting strategies frustrate expectations of dramatic transformation—play on the insecurities of their people by exploiting the distinctive characteristics of identities? As yet these important questions cannot be answered, although the election of a new, Fiji Labour Party-led government in May 1999 suggested that one turning point had at least been successfully navigated. Nonetheless, in the days preceding Mahendra Chaudhry's appointment as the country's first Indo-Fijian Prime Minister, calls for his replacement by an aboriginal Fijian suggested that even opponents of Rabuka's government and the Fiji Labour Party's allies remain deeply affected by the rhetoric of ethnicity which has affected Fiji's politics for so long. Reservations concerning the retreat from exclusion thus remain, and will undoubtedly continue to haunt Fiji.

References

Adam, K., 1997. 'The politics of redress: South African style affirmative action', *The Journal of Modern African Studies*, 35(2):231–49.

Adams, J., 1993. 'Institutions and economic development: structure, process and incentive', in M.C. Tool (ed.), *Institutional Economics: theory, method, policy*, Kluwer Academic Publishers, London.

Akram-Lodhi, A. Haroon, 1992. 'Tax-free manufacturing in Fiji: an evaluation', *Journal of Contemporary Asia*, 22(3):373–93.

——, 1996. 'Structural adjustment in Fiji under the Interim Government, 1987–1992', *The Contemporary Pacific*, 8(2):259–90.

——, 1997. 'Structural adjustment and the agrarian question in Fiji', *Journal of Contemporary Asia*, 27(1):37–57.

Alchian, A., 1974. 'Corporate management and property rights', in E.G. Furuboton and S. Pejovich (eds) *The Economics of Property Rights*, Ballinger Publishing Company, New York.

Arms, D.G., 1997. 'Fiji's proposed new voting system: a critique with counter-proposals', in B. Lal and P. Larmour (eds), *Electoral Systems in Divided Societies: the Fiji Constitution Review*, National Centre for Development Studies, The Australian National University, Canberra.

Asian Productivity Organization, 1991. *Improving Quality of Life in Rural Areas in Asia and the Pacific*, Bangkok, ESCAP.

Bacha, E.L., 1990. 'A three-gap model of foreign transfers and the GDP growth rate in developing countries', *Journal of Development Economics*, 32(2):279–96.

Backman, K.F., Backman, S.J., Brett, D. and Wright, A., 1994. 'Ecotourism: a short descriptive exploration', *Trends*, 31(2):23–7.

Barr, K.J., 1990. *Poverty in Fiji*, Fiji Forum for Justice, Peace and the Integrity of Creation, Suva.

Barzel, Y., 1989. *Economic Analysis of Property Rights*, Cambridge University Press, Cambridge.

Bassett, T.J., 1993. 'Introduction: the land question and agricultural transformation in sub-Saharan Africa', in T.J. Bassett and D.E. Crummey (eds), *Land in African Agrarian Systems*, University of Wisconsin Press, London.

Belt Collins and Associates, 1973. *Tourism Development Program for Fiji*, United Nations Development Program, International Bank for Reconstruction and Development and Government of Fiji, Suva.

Bhagwati, J.N. and Srinivasan, T.N., 1980. 'Revenue seeking: a generalisation of the theory of tariffs', *Journal of Political Economy*, 61(88):1067–87.

Binswanger, H. and Rosenzweig, M., 1984. *Contractual Arrangements, Employment and Wages in Rural Labour Markets in Asia*, Yale University Press, London.

Bonnemaison, J., 1978. 'Custom and money: integration or breakdown in Melanesian systems of food production' in E. K. Fisk (ed), *The Adaptation of Traditional Agriculture*, ANU Development Studies Centre Monograph no.11, Australian National University, Canberra.

Booth, H., 1994. *Women of Fiji: a statistical gender profile*, Department for Women and Culture, Suva.

Bradley, H., 1989. *Men's Work, Women's Work: a sociological history of the division of labour in employment*, Polity Press, Cambridge.

Britton, S., 1980. 'The spatial organisation of tourism in a neo-colonial economy: a Fiji case study', *Pacific Viewpoint*, 21(2):144–65.

——, 1983. *Tourism and Underdevelopment in Fiji*, Development Studies Centre Monograph No.31, Australian National University, Canberra.

—— and Clarke, W.C., 1987. *Ambiguous Alternative: tourism in small developing countries*, University of the South Pacific, Suva.

Bryant, J., 1993. *Urban Poverty and the Environment in the South Pacific*, University of New England, Armidale.

Cabaniuk, S., 1989. *Bouma Forest Park and Reserve: a proposal for landowner tourism-oriented development and heritage protection*, Native Lands Trust Board, Suva.

Cameron, J., 1987a. 'Assessing the quality of life for women and men in Fiji using Active Life Profile Analysis', *The Journal of Pacific Studies*, 13:80–93.

——, 1987b. 'Fiji: the political economy of recent events', *Capital and Class* 33:29–45.

——, 1991. *Practical Economics of Food and Nutrition Policy in Small Open Economies: a case study of four Pacific societies*, Nutrition Consultants' Reports Series No.87, Food and Agriculture Organization, Rome.

——, 1994. 'Simione Durutalo: an appreciation', *Journal of Contemporary Asia*, 24(3):420–21.

——, 1996. *Towards the Establishment of a New Generation of Forest Conservation Areas (Parks and Reserves)*, Native Lands Trust Board, Suva.

Chand, G., 1996. The labour market and labour institutions in Fiji in an era of globalisation and economic liberalisation, Fiji Trades Union Congress, Suva (unpublished).

——, 1997. 'The labour market: a decade of restructuring' in G. Chand and V. Naidu (eds) *Fiji: coups, crises and reconciliation, 1987–1997*, Fiji Institute of Applied Studies, Suva.

Chandra, R., 1985. Industrialisation in Fiji, Ph.D. thesis, University of British Columbia, Vancouver (unpublished).

——, 1989. *Fiji and the New International Division of Labour: a study of the tax free system*, School of Social and Economic Development Working Paper No.11, University of the South Pacific, Suva.

——, 1996. 'Manufacturing in Fiji: mixed results', *Pacific Economic Bulletin*, 11(1):47–62.

Chenery, H.B. and Strout, A.M., 1966. 'Foreign assistance and economic development', *American Economic Review*, 56(4):149–79.

Cheung, S., 1970. 'The structure of a contract and the theory of a non-exclusive resource', *Journal of Law and Economics*, 13:49–70.

Chhachhi , A. and Pittin, R., 1996. 'Multiple identities, multiple strategies', in A. Chhachhi and R. Pittin (eds), *Confronting State, Capital and Patriarchy: women organizing in the process of industrialization*, Macmillan Press, London:93–130.

Chung, M., 1989. 'Ethnic politics and small business: the case of the Fiji Poultry Industries', *Pacific Viewpoint*, 30(2):197–206.

Citizen's Constitutional Forum, 1995. *One Nation Diverse Peoples: a submission to the Constitutional Review Commission*, Citizen's Constitutional Forum, Suva.

Citizen's Constitutional Forum, 1995. *One Nation, Diverse Peoples: Building a Just and Democratic Fiji*, Citizen's Constitutional Forum, Suva.

Cleverdon, R. and Brook, M., 1988. *Secondary Tourism Activity in Fiji: opportunities, policies and control*, United Nations Development Program and World Tourism Organisation, Suva.

Coase, R., 1960. 'The problem of social cost', *Journal of Law and Economics*, 3:1–44.

Collier, P., 1998. *The Political Economy of Ethnicity*, Working Paper Series WPS/98-8, Centre for the Study of African Economies.

Coopers and Lybrand Associates, 1989. *Government of Fiji Tourism Masterplan*, Ministry of Tourism and Civil Aviation, Suva.

Demsetz, H., 1967. 'Towards a theory of property rights', *American Economic Review*, 57:347–59.

Department for Women and Culture, 1995. *Country Report—Fiji: review of implementation of the Nairobi Forward-Looking Strategies for the Advancement of Women, 1985–1992*, Department for Women and Culture, Suva.

Devi, P. and Chand, G., 1997. 'Female employment and earnings' in G. Chand and V. Naidu (eds) *Fiji: coups, crises, and reconciliation, 1987–1997*, Fiji Institute of Applied Studies, Suva.

Din, K.H., 1997. 'Indigenisation of tourism development: some constraints and possibilities', in M. Oppermann (ed.), *Pacific Rim Tourism*, CAB International, New York.

Downer, A., 1997, 'Address by HE Alexander Downer, Australian Minister for Foreign Affairs, to the Fiji-Australia Business Council', August, Suva.

Dunning, J.H., 1997. 'Governments and the macro-organisation of economic activity: a historical and spatial perspective', in J.H. Dunning (ed.), *Governments, Globalisation and International Business*, Oxford University Press, New York.

Durutalo, S., 1986. *The Paramountcy of Fijian Interests and the Politicisation of Ethnicity*, University of the South Pacific Sociological Society, Suva.

Durutalo, S., 1993. 'Democracy in the South Pacific Context', *Review 20*, University of the South Pacific, September 1993:1–12.

Eaton, C., 1988. '*Vakavanua* land tenure and tobacco farming', in J. Overton (ed.), *Rural Fiji*, Institute of Pacific Studies, Suva.

Elek, A., Hill, H. and Tabor, S.R., 1993. 'Liberalisation and diversification in a small island economy: Fiji since the 1987 coups', *World Development*, 21(5):749–69.

Emberson-Bain, 'A., 1994a. 'Backbone of growth, export manufacturing and Fiji's tuna fish wives', in 'A. Emberson-Bain (ed.), *Sustainable Development or Malignant Growth? Perspectives of Pacific Island women*, Marama Publications, Suva:149–72.

——, 1994b. *Labour and Gold in Fiji*, Cambridge University Press, Cambridge.

—— (ed.), 1994c. *Sustainable Development or Malignant Growth? Perspectives of Pacific Island women*, Marama Publications, Suva.

—— and Slatter, C., 1995. *Labouring Under the Law*, Fiji Women's Rights Movement, Suva.

Emsley, I., 1996. *The Malaysian Experience of Affirmative Action: lessons for South Africa*, Human and Rosseau Tafelberg, Capetown.

Fairbairn-Dunlop, P., 1994. 'Mother, farmer, trader, weaver: juggling roles in Pacific agriculture', in 'A. Emberson-Bain (ed.), *Sustainable Development or Malignant Growth? Perspectives of Pacific Island women*, Marama Publications, Suva:73–90.

Fallon, J. and King, T., 1995. *The Economy of Fiji: supporting private investment*, AusAID International Development Issues No.10, Canberra.

Fanelli, J.M., Frenkel, R. and Winograd, C., 1987. *Argentina: stabilisation and adjustment policies and programs*, Country Study no.12, World Institute for Development Economics Research, Helsinki.

Faundez, J., 1994. *Affirmative Action: international perspectives*, International Labour Organization, Geneva.

Fei, J.C.H. and Ranis, G., 1964. *Development of the Labour Surplus Economy*, Richard D. Irwin, Homewood.

Fiji Association of Women Graduates, 1994. *Women Market Vendors in Fiji*, Fiji Association of Women Graduates, Suva.

Fiji Bureau of Statistics, (various issues (a)). *Current Economic Statistics*, Government Printer, Suva.

——, (various issues (b)). *Annual Employment Survey*, Government Printer, Suva.

——, 1996. *Annual Employment Survey, 1993: provisional report*, Government Printer, Suva.

——, 1997. *Tourism statistics*, Government Printer, Suva.

——, 1997. *Statistical News*, Suva.

Fiji Central Planning Office, 1980. *Fiji's Eighth Development Plan 1981–1985*, Government Printer, Suva.

Fiji Constitution Review Commission (FCRC), 1996. *The Fiji Islands—Towards a United Future: report of the Fiji Constitution Review Commission*, Parliamentary Paper No.34, Government Printer, Suva.

Fiji Development Bank (various issues). *Fiji Development Bank Annual Report*, Fiji Development Bank, Suva.

Fiji Employment and Development Mission, 1984. *Final Report to the Government of Fiji*, Government Printer, Suva.

Fiji Ministry of Agriculture and Fisheries, 1978. *Census of Agriculture*, Ministry of Agriculture and Fisheries, Suva.

Fiji Ministry of Finance Central Planning Office, 1979. *A Review of Fiji's Seventh Development Plan*, Central Planning Office, Suva.

Fiji Ministry of Finance, 1991. *1992 Budget Address*, Suva (mimeo).

Fiji Ministry of Tourism and Civil Aviation, 1992. *Fiji International Visitor Survey*, Ministry of Tourism and Civil Aviation, Suva.

——, 1995a. *Annual Report for the Year 1994*, Parliamentary Paper No.46, Government Printer, Suva.

——, 1995b. *Fiji International Visitor Survey*, Ministry of Tourism and Civil Aviation, Suva.

——, 1996. *List of Operating Ecotourism Projects as at July 1996*, Ministry of Tourism and Civil Aviation, Suva.

Fiji Native Lands Trust Board (no date). *Logging Licences: guidelines for loggers and landowners*, Native Lands Trust Board, Suva.

——, (various issues). *Annual Report*, Government Printer, Suva.

——, 1985. *Policy on the Logging of Indigenous Forests*, Government Printer, Suva.

——, 1990. *A Policy for Tourism Development on Native Land 1990–1995*, Paper No.18/90, Government Printer, Suva.

——, 1992. *Environmental Charter*, Native Lands Trust Board Landuse Planning Section, Suva.

——, 1996. *A Tourism Policy for Native Land 1997–2000*, Government Printer, Suva.

Fiji Office of the Registrar of Companies, 1987. *Registration List*, Office of the Registrar of Companies, Suva.

Fiji Public Service Commission, 1996. Officers, gender and racial distribution by ministries, 10 December 1996, MIS Unit, Public Service Commission, Suva (unpublished).

Fiji Republic Gazette, 1991. Government Printer, Suva.

Fiji Sugar Corporation, 1996. *Labasa Mill Database*, Fiji Sugar Corporation, Labasa.

Fiji Trade and Investment Board, 1997. Tax-free factory registration figures, Fiji Trade and Investment Board, Suva.

Fiji Trades Union Congress files (various years). Fiji Trades Union Congress, Suva.

Fiji Trades Union Congress, 1976. *Onward Labour, 1951–1976: Silver Jubilee*, Fiji Trades Union Congress, Suva.

Fiji Visitors Bureau, 1995. *Annual Report*, Ministry of Tourism and Civil Aviation, Suva.

Fijian Holdings Company Limited (various issues). *Fijian Holdings Company Limited Annual Report*, Fijian Holdings Company Limited, Suva.

Fijian Initiative Group, 1988. *Nine Points Plan*, Fijian Initiative Group, Suva.

Forsyth, D., 1996. Women workers in Fiji's formal sector, report, University of the South Pacific, Suva (unpublished).

Forum Economic Ministers, 1997. *Statement*, 11 July.

Forum Finance Ministers, 1995. *Joint Statement*, 21 February.

——, 1995. *Joint Statement*, 8 December.

Foster, P., 1990. *Policy and Practice in Multiculturalism and Anti-racism in Education*, Routledge, London.

Francis, J., 1994. 'Beyond the sea, sun, and sand: the emerging world of Fiji ecotourism', *Islands*, 1:13–7.

Ghai, Y., 1997a. 'The recommendations on the electoral system: the contribution of the Fiji Constitution Review', in B. Lal and P. Larmour (eds), *Electoral Systems in Divided Societies: the Fiji Constitution Review*, Research School of Pacific and Asian Studies, Canberra.

——, 1997b. 'Establishing a liberal political order through a constitution: the Papua New Guinea experience', *Development and Change*, 28(2):303–30.

Goffman, E., 1963. *Behavior in Public Places: notes on the social organisation of gatherings*, Free Press of Glencoe, New York.

Gometz, E., 1994. *Political Business: corporate involvement of Malaysian political parties*, James Cook University, Townsville.

Government of Fiji, 1985. *Laws of Fiji*, Government Printer, Suva.

——, 1986. *Fiji's Ninth Development Plan 1986–1990: policies, strategies and programs for national development*, Government Printer, Suva.

——, 1993. *Opportunities for Growth: policies and strategies for Fiji in the medium term*, Parliamentary Paper No.2, Government Printer, Suva.

Gramsci, A., 1971. *Selections from Prison Notebooks*, Lawrence and Wishart, London.

Griffen, A. (ed), 1997. *With Heart and Nerve and Sinew: post-coup writing from Fiji*, Suva.

Grynberg, R. and Osei, K., 1996. 'Rules of origin disputes and competitiveness in the Fiji garment export industry', Economics Department, University of the South Pacific, Suva.

Haley, J., 1986. 'The politics of entrepreneurship: affirmative action policies for ethnic entrepreneurs', *Small Enterprise Development*, 2(2):2–10.

Harrington, C., 1994. Migration of garment workers: a case study of three Suva factories, Ministry of Women, Ministry of Labour, and the Department of Geography, University of the South Pacific, Suva (unpublished).

——, 1996. Impact of global restructuring on women in the garment industry, Paper presented to Women in Politics Conference, UNIFEM, 18 November, Fiji (unpublished).

——, 1999. The seams of subjectivity and structure: women's experiences of garment work in Aotearoa New Zealand and Fiji, PhD thesis, University of Otago.

Harrison, D., 1997. *Ecotourism and Village-Based Tourism: a policy and strategy for Fiji*, Ministry of Tourism and Civil Aviation, Suva.

Harrison, D., and Brandt, J., 1997. *Ecotourism in Fiji: making sense of the muddle*, paper presented to the Fiji Annual Tourism Conference, 17–18 October, The Warwick Hotel.

Harriss, J., Hunter, J. and Lewis, C. M. (eds), 1995. *The New Institutional Economics and Third World Development*, Routledge, London.

Helu-Thaman, K., 1992. 'Ecocultural tourism: a personal view for maintaining cultural integrity in ecotourism development', in E. Hay (ed.), *Ecotourism in the Pacific: promoting a sustainable experience*, Proceedings of the Ecotourism Conference, 12–14 October, Auckland.

Herrmann, R. and Weiss, D., 1995. 'A welfare analysis of the EC–ACP sugar protocol', *The Journal of Development Studies*, 31(6):918–41.

Hirschman, A.O., 1958, *The Strategy of Economic Development*, Yale University Press, New Haven.

Hodgson, G., 1989. 'Institutional rigidities and economic growth', *Cambridge Journal of Economics*, 13:79–101.

Horowitz, D., 1997. 'Encouraging electoral accommodation in divided societies', in B. Lal and P. Larmour (eds), *Electoral Systems in Divided Societies: the Fiji Constitution Review*, Research School of Pacific and Asian Studies, Canberra.

Illich, I., 1976. *Medical Nemesis*, Marion Boyars, New York.

Institute for Democracy and Electoral Assistance, 1998. *Code of Conduct: ethical and professional administration of elections*, Institute for Democracy and Electoral Assistance, Varberg.

International Confederation of Free Trade Unions, 1997. *Internationally recognised core labour standards in Fiji*, report prepared for the WTO General Council Review of Trade Policies in Fiji, 8–10 April, Fiji.

International Labour Organization, 1992. *Complaints against the Government of Fiji presented by the International Confederation of Free Trade Unions and the Public Services International*, Case No. 1622, International Labour Organization, Geneva.

International Labour Organization/South East Asia and the Pacific Multidisciplinary Advisory Team, 1997. *Towards equality and protection for women workers in the formal sector*, report prepared for the South East Asia and Pacific Multidisciplinary Advisory Team, Suva.

International Monetary Fund, 1994. *International Financial Statistics Yearbook*, International Monetary Fund, Washington, DC.

Jones, S., 1996. *In the Blood: God, genes and destiny*, Harper Collins, London.

Kahlenberg, R., 1996. *The Remedy: class, race and affirmative action*, Basic Books, New York.

Kamikamica, J. and Davey, T., 1988. 'Trust on trial: the development of the customary land trust concept in Fiji', in Y. Ghai (ed.), *Land, Government and Politics in the Pacific Island States*, Institute of Pacific Studies, Suva.

Khan, A.S., 1994. Impact of labour reforms of 1991 and 1992 on industrial relations in Fiji, Diploma Paper in Industrial Relations (unpublished), Victoria University of Wellington, New Zealand.

Korovulavula, M., 1994. Speech to Senate, 12 July, Suva.

Kumar, S., 1997. 'Institutionalised discrimination' in G.Chand and V. Naidu (eds), *Fiji: coups, crises and reconciliation, 1987–1997*, Institute of Applied Studies, Suva: 81–100.

Kymlicka, W. (ed.), 1995. *The Rights of Minority Cultures*, Oxford University Press, Oxford.

Kymlicka, W., 1989. *Liberalism, Community and Culture*, Clarendon Press, Oxford.

Lal, B. and Vakatora, T., 1997a. *Fiji in Transition*, School of Social and Economic Development, University of the South Pacific, Suva.

Lal, B. and Vakatora, T., 1997b. *Fiji and the World*, School of Social and Economic Development, University of the South Pacific, Suva.

Lateef, S., 1990a. 'Current and future implications of the coups for women in Fiji', *The Contemporary Pacific*, 2(1):113–30.

Lateef, S., 1990b. 'Rule by the *danda*: domestic violence among Indo-Fijians', *Pacific Studies*, 13(3):43–62.

Lawson, S., 1991. *The Failure of Democratic Politics in Fiji*, Clarendon Press, Oxford.

Leckie, J., 1988. 'Confrontation with the state: industrial conflict and the Fiji Public Service Association during the 1970s and 1980s', *South Pacific Forum*, 4(2):137–79.

——, 1991. 'State coercion and public sector unionism in post-coup Fiji', *South Pacific Forum*, 4(2).

——, 1992. 'Industrial relations in post-coup Fiji: a taste of the 1990s', *New Zealand Journal of Industrial Relations*, 17:5–21.

——, 1997a. 'Gender and work in Fiji: constraints to re-negotiation', *Women's Studies Journal*, 13(2):127–53.

——, 1997b. *To Labour with the State: the Fiji Public Service Association*, University of Otago Press, Dunedin.

Leibenstein, H., 1957. *Economic Backwardness and Economic Growth*, John Wiley and Sons, New York.

Li, Y. and Butler, R.W., 1997. 'Sustainable tourism and cultural attractions: a comparative experience', in M. Oppermann (ed.), *Pacific Rim Tourism*, CAB International, New York.

Libecap, G.D., 1992. 'Douglass C. North', in W.J. Samuels (ed.), *New Horizons in Economic Thought: appraisals of leading economists*, Edward Edgar, London.

Lijphart, A., 1977. *Democracy in Plural Societies*, Yale University Press, New Haven.

Lipsey, R.G. and Lancaster, K., 1956. 'The general theory of second best', *Review of Economic Studies*, 24(1):11–32.

Lustick, I., 1980. *Arabs in the Jewish State: Israel's control of a national minority*, University of Texas Press, Austin, Texas.

MacDonald, S., 1996. 'Reform of the EU's sugar policies and the ACP countries', *Development Policy Review*, 14(2):131–49.

Madraiwiwi, J., 1994. The role of the Arbitration Tribunal, Paper presented to the Fiji Employers' Federation Seminar on Industrial Relations, 29 April, Sigatoka, Fiji.

Maki, U., 1993. 'Economics with institutions: agenda for methodological enquiry', in U. Maki, B. Gustafsson and C. Knudsen (eds), *Rationality, Institutions and Economic Methodology*, Routledge, London.

Mara, Ratu Sir K., 1997. *The Pacific Way: a memoir*, University of Hawai'i Press, Honolulu.

Matararaba, S. and Cabaniuk, S., 1996. *Vanua Tours*, Fiji Museum and Native Land Trust Board, Suva.

McKenzie Aucoin, P., 1990. 'Domestic violence and social relations of conflict in Fiji', *Pacific Studies*, 13(3):23–42.

Ministry of Fijian Affairs, 1995. *Provincial Profile Project*, Ministry of Fijian Affairs, Suva.

Ministry of Finance, 1991. *Budget Address 1992*, Government Printer, Suva.

Ministry of Finance and Economic Development, 1996a. *1997 Budget Address*, Government Printer, Suva.

——, 1996b. *Supplement to the 1997 Budget Address*, Government Printer, Suva.

Ministry of Finance and Ministry of National Planning, 1997a. *Budget Address 1998*, Government Printer, Suva.

——, 1997b. *Supplement to the 1998 Budget Address*, Government Printer, Suva.

Mohanty, C.T., 1988. 'Under western eyes: feminist scholarship and colonial discourses', *Feminist Review*, 30 (Autumn):61–88.

Morris, M., 1997. 'Correct speech helps us all', *The Australian*, 9 June.

Moynagh, M., 1981. *Brown or White: a history of the Fiji sugar industry, 1873–1973*, Australian National University, Canberra.

Mulgan, R., 1989. *Maori, Pakeha and Democracy*, Oxford University Press, Auckland.

Myint, H., 1965. *Economics of the Developing Countries*, Praeger, New York.

Myrdal, G., 1957. *Economic Theory and the Underdeveloped Regions*, Gerald Duckworth, London.

Narayan, J., 1984. *The Political Economy of Fiji*, South Pacific Review Press, Suva.

National Federation Party and the Fiji Labour Party, 1995. *Towards Racial Harmony and National Unity: submission to the Fiji Constitution Review Commission*, National Federation Party and Fiji Labour Party, Suva.

Nayacakalou, R., 1971. 'Fiji: manipulating the system', in R. Crocombe (ed.), *Land Tenure in the Pacific*, Oxford University Press, Melbourne.

New Zealand Ministry of Foreign Affairs and Trade, 1995. *NZODA Support for Eco-Tourism in Fiji: a report of a study*, Development Cooperation Division, Ministry of Foreign Affairs and Trade, Wellington.

Newbery, D.M.G., 1979. 'Institutional responses to the existence of agricultural risk: an introduction', in J.A. Roumasset, J.M. Boussard and I. Singh (eds), *Risk, Uncertainty and Agricultural Development*, SEARCA and ADC, New York.

North, D.C., 1955. 'Location theory and regional economic growth', *Journal of Political Economy*, 63(3):243–58.

——, 1990. *Institutions, Institutional Change and Economic Performance*, Cambridge University Press, Cambridge.

—— and Thomas, R., 1973. *The Rise of the Western World: a new economic history*, Cambridge University Press, Cambridge.

Nurkse, R., 1953. *Problems of Capital Formation in Underdeveloped Countries*, Oxford University Press, New York.

Overton, J., 1987. 'Fijian land: pressing problems, possible tenure solutions', *Singapore Journal of Tropical Geography*, 8(2):139–51.

—— (ed.), 1988. *Rural Fiji*, Institute of Pacific Studies, Suva.

Parliament of Fiji, 1997a. *Deregulation Review Panel Report*, Parliamentary Paper No. 33, Government Printer, Suva.

——, 1997b. *Inquiry into Allegations of Corruption in the Department of Customs & Excise*, Parliamentary Paper No. 38, Government Printer, Suva.

Pejovich, S., 1990. *The Economics of Property Rights: towards a theory of comparative systems*, Kluwer Academic Publishers, London.

Plange, N., 1996. 'Fiji', in C.M. Hall and S.J. Page (eds), *Tourism in the Pacific Rim: issues and cases*, International Thomson Business Press, London:205–18.

Prasad, B. and Asafu-Adjaye, J., 1998. 'Macroeconomic policy and poverty in Fiji', *Pacific Economic Bulletin*, 13(1):47–56.

Prasad, B.C., 1984. 'Fiji sugar cane production and land tenure' in B. Acquaye and R. Crocombe (eds), *Land Tenure and Rural Productivity in the Pacific Islands*, Food and Agriculture Organisation, SPREP and Institute of Pacific Studies, Suva.

—— and Tisdell, C., 1996a. *Institutional Constraints to Economic Development: the case of native land rights in Fiji*, Discussion Paper 190, Department of Economics, The University of Queensland, Brisbane.

—— and Tisdell, C., 1996b, 'Getting property rights "right": land tenure in Fiji', *Pacific Economic Bulletin*, 11(1):31–46.

Prasad, S., 1995. *Socio-Economic Features of Fiji's Sugar Industry and their Implications for Reviewing ALTA, volumes 1 and 2*, Fiji Sugar Cane Growers Council, Suva.

——, 1999. Fiji's 1999 general elections: falling short on constitutional aspirations, Seminar presented to the University of the South Pacific Sociology Department, 10 May, Suva.

—— and Akram-Lodhi, A. Haroon, 1998. 'Fiji and the sugar protocol: a case for trade-based development co-operation', *Development Policy Review*, 16(1):39–60.

Public Service Commission, 1996. Officers Gender and Racial Distribution by Ministries 10 December 1996, unpublished data, MIS Unit, PSC, Suva.

Putman, R., 1993. *Making Democracy Work: civic traditions in modern Italy*, Princeton University Press, Princeton.

Qarase, L., 1995. *Ten Year Plan for Fijian Participation in Business*, ESCAP, Suva.

Ralston, C., 1990. 'Women workers in Samoa and Tonga in the early twentieth century', in C. Moore, J. Leckie and D. Munro (eds), *Labour in the South Pacific*, James Cook University Press, Townsville:67–77.

Ram, K., 1994. 'Militarism and market mania in Fiji', in 'A. Emberson-Bain (ed.), *Sustainable Development or Malignant Growth? Perspectives of Pacific Island women*, Marama Publications, Suva:237–49.

Randall, A., 1987. *Resource Economics*, John Wiley and Sons, New York.

Ravuvu, A., 1987. *The Fijian Ethos*, Institute of Pacific Studies, Suva.

Reddy, M., 1997. 'Devaluation and economic stimulation: the Fiji economy post-coup', *Pacific Economic Bulletin*, 12(2):85–94.

Reserve Bank of Fiji (various issues). *Quarterly Review*, Reserve Bank of Fiji, Suva.

Riker, W.H. and Weimer, D.L., 1994. 'The economic and political liberalisation of socialism: the fundamental problem of property rights', *Social Philosophy and Policy*, 10(2):67–81.

Roberts, D.F., 1996. Address to the International Sugar Organisation International Policy Council on Agriculture Conference (mimeo).

Robertson, R.T., 1998. *Multiracialism and Reconciliation in an Indulgent Republic: Fiji after the coups, 1987–1998*, Fiji Institute of Applied Studies, Suva.

Robertson, R. T. and Tamanisau, A., 1988. *Fiji: shattered coups*, Pluto, Sydney.

Rutz, H.J., 1987. 'Capitalising on culture: moral ironies in urban Fiji', *Comparative Studies in Society and History*, 29(3):533–57.

Sainath, M., 1997. Women entrepreneurs in Fiji: challenges and opportunities in the twenty-first century, Paper presented to the Pan-Pacific and Southeast Asia Women's Association Twentieth International Conference, 25 August–2 September, Kuala Lumpur.

Sartori, G., 1968. 'Political development and political engineering', in J. Montgomery and A. Hirschmann (eds), *Public Policy*, Harvard University Press, Cambridge, Mass.

Sawailau, S.T., 1994. *General information on tourism in Fiji: its past and future and impact on the economy and society*, Ministry of Tourism and Civil Aviation, Suva.

——, 1996. *Ecotourism/secondary tourism in Fiji: a brief overview*, Ministry of Tourism and Civil Aviation, Suva.

Schuller, W., 1996. Transcribed interview.

Scully, G., 1988. 'The institutional framework and economic development', *Journal of Political Economy*, 96:652–62.

—— and Slottje, D.J., 1991. 'Ranking economic liberty across countries', *Public Choice*, 69:65–76.

Seers, D., 1977. 'Life expectancy as an integrating concept in social and demographic analysis and planning', *Review of Income and Wealth*, 23.

Sharma, A N.,1997. 'Positive discrimination policy in education: a critical review' in G. Chand and V. Naidu (eds), *Fiji: coups, crises and reconciliation, 1987–1997*, Institute of Applied Studies, Suva:101–115.

Sharma, P., 1996. 'Lifting the night work ban', *Balance*, May–June:1–2.

Slatter, C., 1987. 'Women factory workers in Fiji: the "half a loaf" syndrome', *The Journal of Pacific Studies*, 13:47–59.

Smith, A., 1937. *The Wealth of Nations*, Modern Library, New York.

Solimano, A., 1993. 'Chile', in L. Taylor (ed.), *The Rocky Road to Reform: adjustment, income distribution, and growth in the developing world*, MIT Press, Cambridge, Mass.

South Pacific and Oceanic Council of Trade Unions, 1993. Survey of trade union development in the Pacific, report, South Pacific and Oceanic Council of Trade Unions, Brisbane (unpublished).

South Pacific Forum (various years). *Communiqué*, South Pacific Forum, Suva.

Sowell, T., 1990. *Preferential Policies*, Morrow, New York.

Spate, O.H.K., 1959. *The Fijian People: economic problems and prospects*, Council Paper 13 of 1959, Government Press, Suva.

Stiglitz, J., 1986. 'The new development economics', *World Development*, 14(2):257–65.

Sutherland, W., 1992. *Beyond the Politics of Race: an alternative history of Fiji to 1992*, Department of Political and Social Change, Research School of Pacific Studies, Australian National University, Canberra.

——, 1998. Global Imperatives and Island Futures: the case of the South Pacific, Paper presented to the Islands V Conference of the International Small Islands Studies Association, University of Mauritius, Le Reduit, Mauritius, July.

Tabua, S., 1996. *Fiji Country Paper: study meeting on ecology and tourism planning and development*, Native Lands Trust Board, Suva.

Taylor, C., 1994. 'The politics of recognition', in A. Guttman (ed.), *Multiculturalism*, Princeton University Press, Princeton.

Taylor, L., 1991. *Income Distribution, Inflation and Growth*, MIT Press, Cambridge, Mass.

——, 1993. 'A three-gap analysis of foreign resource flows and developing country growth', in L. Taylor (ed.), *The Rocky Road to Reform: adjustment, income distribution, and growth in the developing world*, MIT Press, Cambridge, Mass.

Thaman, R. R., 1983. 'Food for urbanising Polynesian peoples', *Proceedings of the Nutrition Society of New Zealand*, Volume 8.

Thomas, L., 1995. *Three Plays: Outcasts, Yours Dearly, Men Women and Insanity*, University of the South Pacific, Suva.

Thomas, N., 1992. 'Tin and thatch: identity and tradition in rural Fiji', *Age Monthly Review*, March:17–18.

Tietenberg, T.H., 1992. *Environmental and Natural Resource Economics*, Harper Collins, New York.

Torstensson, J., 1994. 'Property rights and economic growth: an empirical study', *Kyklos*, 47:231–47.

Troyna, B. and Hatcher, R., 1992. *Racism in Children's Lives: a study of mainly white primary schools*, Routledge, London.

Tullock, G., 1980. 'The welfare cost of tariff, monopolies and theft', in J.M. Buchanan and G. Tollison (eds), *Towards a Rent Seeking Society*, Texas A. and M. University Press, College Station, Texas.

Tully, J., 1996. *Strange Multiplicity: constitutionalism in an age of diversity*, Cambridge University Press, Cambridge.

Turner, V., 1978. *Image and Pilgrimage in Christian Culture: anthropological perspectives*, Columbia University Press, New York.

Twyford, L.T. and Wright, A.C.S., 1965. *The Soil Resources of Fiji Islands*, Government Printer, Suva.

United Nations (various issues). *International Trade Statistics Yearbook*, United Nations, New York.

United Nations Development Programme, 1994. *Pacific Human Development Report*, United Nations Development Programme, Suva.

United Nations Development Programme/Government of Fiji, 1997. *Fiji Poverty Report*, Government Printer, Suva.

Unpublished data held at the Ministry of Labour, Suva.

Urry, J., 1990. *The Tourist Gaze: leisure and travel in contemporary societies*, Sage Publications, London.

US Department of State, 1999. Fiji Country Report on Human Rights Practices for 1998, Bureau of Democracy, Human Rights, and Labour, US Department of State, Washington, DC.

Vesikula, *Ratu* M., 1989. Transcribed interview, Melbourne, 9 August.

Wakelin, D., 1991. *A Management Plan for Bouma Forest Park, Taveuni, Fiji Islands*, New Zealand Ministry of External Relations and Trade, Wellington.

Wallis, J.J. and North, D.C., 1986. 'Measuring the transaction sector in the American economy, 1870–1970', in S.I. Engerman and R.E. Gallman (eds), *Long-Term Factors in American Economic Growth*, Chicago University Press, Chicago:95–161.

Ward, M., 1995. 'Land, law and custom: diverging realities in Fiji', in R.G. Ward and E. Kingdon (eds), *Land, Custom and Practice in the South Pacific*, Cambridge University Press, Cambridge.

Waring, M., 1990. *Counting For Nothing: what men value and what women are worth*, Allen and Unwin, Sydney.

Watling, D. and Chape, S., 1993. *The National Environment Strategy*, Government of Fiji and World Conservation Union, Suva.

Weaver, S., 1994. A postmodern approach to ecological sustainability, PhD thesis, University of Canterbury, New Zealand.

World Bank, 1986. *Fiji: a transition to manufacturing*, The World Bank, Washington, DC.

——, 1991. *Towards Higher Growth in Pacific Island Economies: lessons from the 1980s*, Washington, DC.

——, 1993. *Pacific Island Economies: toward efficient and sustainable growth*, Volume 1, The World Bank, Washington, DC.

——, 1994. *Development in Practice: governance—the World Bank's experience*, The World Bank, Washington, DC.

——, 1995a. *Fiji: restoring growth in a changing global environment*, The World Bank, Washington, DC.

——, 1995b. *Pacific Island Economies: building a resilient economic base for the twenty-first century*, Washington, DC.

——, 1997. *Global Development Finance*, The World Bank, Washington, DC.

World Bank and United Nations Development Programme, 1989. *Africa's Adjustment and Growth in the 1980s*, The World Bank, New York.

World Trade Organization, 1997. 'Trade Policy Review Body: review of Fiji', April, World Trade Organization, Geneva.

Index

A

active life profiles 139
Adam, K. 227
Adams, J. 112
adult literacy rate xii
age-specific death rates 141
Agreement on Agriculture 89
agricultural census (1991) 180
Agricultural Landlord and
  Tenant Review Research
  Unit 127
Agricultural Landlord and
  Tenants Act, 1977 (ALTA) 123,
  125–30, 132, 185, 207, 217, 229
Agricultural Landlord and
  Tenants Ordinance, 1967
  (ALTO) 123, 229
Agriculture, Forestry and
  Fisheries, Ministry of 119, 185
Aidney, Don 215
Air Fiji 262
Akram-Lodhi, A. Haroon xiii, 71,
  74, 76–79, 88, 89, 125, 210, 229
Alchian, A. 114
alcohol abuse 148
All National Congress
  (ANC) 56, 222
Alliance Party 6, 25, 36, 207, 210,
  274, 277, 290
alternative vote (AV) system 33,
  35, 51, 53, 54, 58, 61–64, 66–69
Arbitration Tribunal 164
Arms, D.G. 34
Asafu-Adjaye, J. 87
Asian crisis 85, 198, 199
Asian Productivity
  Organisation 145

B

Ba Provincial Council 129, 197,
  223
Bacha, E.L. 72, 90
Baisagale, Mesake 271
Barr, K.J. 144, 147
Barzel, Y. 114
Basic Industries Limited 239, 241
Bassett, T.J. 130
Bavadra, Adi Kuini 224
Bavadra, Timoci 7, 55, 224, 277,
  280, 285
Belt Collins Report (1973) 253–55
Bhagwati, J.N. 115
Binswanger, H. 115
Bole, Filipe 285
Bonnemaison, J. 145
Booth, H. 192
Bose Levu Vakaturaga see Great
  Council of Chiefs
Bose, Isimeli 214
Bradley, H. 190
Brandt, J. 250, 264
breastfeeding 147, 148
Britton, S. 252
Bryant, J. 192
Budgets
  1990 78
  1991 153
  1992 79
  1994 222
  1998 84, 85, 220
Burns Philp and Co. Ltd 239
Business Development and
  Investment 76
Butadroka, Sakeasi 207, 277, 282
Butler, R.W. 265

C

Cabaniuk, S. 250, 258, 259
Cakabau, Sir George 242
Cameron, J. 76, 138, 145
Candra Mai 223
Capital Market Development
  Authority 219
Carlton Brewery (Fiji)
  Limited 239, 241, 244
Carpenters Properties
  Limited 241
CBM Holdings 231, 242, 243
Chand, G. 154, 156, 165, 172, 173
Chandra, R. 77, 255
Chape, S. 259
Chaudhry, Mahendra xiii, xiv,
  64, 291
Chenery, H.B. 91
Cheung, S. 114
Chhachhi, A. 186
Christian fundamentalism 7
Christianity 191
Citizens Constitutional
  Forum 26, 43, 228
Clarke, W.C. 252
Cleverdon and Brook Report 256
Coalition government 7
Coase, R. 114
Code of Conduct 32, 43
Collier, P. 99
Colonial Sugar Refinery
  (CSR) 121
Commercial Loans to Fijians
  Scheme (CLFS) 235
communal seats 33, 34, 35
community collection 230
community relations 150, 151
Companies Office 85
Compulsory Recognition
  Order 159

conflicts
  mataqalis 126
  tenants 126
conservation 267
consociationalism 24, 31
Constituency Boundaries
  Commission 46, 62
Constitution (Amendment) Act
  (1997) 56, 74, 205, 228
Constitutional Review
  Commission (FCRC) 22, 25, 27,
  32–34, 42, 44, 51–54, 66, 67, 290
Constitutions
  1970 Constitution 23–25, 29,
    30, 31, 35, 46, 53, 227, 229, 277
  1990 Constitution 24–26, 30,
    49, 51, 53, 82, 200, 205, 228,
    271, 286, 291
  1997 Constitution xii, 14, 24–28,
    31, 36, 39, 48–53, 64–65, 69,
    101, 111, 175–76, 234, 270, 286
Coopers and Lybrand
  Associates 257
  Tourism Masterplan 257
corporation tax 80
Council of Social Services 184
Counter Inflation Act 155
Country Report on Human
  Rights Practices (1998) 173
coups (1987) xii, 2, 3, 7, 77, 111,
  134, 240
cross voting 35
Crown Land 118
  privatisation 130
Customs Department 85, 220
customs duties 80
cyclone Oscar 142

D

Davey, T. 124
demographic data 139

Demsetz, H. 114
deregulation 211
  internal deregulation 80
devaluation 85, 86, 87
Development Plans
  Sixth Development Plan 6, 7, 77
  Eighth Development Plan 145
  Ninth National Development
    Plan 255
Devi, P. 172, 173
discrimination 200
dispute resolution 167, 169
diwali 5
Douglas, Sir Roger 217
Downer, Alexander 217
Draft United Nations
  Declaration on the Rights of
    Indigenous Peoples 290
Dunning, J.H. 111
Durutalo, S. 208, 226, 229, 266,
  289

E

Eaton, C. 124, 125
economic affirmative action 226,
  230
economic reforms 209
Ecotourism Unit 249–53, 259–63,
  265–67
education 148, 151
  compulsory 185
  education and gender 183
Education, Women and Culture,
  Ministry of 180
Elections
  1987 general election 55
  1992 general election 79, 82
  1999 general election xiii, 14,
    19, 32, 38, 39, 42, 46, 49, 51,
    53, 58, 62, 64, 66, 67, 69, 101,
    132, 134, 150, 224, 248

Electoral Commissions 46
electoral rolls 35
Elek, A. 71, 79, 80, 88, 99
Emberson-Bain, A. 179, 182
emergency powers 32
Emperor Gold Mines 88
Employment Act of 1965 154
employment structure 170
Emsley, I. 236
enterprise-based bargaining 169
Environment, Ministry of 258
Environment, Ministry of State
  for the 261
Equity Investment Management
  Company Limited 235
ethnic constitutionalism 22
ethnic differentials in the labour
  market 173
European Economic Community
  74
European Union (EU) 72, 74, 218
  sugar market 105
  Common Agricultural Policy
    74, 89
  internal sugar price 89
  preferential access for sugar
    exports 100
export-promotion 209
external trade liberalisation 80

F

Fairbairn-Dunlop, P. 182
Fallon, J. 181
Fanelli, J. 90
Faundez, J. 227
Fei, J.C.H. 112
female
  farmers 182
  garment workers 193
  participation in postgraduate
    studies 185

female-headed and sole parent households 193
feminist movements 194
Ferry Freights Company 231
Fiji Association of Garment Workers (FAGW) 195
Fiji Association of Women Graduates (FAWG) 182, 183, 184, 193, 196
Fiji Aviation Workers Association 163
Fiji Bank Employees Union 167
Fiji Broadcasting Aviation Authority of Fiji 219
Fiji Bureau of Statistics 74, 116, 154, 180, 251
Fiji Central Planning Office 145
Fiji College of Agriculture 185
Fiji Development Bank (FDB) 209, 213, 237, 258, 288
loans to indigenous Fijians 212
Fiji Ecotourism Association 260
Fiji Employment and Development Mission 77
Fiji Forest Industry (FFI) 242, 243
Fiji Garment Workers Association 158
Fiji Garment, Textile and Allied Workers Union 160, 163
Fiji Hotel Association 260
Fiji Housing Authority 85
Fiji Industries Limited 239
Fiji Labour Party (FLP) xii, 6, 38, 43, 45, 55, 57, 58, 61–70, 134, 143, 156, 205, 206, 210, 222, 224, 248, 280, 286, 291
Fiji Mine Workers Union 164
Fiji Museum 258, 259, 261, 262
Fiji National Archives 190
Fiji National Heritage Posters 261

Fiji Nursing Association (FNA) 188, 192, 195
Fiji Pine Commission and the Marketing Authority 218
Fiji Pine Limited 258, 264
Fiji Poverty Report (1996) 288
Fiji Revenue and Customs Authority 85
Fiji Sugar and General Workers Union 167
Fiji Sugar Corporation 120–21, 241
Fiji Trade and Investment Board 80, 232, 260
Fiji Trades Union Congress (FTUC) 55, 143, 155–57, 162, 166, 174, 195
Fiji Visitors Bureau 251
Fiji Women's Crisis Centre (FWCC) 196, 197
Fiji Womens' Rights Movement (FWRM) 196
Women, Employment and Economic Rights Project 197
campaign against sexual harassment 200
Fijian Affairs Act of 1940 244
Fijian Affairs Board 76, 207–8, 229–30, 234, 239, 241–47, 258
Fijian Association Party (FAP) 55, 57, 61, 62, 64, 67, 69, 221, 222, 224
Fijian Christian Party 223
Fijian Development Fund 229
Fijian Holdings Company Limited (FHC) 208, 209, 229, 234, 238–41, 243, 245–47, 270
Fijian Initiative Group 234
Fijian Nationalist Party 207
Fijian Property Trust 241
Fijianisation of the public sector 208

Fiji–Australia Business Council
  217
Finance and Economic
  Development, Ministry of 77,
  78, 153, 218
FLP/FAP/PANU combination 57
FLP-NFP Coalition government
  6, 55, 224
Food and Nutrition Committee
  148
food imports 146
foreign direct investment 82, 88
Forestry, Department of 258
formal employment
  opportunities 180
Forsyth, D. 181, 194, 195
Forum Economic Ministers
  Meeting (FEMM) 216, 217
Foster, P. 149
Foundation for the Peoples of the
  South Pacific 260
Francis, J. 260, 261
Freedom of Information Act 32
freehold land 118
Frenkel, R. 90

G

Ganilau, Sir Penaia 243, 277, 282
garment sector xii
  exports 79, 83, 88, 182, 199
  production 181, 211
  workers 197, 199
  workers conditions 181
GDP per capita xiv
gender
  discrimination 190
  stereotypes 189
General Agreement on Tariffs and
  Trade (GATT) Article 24 89, 90
Geraghty, P. 271
Ghai, Y. 34, 38, 44, 48, 284

Goffman, E. 265
gold 5, 88
Gometz, E. 236
Goodman Fielder Watties 241
Government Shipyard 84, 219
Gramsci, A. 229
Great Council of Chiefs 6, 7, 27,
  31, 48, 57, 70, 224, 229, 230, 238,
  239, 244, 273, 280, 284, 287
Grynberg, R. 189

H

Haley, J. 232
Harrington, C. 181, 194
Harrison, D. 250, 264
Harriss, J. 137
Hatcher, R.   149
health 145, 146, 148, 151
Health and Safety at Work Act of
  1996 219
Health, Ministry of 180
Helu-Thaman, K. 250
Hermann, R. 75
Hill, H. 71, 79, 80, 88, 99
Hirschman, A.O. 112
Hodgson, G. 112
Horowitz, D. 33
Hotel Aid Ordinance of 1958 252
House of Representatives 34, 35,
  68
Household Income and
  Employment Survey 193
Housing Assistance and Relief
  Trusts 192
Human Rights Commission 32,
  40, 44, 47
Hunter, J. 137

I

IKA Corporation 218
Illich, I. 147

import licensing 80, 212
imported food 146
import-substitution 209
income per capita 87
indigenous culture 265
Industrial Associations Act 157, 166
Industrial Relations Code of Practice 155
industrial disputes 164, 166, 167
infant mortality rates xii, 141
Inland Revenue and Customs, Department of 219
Institute for Democracy and Electoral Assistance 58
Institute of Development Studies 210
Interim Government xii, 72, 77–81, 152, 234, 281
International Bank of Reconstruction and Development 253
International Confederation of Free Trade Unions 174, 199
International Labour Organization (ILO) 160, 174, 197
   Convention 87, 162
   Committee of Experts 162
   South East Asian and the Pacific Multidisplinary Advisory Team 180
International Monetary Fund 78, 248
Investment Policy Statement 219

J

Jalal, Imrana 189, 289
Joint Parliamentary Select Committee (JPSC) 26, 52, 66
Jones, S. 289

K

Kabuna Confederacy 242
Kadavu Province 60, 61, 246
Kahlenberg, R. 227
Kamikamica, J. 55, 124, 221, 242
Kavekini-Navuso 222
Khan, A.S. 160, 162, 163
King, T. 181
Kolinio Qiqiwaqa 278
Koroi, Reverend Josateki 290
Korovulavula, M. 246
Koroyanitu 264
Koy, Jim Ah 220, 272, 273
Kubuabola, *Ratu* Inoke 277
Kumar, S. 208
Kymlicka, W. 22

L

Labasa 197
Labasa mill 120
Labour Advisory Board 155
Labour and Immigration, Minister for 280
Labour and Industrial Relations, Department of 76
labour laws 176
   amendments 157
labour market 176
   deregulation 152, 153, 175
   reform 164, 167, 169, 173
labour relations 175
Labour, Ministry of 158, 164, 167, 176
Laisenia Qarase 235, 288
Lal, B. 25
Lancaster 130
land classification 119
land tenure
   arrangements 126

institutions 121
termination of land leases xiii
land-owning units 245
Lands Department 260
Landuse Planning Section 258, 259
Lasaro, Reverend Manasa 223
Lateef, Shireen 187
Lau Province 5, 6, 129, 246
Lautoka 197
Lawson, S. 188
Leckie, J. 155, 184, 190–92, 208, 260
Leibenstein, H. 112
Lewis, C.M. 137
Li, Y. 265
Libecap, G.D. 113
life expectancy xii, 140, 141
Lijphart, A. 24
Lipsey, R.G. 130
Lomaiviti Province 246
Lomé Convention 74, 89, 217
Lotus Garments 195
Lustick, I. 23

M

MacDonald, S. 75
macroeconomic stabilisation 78
Madraiwiwi, *Ratu* Jone 168, 281
Maki, U. 112
Management Advisory Services Department 234
manufacturing
production 83
sector 210
Mara, *Ratu* Sir Kamisese 7, 274
Mara, *Ratu* Sir Kamisese 7, 8, 274, 276–78, 281–84
Mara, *Ro* Lady Lala 280
mataqali 118, 123, 125, 129, 245

Matararaba, S. 259
McKenzie Aucoin, P. 188, 190
Merchant Bank of Fiji Ltd 241
Methodist Church 8, 223, 232, 234, 244, 290
military regime 4
Motibhai and Company Limited 241, 244
Mount Kasi mine 88
Moynagh, M. 121
Mulgan, R. 288, 291
multiethnic parties 33
multiparty government 36–39, 41
multi-racialism xiv
Myint, H. 112
Myrdal, G. 112

N

Nacola, Jo 272
Nadi 251
Narayan, J. 226
Narsey, Wadan 189
National Bank of Fiji (NBF) 83, 84, 85, 231, 270
National Economic Summit 213, 282
National Environment Strategy 259
National Farmers Union 166, 173
National Federation Party (NFP) xiii, 6, 23, 25, 36, 45, 52, 55, 58, 64, 67–70, 157, 205, 224, 282
national seats 35
National Trust for Fiji 258
National Union of Factory and Commercial Workers 165
Pacific Fishing Corporation 163
Nationalist *Vanua Takalavo* Party (NVTLP) 68, 222

native land 118
Native Land and Fisheries
   Commission 229
Native Land Trust Board (NLTB)
   76, 121–30, 132, 229, 239, 241–
   43, 247, 250, 253, 257, 259, 261
   Environment Charter 258
   Policy on the Logging of
   Indigenous Forests 258
   Policy for Tourism
   Development on Native Land
   1990–95 258
   Tourism Policy for Native
   Land 1997–2000 258
Native Land Trust Board Act 124
Native Lands Conservation and
   Preservation Projects Steering
   Committee (NLCPPSC) 258, 260
Native Lands Trust Act (NLTA)
   122–24, 243
'native policy' 229, 247
natural capital 151
Nayacakalou, R. 118, 124
neoliberal ideology 135
neoliberalism 137
new institutional economics
   (NIE) 137
New Zealand and Fiji Business
   Councils 217
New Zealand Ministry of Foreign
   Affairs and Trade 1995 250
New Zealand Official
   Development Assistance
   (NZODA) 249, 258, 260, 264
Newbery, D.M.G. 128
night work 197
nine o'clock curfew 3
Nine Points Plan 236, 238, 240,
   244
North, D.C. 113–14, 116, 131

nuclear-free Pacific 7
Nurkse, R. 112
Nurses' Christian Fellowship 191
nutrition 147, 148, 151
   overnutrition 147
   policies 146

O

O'Callaghan, Mary-Louise 282
Office of the Registrar of
   Companies 232
Ombudsman 32, 40, 44, 47
open general license scheme 80
Organisation for Economic
   Cooperation and Development
   (OECD) 102
Osei, K. 189
Overton, J. 124, 125, 226

P

Pacific Fishing Company
   (PAFCO) 182
Pacific Harbour Cultural Centre
   262
Pacific Island Gold 88
'Pacific Way' 143
parliamentary seats
   communal 51
   ethnically reserved 51
   open 33, 34, 51, 62
Party of National Unity (PANU)
   56, 57, 61, 62, 64, 67, 69, 221–24
Pejovich, S. 114
Permodalan National Berhad 238
pine plantations 5, 8
Pittin, R. 186
Plange, N. 252
Port Workers and Seafarers
   Union 163

Post and Telecommunications,
Department of 218
Prasad, B.C. 54, 74, 87, 89, 123,
125, 127
Price Control Legislation 155
Prices and Income Board (PIB)
75, 155
property rights 114, 115, 116
Provincial Councils 230, 247
Public Enterprise Act 219
Public Enterprise Unit 76, 81,
211, 220
Public Service Association (PSA)
160
Public Service Commission 180
Public Services International 174
Putman, R. 136

Q

quality of life 141

R

Rabuka, Sitiveni xii, 3, 6, 8, 9, 10,
55, 56, 77, 82, 183, 187, 217, 223,
224, 271, 278–85, 291
Ralogaivau, *Ratu* Filimone 9
Ralston, C. 184
Ram, C. 181
Ramphal, Sir Shridath 283
Randall, A. 114
Ranis, G. 112
Ravuvu, A. 188
Reddy, Jai Ram 56, 282, 286
Reddy, M. 86
Reeves Commission 27, 33–37,
40, 42–44, 47, 48
Registrar of Trade Unions 158,
163
Registrar-General's Department
85
regulation of imports 212

rents for sugarcane land 123
Reserve Bank of Fiji 8, 78, 85
Riker, W.H. 114, 115
Roberts, D.F. 89
Robertson, Robbie xiii
Rotuman community 58
Rutz, H.J. 124

S

Sainath, M. 189
salary data 169
sale of native land 130
Sartori, G. 47
Sawailau, S.T. 254, 260
scholarships 207
Schuller, W. 259
Scully, G. 115
Seaqaqa project 119, 120
Seers, D. 138
Select Committee 27, 34
Senate of Chiefs 281
Sharma, A.N. 197
Shop (Regulations of Hours and
Employment) Act of 1965 154
Siwatibau, S. 273
Slatter, C. 189
Slottje, D.J. 115
small-scale businesses 232
Smith, Adam 115
social policy 133, 135, 148, 151
social wealth 133, 151
Solimano, A. 91
Soqosoqo Ni Vakavulewa Ni Taukei
(SVT) xiii, 52, 54, 58, 61, 62, 64,
68–70, 82, 205–7, 222–24, 290
South Pacific and Oceanic
Council of Trade Unions
survey 195
South Pacific Forum 215, 216
South Pacific Regional Trade and
Economic Cooperation

Agreement's (SPARTECA) 88, 90, 199, 217
Sowell, T. 226
Spate, O.H.K. 124
Standard Concrete Industries Limited 239
Standing Orders 45
statutory wage guidelines 81
Stiglitz, J. 128
Stinson and Pearce Limited 231
Street Commission 30
strikes 166
Strout, A.M. 72, 91
structural adjustment program 78, 82, 105, 152, 181
Subcommittee on Indigenous Fijian Participation in Business 213
subsistence affluence 206
sugar 5
  farmers 119
  farming 116, 117
  industry 74
  processing 116
  production 8, 119
Sugar Cane Growers Council 127
Sugar Protocol 74, 89, 103
Sunday ban xii, 7, 8
sustainable tourism 260
Sutherland, W. 99, 138, 206–10, 215, 222, 275

T

Tabor, S.R. 71, 79, 80, 88, 99
Tabua, S. 252
Taukei movement 7, 8, 10, 272, 273, 275, 285, 290
Tavuni Hill Fort 261
tax concessions 79, 88
tax-free factories 76, 79, 83, 88, 210
tax-free manufacturing 79, 171

tax-free zones 232
Taylor, C. 22, 90, 96
Taylor, L. 72
Thaman, R.R. 145
Thomas, L. 275
Thomas, N. 289
Thomas, R. 113
three-gap model of growth 90, 91
  results 95
Tietenberg, T.H. 114
Tisdell, C. 125, 127
Tiy, Francis Hong 289
Tora, Apisai 221, 223
Torstensson, J. 115
Tourism and Civil Aviation, Ministry of 75, 250–51, 258–63
Tourism Council of the South Pacific 260
tourism industry 86, 251–53, 256, 257, 261, 263
tourism (sustainable) 260
Town and Country Planning, Department of 260
Trade and Commerce, Minister for 81, 233
Trade Disputes Act 155, 157, 163, 168, 174
trade liberalisation 79
trade unions 157–59, 167, 176, 194
  ballots 162
  leaders 157, 176
  membership 164
  representation 194
  Trade Union (Recognition) Act 155, 157, 159, 174
  Trade Unions Act of 1964 154, 157, 161–64, 174, 196
  Trade Unions (Collection of Union Dues) Regulations 157, 160, 162
  unionisation rates 164

tripartite era (1978–84) 166–69
Tripartite Forum 156, 219
Troyna, B. 149
Trudeau, Pierre 283
Tuisolia, *Ratu* Sakuisa 199
Tullock, G. 115
Tully, J. 22
Turner, V. 265
Twyford, L.T. 117, 118

U

ULO/SEAPAT 185
Unit Trust of Fiji 241
United General Party (UGP) 67
United Nations Convention on
  the Elimination of All Forms of
  Discrimination Against Women
  (CEDAW) 191
United Nations Development
  Programme (UNDP) 87, 192,
  193, 198, 249, 253, 256, 260, 290
University of the South Pacific
  (USP) 4, 9, 10
Urry, J. 265
Uruguay Round 215
  Agreement on Agriculture 89
US Department of State 173

V

Vakatora, T. 25
vakaturaga 243
vakavanua 125
value-added tax 79, 211
vanua 125, 230, 233, 243, 245
Vanua Levu 6
Veitata, Taniela 278
*Veitokani Ni Lewenivanua
  Vakaristo* (VLV) 62
violence
  against wives 187

against women and children
  196
Viti Levu 5, 56, 60, 61, 251, 281
  Viti Levu Council of Chiefs 281
  Viti Levu Multiracial Democratic
  Dynamic Party 222
Vula ni Kawa Bula (VKB) 240, 271,
  272, 290
Vunibobo, Berenado 213
wage freeze 165
wages 164, 169, 171
  wage and salary trends 168

W

Wages Council Act of 1960 154
Wages Council Order 181
Wages Councils 156
Wakelin, D. 250
Wallis, J.J. 114
Ward, M. 122, 124, 125, 129
Waring, M. 180
Watling, D. 259
Weimer, D.L. 114, 115
Weiss, D. 75
Westminster system 39, 40, 41, 45
Westpac Bank 182
Westpac Pacific 282
Westralian Forest Industries 242
Winograd, C. 90
Women and Culture,
  Department of 180, 183, 185
women
  access to land 188
  and poverty 192
  and work 179
  education levels 184
  in business 190
  involvement in paid workforce
  179
  mobility 187

older and widowed 193
unpaid labour 179
violence against women 187
working conditions 190
Women, Employment and
Economic Rights Project 197
Women's Coalition for Women's
Citizenship Rights 200
Women's Network 194
Wong, Pio 273
Workmen's Compensation Act of
1965 154
workplace
discrimination 197
relations 190
Works and Energy, Department
of 75
World Bank 215
World Trade Organization (WTO)
xii, 77, 78, 84, 89, 115–17, 120,
123, 126, 133, 217, 218, 248, 256
multilateral trade negotiations
in agricultural products 89
Wright, A.C.S. 117, 118

www.ingramcontent.com/pod-product-compliance
Lightning Source LLC
Chambersburg PA
CBHW040152270326
41927CB00034B/3410